India's Agony over Religion

SUNY series in Religious Studies
Harold Coward, editor

R

India's Agony over Religion

Gerald James Larson

STATE UNIVERSITY OF NEW YORK PRESS

Published by
State University of New York Press, Albany

Printed in the United States of America

For information, address State University of New York Press,
State University Plaza, Albany, N.Y., 12246

Production by Marilyn P. Semerad
Marketing by Nancy Farrell

Library of Congress Cataloging-in-Publication Data

Larson, Gerald James.
India's agony over religion / Gerald James Larson.
p. cm.
Includes bibliographical references and index.
ISBN 0-7914-2411-1. — ISBN 0-7914-2412-X (pbk.)
1. India—Religion. 2. Civil religion—India. 3. Religion and state—India. I. Title.
BL2003.L37 1995
291.1'72'0954—dc20 94-18318
CIP

10 9 8 7 6 5 4 3 2 1

To
Claire, Karen, Chandra, Jennifer
Amanda and Grace

Contents

Preface

The present book began as an inquiry into the contemporary religious crisis in India with special reference to the on-going debate between those who argue that India ought to maintain its identity as a "secular state" without any special consideration for a particular religious tradition and those who argue that the modern nation-state of India should give greater prominence to its specifically "Hindu" heritage. The crisis with the Sikhs in the State of Punjab, the crisis in the Muslim majority State of Jammu and Kashmir, the crisis between Hindus and Muslims over the Shah Bano case and the Muslim Women's (Protection of Rights on Divorce) Bill of 1986, the crisis over caste-reservations and special privileges for Other Backward Classes as evidenced in the Mandal Commission Report, and the crisis in Ayodhya between Hindus and Muslims regarding the disputed (and now destroyed) Babri Masjid and its purported location on the sacred site of the birth of the Hindu god, Rāma (Ramjanmabhoomi), are the most salient if not the only symptoms of India's contemporary religious crisis.

As my research proceeded, however, it became clear that these contemporary issues could not be seriously addressed in depth without looking at the broader dimensions of the overall history and culture of the subcontinent. Moreover, it became clear that when one does begin to get a handle on the dense texture of India's cultural heritage(s), the contemporary religious crisis begins to appear in a very different light. First, it becomes clear that many layers of culture and history are operating in contemporary India, not simply as background elements for understanding modern India but as present-day living traditions demanding to be heard in the current struggles to shape India's future. Second, it becomes clear that the so-called post-Independence "secular state" is to a significant degree a forward-caste Neo-Hindu state, or, in other words, that the "secular state" in the Indian context has a number of religious aspects and may even represent in some respects a religious entity, that is, a kind of civil religion on analogy with the notion of a civil religion that some have noticed in American culture and history. Third, it becomes clear that the Indian context is most instructive by way of challenging and criticizing many of the conventional notions in the academic study of religion or religious studies, such notions, for example, as "Hinduism," "secularization" and even the term "religion" itself. Indeed, these three points taken together, namely,

1. that ancient layers of India's religious life are alive and well in contemporary India;
2. that the hybrid discourse of the "secular state" is itself a religious discourse in modern India; and
3. that India's unique agony over religion is instructive for rethinking some of our most general notions about "religion" and "secularization,"

may well serve as a useful summary statement of the overall thesis or argument of this book.

Put directly, what began as a relatively simple inquiry into contemporary Indian religious life has become instead a much more wide-ranging inquiry into the depths of India's multiform religious identities, an inquiry that also has implications for the study of religious identities and state formations outside of the Indian context. The overall argument is developed in the following manner. In chapter 1 I provide an overview of contemporary India as a modern nation-state in terms of its demography and political economy and its cultural and religious diversity. I also discuss a variety of methodological and theoretical issues pertaining to the overall analysis. In chapters 2 and 3 I provide an historical overview, beginning with the British "layer" (or what I eventually identify as the the Indo-Anglian dimension) but also ranging into the deeper layers of the Indus Valley, the Indo-

Brāhmaṇical, the Indo-Śramaṇical, the Indic, and the Indo-Islamic. On one level, the purpose of the historical overview is to provide the non-specialist or general reader with a summary perspective of India's rich cultural and religious history. On another level, however, the point of the overview is to develop the somewhat unusual historical argument that these "layers" or "branches" of India's culture and history are very much alive and operating in modern India and must be understood as part of the texture of modern Indian social reality. In chapter 4 I attempt to identify the salient intellectual features in the various "layers" or "branches" of India's culture and history and to highlight what I see as a continuing cultural dialogue between the "Old Indic" and the "New Indic" in India's search for self-understanding. In this chapter I also tackle the difficult problem of "religion" as a concept in the South Asian environment, and I construct a typology of "religions" based upon South Asian traditions which focusses the discussion of "religion" and "religions" in a somewhat new way. In chapter 5 I turn to the contemporary scene and attempt to show that the discourse of modernity in India is really a "hybrid" discourse that can only be properly understood when viewed from the perspective of the earlier historical and theoretical discussion. I argue that the notions of "religion," "secular," "secular state," "community," "citizen" and "citizenship" all have unique and/or eccentric meanings in the modern Indian context that can only be properly understood within the layered complexity of India's total cultural life. I then apply the overall analysis to the five salient religious crises in contemporary India: (1) the Sikhs in the Punjab; (2) the Muslim issue in Kashmir; (3) the Shah Bano case and the Muslim Women's Bill; (4) the Mandal Commission Report on Other Backward Classes; and (5) the controversy in Ayodhya. Finally, in a brief concluding chapter 6 I outline some possible recommendations for resolving some of the difficult religious issues.

I recognize that many of the discussions in the chapters that follow are rather dense and difficult, especially the lengthy historical overview in chapters 2 and 3 and the technical discussions of philosophy and religion in chapter 4. My defense for these discussions is simply that the complexity of the material demands a serious and sustained treatment, especially if the non-specialist or general reader is to be given some sense of the depth of India's religious crisis and its historical antecedents. The risk, of course, is that the non-specialist or general reader will find the level of discourse too demanding while the specialist reader may want a good deal more. I have tried, however, to find an appropriate balance. The book is primarily designed for the non-specialist or general reader, but it is not by any means designed to be easy or elementary, any more than India's agony over religion is easy or elementary .

The same can well be said, I suppose, about my final conclusions regarding religion and the state in modern India. The problems are deep, complex, exceedingly difficult, and frequently intractable. There are no simple diagnoses or simple treatments for India's agony over religion. There is only the painful path of sustained critical analysis, attention to detail and nuance, the systematic debunking of name-calling and ideological rhetoric whether of the left or the right, and the patient search for a consensus that is broadly inclusive of the many voices that deserve to be heard.

As already mentioned, this book began as a simple inquiry into the contemporary religious crisis in India. The book was to be part of the Princeton Project on Church and State. Early along, however, the inquiry went beyond the narrow boundaries of the Princeton project, but I would nevertheless like to thank Professor John F. Wilson, director of the Princeton project, for the support and encouragement to start thinking about modern India's religious crisis. Heretofore my primary scholarly work had been in classical Indian philosophical traditions, classical Sanskrit texts and other dimensions of Indology and the general history of religions in India, and it was something of a challenge and risk for me to venture into the modern period. Indeed, if the present book brings a unique perspective to current discussions about religion in modern India, it is probably because the work has been constructed by someone coming at the subject-matter from behind or underneath, as it were, that is, someone approaching the subject from the perspective of India's long intellectual history.

Various colleagues and friends have read the work in typescript and have offered valuable suggestions for improvements. In this regard I would especially like to thank Dr. Pratapaditya Pal, Senior Curator for Indian and Southeast Asian Art at the Los Angeles County Museum of Art; Professor André Béteille, Department of Sociology in the Delhi School of Economics, Delhi University; Professor Stephen Hay, professor emeritus of modern Indian history at the University of California, Santa Barbara; and two of my colleagues in the academic study of religion at UC Santa Barbara, Professors Robert S. Michaelsen and Ninian Smart. Although the critical comments of all of these helped me a great deal, I am, of course, fully responsible for all of the views expressed in the book.

During the early stages of research for the book, I was fortunate to serve as Academic Director of the India Study Centre (in Delhi) of the

University of California's Education Abroad Program (1984–91). I was able in those years to visit India on a regular basis and to benefit from discussions and contacts with a variety of persons representing the whole range of views about contemporary Indian life, including such persons as Ramachandra Gandhi, T. N. Madan, Daya Krishna, L. K. Advani, H. V. Seshadri, K. R. Malkani, Syed Shahabuddin, T. S. Rukmani, Margaret Chatterjee, Upendra Baxi and many, many others. I have learned a great deal from all of these contacts and would like to express my gratitude for their pointing me in this or that useful direction in my continuing research. I would also like to thank my good friend and colleague, Mr. Vijayan Puliampet, Administrative Director of University of California programs in India. He has been a trusted friend for many years. Certain nuances about modern Indian life cannot be conveyed in books and articles. They can only be conveyed through personal friendship. I have been fortunate in having such a friend in Viji.

A special word of thanks should also be expressed to Dr. Ravinder Kumar, Director of the Nehru Memorial Library in New Delhi, not only for several useful discussions about religion and the state in modern India but also for the invitation to lecture at the Nehru Memorial Library about the theoretical grounding of the present book. Also I am grateful to the Rev. Dr. G. Gispert-Sauch who invited me to lecture regarding the basic argument of the book to the faculty and students of the Vidya Jyoti Theological Seminary in Delhi. Both lecture opportunities provided a context for valuable feedback as the book was developing. I should perhaps also mention in this regard a Conference on "Religion and Law in India," held at the Law School of the University of Iowa, Iowa City, in 1991, under the direction of Professor Robert Baird of the Iowa School of Religion, yet another occasion for valuable feedback. A word of thanks, finally, to the Interdisciplinary Humanities Center of the University of California, Santa Barbara, for my appointment as a Fellow in 1991–92 to work on the final phases of the manuscript, to Dr. Knut Jacobsen, my research assistant and a former doctoral student of mine from Norway, who helped me at numerous points in the preparation of this book, especially in tracing bibliographical references and gathering statistical data, and to Dr. Antonio Rigopoulos, also a former doctoral student, who assisted me in preparing the index.

One final word about the transliteration of terms in the South Asian languages. For the ancient and classical traditions of Indian culture and history, I have used the standard diacritical marks for all Sanskrit words. Sanskrit terms are cited in their proper stem (or lexicon) form. Plural formations are cited in their proper stem form with an "s" (the English plural) added after a dash—for example, Upaniṣad-s. For Indo-Islamic terms (derived from Arabic, Persian, Urdu, and so forth), since there is no standard pattern of transliteration, I have used the simplified transliterations that Ira M. Lapidus uses in his work, *A History of Islamic Societies* (Cambridge: Cambridge University Press, 1988). For modern terms in Hindi and for Indic words generally in the modern period, I have followed transliterations which for the most part eliminate diacritical marks as is the practice in modern Indian publishing and in the Indian media generally.

1

Introduction: Beating the Retreat

The European in considering India has not only to deal with a people of alien history, traditions, climate, and habits, but with differing modes of thought, fundamental assumptions and standards of value.
—Percival Spear, *India, Pakistan and the West*

The British in India have understood as much of the country as is necessary for policing it, but no foreigner has ever adequately understood our land.
—S. N. Dasgupta, *Hindu Mysticism*

Permanences Amid the Inescapable Flux

In January 1987 I had the privilege of attending for the first time an annual ceremony held in New Delhi on the occasion of the various activities related to Republic Day (26 January), a ceremony entitled "Beating the Retreat." It is an old British military ceremony, transformed now by the Government of India into a ceremonial remembrance of Great Britain's withdrawal from power in India on 15 August 1947 and the transfer of power to the Sovereign Democratic Republic of India which finally became official with the adoption of The Constitution of India on 26 January 1950. The ceremony occurs at sunset on the great avenue at the base of the hill leading to South Block and North Block (the main buildings of the government's ministries). As one looks up the hill towards the government buildings, one sees in the distance the looming presence of Rashtrapati Bhavan, the official residence of the president of India and formerly the home of the viceroy. One also sees the turbaned soldiers of the Camel Corps with their magnificent red and gold uniforms and mounted on their splendid camels on the high walls of South Block and North Block. Looking the other way down the avenue, one sees the majestic India Gate.

Just before sunset, government officials with their families, the diplomatic community, and various invited guests arrive at the ceremonial enclave. When everyone is seated, a motorcade of Ambassador cars arrives, bringing the various members of the cabinet and the prime minister of India. Shortly thereafter, the president of India arrives accompanied by a platoon of cavalry guards. The president is then ushered to a great throne-chair placed in the center of the avenue and facing up the hill. For a few moments there is an uneasy silence and the spectators simply absorb the extraordinary panorama—the deep red and purples of twilight, the camels silhouetted on the high walls of the government buildings against the gathering darkness, and the shadowed dome of Rashtrapati Bhavan.

Then, from a distance one hears the first faint sounds of music as the Pipe and Drum Corps begins its slow march down the hill, followed after a few minutes by the Army, Navy, and Air Force bands. The bands play separately, demonstrate their various disciplined maneuvers, and then finally, all together assemble directly in front of the president of India and the leadership of the Government of India. At the moment of the setting of the sun over the horizon, the bands then play together some final tunes before "beating retreat" back up the hill, one of which tunes is the music for the old Christian hymn:

> Abide with me; fast falls the eventide;
> The darkness deepens; Lord with me abide;
> When other helpers fail, and comforts flee;
> Help of the helpless, O abide with me.[1]

I was profoundly moved on that occasion, and among the many impressions I had, I want to mention three which are relevant by way of introducing the theme of the present book. First, as a student of Sanskrit and Indology, I found myself reflecting upon this strange embodiment of the contrast of tradition and modernity—on one level (hidden or latent), one of the world's oldest collection of cultures with its *kāvya* (formal poetry), *vyākaraṇa* (science of grammar), *purāṇa* (old tales), *itihāsa* (tradition), *darśana* (philosophical reflection), its Yogins and *sādhu-s* (holy men) and pilgrims, and its plurality of tongues old and new, still "abiding" into the last decades of the twentieth century; on another level (apparent or manifest), that same culture celebrating its identity by cloaking itself with the symbols of imperial power, pageantry and ritual reenactment borrowed from the "eventide" of Western civilization's expansion to the ends of the earth, namely, the British Raj, symbol par excellence of the hoped-for Pax Britannica.

Second, as a student of the history of religions, I was aware of the strange juxtaposition of the state and religion. Here was the modern, secular nation-state of India with its largely Hindu and Muslim population and with its continuing agony over religion on almost all sides (Sri Lanka in the South, Bengal and tribal difficulties in the Northeast, Kashmiri and Punjabi separatism by Muslims and Sikhs in the Northwest), nevertheless celebrating and remembering its emergence into freedom after centuries of imperial domination with the music of an old Christian hymn, "Abide with Me."

Third, and finally, as a student of comparative philosophy, I vaguely recalled the passage in the writings of Alfred North Whitehead in which the old Christian hymn "Abide with Me" somehow played a role. At the actual time of the ceremony, I could not quite recall the passage, and it was some weeks later when I had returned to the United States and to my personal library that I finally found the passage. It is from *Process and Reality*:

> The best rendering of integral experience, expressing its general form divested of irrelevant details, is often to be found in the utterances of religious aspiration. . . . Accordingly we find in the first two lines of a famous hymn a full expression of the union of the two notions in one integral experience:
>
> Abide with me;
> Fast falls the eventide.
>
> Here the first line expresses the permanences, 'abide,' 'me' and the 'Being' addressed; and the second line sets these permanences amid the inescapable flux. Here at length we find formulated the complete problem of metaphysics. Those philosophers who start with the first line have given us the metaphysics of 'substance'; and those who start with the second line have developed the metaphysics of 'flux.' But, in truth, the two lines cannot be torn apart in this way; and we find that a wavering balance between the two is a characteristic of the greater number of philosophers.[2]

Later, in the concluding passages of *Process and Reality*, Whitehead returns to the theme of the old hymn:

> In the inescapable flux, there is something that abides; in the overwhelming permanence, there is an element that escapes into flux. Permanence can be snatched only out of flux; and the passing moment can find its adequate intensity only by its submission to permanence. Those who would disjoin the two elements can find no interpretation of patent facts.[3]

The present book is an attempt to analyze and understand the relation between the state and religion in India, and the ceremony "Beating the Retreat" is diagnostically interesting by way of illustrating the problems involved in such an undertaking. From one point of view, it can plausibly be argued that "Beating the Retreat" is typical of the sorts of patriotic rituals that any modern nation-state undertakes periodically in order to show forth its founding myth and to legitimate its contemporary identity as an independent nation-state. In this sense there is nothing especially "Indian" about "Beating Retreat," and one thinks of K. M. Panikkar's comment shortly after independence: "Clearly, our new democratic, egalitarian and secular state is not built upon the foundations of ancient India, or of Hindu thought."[4] Many interpreters would agree with this assessment, and would trace the intellectual origins of the modern state in India to the influence of Western democratic ideas that became operative on the subcontinent in the middle and latter portions of the nineteenth century and the first half of the twentieth century (the Gandhian nationalist movement and other reformist and revolutionary movements of the first half of the century). Western science and technology, the rationalism and skepticism of the Enlightenment, the industrial revolution, humanist liberalism, Marxism, democratic socialist theories, pragmatism, and so forth, all were important conceptual frameworks in the minds of the Indian elite who wrote the Constitution for India's "Sovereign Democratic Republic and Union of States." Moreover, to the extent that the British made use of older Mughal models of imperial administration (for example, revenue collection, judicial procedure, and so forth), at least in the early phases of the Raj, one can also point to Muslim influences in the formulation of the notion of the state in South Asia.

In a similar manner it can be argued that the modern Indian notion of religion and the closely related notions of secularism and the secular state are ". . . not built upon the foundations of ancient India, or of Hindu thought," and that there is, again, therefore, nothing especially "Indian" in the ritual ceremony of "Beating the Retreat." That an old Christian hymn, "Abide with Me," should provide the culminating point of the ritual reenactment is more than a little symptomatic in this regard. Modern Indian notions of religion derive from a mixture of Christian (and mainly Protestant) models, Orientalist and largely Western reconstructions of India's religious past, and nineteenth century indigenous reform movements most of which were defensive reactions against the onslaught of Westernization and Christian missionizing. "Neo-Hinduism" and "Neo-Buddhism," rather than being authentic products of India's ancient cultural heritage, are really much closer in spirit to traditions of late-nineteenth century European notions of universal religion or liberal Protestant religion. Moreover, even prior to the modern period, India's notion of religion was shaped for many centuries by an alien, non–South Asian tradition, namely, Islam. Thus, to write about the relation between the state and religion in India or to interpret the meaning of "Beating the Retreat" is in one important sense not to write about traditional or Hindu India at all, except perhaps for the most recent period since Independence when Western or non–South Asian notions of the nation-state and religion were fully embraced by the newly emergent state of India. In other words, the task of writing about the relation between the state and religion in modern India is really one of identifying a set or network of ideas that originate mainly outside of South Asia but become exemplified in the subcontinental region when an entity called "India" emerges as a "secular" nation-state in 1947.

One can push this point one step further by asserting that "Beating the Retreat" is not only not especially Indian, at least in its explicit and manifest celebration of the state and religion, but that prior to the modern period there was no such thing as "India" at all. As John Strachey baldly put it in his *India*, published in 1888:

> . . . there is not, and never was an India, or even a country of India, possessing, according to European ideas, any sort of unity, physical, political, social or religious.[5]

Ainslie Embree, commenting on this remark by Strachey, goes on to say:

> Strachey and the authors of *Hobson-Jobson* were speaking for a class that knew India well, but who were convinced that the India of the late nineteenth century was a political artifact created by

> British imperial power and that it was essentially artificial, with its existence dependent upon the careful exercise of that power.[5]

A philosophical statement of the same sort of viewpoint is the famous comment by Hegel: "A State is a realization of Spirit, such that in it the self-conscious being of Spirit—the freedom of the Will—is realized as Law . . . if China may be regarded as nothing else but a State, Hindoo political existence presents us with a people, but no State."[7]

The key phrase for understanding Strachey's point as well as Hegel's, and indeed for understanding "Beating the Retreat" as a ritual celebration of "India" as a modern nation-state is, of course, the phrase "according to European ideas" (in the Strachey quote), and it is important to recognize, at least at the starting-point of any inquiry, that the basic notions of the state and religion in modern India derive from non–South Asian sources and that to the extent that India has defined itself as a modern secular, nation-state, it has only existed as such since 1947 (or, perhaps better, 1950, when its Constitution became law).

That, however, can only be the starting-point of the inquiry, for it must also be recognized that this is very much the "flux" side of Whitehead's permanence-flux metaphor and that this non–South Asian "flux" is unfolding within the "permanence" of that assimilative matrix known as Indic civilization that stretches back over millennia. As Whitehead puts it: "In the inescapable flux, there is something that abides; . . . and the passing moment can find its adequate intensity only by its submission to permanence."[8] In the case of South Asian Indic civilization, the "permanence" that "abides" is massive, all-encompassing and in many ways the antithesis of India as a modern secular nation-state. Interestingly enough, and perhaps understandably so, the ceremony "Beating the Retreat" makes no reference whatever to this "permanence" side, or putting the matter another way, "Beating the Retreat" neglects to portray that *from* which retreat is being made. It is almost as if modern India is acting out a double retreat; on one level, the retreat of the British, on another level, modern India's retreat from its own heritage, its own "permanence." The ceremony would have us believe that one modern nation-state retreats and another modern nation-state emerges in its place. That, of course, is true enough, but the repression (in the psychoanalytic sense) of the "permanence" side in the ritual transaction is truly staggering in its scope, and it is hardly a matter for surprise that there has been a good deal of "the return of the repressed" since 1947 (with the intensity of symptoms increasing in inverse proportion to the distance from Independence).

To shift from the Whiteheadian "permanence-flux" metaphor to an Indic metaphor (to be found in both Hindu and Buddhist thought), it is as if there are two levels of truth in contemporary India, one level representing the changing, empirical dimensions of everyday life (*saṃvṛti-satya*), another level representing what truly *is*, or what truly is the case—namely, the level of absolute truth (*paramārtha-satya*). The Advaita Vedāntins tended to interpret the former or empirical level as ultimately illusory or, at least, as ontologically uncharacterizable, while the latter is what truly is the case as qualityless (*nirguṇa*) Brahman; and they often illustrated the notion of more than one level of truth with the analogy of the rope-snake, wherein the terrified reaction of a person apparently (but wrongly) perceiving a snake immediately disappears when the same person recognizes that the perception is mistaken and that, finally, there is only a rope. The Mādhyamika Buddhists tended to interpret the changing, empirical level as the set of all possible and meaningful discursive statements that can be derived from the ordinary experiences of everyday life, while the level of absolute truth (or what truly is the case) is an ultimate intuition of voidness or emptiness (*śūnyatā*) in terms of any attempt to extrapolate discursive accounts beyond their limited and relative contexts. Regardless of their differing valuations of the relative and the absolute, however, both traditions stressed the importance of both levels of truth and the crucial need to discriminate one from the other, and in this sense the Hindu-Buddhist notion of two levels of truth comes close to the "permanence-flux" metaphor of Whitehead. In other words, whether one argues that the "flux-level" of India as a modern secular nation-state is ultimately illusory (à la the Hindu Vedāntin, a John Strachey or a Hegel) or is, rather, a provisional, empirical formulation that has a certain plausibility within an appropriate context (à la the Mādhyamika Buddhist or the Whiteheadian), all would surely agree that it is crucial to take full account of the "permanence-level" of Indic civilization within which the "flux-level" operates and to attempt to understand the manner in which the permanence-level and flux-level interact historically, ontologically and epistemologically. In the idiom of Whitehead: "Those who would disjoin the two elements can find no interpretation of patent facts."[9] In the idiom of Hindu and Buddhist discourse: those who would fail to distinguish between the two levels of truth are ignorant and insufficiently discriminating (*avidyā*, *aviveka*).

As mentioned earlier, the present book is an attempt to analyze and understand the relation between the state and religion in India, and I have used "Beating the Retreat" as a point of departure by way of suggesting that my interest in the relation between the state and religion in modern India is not just with respect to the current social, economic and political aspects of the relation, although, of course, there will be continuous reference throughout the book to these dimensions, but, rather, to the concern about the manner in which the much more elusive and subtle relation between the state and religion in modern India plays itself out within the larger framework of Indic civilization as a whole. I am interested, in other words, in a double set of relations, the relation between the state and religion in modern India and the relation of that relation to Indic civilization as a whole, and I want to argue that the narrative of the former, that is, the relation between the state and religion in modern India, only becomes intelligible when interpreted in relation to the narrative of the latter, that is, the narrative of Indic civilization as a whole. There is, as it were, a double narrative unfolding simultaneously, a continuing *double entendre* in historical understanding that is often elusive and puzzling. W.H. Morris-Jones had something similar in mind when he formulated his metaphor of "a play within the play" with respect to understanding Indian politics:

> One very general way of putting the problem is to point out that the student of Indian political institutions soon forms the impression that the main thing he has to learn is that nothing is ever quite what it seems or what it presents itself as being. . . .
>
> The observer of Indian politics will not look at his subject for long before he gets the feeling that he is missing something. This feeling can perhaps be described only by metaphors. . . .
>
> Such a feeling with regard to Indian politics is perfectly justified; what the observer has so far not taken into account is a play within the play.[10]

Before turning to the problem of interpreting the "play within the play," however, it will be helpful to provide a brief picture or snapshot of present-day India together with a discussion of the manner in which certain crucial terms will be used in the book, namely, "state," "nation-state," "civilization," and, of course, "religion." Also, it will be helpful to indicate at the outset the theoretical perspective from which the present book emerges. So let us turn, then, to these preliminary matters.

Present-day India: An Introductory Profile

Demography

The Census of India for 1991 indicates that the total population of the country has reached 843,930,861, making India the second largest nation in the world (after China with its population of 1,160,017,381).[11] About 16 percent of the total population of the world is in India. China and India combined account for just under 40 percent of the population of the planet. India's population growth rate for the past decade has been 23.5 percent. In actual numbers this means that over 160,000,000 have been added to the population in the last ten years, an addition that is more than the total population of Japan. Between 1947 (the date of India's independence from the British) and 1981, the population of India doubled. Given the current growth rate, by the year 2011 the population of India will most likely double again (over the 1981 figure of 665,287,849) to more than 1 billion, 330 million. Possibly, given present growth rates and the relative youthfulness of India's population (40 percent under 15), the population of India will surpass that of China at some point fairly early along in the next century.[12]

To the overall figure of roughly 844,000,000, one should perhaps also add another 10 million for the Asian Indian "diaspora," that is, Asian Indians (frequently referred to as "NRIs" or "non-resident Indians") that do not currently reside in India, with the largest concentrations (of 100,000 or more) in Sri Lanka (1,350,000), Malaysia (1,209,500), South Africa (821,000), the United States (815,447 as of 1990), the Persian Gulf region (800,000), the United Kingdom (675,000), Guyana (500,000), Trinidad (421,000), Fiji (326,015), Burma (300,000), Canada (200,000), Singapore (159,000), the Netherlands (102,000) and East and Central Africa (just under 100,000).[13]

India now has the third largest military in the world, stands about twelfth in total GNP, is roughly fifteenth in industrial production, ranks third in the world in its number of technical and scientific personnel, and can boast a middle class of nearly 150,000,000.[14] Literacy in India, according to the recent 1991 census, has increased to 52.11 percent (roughly two-thirds male and one-third female), up from the 36 percent of the 1981 Census. Sex ratio for 1991 is 929 females for every 1,000 males, down from 1981 and considerably down from the optimal 950 or higher required to sustain a context "favorable to females" in India.[15]

Per capita income is one of the lowest in the world: $340, according to 1991 World Bank figures, or, in other words, fourteenth from the bottom of the nations that currently make up the United Nations.[16]

Much of the population still endures poverty and social deprivation. This grouping includes the "Scheduled Castes" (usually referred to as "untouchables" and making up 15% of the total population), "Scheduled Tribes" (indigenous tribal groups making up about 7.5% of the population), and the so-called "Other Backward Classes" (groups higher than "untouchables" and "tribals" but lower than the high or "forward" castes and numbering anywhere from 25% to 50% of the total population). The so-called "forward" or high castes make up about 18 percent of the population, including such caste groups as Brahmins (3.5% of the total population), Rajputs (3.9%), Bhumihars (2.02%), Vaishya-Banias (1.8%), Kayasthas (1.07%), Jats (1%), and so forth, and coinciding to a large extent with the growing middle class.[17]

Government

The Preamble to the Constitution of India, which came into force on 26 January 1950, describes the country as a "SOVEREIGN SOCIALIST SECULAR DEMOCRATIC REPUBLIC."[18] The original 1950 text of the Constitution used only the words "sovereign democratic republic." The addition of the terms "socialist" and "secular" came by way of the forty-second amendment to the Constitution Act of 1976, enacted, it should perhaps be noted, during the national emergency proclaimed by Indira Gandhi from June of 1975 through January of 1977. The president of the Republic (a largely ceremonial office) is officially head of state. The head of government is the prime minister, and the prime minister and all other ministers must be duly elected members of Parliament. There is an upper house of Parliament known as the Rajya Sabha or "Council of States," whose members are elected indirectly (by the various State Legislative Assemblies) or by appointment, and a lower house of Parliament known as the Lok Sabha or "Assembly of the People," whose members are directly elected. The country, in other words, is basically a parliamentary democracy, with an independent judiciary and a remarkably free press.

In addition to the Union or central government, India is made up of twenty-five states and seven Union territories. Each state has a governor, who is appointed by the president, and a popularly elected Legislative Assembly (and in some states a Legislative Council as well) with a chief minister. The chief minister is the head of administration. Each Union territory is administered by the president through an appointed administrator. The term of office for the president as well as popularly elected state and Union representatives is five years.

Languages and Cultural Regions

The twenty-five States and seven Union territories range from the state of Jammu and Kashmir in the far North (in the cold foothills of the Himalayas and bordering Tibet and China on the East and Pakistan on the West) to Tamil Nadu in the far, subtropical South (almost reaching to Sri Lanka), and from the dry, arid states of Gujarat and Maharashtra in the West (bordering on the Arabian Sea) to the damp states of West Bengal and Orissa in the East (touching on the Bay of Bengal). Eighteen official languages are recognized by the Constitution: Hindi (spoken by just under 40%), Telugu (8.2%), Bengali (7.8%), Marathi (7.5%), Tamil (6.8%), Urdu (5.3%), Gujarati (5%), Kannada (4.1%), Malayalam (3.9%), Oriya (3.5%), Punjabi (2.8%), Assamese (1–2%), Kashmiri (.5%), Sindhi (.3%), and Sanskrit (the classical, learned language spoken only by some pandits), and the three most recent additions to the list, Nepali, Konkani and Manipur. Most of the languages of the North are in the Indo-Aryan family of languages, namely, Hindi, Bengali, Marathi, Gujarati, Oriya, Punjabi and Kashmiri. The languages of the South are usually characterized as Dravidian languages, namely, Kannada, Malayalam, Telugu and Tamil. In addition, English is recognized as an official language (spoken perhaps by 3% to 5%), and both Hindi and English are approved for official, government communications.[19]

Apart from these official statistics about language, however, it should be noted that the actual linguistic texture of India is even more complex than the official picture indicates. The Anthropological Survey of India, for example, in its first report of the new "People of India" project, has identified the staggering number of 4,599 distinct communities in India and as many as 325 languages in 12 language families with some 24 different scripts.[20] Moreover, most of the communities surveyed did not consider themselves indigenous or non-migrant. In other words, in the folklore and history of the various communities, most consider themselves as having come to India from outside the subcontinent. Nevertheless, the survey also found that an "all-pervasive sense of Indianness prevails through the linguistic, cultural and ecological diversities of the communities of the country."[21]

The country as a whole is made up of 600,000 villages, some 4,000 towns, over 400 administrative districts and 12 major urban centers of over a million, namely, Calcutta, Bombay, Delhi, Madras, Bangalore, Hyderabad, Ahmedabad, Kanpur, Pune, Nagpur, Lucknow and

Jaipur. Just over 25% of India's population is urban; roughly 73% is rural. The greatest density of population is in the northern "Hindi heartland" states of Uttar Pradesh and Bihar, which together account for over 25 percent of the entire population of the country.

One way of simplifying the rich complexity of India's multicultural, multilinguistic and multinational texture is to identify certain key regions that have tended to coalesce and interact with one another historically and continue to do so even now in the latter part of the twentieth century. More will be said about each of these regions in the sequel (see chapters 2 and 3), but suffice it for this introductory profile simply to identify the basic regions as follows:

1. *The Northwest region*, involving Indus Valley cultural traditions, Brāhmaṇical, Hindu-Buddhist, Muslim and Sikh cultural traditions together with the Punjabi, Urdu, Kashmiri and Hindi literary traditions of the Indus region and the Punjab area, and including the states of Punjab, Jammu and Kashmir and Himachal Pradesh;
2. *The "Hindi heartland" region of north central India*, involving Hindu-Buddhist, Jain and Muslim cultural traditions together with the Hindi and Urdu literary traditions of the Ganges River basin and the Gangetic plain, and including the states of Uttar Pradesh, Bihar, Haryana, Madhya Pradesh and Rajasthan;
3. *The Northeast region*, involving Hindu-Buddhist, Muslim, tribal and Christian cultural traditions together with the Bengali, Oriya and Assamese literary traditions of the large states of West Bengal and Orissa and the smaller, newly emerging tribal states of Assam, Arunachal Pradesh, Nagaland, Meghalaya, Manipur, Tripura, Mizoram and Sikkim;
4. *The Western region*, involing Jain, Muslim, Parsi, and Bhakti Hindu and Maratha cultural traditions together with the Gujarati and Marathi literary traditions of the states of Gujarat and Maharashtra;
5. *The Southern region*, involving Hindu, Buddhist, Muslim, and Christian cultural traditions together with the great Dravidian language traditions in Tamil, Telugu, Kannada and Malayalam of the States of Tamil Nadu, Andhra Pradesh, Karnataka, Kerala and Goa.

Geography and Climate

The Northwest region of the subcontinent is the location of the first of the two great river systems of North India, namely, the Indus River. Originating in the high Himalayas in the far north, the Indus River finally turns south and eventually empties into the Arabian Sea. The Indus River region together with its five tributaries (the Jhelam,

Chenab, Ravi, Beas and Satlaj) came to be known as the "land of the five rivers" or the "Punjab," and the region as a whole was the site of the first major civilization in South Asia known as the Indus Valley civilization (to be discussed later). The other great river system, namely, the Ganges, is further to the east in the north central region, like the Indus also originating in the Himalayas in the far north, then flowing south and east through what is now the states of Uttar Pradesh, Bihar and West Bengal and finally emptying into the Bay of Bengal. The vast north central plain, known as the Gangetic plain or the Ganges River basin, is the other major site for the development of civilization in North India. This eventually became what we know today as the "Hindi heartland." It is also the region in which the classical culture of India took shape. Both river systems, the Indus and the Ganges, provide much of the water that is essential for survival in India.

In addition to the two great river systems, the peoples of the subcontinent are also dependent on the monsoon, the "winds" that bring the season of rains. From late September or early October through May, there is very little rainfall in most parts of northern and central India. By the end of May most of north India has become a dry inferno. Then, in June the winds blow from the Indian ocean in the south, gradually forming rain clouds that issue in the heavy monsoon rains that fall from June through September. Prior to the coming of the monsoon, temperatures in north India can easily reach 110 degrees Fahrenheit or higher. By late September, after several months of monsoon rains, the intense heat begins to subside, and one moves into the season of autumn or "winter" (roughly October or November through February). In north India, therefore, there are basically three seasons: (1) the dry season culminating in the intense heat of May (March through May), (2) the rainy season of the monsoon (June through September), and (3) a cooler autumn or winter season (October or November through February). The natural environment of the subcontinent, though characterized by extremes of temperature and a contrasting variety of climatic features, is nevertheless lush and fertile overall, so long as the monsoon makes its annual appearance. When the monsoon fails to appear, however, the lush productivity quickly disappears, and the spectre of famine haunts the land.

South India is separated from north India in the middle of the subcontinent by the Vindhya mountains, nowhere near as high as the Himalayas but nevertheless a significant natural barrier that has been partly responsible for some of the historical differences between the cultures of north and south India. South of the Vindhyas is the Deccan ("south") plateau and further to the south, the Tamil plain and the region of Kerala. Climate on the Deccan plateau is generally moderate and comfortable because of its elevation. The Tamil country, on the other hand, as well as the region of Maharashtra and further south is largely subtropical, always hot but not having the extremes of heat typical of north India. Two other mountain systems should also be mentioned, the Western Ghats ("steps") which border the west coast of India from south of the Vindhyas down to Cape Comorin and provide the backdrop for the narrow and fertile coastal region known as the Malabar coast (famous for its spice production), and the Eastern Ghats which border the east coast of south India and provide the backdrop for the coastal region known as the Coromandal coast. As mentioned earlier, South Indians are often referred to as Dravidian peoples whose languages (Tamil, Telugu, and so forth) and ethnic backgrounds differ considerably from the peoples of the north, although there has been a great deal of mixing throughout the entire history of the subcontinent.

Political Economy

India is best described as a low income, semi-industrialized, mixed economy, partly capitalist and partly socialist, an economy in which the central government controls the "commanding heights" and is highly interventionist in the organized sector of the economy by way of encouraging import substitution and a self-reliance strategy of rapid industrialization. Currently a vigorous program of economic liberalization is being pursued together with much greater attention to the agricultural sector, but it will be many years before liberalization will seriously alter the basic structures of the political economy of present-day India. Since independence in 1947, India has had a series of five-year economic plans, the first for 1950–56 and the current eighth plan running from 1990 to 1995. Basic or primary industrialization was accomplished during the second and third five-year plans, and by the end of third five-year plan an elaborate legal and bureaucratic structure was in place that enabled the state to control almost the whole of the organized economy. According to Lloyd I. and Susanne H. Rudolph,

> After primary industrialization (second and third five-year plans, 1957–67), two-thirds of the workers and the industrial capital in the organized economy and all of the finance capital are in the state sector, conditions that help make private capital and organized labor dependent on the state.[22]

The modern (industrialized) sector of the economy, however, is only about 10% of the total economy. The traditional economy accounts for the remaining 90%, 67% of which is in agriculture and 23% of which is made up of small-scale trade, cottage industries, and so forth.[23]

The modern, industrial sector of the economy produces 24% of the country's income. The agricultural sector represents 39% of the national income, and the remaining 37% derives from services of one kind or another.[24] In terms of income distribution, some 34% of all wealth is held by the top 10% of the population. A full 50% of wealth is held by the top 20%. The bottom 40% of the entire population controls only 16% of the wealth.[25] Similar imbalance occurs in terms of land distribution, although the worst inequities were eliminated by the land reform efforts of 1950 which eliminated the group of "quasi-feudal" landlords (*zamindars* and *jagirdars*) who for centuries had been intermediaries between the state and the cultivator.[26]

Even with land reform, 39% of all land is still held by 6% of the rural population who were and are large landowners, and another 10% of the land is owned by some 33% who were and are small landowners. What emerged as something new as a result of land reform is a group of what the Rudolphs have called "bullock capitalists," a group of self-employed, self-funded "yeoman"-like farmers who have a pair of bullocks and a small parcel of land and have benefitted from the "green revolution."[27] These new bullock capitalists represent some 34% of the rural population (and at least 25% of the total population) and control some 51% of the land. The category of "bullock capitalist" (an economic notion) largely overlaps with the category of "backward classes" (a status notion), and throughout the decades of the 1970s and the 1980s this group has been becoming more and more politically visible and influential.[28] Finally, it should be noted that some 27 percent of the agricultural population is landless.[29]

Regarding the 10 percent of the modern economy, the government controls fully two-thirds. All basic and heavy industry is in government hands together with the infrastructural components of transportation (railways, airlines, roads) and communications (telephone, telegraph, radio, television, and so forth). All financial institutions, banks and insurance, are government-controlled as is almost all industrial and finance capital. Almost all higher education institutions (including some 142 universities, 9 of which are "central" or national universities and the remainder of which are state institutions, enrolling some 3.5 million students), and hence, most research and development and almost all teachers, scientists, technical personnel and intellectuals, are under direct government funding and supervision. Fully two-thirds of all employment in the organized sector is public employment.[30] Among the 100 largest firms in India, the 8 largest are public. Eighteen of the top twenty are public, as are 24 of the top 30. Among the bottom 50, 35 are private.[31] Clearly the state controls the "commanding heights" of the economy, or, as the Rudolphs put it: "Private capitalism in India is dependent capitalism."[32]

As the Rudophs also point out, such thorough-going control of the "organized" economy in India has led to (*a*) the "marginality of class politics," (*b*) the state as a "third actor" in any analysis of economic development, and (*c*) "the predominance of centrist politics." Regarding "marginality," the point is that the modern notion of class-oriented "workers" is so small (only about 3% of the work force) that their influence is severely limited. Regarding the state as "third actor," the point is that in any economic context, in addition to "owners" and "workers," one must also take account of the overwhelming importance of the state as the "third actor." Finally, regarding "the predominance of centrist politics," the point is that since independence, India's political parties on the national level have been largely "centrist" and "pluralist," the paradigmatic example being, of course, the Indian National Congress Party (founded first in 1885) which has for the most part ruled India since independence (under the prime ministerships of Jawaharlal Nehru, Lal Bahadur Shastri, Indira Gandhi, Rajiv Gandhi and currently, P.V. Narasimha Rao).

> Among the Indian state's sources of strength has been a centrist pattern of partisan politics that minimizes the political salience of major cleavages. The country seems agreed ideologically on secularism, socialism, and democracy, on the merits of a mixed economy—part socialist, part capitalist—and on a nonaligned foreign policy.[33]

It must be continually kept in mind, however, that this "persistent centrism" and "pluralism" pertains for the most part to the modern sector of Indian social reality, that is to say, to little more than a small portion of the political economy and to the small elite group of secular, modern leaders (hardly more than 3–5%) who have ruled the country since independence. It was primarily Jawaharlal Nehru who first fashioned the ideology of centrism and pluralism with its components of secularism, socialism, democracy and non-alignment, and it was Nehru who successfully fashioned the requisite political coalition that would enable the small elite group of secular, modern leaders to rule. The Rudolphs have aptly described how Nehru accomplished this.

> The Nehru settlement had been based on a coalition of urban and rural interests united behind an essentially urban-oriented industrial strategy. Its senior partners were India's proportionately small but politically powerful administrative, managerial and professional English-educated middle classes and private-sector industrialists. Private-sector industrialists welcomed the freedom from foreign competition and dependency that was enabled by the second and third five-year plans' import substitution and industrial self-reliance strategies. The English-educated middle classes manned the senior services, built and managed the public-sector industries, and staffed large firms in the modern private sector. The junior partners in the Nehru settlement were the rural notabilities, mostly large landowners who survived intermediary abolition and blocked the passage or implementation of land ceilings legislation. They consented to the import substitution and industrial self-reliance strategies, middle class control of the central government, and the advantages that accrued to urban elites and organized workers on condition that they themselves control the state governments.[34]

This arrangement worked well up through the decade of the 1960s and had its electoral base in the Congress Party's successful centrist and pluralist coalition of most of the forward castes (including almost all of the professional English-educated middle classes and private-sector industrialists), large landowners and key minority constituencies (Scheduled Castes or untouchables, Scheduled Tribes and Muslims). This Congress coalition has never been a majority, but until recently it has provided a sufficient plurality to insure the formation of a series of reasonably stable governments.[35] As mentioned earlier, however, with the emergence of the "bullock capitalists" and/or the "Other Backward Classes," namely, that sizable segment (ranging from 25% to as much as 52% of the total population) of "middle peasants" below the forward castes but higher than the "Scheduled" groups (untouchables and tribals), the so-called centrist and pluralist consensus has begun to unravel.[36] The recent emergence in the 1970s and 1980s of conservative Hindu groups, the growing defensiveness of minority groups in India, the increasing intensity of communal conflict and violence throughout the subcontinent, and the development of separatist movements in the Punjab, Kashmir and elsewhere, are all symptoms to some extent of the breakdown of the centrism and pluralism of the Nehruvian ideology and political consensus.

Another way of putting the same point is to suggest that India, like a number of other low-income developing countries, has since independence been functioning with "dual economies" that are now beginning to come into conflict. The notion of "dual economies" has been described by E. Wayne Nafziger as follows:

> Virtually all low-income countries and many middle-income countries are *dual economies*. These economies have a traditional, peasant, agricultural sector, producing primarily for family or village subsistence. This sector has little or no reproducible capital, uses technologies handed down for generations, and has low marginal productivity of labor (that is, output produced from an extra hour of labor is less than the subsistence wage).
>
> In the midst of this labor-intensive, subsistence, peasant agriculture (together with semisubsistence agriculture, petty trade and cottage industry) sits a capital-intensive enclave consisting of modern manufacturing and processing operations, mineral extraction, and plantation agriculture. This modern sector produces for the market, uses reproducible capital and new technology, and hires labor commercially (where marginal productivity is at least as much as the wage).[37]

Moreover, these "dual economies" tend to have their own unique political idiom, as has been pointed out by Dipesh Chakrabarty:

> . . . one can discern two kinds of political 'languages.' One is the language characteristic of the project of nation-building and involves the rituals of the state, political representation, citizenship, citizens' rights, etc. This is part of our colonial heritage and it is what Indian nationalism owes to the colonial experience. The other language derives its grammar from relationships of power, authority and hierarchy which pre-date the coming of colonialism, but which have been significantly modified by having been made to interact with ideas and institutions imported by British rule. . . . [I]t would be fair to say that historically the first language has been by and large a privilege of the Indian elite classes, while the lives and aspirations of the subaltern classes have been enmeshed on the whole in relationships articulated in the second.[38]

If one keeps in mind that the elitist, modern sector of the economy and its accompanying political ideology represents only a small portion of the social reality of modern India, whereas the newly mobilizing traditional dimensions of the economy and its accompanying political ideologies (including new religious movements), or what Immanuel Wallerstein would call the "anti-systemic forces" of the social reality of modern India, represent the overwhelming majority of the people of the subcontinent, one begins to get some sense of the historic significance of the great social struggle beginning to act itself out in present-day India.[39]

Religions

According to the 1981 Census of India, the percentage breakdown of the various "world" religions in India was as follows: Hindu—82.64%; Muslim—11.35%; Christian—2.43%; Sikh—1.96%; Buddhist—.72%; Jain—.48%; and Other Persuasions—.42%. The category "Other Persuasions" included Parsis (71,630 in 1981), Jews (5,618 in 1981), tribal traditions (roughly 500,000 in 1981), and so forth.[40] Rounding off the percentages and projecting the rounded off percentages on the population of India in the recent 1991 Census of India (namely, 843,930,861 or about 840,000,000), a reasonable rough estimate of membership in various "world" religion groupings would be the following:[41]

Hindus	690–700,000,000 (82% or 83%)
Muslims	95–100,000,000 (11.5% or 12%)
Christians	20,000,000 (2.5%)
Sikhs	16,000,000 (2%)
Buddhists	6,000,000 (.75%)
Jains	4,000,000 (.50%)
Other	4,000,000 (.50%)

Hindus

The so-called "Hindu" percentage is something of a problem, since it includes Scheduled Castes ("untouchables") and Scheduled Tribes ("tribals") that together account for some 23.5 percent of the total population. If one were to assume that many low-status groups would hesitate or prefer not to identify themselves with the category "Hindu," this could lower the "Hindu" total to as low as 500 million, or, in other words, not much more than 60% or 62% of the population. If one then combined the Scheduled Castes and Scheduled Tribes with the other minority religious groups (Muslim, Christian, Sikh, Buddhist, Jain and

Other), the non-Hindu or minority percentage would be 38% to 40%.[42] Much depends, of course, on precisely what is meant by the term "Hindu" and we shall return to this issue at greater length in chapter 4.

By way of an overall approximation, it can be said that about two-thirds of all Hindus are Vaiṣṇava-s (followers of Viṣṇu or one of his incarnations as Kṛṣṇa or Rāma); about one-third would be Śaiva-s (followers of Śiva) or devotees of the goddess (Śākta-s). These traditions are found throughout India, but it is probably fair to say that Vaiṣṇava traditions (especially the traditions of Rāma and Kṛṣṇa) are particularly strong in the northern Hindi heartland region of north central India as well as in the Northeast region around the state of Bengal and the western region of Gujarat and Maharashtra. Śaiva traditions are particularly strong in Tamil Nadu and Karnataka in the southern region but also in Kashmir in the far Northwest region and in the Northeast region in and around Bengal.

There are several hundred monastic orders within the various Hindu traditions, and estimates run from 1 million to as many as 15 million regarding the number of persons involved in the "professional religious" or monastic life in India.[43] The most famous monastic order is the Daśanāmi (literally meaning "the ten-named" or, in other words, an order with "ten named subdivisions"), founded by the great Vedāntin philosopher, Śankara, probably some time in the eighth century of the Common Era and continuing down to the present, with centers in all the major regions of present-day India, the membership of which is overwhelmingly high-caste Brahmin. In addition, there are numerous other *sampradāya*-s or "orders" belonging to the various Vaiṣṇava and Śaiva groups all around India, as well as various independent monastic groups and a great variety of individual itinerant *sādhu*-s ("holy persons").

In addition to these traditional forms of Hindu spirituality, there are also many varieties of what can be called reformist and revisionist Neo-Hindu religious groups whose emergence in the nineteenth and twentieth century largely represent Hindu India's reaction to Western civilization, secularization, modernization and Christian missionary efforts (and all of which will be subsequently discussed).

The anthropologist, Agehananda Bharati, has usefully distinguished three levels of Hindu religion: (*a*) "village Hinduism" made up of "grassroots," "little tradition" Hindu spirituality, characterized by belief in local demons and spirits, eccentric varieties of magico-religious practices, shamanistic traditions of ecstatic experience, but with some observance of all-India mainline Hindu practices and festivals; (*b*) literate or scripture-based "Sanskrit, Vedic Hinduism," also "grassroots" Hindu spirituality but of a learned, "great tradition" variety, represented by Brahmin priests, pandits (traditionally trained scholars), itinerant ascetics or monastic practitioners; and, finally, (*c*) the "renaissance Hinduism" or Neo-Hinduism of what Bharati calls the "urban alienate," or, in other words, a portion of the new urban middle class, characterized by the modernized, reformed and often Westernized Hindu spirituality of *gurus* such as Ramakrishna, Vivekananda, Satya Sai Baba and many others.[44] Bharati's levels, of course, are not to be taken as hard scientific categories based on survey research. They are, rather, a rough heuristic overview of some of the more obvious types of Hindu social reality.

Assuming, as mentioned above, that the category of "Hindu" includes at least about 500 million (or, in other words, some 60% to 62% of the total population and not including Scheduled Castes and Scheduled Tribes as "Hindu"), possibly as many as 3% to 5% could be included in the category of "renaissance Hinduism" or Neo-Hinduism (or, in other words, between 15 and 25 million, most of whom come from the "forward" castes and many of whom are English-speaking); possibly 13% to 15% could be included in the category of literate, scriptural "Sanskrit or Vedic Hinduism" (or, in other words, between 65 and 75 million, and again largely made up of the higher or "forward" castes, with possibly some few knowing English but with most speaking a modern, regional language such as Hindi, Bengali, Gujarati, and so forth); and the remainder could be included in the category of "village Hinduism" (or, in other words, just over 400 million and largely belonging to the Other Backward Classes or other low-status persons). These, of course, are only rough approximations. Hindus represent a majority in almost all States and Union Territories with the exception of the state of Jammu and Kashmir, in which Muslims represent a two-thirds majority, the state of Punjab, in which the majority (60%) is Sikh, and the tribal States of Nagaland and Meghalaya, in which there are majorities (80% and 53% respectively) of (largely Protestant) Christians.

Muslims

Muslims have been involved in the life of the subcontinent as far back as the seventh century of the Common Era, and even during the long centuries of Muslim rule (first by the Turko-Afghan Muslims of the Delhi Sultanate, 1206–1526, and later by the migrant Iranians and Persianized Afghans and Turks of the Mughal period, 1526–1757), the Muslim population was never more than a minority. Even at the time of Partition in 1947, only 24 percent of the population was Muslim. After partition, when the Muslim populations of Punjab and Bengal were split off from India (to form Pakistan) only the state of Jammu and Kashmir continued to have a majority Muslim population. Moreover, the social and cultural make-up of Muslims in India has always been exceedingly diverse, with only a small elite ruling in north central India and another small elite in what is now Andhra, the remainder of the community being made up of urban artisan groups, petty traders, and peasant agrarian communities. The largest concentrations of Muslims are in Assam (24%),[45] West Bengal (21.5%), Kerala (21.3%), Uttar Pradesh (15.9%), Bihar (14.1%), Karnataka (11%) and Andhra Pradesh (8.5%). Moreover, Muslims tend to be concentrated in urban areas—for example, Hyderabad (38%), Lucknow (29%), Varanasi (26%), Allahabad (24%), Kanpur (20%) and concentrations above the national average in Calcutta, Bombay, Bangalore, Ahmedabad, Agra, Jaipur, Indore and Jabalpur.[46] Roughly two-thirds of all Muslims in India are followers of Sunni Islam (approximately 65 million); one-third follow Shi'a Islam (about 35 million). There is also a small community (less than 200,000) of the heretical Ahmadiyas (a dissident Shi'a group in the Punjab region, founded in 1889, with a following also in Pakistan as well as outside the subcontinent in Africa and the United States).

Christians

Christian traditions have been present in India since at least the sixth century of the Common Era and possibly even earlier. The Malabar Christian community (also called the "Thomas Christian" community) in Kerala and Tamil Nadu claims to have been founded by the Apostle Thomas who purportedly was martyred in what is now Madras in 52 of the Common Era. This is probably a legendary account, but there is some evidence that Christian communities may have been present in south India by the middle of the fourth century, and certainly by the middle of the sixth century.[47] These early Christian communities were of the Orthodox Syrian tradition with ties to both Nestorian and Monophysite traditions in the region of Antioch in Syria. Roman Catholicism came to India with the coming of the Portugese in 1498 and the mission work of the Jesuits, St. Francis Xavier (1506-1552), Robert de Nobili (1577-1656) and others, largely in south India. Protestant missionary work first began with Danish Lutherans at the beginning of the eighteenth century and gained great momentum eventually at the end of the eighteenth century and thereafter with the coming of the Baptist,

William Carey, to the Danish settlement at Serampore near Calcutta in 1793.

Among the estimated 20 million Christians in India, nearly half (over 9 million) are Roman Catholic and follow either the reformed Roman rite or the Syro-Malabar rite (a Syriac liturgy, permitted by Rome, for those in the Orthodox Syrian tradition who have become converted or are in communion with Rome).[48] Nearly 8 million Christians are Protestant, with many belonging either to the united Church of North India (a union of Congregationalists, Presbyterians, Anglicans, Methodists, Baptists and Disciples of Christ dating from 1970, and with a membership numbering about 500,000) or to the united Church of South India (a union of Anglicans, Methodists, Presbyterians, Congregationalists and Dutch Reformed, dating from 1947, and with a membership of 1,500,000). Both united Churches are in communion with the Mar Thoma Syrian Church of Malabar (numbering about one million members), an autonomous Orthodox group that broke away from Syrian Orthodox Church in the nineteenth century. The Syrian Orthodox Church itself or the "Thomas Christian" community numbers about 1,500,000. In addition to these main groups, there are numerous independent Baptist, Lutheran, Methodist, Anglican and Pentecostal churches in India. The majority of all Christians (some 60%) in India are to be found in the southern states of Kerala, Tamil Nadu and Andhra Pradesh. As mentioned above, they also represent majority populations in the small tribal states of Nagaland and Meghalaya. They are also found in the state of Goa (31%), the State of Manipur (26%) and in the Union Territories of the Andaman and Nicobar Islands (26%). For the most part, Indian Christians derive from the lower classes and castes, many from tribal and untouchable groups.

Sikhs

The Sikh tradition is a relatively recent addition to India's potpourri of religious traditions. Founded in the Northwest region (the Punjab area) by Guru Nanak (1469–1539) at the beginning of the sixteenth century as an interesting blend of both Hindu devotionalism and Muslim (mainly Sufi) piety, it attained a more distinctive definition at the time of its final or tenth successor-guru, namely, Guru Gobind Singh (1666–1708), who (*a*) proclaimed that the living tradition of Gurus was to be replaced by the Sikh holy book, the "Ādi Granth" or Guru Granth Sahib ("Book of the Lord"), (*b*) introduced the notion of the "Khālsā" (the "pure" community), a sacred, militant fraternity into which committed followers were initiated by means of a kind of baptismal ritual (called *amrit-dhārī* or "taking the nectar"), and (*c*) required those who had been baptized to take a new surname, "Singh" ("lion"), and to observe the symbolic "five K's" (*pañj-pakke*), namely, *kes* (unshorn hair), *kanghā* (comb), *kaṛā* (steel bangle), *kirpān* (dagger) and *kacch* (special cloth shorts or underwear).[49] Thereafter those who had taken "baptism" and become part of the Khālsā came to be known as *kes-dhārī* ("wearing unshorn hair"), while those who had not taken baptism and not joined the Khālsā were referred to as *sahaj-dhārī* or "non-Khālsā Sikhs" or simply the "not yet committed." Much of the religious sentiment of the Sikhs closely parallels Hindu devotional piety, but it resembles Islam in its clear monotheism and its rejection of any representation of the deity. The Sikhs also reject many aspects of the traditional caste system, although caste-groupings do play a role in Sikh politics and religion—for example, urban-based "forward" caste Khatris in rivalry with rural-based and "forward" caste Jats, or again, low-caste or "scheduled caste" Sikhs who seek entitlement benefits along with Hindu "scheduled castes," and so forth.

The Sikh tradition is probably closer overall to Hindu traditions than to Muslim traditions, and it is not unusual for Hindus to think of the Sikh tradition as a subset of Hindu traditions. Moreover, intermarriage is often allowed between Sikh and Hindu families, something that would never occur between Hindus and Muslims.[50] At the same time, however, it is generally the case that Sikhs, especially the *kes-dhārīs* but probably most others in the community as well, since before independence in 1947, have clearly wanted to differentiate Sikh traditions from Hindu traditions, both in terms of politics and in terms of religion. The Sikhs attained a measure of political independence in 1966 when the two new states of Haryana and Punjab were formed, the former of which is a largely Hindu, Hindi-speaking part of the southeastern portion of the old Punjab region and the latter of which is a largely Sikh, Punjabi-speaking part of the northwestern portion of the old Punjab region. The new state of Punjab has a majority Sikh population of 60 percent (roughly 12 million) with its distinctive regional language of Punjabi (and even a distinctive script known as Gurmukhi or "language of the Gurus"), and minority Hindu and Muslim populations of 38% and 1% respectively. There are many Sikhs, however, outside the state of Punjab. As many as 4 million live in the States of Haryana, Rajasthan, Uttar Pradesh and the Union Territory of Delhi, and there is a sizable Sikh "diaspora" outside of India in Canada, the United States, Great Britain and West Germany.

Even with majority status in the new state of Punjab and with their own distinctive political party called the Akali Dal (the "eternal party"), however, the Sikhs have found it difficult to attain a unified voice either in politics or in religion. Indeed, it was Indira Gandhi and her Congress Party who first brought the extremist Jarnail Singh Bhindranwale into political prominence in order to divide the Sikh vote and to increase the influence of the Congress Party in the Punjab.[51] As is well known, the attempt proved to be a disastrous miscalculation, and eventually Mrs. Gandhi had to send the Indian army into the sacred precincts of the Golden Temple in Amritsar in June of 1984 (Operation Blue Star) in order to uproot Bhindranwale and his followers who had taken refuge there. This in turn triggered the assassination of Mrs. Gandhi by her own Sikh body guards in October of 1984 and the subsequent slaughter of innocent Sikhs in Delhi by enraged Hindus and other communal elements. Since that time there has been a growing hard-core of extremists in the state of Punjab and elsewhere (within India and within the Sikh "diaspora" outside of India as well) who want not simply local autonomy within India and recognition as a distinct non-Hindu religious community, but, rather, who demand a separate state in the region to be known as "Khalistan" ("Land of the Pure"). These militant separatists or Khalistani Sikhs represent only a small minority—current estimates by the Government of India put their number at little more than 2,000[52]—but they exert widespread influence over the political life of the state of Punjab and continue to terrorize both the Sikh and Hindu population of the state, although in the last year or two (1993–94) the level of violence has subsided considerably.

Buddhists

The Buddhist tradition, of course, is one of the oldest non-Hindu or non-brahmanical religious traditions in India dating back to the time of its founder, Gautama (ca. 563–483 B.C.E.), in the north central region of the Gangetic plain in what is now Bihar and the foothills of the Himalayas in the southern part of Nepal. The Buddha rejected Vedic ritualism and the authority of Brahmin priests and, instead, taught a moderate "middle way" of disciplined meditation. Buddhist traditions have a rich history on the Indian subcontinent, ranging from its early or Theravāda ("tradition of the elders") forms which helped in providing the political and religious ideology of *dharma* ("law," "righteousness," "doctrine") for India's first period of imperial unification under the Mauryan emperor, Aśoka (269–232 B.C.E.), through various Mahāyāna ("great vehicle") forms in the first centuries of the Common Era, and finally into later highly ritualistic Tantric or Vajrayāna ("thunderbolt vehicle" or "diamond vehicle") forms from the sixth through the tenth and eleventh centuries. Buddhist traditions were prominent on the Indian subcontinent. Early along, they were exported to South and Southeast Asia (largely in Theravāda forms), and eventually to Tibet, Central Asia, China, Korea and Japan (largely in Mahāyāna and Tantric forms), thus becoming a broad, cross-cultural religious tradition on analogy with the two other broad, cross-cultural religious traditions, the Christian and the Islamic.

In the land of its birth, however, namely, India, Buddhist traditions became for the most part extinct after about the fourteenth century of the Common Era, partly because of the onslaught of the Turko-Afghan Muslim invaders from the tenth century onwards which caused thousands of Buddhist monks to be slaughtered or to flee into Tibet and Central Asia, but partly also because many of its distinctive ideas and practices were simply absorbed by the larger Hindu culture. In any case, when one hears about Buddhists in present-day India, it must be kept in mind that there is almost no continuity between present-day Buddhists in India and the historic traditions of Indian Buddhism. To be sure, Indian nationalists both before and after independence were fully aware of the rich contribution that Buddhist institutions and ideas have made to the larger cultural identity of India, and since independence, various Buddhist show-place monasteries (supported by Buddhist followers from Thailand, Japan, and so forth) have been maintained in and around Sarnath, the suburb of the famous city of Banaras, where Gautama the Buddha purportedly first taught his four noble truths and his eightfold path.

Buddhists in present-day India, however, represent two quite different orientations, both highly political and both largely reintroductions of Buddhist traditions into India. Moreover, both reintroductions occurred in the decade of the 1950s. The first has to do with modern India's great untouchable leader, B. R. Ambedkar (1891–1956). Born to the untouchable Mahar caste in the state of Maharashtra in western India, Ambedkar received a solid education and legal training in Bombay (University of Bombay), New York City (Columbia University) and London (University of London). He became a spokesman for India's untouchables and was a major critic of Gandhi and the Congress-led nationalist movement because of its overreliance on Hindu ideas and institutions.[53]

Ambedkar detested everything Hindu but agreed to serve in Nehru's first cabinet as Minister of Law. He also agreed to chair the drafting committee for India's new constitution and was instrumental in helping to fashion the final constitutional document. Through the years he became more and more attracted to Buddhist ideas, since the

Buddhist tradition was an indigenous and authentic tradition of Indian religion that repudiated the authority of the Brahmins as well as the trappings of the caste system. In 1951 he resigned his cabinet post, travelled to Buddhist countries, lectured and wrote about Buddhism. On 14 October 1956 he led a mass conversion to Buddhism of thousands of untouchables in the city of Nagpur in Maharashtra.[54]

Although Ambedkar himself died soon thereafter, the conversion movement he started spread rapidly among untouchable communities, and within a few years some 4 million people, largely Scheduled Castes or untouchables in Maharashtra, Karnataka, Tamil Nadu and Uttar Pradesh, had converted to Buddhism.[55] Ambedkar was also instrumental in laying the groundwork for a new political party, the Republican Party, specifically designed to serve the needs of Scheduled Castes and other low-status persons. Because of Ambedkar's premature death, the political party has not had any longterm or lasting significance, although it did generate an untouchable political awareness in independent India that has taken a variety of forms in more recent years. At any rate, among the 6 million Buddhists in present-day India, the overwhelming majority are these Neo-Buddhists from the Scheduled Castes in Maharashtra and elsewhere.

The other dimension of the re-introduction of Buddhist tradition into present-day India, of course, is the presence of His Holiness, the fourteenth Dalai Lama, together with the remnant of the Tibetan Buddhist community.[56] The People's Republic of China "liberated" Tibet in 1950, and in 1959 when the Tibetan rebellion in Lhasa against the Chinese was viciously repressed, the Dalai Lama together with thousands of monks fled to India. The Tibetans were given asylum by Prime Minister Nehru in Dharmasala in the northern state of Himachal Pradesh, and since that time the Tibetans have been working diligently to preserve Tibetan Buddhist culture in India and to prepare a Tibetan political movement looking towards a return to Tibet as well as some sort of political settlement with the People's Republic of China.

Jains

Unlike the Buddhist tradition which largely became extinct in India and had to be reintroduced, the Jains have been a small but influential presence in India since their founding in the sixth century B.C.E. by Vardhamāna ("he who is bringing prosperity"), also called Mahāvira (the "great hero").[57] There is some evidence that Jain traditions may be even older than Buddhist traditions, possibly going back to the time of the Indus Valley civilization, and that Vardhamāna rather than being a "founder" per se was, rather, simply a primary spokesman for a much older tradition.[58] Like the Buddhist traditions, the Jains represent a dissident tradition in India. That is to say, like the Buddhists, they too reject the Vedic sacrificial system and the authority of the Brahmin priests, and encourage or teach, instead, a mendicant life of disciplined meditation. Also like the Buddhist traditions, the origins of the Jain traditions are in the north central region of the Gangetic plain in what is now Bihar and the southern part of Nepal. There were a number of other mendicant groups in the same region in the sixth and fifth centuries B.C.E., and these various dissident traditions are referred to as *śramaṇa*-groups or "wandering ascetic"-groups. Jain traditions differ from Buddhist traditions and some of the other *śramaṇa*-groups by being much more extreme in the pursuit of ascetic practices. Jains are usually credited with introducing the notion of "non-violence" (*ahiṃsā*) towards all living things and the tradition of vegetarianism in India.

As early as the fourth century B.C.E., a great schism occurred among the Jain ascetics which continues to divide the community down to the present day. A section known as Digambaras ("sky-clad") which requires a strict, ascetic life including even the giving up of all clothes or garments, hence the name "sky-clad" or naked, broke away from a more moderate section known as Śvetāmbaras ("white or cotton-clad") which is willing to make compromises with ordinary conventional society and is also willing to allow women into the mendicant life.[59] Eventually the Digambaras migrated to south India, to southern Maharashtra and Karnataka, whereas the Śvetāmbaras migrated to the western region of India, the areas of Gujarat, Rajasthan, western Madhya Pradesh and northern Maharashtra. This distribution of the two main sections of Jain traditions continues to a large extent down to the present, and the 4 million Jains in present-day India tend to be settled for the most part in the western regions (Gujarat, Rajasthan and northern Maharashtra) and southern regions (Karnataka, and so forth) of the subcontinent, although smaller groups may also be found in almost every region of India, especially in major urban centers like Delhi and Bombay. They have traditionally been involved in trade and commerce (both before modernization and after), especially in Gujarat and Rajasthan. They tend also to be highly educated and urban-based, although in south India there is a sizable rural population of Jain farmers.[60]

One interesting historical question is why the Jains were able to survive in India for so many centuries down to the present day, whereas the Buddhists became for the most part extinct after the fourteenth century. Part of the answer relates to royal patronage at certain crucial times in the regional histories of western India and southern India. Another part of the answer relates to the extreme puritanical attitude of Jains that has always given them a definite sense of being separate from the larger Hindu environment. A third part of the answer, possibly a major part, relates to certain strategic compromises that Jains were able to make in the areas of ritual behavior, adherence to local customs, and a willingness under certain circumstances to engage in intermarriage with certain Hindu groups. Moreover, the Jain monastic traditions have always maintained close ties with their larger lay communities, and Jain writers, monks and intellectuals have addressed themselves in detail to problems of maintaining the Jain identity within the larger sea of Hindu India.[61]

Parsis and Jews

At least some mention should be made of two additional religious communities in present-day India that are rapidly becoming extinct but have been in former years identifiable and influential. As mentioned above, in the 1981 Census of India, these groups were listed under the category of "Other Persuasions," the number of Parsis being put at 71,630, largely in the city of Bombay and its environs, and the number of Jews being put at 5,618, including the so-called Malayalam-speaking "Cochin Jews" of Kerala, the so-called "Baghdadi" Jews of the northern cities, and the so-called Marathi-speaking "Bene Israel" ("Children of Israel") in Maharashtra (mainly Bombay).[62] In earlier years there were well over 100,000 Parsis in Bombay, and at the time of independence in 1947 there were well over 25,000 Jews. Since the founding of the state of Israel, however, most Jews have left India for Israel, and when the calculations for the 1991 Census of India are published, it may well be the case that there are no longer any Jewish communities in India beyond some few families in Bombay, Calcutta and Pune.

Evidence indicates that Jews first came to India around the thirteenth century along the Malabar coast (the region of Kerala) and were involved largely in trade and commerce.[63] Others settled further to the north in the region of Maharashtra. Some have suggested that the Jewish presence in India is as old as the presence of Christianity, but such a claim is difficult to document. In addition to trade and commerce in modern India, Jews have also been involved in manufacturing, civil administration and the military. They have been largely urban-based.

Parsis are also rapidly disappearing, since one can only be a Parsi if descended from a Parsi male; in other words, there is no possibility of conversion to the Parsi faith by a non-Parsi. The name "Parsi" is a

Gujarati form of "Persian" and refers to a small refugee band of Zoroastrians who came to the northwestern coast of India (Maharashtra, in and around the Bombay area) some time in the tenth century C.E. after prolonged persecution following the Arab Islamic conquest of Iran.[64] Over the centuries the Parsis have built and maintained their sacred "fire temples" (some of which are said to have maintained continuous fire for over a thousand years) and the well-known "towers of silence" in which the dead are placed to be devoured by vultures so that the earth is not polluted by the flesh of the dead. The Parsi community became highly Westernized during the nineteenth century and has played a major role, especially in western India but elsewhere as well, in the development of India as a modern, industrialized state. Being itself a separate caste or ethnic group, it has been free from many of the restrictions that hindered the modernization of many traditional Hindu castes.

This, then, concludes my attempt to sketch an introductory profile of present-day India. It is, to be sure, little more than a preliminary snapshot of a great civilization struggling to survive and to develop itself into a modern, industrialized nation-state, able to support its massive population and to overcome the cruel inequities of its precolonial and colonial past. Obviously "religion" or, perhaps better, the so-called "world religions" loom large in the awareness of the people of modern India, and how the people of modern India understand their "world religions," and even more important, how they negotiate the relations between the various "world religions," on the one hand, and between the "world religions" and the "state," on the other, will be important variables in determining the long-term viability of India as a modern, industrialized nation-state.

But let me move on now quickly to complete this introductory chapter by briefly saying something about some issues of definition and theoretical perspective to be followed in this study.

The Term "Religion"

What begins to become clear even in this rapid and introductory survey is the remarkable diversity within the various "world religions" in India, a diversity so rich in texture that one begins to question whether it is legitimate to make any generalizations at all about the various "religions," and even more than that, to question the very validity of the categories or names employed. To be sure, it might be argued that such labels have at least a heuristic naming utility that enables us to identify certain large populations for purposes of intellectual analysis, but it might well be countered that even as naming terms they are not identifying certain large populations as much as they are identifying overly broad abstractions about certain large populations, overly broad abstractions that finally hinder any serious attempt at intellectual analysis. Robert Frykenberg has argued along precisely these lines with respect to the use of the terms "Hindu" and "Hinduism":

> . . . in what is now often referred to as "popular Hinduism"; what is called "temple Hinduism"; . . . "bhakti Hinduism"; . . . "village Hinduism"; ...and "tribal Hinduism"; not to mention other localistic forms of Indian culture and religion which some think of as being quintessentially "Hindu"—the term "Hinduism" has been and still is often compounded and confused with any or all of the above usages. The result has been a jumbling and scrambling of signals. Vagueness of usage has led this concept into trackless deserts of nonsense.[65]

Peter Hardy has made a similar observation about Islam in India:

> The entry of Muslims into South Asia by so many and separated doorways and their spread over the subcontinent by so many different routes, over a period of centuries, ensured that Islam would present itself to the peoples of South Asia in many different epiphanies seen from many angles. Neither to its own adherents nor to non-Muslims in South Asia has Islam seemed monochromatic, monolithic or indeed mono-anything. It has indeed been said that Islam in South Asia has been united only by a few common rituals and by the aspirations of its scholars.[66]

I am inclined to go even further than Frykenberg and Hardy and to argue that much the same can be said about all of the other so-called "world religions" in India as well, including Christianity, Sikhism, Buddhism, Jainism, Judaism and Parsiism (or Zoroastrianism). These designations are for the most part little more than conventional labels that have almost no referential or theoretical validity whatever. Each is a singular label disguising what is in reality a pluralist array of cultural traditions. As Wilfred Cantwell Smith has shown, such singular labels ("Hinduism," and so forth) are products of the reifying intellectualism of the European Enlightenment.[67] Frits Staal has pushed the issue even more radically, arguing that even the term "religion" itself is little more than a proper name or label derived on analogy from pre-modern Jewish, Christian and Islamic models and then uncritically projected on to cultural traditions in which the label does not fit in any meaningful sense. The term "religion," in other words, is not a general or generic notion such as "language" or "culture," but only a naming term.[68]

Both W. C. Smith and Frits Staal suggest that the use of "world religions" discourse as well as the use of the term "religion" be abandoned or set aside. I would fully concur with the former suggestion, but I would not concur that we stop using the term "religion." Because a term has been uncritically used or applied need not entail that the term be dismissed or eliminated. A better approach might be to set forth a theoretically and analytically useful reinterpretation of the terms at issue, and wherever possible, to reduce the former, uncritical discourse to a meaningful, critical account of what is at stake. I shall attempt such a reinterpretation of the notion of "religion" in chapter 4 of the present book. I mention this important issue now in this introductory chapter in order to make clear that my use of the term "religion" in the sense of "world religions" in this chapter is only a preliminary starting-point that will be reworked in the sequel.

The Terms "State," "Nation-State" and "Civilization"

There is no need to enter into detailed theoretical discussions about the meaning of the terms "state," "nation-state" and "civilization," but there is a need to make clear how the terms are being used in the present book. In this regard I have found the discussions of Ernest Gellner, Anthony Giddens and Ravinder Kumar to be especially helpful, the first two by way of providing useful general discussions about the notions "state" and "nation-state" and the latter by way of providing a useful perspective about the notion of "civilization" and the manner in which these various terms apply to India.

Turning first to the notions of "state" and "nation," Gellner offers the following definitions:

> . . . the state is the specialization and concentration of order maintenance. The "state" is that institution or set of institutions specifically concerned with the enforcement of order (whatever else they may also be concerned with). The state exists where specialized order-enforcing agencies, such as police forces and courts, have separated out from the rest of social life. They *are* the state.[69]

Gellner goes on to point out that the notion of the "state" is a contingent one, as is the notion of the "nation." In pre-agrarian (hunting and gathering) societies, for example, both notions are totally absent. Even in agrarian societies, they are only options, and there is a great variety of types of "state" and "nation." In post-agrarian, industrial society, the notions of "state" and "nation" are everywhere present. Says Gellner: "Paraphrasing Hegel, once none had the state, then some had it, and finally all have it."[70]

Gellner then offers what he calls a "makeshift" definition of the "nation" as follows:

> 1. Two men are of the same nation if and only if they share the same culture, where culture in turn means a system of ideas and signs and associations and ways of behaving and communicating.
> 2. Two men are of the same nation if and only if they recognize each other as belonging to the same nation. . . A mere category of persons (say, occupants of a given territory, or speakers of a given language, for example) becomes a nation if and when the members of the category firmly recognize certain mutual rights and duties to each other in virtue of their shared membership of it.[71]

The notion of "nation," in other words, is not simply a matter of a shared culture or a shared language. It is also a matter of mutual recognition and obligation willingly assumed. To use the idiom of Benedict Anderson, it is always "an imagined community" in an important sense.[72]

Turning next to the more complex or compounded notion of the "nation-state," the work of Anthony Giddens is important and precise. Regarding the definition of "nation-state," Giddens offers the following:

> The nation-state, which exists in a complex of other nation-states, is a set of institutional forms of governance maintaining an administrative monopoly over a territory with demarcated boundaries (borders), its rule being sanctioned by law and direct control of the means of internal and external violence.[73]

The nation-state, says Giddens, differs from "traditional states" and "absolutist states." Prior to the modern period, there had been basically four different types of "traditional" "intersocietal systems," namely, "tribal cultures," "city-state systems," "systems of feudal states" and "imperial systems."[74] Beginning in seventeeth-century Europe, a new system begins to emerge which Giddens calls the "absolutist state."

Impersonal administrative power and bureaucratization are key characteristics of the absolutist state, which paves the way for the development of nation-states with their "administrative orders of high intensity."[75] The notion of the "nation-state" and the system of nation-states is a unique development in European history and closely parallels the development of industrialism and capitalism. Now, of course, all three, namely, the system of nation-states, industrialism and capitalism have become global. We are now living in the time of the "global consolidation of industrial capitalism" and the "global ascendancy of the nation-state system."[76]

Giddens also helpfully summarizes the various attempts at constructing typologies of the kinds of states in the system of nation-states, reducing them to three, namely, (*a*) a geopolitical framework, (*b*) an original-state-formation framework, and (*c*) an institutional-clustering framework.[77] Regarding the geopolitical framework, he identifies the following types:

Focal–Hegemonic
Adjacent–Subsidiary
Central–Aligned
Central–Non-Aligned
Peripheral–Aligned
Peripheral–Non-Aligned.[78]

"Focal–Hegemonic" refers to the United States and the former Soviet Union and the bipolar geopolitical world that flourished from the end of World War II until the end of the Cold War. "Central" refers to "second-order" powers which are nevertheless able to play an important role in global politics because of fairly high levels of industrialism and a strong military. "Peripheral" refers to states with low levels of industrialism and military capacity who are also at a great distance from the main focal areas. Given such a geopolitical typology, present-day India would probably be placed either within the type "Central–Aligned" or "Central–Non-Aligned," depending upon how one would assess the importance of India's relation to the Soviet Union up through the decade of the 1980s.

Regarding the original-state-formation framework, Giddens identifies four types:

1. Classical
2. Colonized
3. Post-Colonial
4. Modernizing[79]

"Classical," of course, is the paradigmatic European nation-state. "Colonized" would include such states as the United States, Canada, Australia and Israel. "Post-colonial" would be those largely Third World states whose polities were brought from the outside by colonial powers but who since have become independent. Sometimes they are referred to as "state-nations" instead of "nation-states" in the sense that the foreign polity has been much more decisive in the formation than has any sense of being a "nation." Many of the new states in Africa would be included under this type. Finally, "modernizing" refers to those states that are moving from a traditional orientation to a modernizing one through a process of internal political mobilization, even though they may have been under direct colonial control for a period of time. Given such a typology, clearly present-day India would be a "modernizing" nation-state. Although India experienced two hundred years of colonialism, it can hardly be described as a "state-nation" of the "post-colonial" type. There is a long heritage of state-formation in India, including Hindu, Islamic as well as British models or paradigms together with over a century of internal political mobilization of a modern type.

Finally, regarding an institutional-clustering framework, Giddens proposes the following:

Industrialized economy	+	–
Capitalistic production	+	–
Political integration	+	–
Military rule[80]	–	+

The classical nation-state is represented by the left column. This is a diagnostically interesting way of looking at nation-states outside of the classical European context. With respect to present-day India, one would have to say that India is obviously aspiring to the classical model but has some considerable way to go. Industrialism and capitalism represent only a small percentage of the total Indian economy. Political integration has, of course, been achieved over nearly fifty years of independence, but it is now seriously threatened in the states of Punjab and Jammu-Kashmir and in the Northeast region as well (the tribal states and West Bengal). The military in India has not played a political role since the time of independence, but the absence of internal pacification in many parts of India (Punjab and Kashmir being the main examples) could trigger the beginning of a political role for the military, at least in the troubled states.

As helpful as Gellner and Giddens are by way of helping us understand the notions of "state," "nation," and "nation-state" and the manner in which one might place present-day India within the contemporary system of nation-states, there is something still missing from the analysis. To be sure, India is a modern nation-state or at least an aspiring modern nation-state, but it is also more than that. Here we return to something mentioned at the beginning of the chapter, namely, that abiding sense of permanence within the flux of modernity, or perhaps better, that "play within the play" mentioned by W. H. Morris-Jones. India is not only a modern nation-state. It is also a world-class "civilization," and here the work of Ravinder Kumar is instructive. Kumar delineates the basic issue as follows:

> As a result of the development in material conditions and growth in political awareness that has taken place after 1947, the deep contradiction between the sharply focussed identity of a Nation-State, on the one hand, and the truly epic diversity of the local and regional cultures which underpin Indian civilisation, on the other, can no longer be brushed aside. Indeed, without focussing upon the centres of disquiet within the subcontinent, it is clear that the notion of India as a Nation-State sends tremors of alarm through wide swathes of the people, who look to their location in regional or local communities as the primary basis of their identity formation. Even in the great heartland, where Hindi (or one of its variants) constitutes the language and shapes the culture of the people, the primary basis of identity formation remains the locality and the region; beyond which stands the amorphous concept of a pan-Indian civilisation and the partially crystallised notion of a Nation-State.[81]

Kumar then goes on to suggest that instead of thinking about India as a nation-state, it might be more appropriate to refer to it as what he calls a "Civilisation-State." Kumar defines "civilisation" as follows:

> . . . a civilisation consists of a major segment of humanity, characterized by some distinctive traits which confer on it a unique

> social character. . . . the mechanisms of wealth generation; the character of social and political institutions, and the texture of moral values—confer on it a distinctive identity and an autonomy which have been major features of world history over the past few millennia.[82]

By the expression "texture of moral values," Kumar means the "unique moral vision" or "view of the 'good life . . . which illumines both the sacred and the profane worlds." Kumar, then, concludes:

> The objectives of the liberation struggle—the transformation of an agricultural into an industrial society; the creation of a cohesive pan-Indian State; and the creation also of representative institutions within India—can be achieved with greater facility within the framework of a "Civilisation-State" than within the framework of a "Nation-State." However, crucial to such a consummation is the concept of a subcontinental culture resting upon a multiplicity of religious visions; and drawing into its matrix the richness of the regional constituents of Indian society.[83]

The Rudolphs are struggling with a similar conceptualization when they refer to modern India as a "subcontinental multinational state," or "the state Europe would have become had the Holy Roman Empire embodied itself in a modern polity."[84] A somewhat similar point has been made by Sir Percival Spear but with the slightly more pessimistic twist that the "Civilisation-State" or "subcontinental multinational state" that India aspires to become has always eluded it.

> Though India has been the seat of a single culture, however diversely expressed, this culture has neither articulated itself in a number of independent national states as in Europe, nor as a single stable cultural empire as in China. There has been a constant striving for unity without the power of achieving it.[85]

Theoretical Perspective

There remains one final task for this introductory chapter, and that is briefly to indicate the theoretical perspective from which the present book is written. Regarding theoretical perspective, perhaps the best way to proceed is to characterize some of the more important theoretical perspectives that are currently employed in South Asian studies and the manner in which the perspective of this book is dependent upon but also different from these perspectives.

Modernization-Secularization Theorizing

I have in mind here the tradition of modern, liberal social scientific work, beginning with Durkheim and Weber and coming down to most of the sociological and social-anthropological work currently being done in the United States, Western Europe and India (for example, Peter Berger, Milton Singer, Louis Dumont, McKim Marriott, M. N. Srinivas, André Béteille, and a host of others).[86] I am also inclined to include the "critical theory" tradition of Jürgen Habermas and the Frankfurt School under this heading. There is, of course, great diversity among these theorists, but they all also operate with certain basic (largely Weberian) assumptions, namely, (*a*) that modernization entails the "disenchantment of the world" and a continuing process of secularization, (*b*) that industrialization and economic growth depend upon "rationalization," the free play of ideas (pluralism) in the academy, the free play of commodities (free trade) in the market (at least for fully developed economies), and a this-worldly humanistic orientation, (*c*) that there is a continuum of development from less developed "traditional" societies to more developed "modern" societies and that one can rationally "plan" for the transition from the former to the latter, (*d*) that the model for modernization and the resulting secularization is industrialized (and largely Protestant) Western Europe and the United States (and to some extent Japan), and (*e*) that "traditional" societies are best understood when compared and contrasted with modern western civilization and its development from the sixteenth and seventeeth centuries onward. The philosophical grounding of this sort of theorizing is Neo-Kantian (in Durkheim, Weber, and so forth) or Neo-Hegelian (in Habermas and the Frankfurt School tradition), and its economic grounding is capitalism or democratic socialism. It is largely the theoretical basis from which Nehru and other secular Indian nationalists (and even to some extent Gandhi) developed the notion of independent India as a "sovereign democratic republic" (in the 1950 version of the preamble to the Constitution of India) or later as a "sovereign socialist secular democratic republic" (with the addition of the forty-second amendment to the Constitution in 1976).

Orientalist Theorizing

Here, of course, I have in mind the traditions of humanistic scholarship as they pertain to non-Western traditions, including philology, archaeology and art history, ancient history, language and literature, history of religions, and the great area specializations of Islamic studies, Buddhist studies, Indology, Sinology and Japanology. In contrast to modernization-secularization theorizing with its trajectory of future-oriented development, Orientalist theorizing focuses on the "classical" and essentialist formulations coming from the past of the world's great non-Western civilizations and religions as they are set forth primarily in textual, art historical and archaeological sources. Edward Said has described the "features of the Orientalist projection" as follows:

> To restore a region from its present barbarism to its former classical greatness; to instruct (for its own benefit) the Orient in the ways of the modern West; . . . to formulate the Orient, to give it shape, identity, definition with full recognition of its place in memory, its importance to imperial strategy, and its "natural" role as an appendage to Europe; . . . and, above all, to transmute living reality into the stuff of texts.[87]

Said's account, of course, is not a little tendentious and something of a caricature. Moreover, it treats mainly Islamic and Middle Eastern studies thereby leaving out most of Orientalist theorizing. A better recent account is that of Ronald Inden who refers to "Orientalist discourse" being made up of "two major clusters" of "language and area studies." These "two major clusters"

> . . . correspond rather closely to the two Orients their practitioners represent in their discourse. The one consists of the study of the Arabic, Persian, and Turkish languages and has Islam as its unifying subject. This is the orientalism about which we have heard so much since the publication of Edward Said's book of that name.
>
> The other cluster of disciplines consists of the study of 'classical' Chinese (and of Japanese and other central and east Asian languages) and of Sanskrit, India's 'classical' language, along with other 'regional' languages of the subcontinent. It is unified only very loosely by the religion of Buddhism. The first of these clusters has as its professional organ in the United States, the Middle Eastern Studies Association. Scholars of the second cluster congregate annually under the rubric of the Association for Asian Studies.[88]

He might well have added the American Oriental Society and such journals as the *Journal of Asian Studies*, the *Journal of the American Orien-*

tal Society, the *Journal of the Royal Asiatic Society*, the *Indo-Iranian Journal*, the *Wiener Zeitschrift fur Kunde Sud Asiens*, and a host of others. What I am calling "Orientalist theorizing," even after the critique of Said and the more recent critique of Inden, is still the dominant mode of theorizing among European, American and Japanese humanists who work in non-Western traditions.[89] It was also strong among Indian scholars up to and after India's independence—one thinks, for example, of such figures as Surendranath Dasgupta, G. Jha, R. G. Bhandarkar, R. N. Dandekar, and P. V. Kane—but interestingly enough it is rapidly disappearing among contemporary Indian scholars.

World-System Theorizing

Here I would include, of course, the work of Immanuel Wallerstein along with other "economistic" approaches, including the original work of Marx himself and such spin-offs as dependency theory, and other Marxian approaches.[90] Two primary characteristics separate this sort of theorizing from the liberal modernization-secularization theorizing mentioned earlier. First, world-system theorizing stresses a holistic, systemic approach. One cannot speak about India in isolation from the world-economy as a whole. In terms of the core of the world-economy, its semi-periphery, and its periphery, India clearly belongs in the semi-periphery, as a necessary mediating economy between the core and the periphery. Second, unlike modernization-secularization theorizing which focuses more on a Weberian "elective affinity" model of relating ideas and political movements (superstructure) to economic institutions or "modes of production" (infrastructure), world-system theorizing stresses the causal significance of the material base (the economy). Hence, "anti-systemic movements" (for example, activist religious groups) are seldom significant in terms of their ideas or intellectual content. The content, rather, is a veiled symptom of changing modes of material production within a national economy and the world-system as a whole. The great advance, of course, of Wallerstein's "world-system" theorizing over traditional Marxian analysis is its taking seriously of nationalism and the system of nation-states. Also it takes much more seriously the emergence of new religious groups as "anti-systemic movements" within the larger exploitative "world-system," although it is still naively reductive in its treatment of religion as conventional Marxian analysis. While Wallerstein's world-system theorizing and its basically Marxian orientation is only a minor intellectual tradition in European and American scholarly circles (especially since the end of the Cold War and the collapse of the Soviet system), such leftist theorizing is still very strong in Indian intellectual circles.[91] This is somewhat ironic, since a Marxian-type analysis only pertains to a small segment of the Indian economy—that is to say, that portion of the economy that is "organized" along "class" lines in the Marxian sense. Even more ironic is that leftist intellectuals in India have consistently supported the policy of import substitution and the relative isolation of the Indian economy within the world-system and represent currently the most vigorous critics of the new liberalization policy. One can only conclude that leftist rhetoric in India has a very different referent than was meant by Marx or that is currently meant by Wallerstein and other world-system theorists.

Subaltern Theorizing

Some of the most intriguing and important new theoretical work in Indian studies has come from what is known as "subaltern studies."[92] A group of (largely) young scholars and intellectuals in India, including Ranajit Guha, Gautam Bhadra, Dipesh Chakrabarty, Partha Chatterjee, Ramachandra Guha, Gyanendra Pandey and others have been pursuing research which tries to break free of what they call the "elite historiography" on India by both Western and Indian historians. In a way it could well be said that this group of theorists calls into question all three of the theoretical perspectives just mentioned, that is, modernization-secularization theory, Orientalist theory and world-system theory because all of these theories pertain only to a small segment of Indian social reality. Gayatri Chakravorty Spivak, the well-known post-modernist critic (and translator of Derrida), nicely captures the thrust of this movement in the title to her review essay, namely, "Subaltern Studies: Deconstructing Historiography."[93] The task, as she sees it, is to get beyond the broad, mainstream and biased overview of the "official" or "elitist" history of India in order to find the concrete and particular historical struggles of the "subaltern" masses in India. Hence, "subaltern studies" often focus on microscopic and local or regional issues the only evidence for which is local archival material, village birth records, regional court cases and oblique or passing references in "official" accounts. Essay titles such as "Four Rebels in 1857" (by Gautam Bhadra), "Trade Unions in a Hierarchical Culture: The Jute Workers of Calcutta, 1920–50" (by Gyanendra Pandey) or "Adivasi Politics in Midnapur, c. 1760–1924" (by Swapan Dasgupta) are typical of the specific topics addressed by the subaltern group.[94] "Subaltern studies" look for "an-other India" which is not yet a "nation," or, as Dipesh Chakrabarty puts it: "Subaltern studies begins by questioning the category of the 'nation' and poses the failure of the 'nation' to come to its own as a fundamental problem of modern Indian history."[95] Or again: "The central aim of the Subaltern Studies project is to understand the consciousness that informed and still informs political actions taken by the subaltern classes on their own, independently of any elite narratives."[96] "It is in this context that the 'religious consciousness' of the peasant remains an extremely vital subject of study."[97] It must be said, of course, that the subaltern group has not made much progress in its treatment of the "religious consciousness," but it is very much to the credit of the group to have recognized the singular importance of the religious perspective. The problem with subaltern theorizing is that it is intellectually derivative from post-modernist and post-structuralist western "critical theory" and thereby runs the risk of being little more than a kind of Neo-Orientalist theorizing.[98]

Towards a "Religionization" Theorizing

I would characterize my own approach in the present book as an attempt at developing a theory of "Religionization."[99] Although the importance of religion is recognized by all of the types of theorizing mentioned above, no one of the approaches adequately deals with the high salience of the religious question. Modernization-secularization theorizing focuses on the disappearance of traditional religious perspectives but has little to say about how religious perspectives come into play beyond rather thin theories of functionalism (or structural-functionalism, largely following Durkheim) or an unapologetic historicist positivism (so-called substantive accounts like that of Peter Berger). Orientalist theorizing tells us a great deal about the great, pre-modern "world religions," especially as these classical "essences" are described in the belief systems of the great textual traditions, but such theorizing seldom takes us beyond essentialist formulations, as Ronald Inden has cogently shown in his *Imagining India*.[100] World-system theorizing clearly recognizes the importance of the religious perspective as a crucial component in many "anti-systemic movements" but then treats the perspective in a reductive fashion, as something other than what it appears to be. Finally, subaltern theorizing realizes that the "religious consciousness" is a "vital subject of study" but frankly admits that it has not made a great deal of progress in treating it.

Lest I be misunderstood, let me hasten to add that my intention here is to be descriptive, not polemical. My own training has been largely in the tradition of Orientalist theorizing, and I have learned much and greatly benefitted from the corrective perspectives of modernization-secularization theorizing, world-system theorizing and subaltern theorizing. What is missing in all of these traditions of theorizing, however, is what I would call a religious studies perspective. By a religious studies perspective, I mean a perspective that focuses on the high salience of religious experience, not simply in terms of its manifestation in historical, social, economic and political contexts, but also in terms of its substantive content, that is, its basic intellectual and spiritual claims. This is not to blame or censure any of the other traditions of theorizing, since, after all, they do not intend nor, for that matter, should they intend to do a religious studies analysis. My only point is to say that a religious studies perspective is what I intend to offer in this book, not as a substitute for any of the traditions of theorizing briefly described, but, rather, as what I hope will be a useful supplement to all of our varied attempts to understand the problem of the relation between "religion" and the "state" in modern India.

2

Discontinuity as Continuity (i): Old Indic Formations

One of the distinctive features of South Asian culture in historic and recent times is the way in which it has encapsulated communities at many different cultural and technological levels, allowing them, to a large extent, to retain their identity and establish inter-community relationships.

—B. and R. Allchin, *The Rise of Civilization in India and Pakistan*

The World Turned Upside Down

The siege at Yorktown in Virginia (28 September through 19 October 1781) had been long and painful for Lieutenant General Charles (the second Earl) Cornwallis, commander of His Majesty's army in the southern part of North America, and for his six thousand troops.[1] The earl's commanding officer, General Henry Clinton, based at British headquarters in New York, had promised repeatedly to provide relief both by land as well as by sea, but no help had materialized by the middle of October. What neither Clinton nor Cornwallis had fully realized at the time was that a sizable French fleet under the Comte de Grasse had secured control of the sea access to Yorktown by blocking the entrance to Chesapeake Bay, while George Washington's American army, accompanied by a French land force commanded by the Comte de Rochambeau, had already advanced from New York by late September and had secured complete control of the land access to Yorktown. In other words, neither realized that by the first days of October of 1781 Lieutenant General Cornwallis and his six thousand troops were hopelessly trapped.

When he finally realized the tragic reality of his situation, Cornwallis, of course, sued for peace, and by mid-day on 19 October the terms of surrender had been agreed to by all concerned. Basically it was a generous surrender which General George Washington proposed and to which General Cornwallis acceded, allowing, for example, a broad-based parole for Cornwallis and his officers and men, even going so far as allowing them to return to Europe, but there was one humiliating exception. General Cornwallis and his British army were to be denied the honors of war by General Washington, a tradition which allowed the surrendering army to leave with flags unfurled and playing a march of the victorious army.[2] Instead, Washington insisted that the British leave with their flags furled or encased, playing only a British or a German march. The reason for this humiliation is that a year earlier the British general, Henry Clinton, had denied the honors of war to the defeated American army of General Benjamin Lincoln at Charleston, South Carolina.

In mid-afternoon, then, the British army marched out of Yorktown with its flags encased, its drums pounding and its fifes or shrill flutes purportedly playing, at least according to one eye-witness account, a British tune entitled, ironically enough, "The World Turned Upside Down."[3] Cornwallis himself did not lead his troops to the formal surrender ceremony on that October afternoon; the troops were led, rather, by Brigadier General Charles O'Hara. Cornwallis had become ill with fever, possibly feigned because of the humiliation, but more likely real enough, for whatever else might be said about Lord Cornwallis, all would agree, then as well as now, that he was a man of personal courage, integrity and honor. In many ways he was one of the ablest military men that the British had sent to North America to put down the American insurrection. Just months earlier he had scored a major victory at Camden, South Carolina, over General Horatio Gates, and generally speaking, he has been given high marks for his military work in the southern theater of the American Revolutionary War, his surrender at Yorktown notwithstanding. Cornwallis himself was never really blamed for the British defeat in North America, even though the surrender at Yorktown was the *coup de grâce* in the American War of Independence. The ineptitude of Henry Clinton and British policy generally were much more to the point in determining the reasons for the British failure in colonial America.

In any case, I begin this second chapter with this little anecdote about Charles Cornwallis at Yorktown and the ironic British tune, "The World Turned Upside Down," not because of the failure of the British in the "New World," but, rather, because of the success of the British in the "Old World." Putting the matter somewhat differently, the irony of the title, "The World Turned Upside Down," resonates far beyond the surrender at Yorktown and the British loss of the American colonies. For the very same Lieutenant General Charles, second Earl Cornwallis, was to have a remarkably different September-October just five years later in 1786. His second September-October, five years later in 1786, would mark the time of his arrival on the other side of the earth, in Calcutta (on Monday, 11 September 1786) as Governor-General of India and commander-in-chief of all British forces.[4]

For the next seven years (1786–93) Cornwallis would preside over the consolidation of the East India Company's rule (in other words, British rule) in India, (*a*) by devising the famous Permanent Settlement regarding land tenure for the *zamindars* (traditional tax or revenue-collectors who now became "land-owners" with a fixed or "permanent" revenue obligation) in Bengal and Bihar, (*b*) by bringing about the separation of civil, judicial and commercial tasks for British officials in India together with greatly improved salaries for the various positions, thereby professionalizing the British civilian presence in India for the first time and ending the corruption of the so-called "Nabob" period, (*c*) by codifying older traditions of Muslim and Hindu law with an overlay of British law (the so-called Cornwallis Code of 1793), (*d*) by regularizing policies and procedures for the professionalization of the military (including government troops, "Company" troops and "native" Sepoys), and (*e*) by accomplishing all of this while also insisting that Indian nationals be excluded from any significant role beyond the lowest levels of civilian and military functioning—as a result of the "reforms" of Cornwallis, no Indian could occupy a civilian or military position paying more than 500 pounds per year.[5] Regarding this latter point, Cornwallis writes the following in one of his communications to the Court of Directors back in England:

> It must be universally admitted that without a large and well-regulated body of Europeans, our hold of these valuable dominions must be very insecure. It cannot be expected that even the best of treatment would constantly conciliate the willing obedience of so vast a body of people, differing from ourselves in almost every

> circumstance of laws, religion and customs; and oppression of individuals, errors of government, and several other unforseen causes, will no doubt arouse an inclination to revolt. On such occasions it would not be wise to place great dependence upon their countrymen who compose the native regiments to secure their subjection.[6]

Cornwallis himself knew next to nothing about India when he first became governor-general nor did he ever make a serious effort to develop either an intellectual appreciation or a fondness for India or Indians. He never overcame what Aspinall has called his "deeply rooted conviction that Indians were unworthy of trust, that they must no longer be allowed to hold high and responsible offices, but that they must be replaced by Europeans in whose capacity and integrity he had confidence."[7] Furthermore, even those remarkable persons who assisted Cornwallis and who knew a good deal more about India than the governor-general, including John Shore (an expert on traditions of land tenure in the Bengal region), Charles Grant (an expert on the commercial operations of the East India Company), and the famous William Jones (an expert on law and the "father" of Orientalism), in spite of their expertise, did not diverge greatly from the basic attitudes towards India and Indians of Cornwallis himself. In this sense Cornwallis's mind-set was diagnostically symptomatic of his time.

The career of Cornwallis, however, was to extend considerably further than even Yorktown and Calcutta. To be sure, after his return from India (now as the first Marquess as well as the second Earl), he had a few brief years as a conventional English gentleman dealing with family affairs and local political matters in and around his beloved estate at Culford in Suffolk,[8] but then from 1798 to 1801, "The World Turned Upside Down" again for Cornwallis with his appointment as Viceroy of Ireland and commander-in-chief of all British forces. Here he dealt with Protestant-Catholic tensions and was deeply involved in bringing about the parliamentary union of Great Britain and Ireland in January of 1801. Then, the very next year he became embroiled in yet another great revolutionary conflict of his time, namely, the French Revolutionary and Napoleonic Wars. In 1802 he was named plenipotentiary to the France of Napoleon Bonaparte, negotiating, mainly with Joseph Bonaparte but also to some extent with Napoleon himself, the Anglo-French peace Treaty of Amiens of 27 March 1802.

Moreover, his encounter with the French had much deeper roots than his negotiating the Treaty of Amiens in 1802. His first encounters had been at the outset of his military career, following his early education at Eton, when he was learning the skill of soldiering on the continent during the Seven Years War (1756–63), a war that pitted Prussia and Great Britain against France, Austria and Russia, and a war that itself marked the end of a much longer struggle known as the French and Indian Wars (1689–1763), the great struggle between the English and the French over colonial expansion in North America and India. That great struggle between Britain and France would finally end only in 1815 with Napoleon's final, decisive defeat at Waterloo and the emergence thereafter of Great Britain as a preeminent imperialist power. In any case, Cornwallis as a young man had his first combat and command experience during the famous Battle of Minden of the Seven Years War. That war ended with the Treaty of Paris (10 February 1763), in which the French relinquished all military and political power in colonial North America and India to Britain.

But "The World Turned Upside Down" had yet one final dimension of meaning for the first Marquess and second Earl Cornwallis, and again, oddly enough, it was to be an event in September-October. In 1805, at the age of sixty-seven, he was appointed a second time as Governor-General of India and commander-in-chief of all British forces, primarily to stabilize the Indian political scene after the aggressive excesses of Governor-General (Richard Colley) Wellesley and his younger brother, Arthur Wellesley (later to become the Duke of Wellington, the nemesis of Napoleon at Waterloo). Cornwallis arrived in Calcutta in September of 1805 and shortly thereafter began a boat journey up the Ganges River to visit various collectors' stations in Bengal, Bihar and what is now Uttar Pradesh. This time, however, he was a much older man, and the demands of the Bengali climate in September together with a lifetime of physical exertion finally broke his health. In late September, just a few weeks after his return to India, burning with fever, he was taken from his boat and placed in a guesthouse in the town of Ghazipur in what is now Uttar Pradesh, and on 5 October 1805 he died there.[9] The young warrior at the Battle of Minden, the general who surrendered his army at Yorktown, the Governor-General of India and commander-in-chief of all British forces, the Viceroy of Ireland, the plenipotentiary to Napoleon Bonaparte for the Treaty of Amiens, was quietly buried in Ghazipur in the interior of India where he rests in peace to this day, far indeed from his beloved Culford in Suffolk.

What is so striking about Cornwallis is his involvement in so many crucial events having to do with the emergence of modernity. The beginning of industrialism, mercantile capitalism, colonial expansion in North America and India, the beginnings of the modern nation-state system, the Seven Years War, the American Revolution and the

War of Independence, the first consolidation of the British Raj, the parliamentary union of Great Britain and Ireland, the French Revolution and the French Revolutionary and Napoleonic Wars—Cornwallis was involved in all of these as more than a casual player.

What is also striking about Cornwallis, however, is that he understood so little of what he was involved in. He seems to have had hardly any sense of the import of the momentous historic events unfolding around him. "The World Turned Upside Down" for him again and again, but he apparently was never quite able or even inclined to try to put the pieces together. He knew almost nothing about North America or India, even though major portions of his career involved both contexts. He disliked the American South and Americans (although he was sympathetic to some of the grievances of the colonists even prior to the Revolutionary War). He despised India and felt that Indians were unworthy of trust. He hated the French Revolution and everything it represented. He detested Napoleon and almost all things French. He has been described variously as "the highest order of commonplace," "utterly destitute of originality," and "the Founder of all sound Indian Administration."[10] He thought of himself only as a competent soldier, a servant of his king, an aristocrat and peer of the realm, a loyal member of the Church of England and the support of his family. In many ways one could well argue that there is perhaps no better illustration than Charles, the first Marquess and second Earl Cornwallis, of the wry observation that the British empire was accrued in a fit of absentmindedness.

But such a wry observation misses a fundamental point, namely, that what appears subsequently as the easy and obvious continuity of hindsight is often in its own time a blundering, ignorant and clumsy discontinuity in which there is little if any mature foresight, and it is this very discontinuity, this very lack of insight, that makes the career of Cornwallis so diagnostically interesting. And whether it is the life and career of a Cornwallis or the history of the Indian subcontinent or the manner in which the former encounters the latter as a result of the radical contingency of historical process, it is easy enough for us looking back to weave together the various threads into a continuous fabric or narrative, but it is often the case that the continuity is largely our hindsight which we build out of the discontinuities of what has gone before. Put somewhat less strongly, although there may well be a fundamental continuity, it is almost always a continuity fashioned from radical discontinuities. This seems particularly clear in the case of Cornwallis, and is perhaps even clearer in the case of a civilization as complex and dense as that of India.

Two Metaphors: Fault Lines and Banyan Trees

In discussions of the history and cultures of the subcontinent, there have been two illuminating metaphors, in my view, that help to articulate the peculiar relation between discontinuity and continuity in India. The first is derived from the earth sciences of geology, archaeology and geography, in which Indian civilization is viewed in terms of layers or levels of sedimentation together with the juxtaposition of discrete tectonic plates that interact with one another, forming fault lines that become foci over long periods of time for the release of gigantic pressures, a release of pressures exhibiting on occasion catastrophic violence and upheaval. From one point of view, there is great stability which derives from the preservation of many layers and the peculiar balance of forces that are largely distinct from one another but nevertheless interdependent at certain crucial pressure points. From another point of view, there is always the risk of violent upheaval and dissolution.

One thinks here, of course, of the work of Fernand Braudel and Michel Foucault both of whom have made use of geological metaphors in their discussions of world history, stressing, on one level, the need for a broad perspective over time (*la longue durée*), while stressing, on another level, the need for an appreciation of basic discontinuities in the historical process, disruptions and upheavals that belie all attempts at fashioning simple continuities. It is hardly my intention, however, to attempt a Braudelian or Foucaultian analysis. Such would require a multivolume undertaking. I am simply calling attention to their use of a geological metaphor.

Perhaps more to the point in the South Asian area is the more context-specific perspective of Bridget and Raymond Allchin in their work, *The Rise of Civilization in India and Pakistan*.[11] As a work primarily of archaeology and prehistory, much of their discourse is, of course, literally concerned with the geology and geography of the subcontinent, but there is also present an intriguing metaphorical extension as in the following passage:

> Like all major enduring cultures of the world it [South Asian culture] draws upon the resources and the genius of contrasting but complementary regions. In this case it is that of two already highly complex regions. . . . It survives not as a monolith—such cultures quickly pass into fossilized obscurity—but as a highly sophisticated structure maintained by many balances and coun-

> terbalances, and capable of lending itself to revival, additions and adaptation.[12]

The epigraphs by the Allchins quoted at the head of this chapter as well as at the head of chapter 3 likewise make use of a geological metaphor of "layers" or "levels" of culture that are carried in South Asia over long periods of time very much like the layers or levels of rock-formations or tectonic plates that make up the earth in a given region.

The other metaphor is derived from the biological sciences and is that of the banyan tree, or in Sanskrit the *nyagrodha* (from the root, *ruh*, or *rudh*, plus the adverbial particle *nyañc*, meaning "down-grown" or "down-grower") tree. Many have utilized this metaphor—indeed, its origin is as old as the ancient Upaniṣad-s—but perhaps the best statement of it is that of the Indologist W. Norman Brown:

> In viewing Indian civilization I am reminded of the banyan tree, a fig tree, in Sanskrit called *nyagrodha*, a word which means "the down-grower." Though this tree begins life with a single trunk rising from a minute seed, its wide-spreading branches send down air roots, some of which themselves reach the ground, penetrate it, and become secondary trunks, occasionally to rival in size the first trunk. Thus the tree may come to shade an acre or more of ground. One can imagine a banyan tree of such age and such coverage that it may have a number of secondary trunks capable of being confused at first glance with the primary trunk. Such, it seems to me, has been the history of Indian civilization.[13]

What is especially illuminating in both metaphors is the manner in which a rather messy mixture of apparently discontinuous components can come together to form an overall continuity, in the case of the geological metaphor, the sedimented layers and tectonic plates of diverse origins nevertheless coalescing into a given, continuous portion of earth, and in the case of the banyan tree metaphor, the secondary branches becoming secondary trunks that can easily be confused with the primary trunk in size and importance but all of which trunks and branches and air roots nevertheless make one, continuous tree. In the preceding chapter reference was made to a report of the new "People of India" project of the Anthropological Survey of India in which it is suggested that there are as many as 4,599 distinct communities in India speaking some 325 languages in 12 language families. At the same time, it may be recalled, the report also asserts that an "all-pervasive sense of Indianness prevails through the linguistic, cultural and ecological diversities of the communities of the country."[14]

It is this continuity in the midst of discontinuities that must be grasped if one is to understand South Asian cultural life. It might even be said that the continuity *is* the discontinuity in the sense that in phase after phase of the unfolding of the history of cultures in India, what is apparently extraneous, foreign, and utterly different is absorbed or assimilated, not by being transmuted into something other than itself in order to conform with some pre-existing Indic identity, but, rather, by being allowed to stand in its very extraneous and foreign otherness as one more component of an identity that is indeterminate and always yet to be, but with the attendant paradoxical claim that somehow all such components have always been present at least implicitly.

Discontinuity as Continuity

I began this chapter with one of the more blatant and obvious manifestations of discontinuity, namely, "The World Turned Upside Down" of Lord Cornwallis who initiated in the later eighteenth century the most recent sedimentary layer or secondary branch of the "indeterminate and always yet to be" Indic identity, known as the Indo-Anglian layer. It is the layer in which India becomes a modern nation-state, or perhaps somewhat more accurately, a multinational civilisation-state, one among many modern nation-states in a multipolar world of global, industrial capitalism. Modern India on this most recent sedimentary layer is self-described in the preamble to its Constitution as a "sovereign, socialist, secular, democratic republic." It is nonaligned in its foreign policy, and a member in good standing of the British Commonwealth and the United Nations.

There are, of course, numerous other sedimentary layers or secondary branches throughout the long history of the subcontinent, but five layers in particular (in addition to the Indo-Anglian) require at least some treatment by way of providing an historical overview of India's cumulative trajectory: the Indus Valley layer, the Indo-Brāhmaṇical layer, the Indo-Śramaṇical layer, the Indic (Hindu-Buddhist-Jain) layer, and the Indo-Islamic layer. What follows, it should be clearly noted, is not by any means a detailed history of the development of the layers but only a capsule overview for the sake of the nonspecialist or general reader and for the sake of highlighting some of the more important cultural components that are present in modern Indian social reality. It should also be noted that in what follows the primary focus is on the unfolding of the religious dimensions in the South Asian cultural traditions.

In terms of overall periodization, the layers or branches can be characterized as follows:

1. The Indus Valley (c. 3000–1500 B.C.E.),
2. The Indo-Brāhmaṇical (c. 1500–600 B.C.E.),
3. The Indo-Śramaṇical (c. 600 B.C.E.–300 C.E.),
4. The Indic (Hindu-Buddhist-Jain) (c. 300–1200),
5. The Indo-Islamic (c. 1200–1757), and
6. The Indo-Anglian (c. 1757–present).[15]

Before treating each of these layers, two additional points should be made regarding the overall perspective. First, although we shall proceed chronologically begining with the Indus Valley layer, it should be remembered that the actual progression is more accurately described as a regression. That is to say, in thinking about the history of the cultures of the subcontinent, the beginning has really been the sixth layer or the Indo-Anglian period, since it is in this most recent layer that modern historians (both European and Indian) have become aware of the earlier layers. As the earlier Indo-Islamic layer came into focus, historians became increasingly sensitive to the yet older Hindu, Buddhist and Jain layers. The study of the Hindu, Buddhist and Jain layers led to examinations of the original Indo-Aryan migrations and early Vedic traditions. Finally, largely through careful archaeological research, the Indus Valley layer came into view, and debates continue even now as to whether the Indus Valley layer is discontinuous or continuous with mainstream Indic civilization. Thus, in an important sense it can be argued that any treatment of the historiography of the subcontinent should properly begin with the Indo-Anglian layer of Lord Cornwallis and his mid-eighteenth-century cohort and work its way regressively backwards and then, of course, progressively forward to post-independence India.[16]

Second, it should be noted that in an important sense one can plausibly argue that all of the layers come from the "outside," as it were, that is to say, the layers are not indigenous to the subcontinent. This is obviously true for layers (2) through (4). The Indo-Brāhmaṇical, Indo-Śramaṇical and Indic all owe many or most of their distinctive characteristics to the waves of migrating Indo-Aryans who first came to the subcontinental region in the second millenium B.C.E. This is probably true also for the Indus Valley layer as well. There is increasing evidence that the cultural characteristics of the Indus Valley civilization, so far as they can be determined, can be traced to the older village cultures of Sind, Baluchistan and to the eastern reaches of the Iranian plateau, in other words, to what is now Pakistan and areas even further west from the subcontinent. The Indo-Islamic layer is also obviously "outside," with its Turkic, Afghan, Perso-Arabic and Iranian components, as, of course, is the Indo-Anglian as well.

This, of course, is the reason for the title of both this chapter and chapter 3: Discontinuity as Continuity. Each of the layers of the subcontinental civilization is interestingly discontinuous with all of the others and needs to be understood in terms of its own unique or particular texture. At the same time, however, layers (1), (2), (3) and (4) (the Indus Valley, the Indo-Brāhmaṇical, the Indo-Śramaṇical and the Indic), as we shall see, have a number of "family resemblances," as do layers (5) and (6) (the Indo-Islamic and the Indo-Anglian). For convenience I shall refer to the former "family resemblances" simply as "Old Indic" formations or layers, and these will be the focus of attention in the present chapter. I shall refer to the latter "family resemblances" as "New Indic" formations or layers, and they will be the focus in chapter 3. Throughout the discussion in chapters 2 and 3, however, the primary focus will be on the particular texture in each formation or layer. In chapter 4 the issue of overall continuity or coherence will be addressed.

To shift to the banyan tree metaphor, the point here is that it is exceedingly difficult to find the "primary trunk" of the subcontinental banyan tree. For those who focus on premodern India, a possibly plausible case could be made, perhaps, for the Indus Valley as a "primary trunk" or possibly the Indo-Brāhmaṇical. Both claims, however, would be considered highly dubious by other researchers, especially since layer (4) (the Indic) is so obviously a composite of the Indus Valley, the Indo-Brāhmaṇical and the Indo-Śramaṇical. For those who focus on modern India, clearly the Indo-Islamic and the Indo-Anglian are candidates for the "primary trunk" with the implicit claim that there simply was no "primary trunk" prior to the Indo-Islamic period.

The Indus Valley (c., 3000 - 1500 b.c.e.)

From ancient times, according to Bridget and Raymond Allchin, the Indian subcontinent has been characterized by its "frontier regions" and its "interior regions."[17] The "frontier regions" are twofold: (1) the Northwest, including both the area of Baluchistan in contact with the Iranian plateau as well as the Northwest frontier in contact with Central Asia and China, and (2) the Northeast, including both the

Himalayan zone in contact with Tibet as well as the area of Bengal and Assam in contact with Burma, south China and southeast Asia. The "interior regions" of the subcontinent include (*a*) the western, with its focus on the Indus River system and the Punjab, (*b*) the northern and eastern, with its focus on the Ganges River system, and (*c*) the Southern or Peninsular, with its focus on the Deccan and the Tamil plain. The latter "interior region" is separated from the two other interior regions by the forested Vindhya mountains. Two major corridors or paths have historically been the trajectories through which communication and peoples have passed through the "interior regions", first, a "northern corridor" stretching from the Northwest frontier and the region of the Indus, through the Punjab, the Gangetic plain, and on into what is now Bengal; and, second, a "southern corridor" stretching from Sind to Gujarat, Malwa and the southern part of Rajasthan, and then into Maharashtra, the southern peninsula and the Tamil Nadu region. The "northern corridor," encompassing the agricultural regions related to the Indus and Ganges river systems, passes through what the Allchins have designated as the "Northern Nuclear Region."[18] The "southern corridor," encompassing the agricultural areas of the western and southern regions of the subcontinent is designated by them as the "Southern Nuclear Region." These, then, are the basic geographical parameters within which the cultural histories of South Asia unfold.

There has been some sort of human habitation in South Asia from 400,000 to 200,000 B.C.E., based on the discovery of pebble tools coming from the paleolithic Soan Culture.[19] Domestication of various sorts of animals may have occurred as early as 10,000 years ago or earlier in West and South Asia, thus making possible pastoral nomadic and semi-nomadic life. Nearly as old are some examples in West Asia of the planned growth of certain strains of wheat and barley, suggesting the beginnings of sedentary settlement.[20] The further development of agriculture and the emergence of organized village life probably began in the Middle East some time after the beginning of the neolithic period (roughly 6000 B.C.E.), and the first evidence for settled village life in South Asia can be dated approximately in the fourth millenium (4000–3000 B.C.E.) in such areas as Baluchistan and Sind in the Northwest of the subcontinent (in what is now Pakistan).[21] We know very little about the religion of these village settlements beyond what we know about comparable village cultures of other early agricultural groups in the Mediterranean and the Middle East generally. The Allchins have commented as follows about this pre-historic phase of religion:

> Throughout the length and breadth of India there are found today, at the folk level, rites and festivals which are intimately associated with the changing seasons, the sowing and harvesting of crops and the breeding of cattle and other livestock. There is also a whole pantheon of local gods and goddesses some of whom remain unassimilated while others have been absorbed at different levels into the sanskritized hierarchy of gods of the 'great' or classical Indian tradition. There can be no doubt that a very large part of this modern folk religion is extremely ancient and contains traits which originated during the earliest periods of stock raising and agricultural settlement.[22]

It may be recalled from chapter 1 that as many as 400 million in modern India follow some sort of "village Hindu" religiosity in contrast to literate, scripture-based, so-called "great tradition" Hindus and "renaissance" or modernist Hindus (the latter of which groups make up about 100 million). To the extent that this "village Hindu" spirituality is not unlike the folk religion described above by the Allchins, it is not implausible to suggest that a majority of Hindus in present-day India still follow a prehistoric spirituality that predates even the Indus Valley layer of civilization.

Be that as it may, the Indus Valley civilization, sometimes called the Harappan Civilization (after the name of one of its principal cities), flourished from the third through the first half of the second millenium B.C.E. in the region of the Indus valley and in the areas known as the Punjab and Gujarat.[23] To some extent it resembles the older village cultures of Baluchistan and Sind, but it also represents a significant advance beyond scattered village life. It was a sizable civilization, covering as much as half a million square miles (covering what is now Pakistan and much of Northwest India as well) and including several large cities, the two most prominent of which were Mohenjo-daro and Harappa. Very little is known about the origins of the civilization or about its end. Regarding origins, there is some evidence from archaeological excavations that there had been some minimal contact between the Indus Valley and Sumeria and Mesopotamia in the ancient Near East, but the evidence is insufficient by way of establishing any extensive borrowing or dependence either way. Regarding the decline of the civilization in the middle of the second millenium, some have speculated that its decline was caused by invading nomadic Aryans (see below, "The Indo-Brāhmaṇical"). Others have suggested that the civilization was the victim of a major natural disaster, possibly a flood, earthquake or famine.

Excavations of the two large urban sites, Mohenjo-daro and Harappa, have yielded some intriguing clues about the culture and religion of the Indus Valley civilization. Each city, for example, had a large artificial hill or citadel with what appear to be sizable official buildings (possibly governmental, religious, or both). There was also in Mohenjo-daro what appears to be a large, rectangular bathing area in the main part of the citadel area with steps leading down into it, suggesting some sort of ritual bathing practice (not unlike the ritual bathing "tanks" connected to Hindu temples in later Indian culture). The cities themselves are rather sophisticated in design with carefully planned streets and houses facing inwards away from the street.

In terms of artifacts, numerous small (about one-inch or two-inches square) soapstone seals have been uncovered, depicting various animals (for example, bulls, tigers, and monkeys), trees, and human figures. There are also inscriptions on many of the seals in some sort of pictographic script that has unfortunately never been deciphered. One seal shows a strange, horned figure sitting in what could be described as a Yogic or meditation posture and surrounded by four animals. Some older archaeologists have suggested that this might be some sort of "proto-Śiva" figure, since in later Hindu traditions the great Hindu god, Śiva, is considered to be the lord of Yoga. Moreover, the four animals might suggest Śiva as "lord of animals" (*paśupati*), a well-known designation of Śiva in later times. Some more recent archaeologists and art historians have disputed this interpretation. In any case, in addition to the seals, archaeologists have also uncovered what appear to be phallus-shaped stones and crude terra-cotta female figurines, suggesting some sort of fertility cult and belief in a mother goddess. All of this is highly speculative and debatable, mainly because the Indus Valley script and language has not yet been deciphered. One is left largely with scholarly guesses, but it is intriguing to entertain the possibility that traditions of ritual bathing, some sort of tradition of meditation or Yoga, possible prototypes of Śiva and a mother goddess, and a cult of sacred animals, all of which are prominent features in later Hindu traditions, may indeed be traceable ultimately all the way back to the third millenium B.C.E., and possibly earlier to the Baluchistan and Sind village cultures that go back to time immemorial.[24]

THE INDO-BRĀHMAṆICAL (C. 1500–600 B.C.E.)

As already mentioned, it is not clear how the old Indus Valley civilization ended, whether by natural disaster some time before the coming of the Indo-Āryans or by conquest as a result of the marauding warrior nomads. What is reasonably clear is that some time in the early part of the second millenium (just after c. 2000 B.C.E.), semi-nomadic warrior tribes who had been living in the steppeland that ranges from Eastern Europe to Central Asia began to undergo extensive migrations. No one is quite sure about the reasons for the migrations. Possibly the migrations were occasioned by famine, some sort of natural disaster or by some dread disease. Whatever the reasons, some tribes migrated westwards, finally finding their way to Europe, becoming the cultural and linguistic ancestors of the Greeks, Romans, Celts and Teutons. Other tribes remained in the same general steppeland region becoming the cultural and linguistic ancestors of the Baltic and Slavonic peoples. Still others migrated southwards and eastwards, moving into Persia, then on further into Afghanistan, Baluchistan and finally into the Indus Valley region. The tribes conquered local peoples as they moved, intermarried with the indigenous population and developed into a ruling elite. They were known as Ārya-s or Āryan-s (meaning "noble ones"), and those Āryan tribes that reached Persia and India are known as Indo-Iranians or Indo-Āryans. These migrations did not occur all at once. There were probably waves of migrating Indo-Āryan tribes over a period of some years.[26]

These Indo-Āryan nomadic tribes brought with them into India in the middle of the second millenium (c. 1500 B.C.E.) a number of cultural characteristics that were to prove determinative for the development of later Indian civilization: (*a*) a form of the Sanskrit language called simply Old Indic (or Vedic Sanskrit), later to develop into the classical language of India known as classical Sanskrit; (*b*) a patrilineal system of social organization centering around a tripartite division of social functions consisting of priests (*brāhmaṇa*-s), warriors (*rājanya*-s or *kṣatriya*-s) and food-producers (cattle raisers, cultivators, traders, and so forth) (*vaiśya*-s), later to develop after some centuries into what we now know as the caste system; (*c*) an elaborate ritual system of sacrifice (*yajña*) on open-air altars involving offerings of milk, honey, clarified butter or ghee, and animals into the sacred fire (*agni*) together with imbibing a sacred drink called Soma that brought about hallucinogenic effects; and (*d*) the worship of an elaborate pantheon of sky, atmospheric and earth gods.

In order to perform the fire ritual the priests or *brāhmaṇa*-s had to master an extensive body of what can be called sacred "utterances," including hymns, chants and ritual instructions of one kind or another. These liturgical utterances, not yet written texts since writing was not extensively used by these Indo-Āryans until many centuries later, are referred to as the Veda-s, from the root meaning "to know." In other words, the Veda-s are what the priests had to know in order to perform the ritual sacrifice (*yajña*). Originally there were three basic ritual collections, namely, the Ṛg Veda (meaning the "Hymn Veda," a collection of over one thousand hymns), the Sāma Veda (meaning the "Chant Veda," a collection of selected chants derived largely from verses of the Ṛg Veda) and the Yajur Veda (meaning the "Instruction Veda," a collection of instructions about the ritual performance). Somewhat later a fourth set of sacred utterances was added called the Atharva Veda (not so much a ritual collection as a collection of incantations, chants and spells for curing illness).

The purpose of the ritual sacrifice was to propitiate and "feed" the gods. In return the gods would assist their Indo-Āryan devotees with long life, much cattle, and earthly happiness. This reciprocity between gods and priests maintained the cosmic order or "*ṛta*." Especially important was Agni, not only the literal word for "fire" but also the name of a kind of priestly god who would carry the prayers and hymns of the priests to the realms of the gods. Also important was the god Indra, an atmospheric warrior god who assisted the Indo-Āryans in their wanderings and their battles, and according to one old Vedic creation myth, destroyed the demon, Vṛtra, a cosmic serpent who had devoured all of the sources of creation and life (the sun, water, and so forth). Indra killed Vṛtra with a great spear or weapon called the *vajra* ("thunderbolt" or "diamond-hard weapon") splitting open the body of the demon and thereby allowing the sources of creation to escape their bondage in the demon's body (Ṛg Veda I.32).

Another important creation myth refers to a Cosmic Man or Puruṣa (Ṛg Veda X.90) who is sacrificed on the sacred fire altar. From his sacrificed body, the world is created. Says the hymn (in verses 10–11): "When they divided the Man (*puruṣa*), into how many parts did they apportion him? What do they call his mouth, his two arms, and thighs and feet? His mouth became the Brahmin; his arms were made into the Warrior, his thighs the People, and from his feet the Servants were born."[26] Some have suggested that this may represent one of the first references to the caste system, known as the *varṇa* (literally "color") system, but that is perhaps to read too much into the passage. It may simply be calling attention to a division of labor among the Indo-Āryans and nothing more.

Yet another creation myth (Ṛg Veda X.129), probably one of the latest in the Vedic hymn collections, concerns a mysterious "That One" (*tad ekam*) who "breathed windless, by its own impulse." "Other than that," the hymn continues, "there was nothing beyond. Darkness was hidden by darkness in the beginning. . . . Desire came upon That One in the beginning; that was the first seed of mind." The hymn ends on a paradoxical, skeptical note: "Whence this creation has arisen—perhaps it formed itself, or perhaps it did not—the one who looks down on it in the highest heaven, only he knows—or perhaps he does not know."[27] Somewhat later the Cosmic Man or Puruṣa and the mysterious "That One" are combined into a more personal, but still largely abstract, Prajāpati ("lord of creatures").

Other important gods were Varuṇa and Mitra, high celestial gods of cosmic power and order, Vāyu, god of the wind, Dyaus and Pṛthivī, the gods of heaven and earth, Sūrya, god of the sun, Viṣṇu, the god who maintains or sustains the cosmos, Rudra, the "howling" god of storm, thunder and the mountain, later to be combined with the god, Śiva. Interestingly enough, in this early Indo-Brāhmaṇical context, Indra and Agni, and Varuṇa and Mitra were considerably more important than Viṣṇu or Rudra-Śiva. It would be almost a millenium later that Viṣṇu and Śiva would emerge as principal gods in classical Hindu traditions. The tendency in this Indo-Brāhmaṇical context is to move away from personal gods in the direction of speculative abstractions that put ever greater emphasis on the importance of the priests for the performance of the ritual as well as for the interpretation of its meaning.

As mentioned earlier, these Indo-Āryan nomadic tribes entered India about 1500 B.C.E. in the region of the Indus Valley and the Punjab. Over the next thousand years they spread their control over all of North India, intermarrying with the indigenous population and becoming a settled agricultural people. During this thousand-year period many important changes occurred. The sacrificial ritual became much more complex and came to be divided into two basic types: (*a*) what were called Śrauta (from the word *śruti* meaning the sacred utterances of the Veda-s or scripture) or great public rituals involving as many as seventeen priests and three sacred fires and lasting for several days and in some instances up to two years; and (*b*) what were called Gṛhya (meaning simply "domestic") or home-based oblations (called the Agnihotra or "fire offering") into a single fire in the domestic hearth. Also related to the "domestic" rituals were the life-cycle rituals (called *saṃskāra*-s), from twelve to sixteen rites of passage, including such rituals as the marriage ritual, the ritual for conceiving a male child, a birth ritual, a name-giving ritual, and so forth. Whereas most of the Indo-Āryan families were able to maintain the home-based rituals, only rich "sacrificers" (called *yajamāna*-s) such as the chief or local ruler (*rājan*) could afford the great public rituals.

One of the most elaborate public rituals was the Horse Sacrifice (*aśvamedha*) in which a horse was allowed to roam for a year followed by warriors of a particular local ruler or *mahārāja*. Wherever the horse roamed was claimed as land for the ruler and could presumably be challenged by other local rulers. Finally at the end of the year a great Horse Sacrifice was held to celebrate the ruler's power and authority. Other major public rituals were the Enthronement Ritual (*rājasūya*) and the Ritual of Building the Fire Altar (*agnicayana*), involving many days and the ritual use of the Soma drink.

As might well be imagined, as the rituals became more complex and expensive, the priests became more specialized in one or another aspect of the ritual process. Long prose commentaries were composed (first orally but eventually written down) explaining the ritual, called Brāhmaṇa-s (utterances "pertaining to the priestly function"). Also, special schools and branches of specialization developed in centers of learning just outside the settled areas or village-enclosures in various parts of North India, and the products of these specialized schools were calledĀraṇyaka-s (utterances "pertaining to the forest-schools"). Finally, the priests began to speculate on the deeper meaning of the ritual process and even began a kind of elementary philosophizing about the relation of the ritual to the cosmos and to the human community (mainly to the priestly community but to the ruling *kṣatriya* or warrior community as well). These early speculative and proto-philosophical reflections came to be collected in a group of compositions called Upaniṣad-s (meaning literally "to sit down near" the teacher and to learn special, secret teachings). Upaniṣad-s came to be composed already in the ninth and eighth century B.C.E. and continued to be composed well into the first centuries of the Common Era. The Brāhmaṇa-s and Āraṇyaka-s are somewhat older, reaching back to the eleventh and even twelfth century B.C.E. These utterances taken together, namely, the Vedic verse collections (Ṛg, Sāma, Yajur, Atharva), the Brāhmaṇa-s, the Āraṇyaka-s and the Upaniṣad-s are referred to as the Veda or *śruti* (literally "that which has been heard") or "scripture." These Veda-s are considered to be eternal and to have been intuited or "seen" by the ancient *Ṛṣi*-s or "seers" and, thus, not to have a human origin ("not derived from men" or *a-pauruṣeya*). The Upaniṣad-s which come at the end of the collection are sometimes called "Vedānta" which means "the end of the Veda." The ritual portion of the Veda-s are referred to as the ritual Action Portion (*karma-kāṇḍa*), while the proto-philosophical speculations of the Upaniṣad-s are referred to as the Knowledge Portion (*jñāna-kāṇḍa*).

something like a grass roots movement back to basics.

The proto-philosophical speculations in the Upaniṣad-s are interesting by way of showing some of the oldest patterns of reflection in ancient India.[28] While still obviously unfolding in the ritual environment, this first proto-philosophizing is beginning to move away from the old external rituals and to look inward into the nature of human experience and the manner in which the old rituals illuminate human experience. There is a deep concern for finding the true inner Self and for relating the notion of Self to the external ritual and the cosmos as a whole. The external fire rituals, to be sure, continued to be performed, and these priestly proto-philosophical speculations probably represent only a fairly small group of thinkers who wanted to find the deeper meaning of the sacrifice in terms of their inner experience and their interests in cosmology. Thought in this ancient period is, of course, fluid, simple and wide-ranging, but one particular tradition of speculation together with an important variant should be mentioned, since it eventually provided the basis for two of the more important later traditions of Indian philosophy, the monist tradition of the Advaita Vedānta, and the dualist tradition of the Sāṃkhya.[29]

This particular tradition of speculation begins with playing on the word for "priest," the Sanskrit of which is "*brāhmaṇa*," and the relation between the notion of "priest," the notion of the world or cosmos (*viśva, bhuvana, jagat*), and the notion of the Self or Soul (called variously *ātman* or *puruṣa*). The root meaning of the word for "priest" or "*brāhmaṇa*" is "to speak" or "to pray," and there are several derivative terms that can be formed, including *bráhman* (with accent on the first syllable), *brahmán* (accent on the second syllable), Brahman (a neuter abstract noun), Brahmā (a masculine form), and, of course, *brāhmaṇa*, the actual word for "priest." The term *bráhman* (with accent on the first syllable) means something like "prayer" and refers to the actual verses (called *mantra*-s) of the Vedic hymns, referring, in other words, to the objective content that the priest must know. The term *brahmán* (with accent on the second syllable) means something like "pray-er," that is to say, the person doing the praying, referring, in other words, to the subjective capacity of the priest to speak or to pray.

The priests proceeded to speculate, then, on both kinds of *brahman*. The *bráhman* as "prayer" is objective, relates directly to the external fire ritual, which in turn is made possible by the air or wind, which in turn is made possible by the sun and moon and all of the forces of the cosmos. In other words, this is a line of speculation leading in a cosmological direction, and when inquiring into that ultimate first principle which makes all of this objective universe possible, they used the term Brahman (the neuter abstract noun). It is the ultimate first principle of objectivity from which everything is derived. In some other, slightly later Upaniṣadic contexts this first principle of objectivity is called the "principal" one (*pradhāna*) or primal materiality (*prakṛti*).

The *brahmán* as "pray-er," on the other hand, is subjective and refers to the priest's ability to speak or utter prayers. Just as the "prayer" relates directly to the external fire altar, so the "pray-er" has an internal fire or burning (called *tapas* or the inner process of meditation and self-purification that burns off personal impurities). And just as the external fire is dependent on the air or wind, so the internal fire is dependent on the breath or life-force (*prāṇa*), and just as the external world is illumined by the sun, so the subjective inner world of the priest is illumined by knowledge (*vidyā, jñāna*). When inquiring into that ultimate first principle which makes the subjective inner world of the priest possible, they used the term for the reflexive pronoun in Sanskrit, the Ātman (*ātman*) or "Self," or simply the word for "man" or "person" (*puruṣa*).

The obvious question, then, is what, finally, is the difference, or, what is the relation between the Brahman (the first principle of objectivity) and the Ātman (the first principle of subjectivity)? The answer, according to the priestly tradition that will later become the monistic Advaita Vedānta, is that there is no difference. When I have come to understand or "know" (*vidyā, jñāna*) the first principle of subjectivity by means of *tapas* (the inner ascetic "burning" of meditation and self-purification) or what amounts to the same thing, "disciplined meditation" or Yoga, I have come to understand the ultimate first principle of everything that is, the Brahman. Such an answer obviously is tending towards monism, the view that finally objectivity and subjectivity coalesce into the pure consciousness that is Brahman or Ātman. Hence, the priestly refrains in the famous Bṛhadāraṇyaka Upaniṣad (I.4.10) and Chāndogya Upaniṣad (VI.9.4 ff): "I am Brahman" (*ahaṃ brahma-asmi*), and "That are thou, Śvetaketu" (*tat tvam asi, Śvetaketu*). The realm of objectivity or materiality or multiplicity tends to dissolve, and, indeed, in later philosophizing the realm of objective multiplicity is said to be *māyā*, a sort of illusory, shifting kaleidoscope that does not truly exist in the sense that the pure consciousness of Ātman or Brahman may be said to exist.

A possible second answer, given by those Indo-Brāhmaṇical thinkers that will later become the followers of the dualist Sāṃkhya, is that there is a fundamental difference between objectivity or materiality (*pradhāna* or *prakṛti*) and pure consciousness (*puruṣa*). When I have come to understand or "know" (*vidyā, jñāna*), as a result of my disciplined meditation or Yoga, that pure consciousness (*puruṣa*), if it is truly pure, can have no content whatever, and that, therefore, it must be totally distinct from every determinate formulation, then I must realize that pure consciousness is radically separate from all determinate objectivity or materiality (*prakṛti*). There is a truly existing realm of objective multiplicity—the world, in other words, is fully real—but my true Selfhood or my pure consciousness is totally distinct from that realm.

Interestingly enough, both the monistic-tending Vedānta interpretation of what happens as a result of the pursuit of disciplined meditation (*yoga*) and the dualistic-tending Sāṃkhya interpretation of what happens are almost identical with respect to the issue of the nature of Selfhood or pure consciousness (*ātman* or *puruṣa*). They differ mainly with respect to the interpretation of the realm of objective multiplicity, the Vedāntin wanting to reduce multiplicity to the radical oneness of pure consciousness, the Sāṃkhyan acknowledging the separate reality of objective multiplicity but seeking to isolate a pure contentless consciousness over against it.

Clearly these Upaniṣadic speculations are growing out of the sacrificial ritual as attempts to make sense of the relation of the ritual to the world and human experience, but at the same time they are also striking out in new directions. The priests are obviously becoming much more independent. Indeed, they are becoming more important even than the gods, for the priests by their understanding and manipulating of *bráhman*, *brahmán* and Brahman, their internalization or interiorization of the fire-ritual in terms of *tapas* and Yoga, and their cosmological speculations in terms of cosmology, are coming to understand and thereby to control both the objective world and the subjective world. The priests are becoming all-powerful. Domestic rituals, public rituals, the gods who are fed by the ritual process and even the cosmos itself are all now under the control of the priests.

With this Indo-Brāhmaṇical layer we have come close to the threshold of what will later become the "Hindu" traditions in India. The sacred scriptures have been devised (the Veda-s together with the Upaniṣad-s.), basic rituals both public and domestic have been elaborated, a tripartite social order (not quite the caste system, to be sure, but clearly a prototype for it) has gradually transformed itself from a nomadic or semi-nomadic form into a settled or sedentary agricultural base, and patterns of speculation and proto-philosophizing have shown themselves that will prove to be of decisive importance in the development of later Hindu philosophy. Nevertheless, some crucial components of what will later be known as Hindu traditions are glaringly absent. There are no temples, only the open-air fire altars of the priests. There is very little focus on the notion of a personal god. Viṣṇu and Śiva, though present in incipient forms, are not dominant figures. There is little evidence of urban life of any kind beyond the level of village communities or small, settled communities related to local rulers or ruling clans. Kingship has hardly developed beyond the level of local rulers or tribal confederacies in kinship lineages. There are references to "forest schools" that exist outside of settled areas but not much concern with city-life or corporate life beyond the public rituals of local chiefs. There is no mention of pilgrimage of any kind. With one or two minor exceptions, there is little emphasis whatever on notions of Karma and rebirth, so prominent in later Hindu interpretations of the meaning of orthopraxy and ritual behavior (and present possibly also in earlier pre-Āryan village religiosity), suggesting that Karma and rebirth were originally not part of the Indo-Brāhmaṇical layer. There is, to be sure, a growing concern over the possibility of re-death (*punarmṛtyu*), probably growing out of analogies with life-cycle stages. Just as one passes through the various phases of life, so one might pass through death itself, thereby requiring a re-birth and a subsequent re-death. Moreover, there are a few Upaniṣadic passages which mention the notion of Karma and rebirth, but they are always mentioned in the context of secret teachings, as if, in other words, the full doctrines of Karma and rebirth had not yet been developed or had not been assimilated into the Indo-Brāhmaṇical belief-system.

THE INDO-ŚRAMAṆICAL (C. 600 B.C.E. –300 C.E.)

What the Indus Valley layer revealed were the archaic roots of Indic spirituality. The Indo-Brāhmaṇical layer introduced the Indo-Āryan component with its intricate and obsessive sacrificial rituals (*yajña*), its sacred utterances of the Veda-s and Upaniṣad-s (*śruti*), its tripartite social organization of priests, warriors and food-producers destined to become the later caste system, and perhaps most important of all, the centrality of the priests both in terms of the performance of the ritual and in terms of the first proto-philosophical reflections in the Upaniṣad-s. With the Indo-Śramaṇical layer, which may well reflect the resurfacing of pre-Brāhmaṇical traditions, we begin to see some reactions against this powerful religion of the priests, and we begin to see some further dramatic manifestations of the two other kinds of spirituality that will prove to be as important in the formation of Indic religious traditions as ritual sacrifice (*yajña*), namely, ascetic or disciplined meditation (*yoga*), and focused or single-minded devotion to a personal god (*bhakti*).

We will also begin to see new and larger political formations in this period, occasioned probably by the new iron technology which greatly improved agricultural efficiency, enabled land clearance and the development of much more sophisticated weaponry, and provided overall an improved material base for increased trade and commerce. Following Alexander the Great's brief foray into India (in the Indus Valley region, c. 326 B.C.E.), the local regional polities across north central India were finally united for the first time into one coordinated, albeit loose, confederation by a power in the Magadha region of the Gangetic plain known as the Mauryan dynasty, the most illustrious representative of which was Aśoka, who reigned from c. 269–232 B.C.E.[30]

Ravinder Kumar suggests that it is precisely in this Indo-Śramaṇical context that the basic structures or levels of Indic political activity and State formation take shape that will hold for the most part in subsequent centuries, indeed until the establishing of the British Raj in the nineteenth century.

> There came into existence at this stage three distinct, yet related, levels of political activity within India. A local level, which was characterized by the dispersal in space of distinct *jāti* and *jana* communities, a regional level, shaped through interaction between local polities; and a pan-Indian level, holding the country as a whole in a loose federation. These three levels of political activity underpinned State formation within India until the 19th century, notwithstanding substantive changes in modes of social production or in the structure of society. For the same reason, the pan-Indian polity remained a relatively weak institution, until the establishment of the British Empire over India. Indeed, prior to the 19th century, the political history of the subcontinent was largely characterised by a dialogue between the regional States, on the one hand, and between local and regional polities, on the other. The pan-Indian State made its appearance only in a few brief centuries over a period of two millennia.[31]

The older Indo-Brāhmaṇical layer also undergoes some fundamental changes towards the end of what we are calling the formation of the Indo-Śramaṇical layer, mainly in terms of the development of a much more inclusive literature than the older Vedic corpus, including the generation of law-books known as *Dharmaśāstra*-s and the redaction of the two great epics of India, the *Rāmāyaṇa* and the *Mahābhārata*, the lat-

ter of which contains the most important religious text for the formation of the emerging Hindu traditions, the *Bhagavad-gītā* or "Song of the
Lord."

The term "*śramaṇa*" is from the root *śram*, meaning "to exert one-
self" or "to practice austerities," and refers to non-Indo-Brāhmaṇical
mendicant groups that began to appear in North India some time
around the sixth century B.C.E.[32] To some extent, these *śramaṇa* groups
were engaging in the same sorts of speculation about the Self or Soul
that we noticed in the proto-philosophical Upaniṣad-s of the Indo-
Brāhmaṇical tradition. It is possibly the case that most of these groups
got many of their ideas from the speculations of the priests. The search
for inner truth, the turn towards meditation and self-searching, and the
pursuit of disciplined meditation or Yoga, were not simply to be found
among some of the priests. They were to be found as well among all of
these mendicant groups.

The crucial difference, however, is that the *sramaṇa* groups did
not accept the authority of the priests nor did they accept the validity of
the Indo-Brāhmaṇical sacrificial system. They, therefore, also rejected
the sacred utterances of the priests, the Veda-s in their elitist language
of Sanskrit, as well as the supposed superiority of the Indo-Brāhmaṇical priests in the developing hierarchical social reality. They
formed their own separate mendicant communities and represent the
first examples of organized monastic life in ancient India. The *śramaṇa*
ascetic in later classical Sanskrit literature as well as in Buddhist and
Jain texts is frequently contrasted with the *brāhmaṇa* ascetic. One Indian
grammarian introduces the compound word "*śramaṇa-brāhmaṇa*" as
examples of unending hostility, like that between "cat and mouse,"
"dog and fox," and "snake and mongoose."[33] There were, thus, in this
ancient period several separate traditions of disciplined meditation or
Yoga, deriving from both Indo-Brāhmaṇical and Indo-Śramaṇical
sources.[34]

There were many such *śramaṇa* groups, but two in particular
eventually developed into independent religious traditions in ancient
India of great importance: the Jains and the Buddhists. To call to mind
what was briefly mentioned in chapter 1, the founder of the Jain tradition was Vardhamāna ("he who is bringing prosperity"), also known
by the honorific epithet, Mahāvīra ("Great Hero"). He was born into a
warrior (*kṣatriya*) clan and lived in the sixth century B.C.E. (c. 549–477
B.C.E.) in Northeast India in the region of the Gangetic plain in what is
now the state of Bihar. He practiced rigorous asceticism and organized
a Jain monastic community. The word "Jain" comes from the word *jina*,
meaning "conqueror." As was mentioned earlier, according to the Jain

Direct opposition

Buddhism born of rejection of priest'ly caste

tradition, Mahāvīra was not the first ascetic teacher of the tradition. There had been many other teachers before him called *tīrthaṃkara*-s or "crossing-makers," meaning teachers able to cross the rivers of suffering in this world and to attain enlightenment. Some have claimed that these traditions can be traced back to the old Indus Valley layer or earlier, but that is unlikely. It is likely, however, that the Jain tradition is considerably older than the Buddhist tradition.

The literature of the Jains is extensive, and most of it is composed in one or another form of a group of languages or dialects known as Prakrits. These are Middle Indic languages, in the "middle," as it were, linguistically, between the Old Indic languages (Vedic Sanskrit and Classical Sanskrit), on the one hand, and Modern Indic languages (Hindi, and so forth), on the other. The scriptural basis for the Jain traditions are a group of some sixty Prakrit texts (called Āgama-s or "sacred utterances"), including a group of Pūrva or "Ancient Texts" (no longer extant but referred to in later texts), Anga-s or "Limbs" (the basic teachings of the tradition), and Upānga-s or Angabāhya-s or ("subsidiary texts").[35] There is also an extensive non-canonical Jain literature in various Prakrits, Sanskrit and Modern Indic languages as well. Some portions of the Jain canonical literature are very old and can be traced possibly to the time of Vardhamāna. Most of it, however, and certainly all of the non-canonical commentarial literature comes from a much later period, probably not earlier than the end of this Indo-Śramaṇical period, that is to say, the first centuries of the Common Era and even later.

The Jains believe in a rigorous dualism of Self (*jīva*) and Not-Self (*a-jīva*), somewhat like the Self (*puruṣa*) and materiality (*prakṛti*) duality of the Upaniṣadic Sāṃkhya mentioned above, with the important difference that the Jain Self or *jīva* is a concrete, determinate entity that can enter into relations with the Non-Self (*a-jīva*). The Self becomes imprisoned in the Not-Self through *karman* or worldly action, conceived in this tradition as a kind of physical stuff. Especially violent action or any act of killing leads to a great influx of karmic matter which leads to even further imprisonment and suffering of the Self. One ought to avoid ordinary worldly action, especially any violent action or killing. Hence, the Jains practice strict vegetarianism, follow the doctrine of non-violence (*ahiṃsā*) and encourage rigorous ascetic meditation in order to bring about the separation of the Self or Soul from the body. As was mentioned in the last Chapter, in the fourth century B.C.E. a great schism occurred in the community between the Śvetāmbara-s ("white or cotton clad") and Digambara-s ("sky-clad"), with the former mendicants and their lay followers finally settling largely in the Western regions of Gujarat, Rajasthan and northern Maharashtra, and the latter settling largely in the South in southern Maharashtra and Karnataka. Jain communities, both monastic and lay, have existed in India throughout the centuries, and as noted earlier, there are about 4,000,000 in contemporary India and several thousands who live outside of India in Europe, the United States and elsewhere.[36]

The other prominent tradition within the *śramaṇa* context is the Buddhist, and again, to review what was mentioned briefly in chapter 1, the founder of the Buddhist tradition was Gautama, also known by such epithets as *buddha* ("the awakened or enlightened one") *śākyamuni* ("the monk of the Śākya clan) and *siddhārtha* ("he whose goal has been attained" or "he whose goal is perfection"). Like Vardhamāna, he too was from a warrior (*kṣatriya*) clan and lived as an older contemporary of Vardhamāna in precisely the same region of the Gangetic plain. The dates of the Buddha are usually set at 563–483 B.C.E..

According to one tradition, Gautama is born as a prince of the Śakya clan, and it is predicted at the time of his birth that he will become either a great ruler or a great spiritual leader. His father tries to protect him from ordinary life and to direct him towards becoming a great ruler, but the young prince becomes weary of conventional life and leaves his family to seek spiritual enlightenment. At first he becomes a mendicant and learns the various types of disciplined meditation (*yoga*) available in his time, but concludes that they will not lead to enlightenment. Then, he pursues for some six years the extreme opposite of the conventional life of indulgence that he had enjoyed before leaving his family, that is to say, he pursues a regimen of extreme asceticism or *tapas* ("interior burning"), but he concludes that these extreme techniques will also not bring enlightenment. He, then, abandons extreme asceticism and begins to practice a moderate, new form of disciplined meditation (*yoga*) that comes to be known as the "Middle Way," a new moderate form of meditation which brings him to enlightenment. The content of his enlightenment experience, of course, is the well-known formula of the four "noble" (*ārya*) truths and the eightfold path: (l) all of life is frustrating; (2) frustration has a cause (namely, clinging or thirsting after the impermanent as if it were permanent); (3) frustration can be stopped (by means of a moderate form of disciplined meditation); and (4) the method of disciplined meditation to be followed is the eightfold path of right views, right intentions, right speech, right action, right livelihood, right effort, right mindfulness and right concentration.[37] The new "Middle Way" is called the *dharma*, a term which means variously "law," "doctrine," "righteousness" and even "truth" in Buddhist contexts. The term *dharma* also comes to have a technical meaning as the "constituents" or "force factors" that make up the phenomenal, empirical world, as will be seen below.[38]

What is distinctive about the early Buddhist analysis of experience is (*a*) its repudiation of the extreme asceticism of other *śramaṇa*-groups in favor of a "Middle Way" between the extremes of sensuous indulgence and extreme mortification, and (*b*) its declaring of a fresh and original interpretation of the nature of the world and human experience.[39] Whereas the Indo-Brāhmaṇical traditions of Upaniṣadic Vedānta and Sāṃkhya as well as the Indo-Śramaṇical Jain tradition had focused their disciplined meditation or Yoga on the problem of the relation of Self or consciousness (*ātman, puruṣa, jīva*) to the realm of objective multiplicity or the Not-Self (*māyā, prakṛti, a-jīva*), the Buddhists suggested on the basis of their new, moderate method of meditation that a more adequate perspective on the world and human experience revealed a radical and ever-changing process or transience (*anitya*) in which there was neither a substantial "world" nor a substantial "self." Whereas the early Vedānta, early Sāṃkhya and Indo-Śramaṇical Jain traditions tended to think in terms of "things" or "entities," utilizing essentially spatial metaphors, the early Buddhists thought, rather, in terms of "events" and process, utilizing, in other words, a powerful temporal metaphor.

There is only change and transformation, a continuing sequence of unfolding events. Reality is really made up of discrete force-factors, flashes of energy or mathematical point-instants, which these early Buddhists called *dharma*-s. Notions or constructs like "world," or "nature," or "self" are simply verbal conventions (*vikalpa*-s) that may be serviceable enough for purposes of everyday conventional life but, in fact, have no ultimate validity. The early Buddhists suggested, instead, the radical notion of No-Self (*an-ātman*) and, somewhat later, the more radical notion of "substancelessness" (*niḥ-svabhāva*). Because we cling or thirst after permanence when, in fact, there is nothing permanent, we, therefore, get caught up in frustration and suffering (*duḥkha*). We need to break the cycle or wheel of endless thirsting after permanence and pursue, instead, a radical cessation (*nirodha*) of ordinary conventional life. By following the eightfold path, which is, as it were, a new kind of "wheel of the truth" (the *dhammacakka* in Pāli, or *dharma-cakra* in Sanskrit), we can achieve that cessation (*nirodha*) and eventually come to the final peace of complete freedom from frustration or suffering known as *nirvāṇa* (literally meaning "blowing out" or, in other words, complete cessation). Gautama the Buddha is the exemplary figure who shows us the new way. He is not a god; indeed, the notion of a god is only one more verbal convention. We must follow the new path of disciplined meditation and discover the ultimate truth in our own experience.

As was mentioned in chapter 1, the Buddhist tradition plays an important role in both the religious and political history of India. The Buddhist tradition itself refers to three phases in its history in India or what it calls "three turnings of the wheel of the law:"[40] (*a*) an early period of some five hundred years (from the death of the founder in the fifth century B.C.E. to about the first century of the Common Era) during which the Sthaviravāda or Theravāda or "Tradition of the Elders" develops, (*b*) a second period of five hundred years (roughly from the first century C.E. through the fifth or sixth centuries) during which the more inclusive Mahāyāna or "Tradition of the Great Vehicle" develops, (*c*) and a third period of five hundred years (from about the sixth century through the tenth century, after which the Buddhist tradition declines and finally disappears from India) during which a highly ritualized form of esoteric practice develops known as the Vajrayāna or "Tradition of the Diamond Vehicle" develops.

Initially the "Tradition of the Elders" was little more than one among many mendicant *śramaṇa*-groups in the Gangetic plain region, but early along it became linked with some of the dramatic social and political changes occurring in the region: the development of cities, the development of a monied economy, and most important, the development of the first all-India or pan-Indian dynastic state, the Mauryan dynasty, and its most illustrious representative, Aśoka, who reigned c. 269–232 B.C.E. It is not clear whether Aśoka himself ever became a Buddhist—evidence suggests that he supported a variety of religious traditions in addition to the Buddhists—but he did make use of the Buddhist notion of *dharma* ("law," "doctrine," "righteousness") as one of the primary ideological notions for legitimizing his pan-Indian empire.

In this same period of Mauryan ascendancy, that is, the latter part of the fourth century and the third century B.C.E., one finds some of the first reflections about the concept of kingship and the relation between the state and society, on the one hand, and the religious monastic orders, on the other. To what extent theories of kingship are to be traced to Buddhist traditions and notions is difficult to determine. Greek and Persian influences were already present to some extent as a result of the conquests of Alexander the Great (c. 326 B.C.E.), and it could well be the case that the Buddhist texts simply reflect notions of kingship that are generally present in the newly developing cultural environment. Discussions are usually framed within a broad cosmology of periodic decline, and the institution of kingship is understood as a reluctant necessity agreed to by people in order to maintain some semblance of order in an increasingly disordered world. In *Dīgha-nikāya* 3.80vv., for example, after having described how the world had become corrupt, the text continues:

> Then the people gathered together and lamented, saying: "Evil ways are rife among the people—theft, censure, false speech, and punishment have appeared among us. Let us choose one man from among us, to dispense wrath, censure and banishment when they are right and proper, and give him a share of our rice in return."
>
> *Mahāsammata* means approved (*sammata*) by the whole people (*mahājana*), and hence Mahāsammata was the first name to be given to a ruler.[41]

Whether in fact kings were ever selected on such a rational basis of contract, the passage clearly suggests a distinct political domain for the maintenance of law and order apart from the religious domain. Also from about this same Mauryan period one finds the first appearance of the notion of a "universal monarch" (*cakravartin*), a king of kings who will rule over all the earth and maintain proper order (*dharma*).[42] Generally speaking, Buddhists were conservative in their attitudes towards political power and the state. The ruler should rule with righteousness (*dharma*) and should support the Buddhist monastic organization (*saṃgha*) so that the spiritual life of the monks and nuns could be pursued in peace. The members of the monastic order would in turn support the ruler and provide the requisite religious legitimation for the political domain. Louis Dumont has referred to this separation of the political and the religious in Buddhist contexts (as well as Hindu contexts) as a "process of secularization." That is perhaps an anachronistic overstatement, but it must be conceded that there was a clear separation of the political from the religious in ancient India. We will return to this point a bit later when we discuss the Hindu concept of kingship as set forth in the *Dharmaśāstra*-s and Kauṭilya's *Arthaśāstra*.[43]

From this time onwards the Buddhist tradition rapidly became a pan-Indian tradition, supported, on one level, by the new pan-Indian empire, and, on other levels, by rich, regional landowners, urban dwellers, tradespeople, artisans, and so forth, who were coming into prominence with the emerging new social reality. Monasteries (*vihāra*-s) and reliquary or burial monuments (*stūpa*-s) begin to be built in various parts of the subcontinent for housing monks and for providing a network of pilgrimage places (celebrating the various events or acts of the Buddha) for wandering monks and lay people. The "Tradition of the Elders" develops into some eighteen different schools, many of which are related to specific regions in the subcontinent, with the greatest strengths of the tradition in the north central area (the Gangetic plain), the Northeast region (in and around Bengal), the southern region (in what is now Andhra Pradesh and Tamil Nadu) and the far Northwest (in and around Kashmir).

Like the Jain tradition, the early Buddhist traditions for the most part used the Middle Indic Prakrit languages rather than the elitist Indo-Brāhmaṇical Sanskrit. The scriptural base for the "Tradition of the Elders" is referred to as the "Three Baskets" (Tipiṭaka in Pāli, Tripiṭaka in Sanskrit), referring to the three subdivisions of (*a*) monastic rules, (*b*) discourses of the founder and (*c*) speculative and technical writings. Most of this was oral literature in the earliest period, and written texts in the form that we now have them are not much earlier than the time of King Aśoka. Most of them are considerably later, coming from the end of this Indo-Śramaṇical period, or, in other words, the first centuries of the Common Era. Early along the "Tradition of the Elders" or Theravāda became firmly established in what is now Sri Lanka, and a full corpus of the "Three Baskets" has been preserved there in the Middle Indic Pāli language and referred to simply as the Pāli Canon. Some of the other early schools, however, for example, the Sarvāstivāda (the "Tradition that All Exists," a school stressing that the "force-factors" or *dharma*-s "exist" in all three times of past, present and future) and the Sautrāntika (the "Tradition based on the Discourses," a school that puts a special focus on the discourses of the founder) in the far Northwest, purportedly had Sanskrit versions of the "Three Baskets," although these for the most part are no longer extant. Also, the "Tradition of the Great Vehicle" (Mahāyāna) which arises towards the end of the Indo-Śramaṇical period that we are discussing also utilizes the medium of Sanskrit. Evidently as the Buddhist traditions became pan-Indian traditions, the elitist vehicle of Sanskrit became more and more prevalent.

Before concluding our discussion of this Indo-Śramaṇical period, one other development must be mentioned, and that is the first appearance of devotional cults, specifically Śaiva (devotees of Lord Śiva) and Vaiṣṇava (devotees of Lord Viṣṇu) traditions. Although, as mentioned earlier, both Rudra-Śiva and Viṣṇu were known in the older Indo-Brāhmaṇical Vedic religion and are sometimes mentioned in the Upaniṣad-s, they were clearly not dominant figures. It is only here in this Indo-Śramaṇical period that we begin to see the emergence of devotion (*bhakti*) to a personal god for the first time, and it appears to be the case that these devotional cults were originally outside the Indo-Brāhmaṇical sacrificial framework as were the *śramaṇa*-groups themselves. Śiva, Vāsudeva-Kṛṣṇa, Nārāyaṇa, Rāma and many other later Hindu deities all appear to have begun as local traditions outside of the Indo-Brāhmaṇical tradition, their origins in some instances possibly even going back to pre-Indo-Āryan times (as we mentioned when discussing a possible proto-Śiva figure in the Indus Valley period). They begin now, however, to become major cults.[44]

The later Bhāgavata tradition of Vaiṣṇavism (with a focus on Vāsudeva-Kṛṣṇa), the Śaiva-bhāgavata (with a focus on Śiva), the Pāśupata tradition (again with a focus on Śiva) and the Pāñcarātra tradition (with a focus on Viṣṇu) all appear to have their origins in this Indo-Śramaṇical period.[45] Moreover, like the *śramaṇa*-groups themselves, they are all to some extent reactions against the Indo-Brāhmaṇical sacrificial system and the authority of the priests. Emphases in these religious traditions begin to emerge that will achieve great prominence in the future: the making of images and image-worship (*pūjā*) in contrast to the older sacrifice (*yajña*), the appearance of temples (probably greatly influenced by the Buddhist building of *stūpa*-s or relic-shrines of the Buddha), the practice of pilgrimage (again probably due largely to the Buddhist custom of making pilgrimage to certain sacred places), singing devotional songs, observing certain religious festivals, and so forth. All of these go considerably beyond and to a large extent begin to supplant the old Indo-Brāhmaṇical sacrificial cult. Moreover, the Indo-Śramaṇical Jain and Buddhist traditions of reverencing highly realized spiritual persons (Mahāvīra and Buddha) probably had more than a little influence on the development of *bhakti* as a form of personal devotion that moves away from the older hieratic ritual performances. Such influence, to be sure, could easily work the other way as well, and it is frequently difficult if not impossible to trace the influence one way or the other. It is clear enough, for example, that the second period in the history of the Buddhist tradition, that it to say, the rise of the Mahāyāna contains an important dimension of what can only be called Buddha-*bhakti*. Also, the Mahāyāna focus on the spiritual ideal of the *bodhisattva* (the "enlightenment-being" or "the being on the way to enlightenment") who extends great compassion to all suffering creatures is not unlike notions of the compassionate grace (*anugraha* or "grasping after") of the personal deity in later Hindu *bhakti*. It should also be kept in mind that it could well be the case that all of these more popular traditions were always present in the larger culture but never surfaced in the Indo-Brāhmaṇical sacerdotal literature and could only show themselves as a result of the growing success, both spiritually and socio-politically, of the Indo-Śramaṇical protest traditions. In any case, there appears to be a clear affinity between the spirituality of the Indo-Śramaṇical (Jain and Buddhist) traditions and the devotional *bhakti* cults that begin to become prominent in this period.

The Indic (Hindu-Buddhist-Jain) (c. 300–1200)

The reactions by the various priest-communities to all of these complex developments, including the emergent new social reality, the increasing influence of the various *śramaṇa* mendicant communities (especially the power and influence of the Buddhists under the pan-Indian empire of Aśoka and the Mauryan-s), and the surge or resurgence of simple devotional piety, were not, as might be anticipated, defensive rejection or condemnation, but, rather, to a remarkable extent, assimilation and accomodation, and this process of assimilation or accomodation can be seen in the new literature that is taking shape in Indo-Brāhmaṇical circles towards the end of the preceding period (alluded to briefly in the previous section), that is to say, the last two centuries B.C.E. and the first centuries of the Common Era.

Since this new literature attains its final redaction in the first centuries of the Common Era, it is, therefore, best treated in what we are calling the Indic (Hindu-Buddhist-Jain) period (c. 300–1200 of the Common Era), although it should be carefully noted that much of this literature contains material that is much older than the third century of the Common Era. This is also the time when Mahāyāna Buddhist literature emerges together with the later texts of the earlier Buddhist and Jain traditions as well. One also finds the emergence of Tantric traditions (both Hindu and Buddhist) in this period (especially after the fifth century of the Common Era), and this same period also marks the beginning of systematic, classical Indian philosophizing (in Hindu, Buddhist and Jain contexts) that will generate a rich and highly polemical technical literature over the next thousand years or more.

Sometimes writers refer to this period as a "classical Hindu" or "Purāṇic Hindu" period, and it is true enough that one can legitimately begin to use the term "Hindu" in this Indic period.[46] But what is striking is that much more than a "classical Hindu" or "Purāṇic Hindu" tradition is emerging. What is emerging, rather, is a composite Indic tradition with Hindu, Buddhist and Jain components, incorporating various regional cultural identities, and assimilating as well older, archaic village traditions. In other words, what is emerging is a pan-

Indian cultural vision that brings together components of the ancient Indus Valley culture, Indo-Brāhmaṇical traditions and Indo-Śramaṇical traditions in a manner that nicely mirrors the three levels of sociopolitical life on the subcontinent, that is, the local, the regional and the pan-Indian. Put somewhat differently, what is achieved in the Indic period is what Ravinder Kumar calls "a unique moral vision" or "a view of the good life" that is essential for the formation of a great civilization, and what is most characteristic about this emerging moral vision of Indic civilization, that is at once Hindu-Buddhist-Jain, is its profound appreciation for diversity together with an equally profound capacity for accomodating diversity on all levels of cultural formation.[47]

As mentioned above, the Indo-Brāhmaṇical contribution to this emerging Indic civilization can be seen in the new literature coming into prominence in the period. This new literature as a whole is referred to as literature "worthy to be remembered" (*smṛti*) in order to distinguish it from the literature that is considered to be authentic "scripture" (*śruti*), that is to say, the Veda-s (including the Upaniṣad-s) that we have already discussed. Interestingly enough, however, even though Hindus for the most part only accept the Veda-s as *śruti*, in fact, most of the basic ideas and practices of Hindu traditions derive from this new *smṛti* literature. In other words, Hindus for the most part pay little more than lip service to the Vedic *śruti*. The point can also be made in terms of the emerging social reality. Whereas the Vedic *śruti* is taken seriously by a small subset of priests, the *smṛti* texts are taken seriously by the overwhelming majority of Hindus, regardless of class or caste identity.

This new *smṛti* literature includes the following:

1. The great epic of India known as the *Mahābhārata*, the story of the great war between two branches of a family (the Kurus and the Pāṇḍus) that establishes the ancient kingdom of Bhāratavarṣa (the "Land of the Sons of Bharata") and includes within it the most popular and beloved text of the Hindu tradition, the *Bhagavad-gītā* or "Song of the Lord," featuring the teachings of Kṛṣṇa, an incarnation or "descent" (*avatāra*) of the mighty god Viṣṇu, who fights on the side of the victorious Pāṇḍus against the evil Kurus;
2. A second epic known as the *Rāmāyaṇa*, a story of another great war, this time between Rāma, another incarnation or "descent" (*avatāra*) of the mighty Viṣṇu, and the great demon, Rāvaṇa, who had kidnapped Rāma's beloved wife, Sītā, and carried her off to his fortress in the far

South (present-day Sri Lanka), from which captivity Rāma rescues her with the help of a mighty army of monkeys led by the beloved monkey god, Hanumān;
3. A group of texts called *Purāṇa*-s or "Old Tales," repositories of the great myths and legends of the Hindu traditions, largely having to do with cosmogony or how the world came to be, and with the beloved stories and tales about the three high gods of the Hindu traditions, Brahmā, Viṣṇu and Śiva;
4. A group of law-books called *Dharmaśāstra*-s, the most famous of which is the "Law-Book of Manu" (*Mānava-dharma-śāstra*), which provide detailed discussions of such matters as the proper purposes of life, the stages of life, the caste system and the manner in which the community is to be governed. Mention should also be made here to another class of texts, of some importance in terms of Hindu notions of statecraft, namely, the literature of the "science of material gain" (*artha-śāstra*) and especially to the famous *Arthaśāstra* attributed to Kauṭilya, purportedly a minister of state under Candragupta Maurya (the founder of the Mauryan dynasty) in the fourth century B.C.E. The core of the work may well be traceable to the time of Candragupta, but the present redaction of the extant text is probably from the first centuries of the Common Era, or, in other words, a time roughly contemporary with the *smṛti*-literature being described.[48]

As mentioned at the outset of this section, all of these texts contain material that is very old, probably going well back into the earlier Indo-Śramaṇical period already discussed, but they all receive their final form and general acceptance in this Indic period which coincides, at least initially, with the rise of the second great dynastic unification of the Indian subcontinent under the Gupta kings, c. 320–540 of the Common Era.

Regional Polities and the Gupta Consolidation

Following the end of the Mauryan dynasty in 183 B.C.E., which earlier under Aśoka (269–232 B.C.E.) had unified much of the subcontinent for the first time utilizing an essentially Buddhist ideology of *dharma* ("law" or "righteousness") for its legitimation, there had been an Indo-Brāhmaṇical revival under the regional (north central India) Śunga dynasty, beginning with Puṣyamitra Śunga, who reigned from c. 183 B.C.E. to 147 B.C.E., as well as among other regional polities, for example, the Sātavāhana-s in Andhra, c. the first century B.C.E. through the third century C.E., and the Vākāṭaka-s of Madhya Pradesh and northern Maharashtra, c. third and fourth centuries of the Common Era. For the most part, however, the period after the Mauryans (c. 183 B.C.E. to 300 C.E.) was characterized largely by decentralization and a series of invasions of the Northwest region (the Indus Valley area and the Punjab) from the outside by Bactrian Greeks, Śaka-s (Scythians from Central Asia), Pahlava-s (peoples from the Iranian plateau) and, finally, Kuṣāṇa-s (probably Turkish tribesmen from Central Asia), and it would not be until the time of the Gupta consolidation in the fourth century that classical Hindu traditions could develop on a pan-Indian basis.

To be sure, the Kuṣāṇa-s under the leadership of the great Kaniṣka (c. 78–144 C.E.) achieved hegemony over much of North India up to Varanasi, Central Asia (including Gandhāra, the region famous for Greco-Buddhist art), and the Punjab region, a consolidation that somewhat approached the earlier Aśokan achievement. Moreover, Kaniṣka like Aśoka was a great patron of Buddhist traditions (mainly Mahāyāna but older Buddhist traditions as well). Overall, however, the Kuṣāṇa achievement of Kaniṣka was only, finally, a regional one and hardly a match for the earlier Mauryan unification, and, thus, it must be said that from the time of the Śunga dynasty until the rise of the Gupta dynasty (c. 320–540 C.E.), there was little or no political unity of any kind on the pan-Indian level. As A. L. Basham has commented, not simply about this decentralized period but about most of Indian social and political reality in subsequent centuries as well:

> The inspiration of the Mauryas was soon almost forgotten. Later the Guptas tried to build an empire of a more centralized type, and directly controlled much of North India for over a hundred years, but, with this major exception and a few minor ones, all later Hindu imperialism was of the quasi-feudal type, loose and unstable. . . . In general the history of post-Mauryan India is one of the struggle of one dynasty with another for regional dominance, and the political, though not the cultural, unity of India was lost for nearly two thousand years.[49]

Even the Gupta period is to a large extent "quasi-feudal" in the sense that at its height of development under Candra Gupta II (c. 376–415), it hardly controlled more than the north central Gangetic basin, the western region of what is now Gujarat and Rajasthan, and the Northeast region of Bengal and Bihar, the remainder of the various regional polities being largely tributary "vassal"-like "feudatories" with varying degrees of independence. Much of the South was completely outside the Gupta domain, and much of the far Northwest was still under Śaka and Kuṣāṇa control. It is, however, under this period of Gupta consolidation that one can see the emergence of revitalized and resurgent Indo-Brāhmaṇical religious traditions that can now legitimately be called "Hindu." Moreover, this is the case not simply in the area of religious traditions but with respect to the development of Indic culture generally, including literature, art, music, drama, dance, philosophy and so forth.

The Gupta dynasty faltered due to the onslaught of the Hūṇa invasions (Turko-Mongols from Central Asia) in the Northwest region beginning in the middle of the fifth century (c. 454) and recurring again towards the close of the century (c. 495). Thereafter for several decades the Hūṇa-s controlled much of the Northwest and western regions of India. The Gupta dynasty technically continued until the middle of the sixth century (c. 540), but its actual power and influence had ended with the Hūṇa invasions. There was one final attempt at consolidation of north central India by Harṣavardhana (or simply Harṣa) of Kānyakubja (Kanauj) who came to power in 606 and managed to control most of North India by the end of his reign in the middle of the seventh century (c. 646). Like Aśoka and Kaniṣka before him, he was a great patron of Buddhism, both in its Mahāyāna and Tantric or Vajrayāna forms.

Apart from the Gupta consolidation and Harṣa's brief consolidation of much of North India, the remainder of this Indic period (c. 700–1200 C.E. and beyond) marks primarily the emergence of a great variety of regional polities and cultures, including (*a*) the Pratihāra-s of Kānyakubja (c. ninth and tenth centuries), the Cāhamāṇa-s of Ajmer and the Gāhaḍavāla-s of Varanasi (c. the tenth and eleventh centuries) in the north central region; (*b*) the Pāla-s of Bengal and Bihar (c. the eighth through the twelfth centuries), and the Sena-s of Bengal (c. the twelfth century) in the Northeast; (*c*) the Caulūkya-s or Solanki-s of Gujarat (c. the tenth through the thirteenth centuries) in the western region; (*d*) the Paramāra-s or Pawar-s of Mālwā, also in the western region; and, finally, (*e*) the emergence into prominence for the first time of a variety of powers from the Deccan or the South, namely, the Pallava-s of Kāñcī (c. the fourth through the ninth centuries), the the Cālukya-s of the western and central Deccan (c., sixth through the tenth centuries), the Rāṣṭrakūṭa-s of Mānyakheta in the central Deccan (c. eighth through the tenth centuries), the Cola-s of Tamil Nadu (c. the ninth through the thirteenth centuries), the Hoysala-s of Karnataka (c. the eleventh through the fourteenth centuries), the Pāṇḍya-s of Madurai (c. the thirteenth and fourteenth centuries), and others. As Ronald

Inden has shown in his recent book, *Imagining India*, these regional kingdoms were in geopolitical interaction with one another in terms of the unfolding Indic "imperial formations" on the subcontinent.[50]

Another regional kingdom that should be mentioned here, even though chronologically it comes during the later Indo-Islamic period, is the famous Vijayanagara (on the Tungabhadra River in the region of what is now the state of Karnataka, c. 1336–1565), perhaps along with the Pallava, Rāṣṭrakūṭa and Cola kingdoms one of the more important Hindu cultural centers in the history of the South.[51] When it fell to a coalition of Sultans—the term "sultan," meaning "authority," is a title for a Muslim monarch—in the middle of the sixteenth century, it can be said that the tradition of old-style regional Hindu kingdoms had come to an end.[52] Also, two other regional polities, albeit considerably later, warrant perhaps some mention in this brief account of the rise of regional powers, namely, the Maratha-s in the western region of the Deccan (Maharashtra), organized for the first time from a collection of clans and tribes into a unified regional force by the famous Śivājī (1627–1680), and destined to become a major political force in the eighteenth century, and the Sikh-s in the Northwest or Punjab region, transformed from a reformist, devotional, religious movement in the sixteenth century into a powerful political, military movement by their tenth Guru, Govind Singh (1666–1708). Both of these latter regional polities proved to be important resistance movements against both the Mughals and the British in the seventeenth and eighteenth centuries.

It should perhaps also be pointed out here that the above-mentioned regional polities of the North and the West (including mainly the hill or tribal peoples and clans in the larger Rajasthan area related to the Pratihāra-s, Cāhamāna-s, Solanki-s, Paramāra-s or Pawar-s, et al.) probably were the nucleus for the emerging Rajput clans who would prove to be the first and formidable line of defense against the onslaught of the Turko-Afghan Muslim invasions of Mahmud of Ghazni and then of Sultan Muhammad of Ghur in the eleventh and twelfth centuries. The Rajput clans most likely were themselves originally outsiders to the subcontinent. Their ancestors could well have been the earlier Hūṇa invaders who eventually became assimilated in the hill regions of Rajasthan. Possibly the Rajputs are a mix of Hūṇa-s (or even Kuṣāṇa-s) and indigenous tribal clans in the hills of Rajasthan. In any case, regardless of their origins, they were given caste status as "warriors" (*kṣatriya*-s).[53]

The Rajput leader, Pṛthivīrāja (of the Cāhamāna-s) is remembered for his great courage (and victory) at the first battle of Tarain in 1191 against Muhammad of Ghur. A year later, however, Muhammad of Ghur returned with a larger army under the command of his "slave"-general, Qutb ud-Din Aibak, and defeated and killed Pṛthivīrāja.[54] Muhammad of Ghur was himself eventually assassinated and his "slave" general in 1206 proclaimed himself Sultan in Delhi, thereby beginning what has come to be known as the Delhi sultanates (1206–1526), including the so-called "Slave" dynasty (1206–1290), the Khalji sultans (1290–1320), the House of Tughluq (1320–1413), the Sayyid rulers of Delhi (1414–1451) and finally the Lodī Dynasty (1451–1526), a series of Turko-Afghan sultanates finally overthrown by Babar, the founder of the great Timurid or Mughal Dynasty (1526–1757).[55]

For the most part, apart from the later Delhi sultanates and the great Mughal Empire, these regional kingdoms were Hindu in orientation, but there are important exceptions, the Pāla-s of Bengal and Bihar, for example, favoring Buddhist traditions (especially Mahāyāna and Tantric forms) and the Caulūkya-s or Solanki-s of Gujarat patronizing Jain traditions. Moreover, it was not uncommon for ruling families to patronize a variety of religious traditions in addition to the Indo-Brāhmaṇical. Also, the spread of the culture of North India to the South was accomplished in many instances by the spread of Buddhist and Jain institutions (monasteries, lay communities, and so forth). The Pallava-s of Kāñcī appear to have been one of the main vehicles for the spread of specifically Indo-Brāhmaṇical or Hindu institutions in the South, a process that was largely completed after the Gupta age. As Basham has noted, "the contact of Āryan and Dravidian produced a vigorous cultural synthesis, which in turn had an immense influence on Indian civilization as a whole."[56] Especially noteworthy in this regard is the contribution of the great Tamil poet-saints (c. the sixth through the ninth centuries), both Śaiva and Vaiṣṇava, to the development of medieval Hindu *bhakti* traditions in the later Indo-Islamic period.

Hindu Traditions

But let us return now to a discussion of the emergence of what can now in this Indic period be properly called "Hindu" tradition, in contrast to what up until now we have characterized simply as "Indo-Brāhmaṇical." In this section, since the material is so extensive no attempt is made to trace various historical developments. The focus, rather, is on the remarkable synthesis achieved.

By way of a first approximation it is useful to call attention to the following important comment by S. C. Dube:

> Hinduism, such as it is, is a loosely structured federation of faiths rather than a faith. Hindu civilization represents a pattern of stablized pluralism with well developed linkages and patterns of interdependence between its insoluble segments that enjoy varying degrees of autonomy and identity. Birth and minimal cognitive participation are enough to identify one as belonging to the Hindu faith.[57]

Hindu traditions in this Indic period now show themselves as an artful synthesis of ritual action (*yajña* and *pūjā*), disciplined meditation (*yoga*) and devotional piety (*bhakti*), shaped on one level by the old Indo-Brāhmaṇical religion of ritual sacrifice, shaped on another level by the Indo-Śramaṇical and pre-Indo-Brāhmaṇical traditions of disciplined meditation (Buddhist and Jain *yoga*) and devotion (Bhāgavata and Pāśupata traditions), but resonating as well to the spiritual rhythmns of the old Indus Valley civilization and the archaic village spirituality of the fourth and fifth millennia B.C.E. (ritual bathing, local fertility cults, religio-magical practices, and so forth).

This "loosely structured federation of faiths" which is Hindu tradition has a number of interesting features, including certain notions and practices about gods and goddesses, certain notions and practices about living things (including human beings) in terms of *karman* and rebirth together with strategies for attaining salvation or release, and certain notions and practices about social life having to do with the four proper purposes of human life (*puruṣārtha*-s), the four stages of life (*āśrama*-s), the four castes (*varṇa*-s, and the larger framework of *jāti*-s), and a theory of kingship and statecraft. Sometimes it is common for Hindus to refer to all of these features taken together with the expression "eternal law" or *sanātana-dharma*. The term "*sanātana*" means "eternal," "ancient," or "from of old." The term "*dharma*" means "law," "custom," "tradition," "duty," or simply "usage." The term *dharma* can also mean something like "ordinary religion," that is to say, it refers to the conventional practices of ritual behavior and duty to be expected from people as a result of their station in life in terms of family, occupation, region, and so forth. It is interesting to note that no Indian language has a term for our English word "religion." The closest approximation to the English expression "Hindu religion" in an Indian language is "Hindu *dharma*."

Gods and Goddesses

There are, of course, many gods and goddesses in Hindu traditions, but most Hindus think of the various gods and goddesses as manifestations of one ultimate truth. Hindu traditions combine the old Vedic notion of the Brahman, the Ultimate or Absolute, with the notion of a plurality of forms (or *mūrti*-s) that the Ultimate or Absolute assumes, three of which are central in the myths, beliefs and practices of Hindus, namely, Brahmā, the creator god, Viṣṇu, the preserving god, and Śiva, the destroying god. Brahmā, Viṣṇu and Śiva taken together are referred to in later centuries as the "three basic forms" (*trimūrti*) of the Ultimate or Absolute. One can also think of Brahmā, Viṣṇu and Śiva in terms of the flow of time, with Brahmā as the beginning, Viṣṇu as the middle, and Śiva as the end, but the notion of time is cyclical in Hindu thinking so that the beginning, the middle and the end are never once-for-all. Like the seasons of the natural year, so time itself and all of reality unfolds in endless cycles of beginnings, middles and ends.

Brahman or the Ultimate engages in an endless "play" (*līlā*) of unfolding forms that brings into being the endlessly recurring cycles of creation, preservation and destruction. Moreover, the Absolute or the Ultimate does not only assume male forms. There are also female manifestations. Śrī or Lakṣmī is the goddess of abundance, often linked with Viṣṇu. Durgā or Kālī is the awesome power of the Great Goddess, able to devour the demonic and evil forces in the world, often linked with Śiva. Sometimes the Absolute or Ultimate assumes an androgyne form, a composite of male and female, known as the "Lord whose half is woman" (*ardhanārīśvara*).

The Ultimate is boundlessly various, and so too are the cultic forms which everyday *deva-pūjā* or worship takes in the home and in the great temples. The devotees of Lord Viṣṇu are called Vaiṣṇava-s ("followers of Viṣṇu") and have numerous temples and shrines throughout the subcontinent for their *pūjā*.[58] There were many "incarnations" (altogether ten) or "descents" (*avatāra*-s) of Lord Viṣṇu, the two most important of which are as Kṛṣṇa (the divine hero of the *Mahābhārata* as well as certain *Purāṇa*-s) and Rāma (the divine hero of the *Rāmāyaṇa*). As was mentioned in chapter 1, nearly two-thirds of all Hindus are followers of one or another form of Vaiṣṇavism (including devotees of Kṛṣṇa and Rāma). The devotees of Śiva, whose mythology and ritual prescriptions are set forth primarily in certain *Purāṇa*-s, are called Śaivas ("followers of Śiva") and they too have numerous temples and shrines for their *pūjā* throughout India, especially in Tamil Nadu in the South, West Bengal in the North, and Kashmir in the far Northwest. As was mentioned earlier, perhaps as many as one-third of all Hindus are Śaivas of one kind or another. Some "forward" or high caste Hindus (overwhelmingly *brāhmaṇa*-s) are somewhat more eclectic or non-sectarian in their *deva-pūjā*, not following any one particular deity but, rather, five: Sūrya (the sun-god), Śiva, Viṣṇu, Devī (the Great Goddess), and Gaṇeśa (the elephant-headed son of Śiva and his consort, Parvatī). They perform what is known as "*pūjā* or worship of five symbols (deities)" (*pañcāyatana-pūjā*). This tradition was supposedly established by the great Vedānta philosopher, Śankara, in the eighth century. Followers of this high caste tradition are usually called Smārta Hindus.[59]

Ritual performance is still a major component in Vaiṣṇava and Śaiva cultic environments, but there has been an important shift from the old Vedic *yajña* or ritual sacrifice to the newer Hindu focus on *pūjā* or ritual "worship." Whereas the Vedic *yajña* had its primary focus on the ritual process and the ritual sacrifice, the Hindu *pūjā*, whether in great public temples or in the home, focusses on the presence of the personal deity, Viṣṇu or Śiva or whichever deity is the focus of the *pūjā*. There is still the ritual invoking of the presence of the deity, the use of priests, chanting, ritual offerings of flowers, and so forth, and the use of fire, but the *pūjā* ceremony is a much more personalized devotion, involving image-making, image worship, devotional singing, dancing, and so forth.[60] Similarly the great feasts and holy days of the ritual calendar usually center around the great exploits of the personal gods, their birth celebrations and other great events in their sacred narratives. Likewise rituals of pilgrimage and fasting become linked with episodes in the sacred narratives of the personal gods and the various sites of the divine activities.

These cultic changes closely parallel another development in the emergence of Hindu spirituality in contrast to the older Indo-Brāhmaṇical traditions, and that is the focus on *bhakti* or loving devotion. To some extent, of course, some sense of devotion or love had undoubtedly been present in the old Vedic *yajña*, but much of Vedic ritualism creates the impression of emotional detachment. The focus is, rather, on the mechanical functioning of the sacrificial process itself and the overwhelming importance of the priests. There is some sense of devotion to a personal god in the emergence of Prajāpati, the Lord of Creatures, in the later Vedic literature and clearly even a further movement towards devotionalism in such Upaniṣad-s as the Īśā, Kaṭha and Śvetāśvatara, but in all of these contexts the emotional content is limited and constrained. Even the *bhakti* of the *Bhagavad-gītā* (to be discussed below) is restrained and moderate. With the full emergence of Hindu spirituality, however, there is a new focus on personal involvement and loving devotion, and it appears to be clearly the case that Vaiṣṇava and Śaiva theistic movements are absorbing the emotional energy of the local pre-Indo-Brāhmaṇical devotional movements, such as those of the Bhāgavata-s and the Pāśupata-s, as well as the anti-

Brāhmaṇical orientation of the Indo-Śramaṇical traditions with their focus on great hero-saints such as Mahāvīra and the Buddha.[61]

Regarding *bhakti* or loving devotion, it is, of course, also essential to mention the contribution of the Tamil poet-saints, beginning during the Pallava period in the region of the South of the subcontinent, between the sixth and the ninth centuries. The devotional poems or songs of the Vaiṣṇava poet-saints (called Āḷvār-s) and of the Śaiva poet-saints (called Nāyanār-s) became widely popular in Tamil contexts, spread rapidly to Kannada-speaking and Marathi-speaking areas in what is now Karnataka and Maharashtra and finally spread to the Hindi-speaking regions in the North.[62] Here again one can clearly see a reaction against the hieratic Indo-Brāhmaṇical ritualism in favor of a more broadly based personal spirituality. In other words, this exuberant *bhakti* emotionalism appears to have clear linkages both with pre-Indo-Brāhmaṇical local devotional traditions as well as with the old Indo-Śramaṇical repudiation of the authority of the priests.[63] Thereafter from medieval times to the present, a focus on exuberant love and devotion directed to a particular deity or to a particular *guru* has been an important component of Hindu spirituality.

Devotees of the goddess, whether Kālī or Devī or Durgā, are called Śākta-s, a term which means something like "relating to energy or power," referring to the "power" (*śakti*) of the goddess to create and sustain the world, or the "power" of the goddess to destroy the demonic or to bring an end to all things. Whereas many of the traditions about the Vaiṣṇava-s, Śaiva-s and Śākta-s are to be found in the *Mahābhārata*, *Rāmāyaṇa* and the *Purāṇa*-s, it should also be mentioned that there are other classes of texts, called *Tantra*-s ("esoteric manuals") and *Āgama*-s ("esoteric received traditions"), coming from a period beginning with the fourth or fifth century of the Common Era and thereafter, having to do with elaborate ritual practices and relating especially to Śākta or goddess-traditions. These traditions are frequently linked with Śaiva environments and, as already mentioned, may well be very old or, in other words, pre-Indo-Brāhmaṇical or even pre–Indus Valley. They are especially prevalent in West Bengal and Assam in the Northeast and in Kashmir in the far Northwest. In addition to elaborate ritual practices, these *Tantra* and *Āgama* texts also make frequent use of sexual symbols, for example, comparing the manner in which the goddess interacts with the world to the manner in which male and female interact in sexual intercourse.

Finally, it should be noted that *Tantra*-s and *Āgama*-s are not to be found only in Hindu environments. They are also prominent in Buddhist traditions, especially the Vajrayāna or third "turning of the wheel of the law." Indeed, inasmuch as West Bengal, Assam and Kashmir (together also with certain centers in South India) appear to be the original contexts for the Tantra and since these are also centers for Buddhist traditions, it has been suggested that Tantric traditions may have been originally Buddhist. This is unlikely, however, since the tone of Tantric spirituality is so obviously archaic and, thus, probably pre-Indo-Brāhmaṇical and pre-Indo-Śramaṇical—in other words, pre-Hindu as well as pre-Buddhist. It is possible, of course, that although Tantric traditions are archaic, they may have first become part of mainstream or Great Tradition spirituality via Buddhist environments.

Karman, Rebirth and Strategies for Release

As there is boundless variety in the manifestations of the Absolute on the divine level, so too there is boundless variety in the many forms of ordinary life, and human life is only one part of the hierarchy of living beings "from Brahmā down to a blade of grass," as an ancient Hindu text puts it (verse 54 of the *Sāṃkhyakārikā*). The endless cycles of unfolding time and the boundless variety of living forms are controlled not by the gods and goddesses, as one might anticipate, but, rather, by a process or principle known as *karman*. Indeed, even the gods and goddesses are governed by *karman*. The term "*karman*" means "action" and refers to the simple principle that life is governed by behavior or practice, not only from the perspective of human life but from the perspective of the entire hierarchy of living forms. Moreover, just as one passes through various stages of life, so too death is only one more stage. After death, in other words, there will be a re-birth, to be followed in due time by another re-death, to be followed by another re-birth, and so forth.

Through endless cycles of recurring time, depending upon one's karmic heritage or trajectory, one might come to be embodied in any number of life-forms. There is a beginningless cycle of continuing transmigration (*saṃsāra*) and rebirth (*punarjanman*) that parallels the seemingly endless cycles of unfolding time, and all are, as it were, "caught" in this web or network of recurring transmigration, "caught" not because of any divine power, but "caught," rather, by the unfolding effects of past actions. These endless cycles of karmic trajectories are frustrating and painful, and there is a deep urge within all living things to be free or to be released (*mokṣa*) from these endless cycles of recurring rebirth.

The human life-form, though painful like all other life-forms, is nevertheless a potentially liberating life-form, since the human life-form can exercise a good deal of control over an unfolding karmic trajectory, whereas non-human life-forms for the most part are largely victims of a mechanical unfolding of effects. By disciplined meditation that leads to correct insight or wisdom, known as the "discipline of knowledge" (*jñāna-yoga*), or by disciplined meditation that allows one to become engaged in ordinary life but not to be attached to the fruits of one's action, known as the "discipline of action" (*karma-yoga*), or, finally, by disciplined meditation that involves devotion to a chosen deity who will aid the devotee in the quest for release, known as the "discipline of devotion" (*bhakti-yoga*), the human being can begin to control his or her own *karman* and to move towards "release" or *mokṣa* from the endless cycles of recurring transmigration and rebirth.

These three types of *yoga* are discussed at great length in the "Song of the Lord" or *Bhagavad-gītā* , in which Kṛṣṇa engages in a long dialogue with Arjuna, the general of the army of the Pāṇḍu-s in the great epic war of the *Mahābhārata*. As the great war is about to begin, Arjuna loses his nerve for the battle, since he sees his own kinsmen in both armies and realizes that winning the battle will require the death of his own relations. The war, however, is a righteous undertaking, that is to say, one based on *dharma*, inasmuch as the opposing Kuru-s unjustly have deprived the Pāṇḍu-s of their portion of the kingdom. Kṛṣṇa, who is Arjuna's charioteer, then explains that in this instance it is Arjuna's "duty" (again, *dharma*) to fight the war and that larger issues of truth and justice are at stake than simple family loyalty. The *Bhagavad-gītā* is known and beloved by all Hindus, and the process of *karman* and rebirth together with the various strategies of *yoga* or disciplined meditation would be widely accepted by all Hindus down to the present time. If there is any one text that comes near to embodying the totality of what it is to be Hindu, it would be the *Bhagavad-gītā* .

The *Bhagavad-gītā* is important not only because of its artful expression of Hindu spirituality but also because of its historical place within the cultural history of the subcontinent. It was compiled in its final form most likely by a Vaiṣṇava *brāhmaṇa* poet, or poets, in the first centuries of the Common Era, and like Indic civilization itself has many "layers" of meaning. On one level it accepts the older Indo-Brāhmaṇical tradition, but it is highly critical of excessive ritual behavior. On another level it refers to the old Upaniṣadic notions of disciplined meditation or *yoga*, the Ātman-Brahman formulation as well as the Sāṃkhya *puruṣa-prakṛti* formulation, and deals with them largely as forms of the "discipline of knowledge" (*jñāna-yoga*), but makes clear that in many ways the "discipline of action" (*karma-yoga*) and the "discipline of devotion" (*bhakti-yoga*) are superior or to be preferred, partly because these latter are "easier" ways but also partly because these latter are much more relevant for ordinary people. Furthermore, the *Gītā* deliberately makes use of Buddhist and Jain terminology, or, in other words, explicitly takes into account the old Indo-Śramaṇical traditions of *yoga*, and likewise incorporates the old Bhāgavata tradition of *bhakti* or devotion. Finally, the text overall is given a Hindu Vaiṣṇava flavor centering on Kṛṣṇa as an "incarnation" or "descent" (*avatāra*) of Viṣṇu. The Gītā , in other words, is a remarkably syncretic discourse that beautifully illustrates from a Hindu angle a point made early along in this section, namely, the Indic (Hindu-Buddhist-Jain) tradition's profound appreciation for diversity together with an equally profound capacity for accomodating diversity. It is hardly an accident, therefore, that through the centuries the *Gītā* has been commented upon by almost all of the schools and traditions of Hindu thought and practice, including even Gandhi and his political use of the text in the Indian nationalist movement.[64]

The Four Purposes of Life, the Four Stages of Life, the Four Castes and the Hindu Conceptions of Kingship and the State

In addition to notions and practices related to the gods and goddesses, cultic and sectarian developments, and basic attitudes about *karman*, rebirth and the various kinds of disciplined meditation (*yoga*) for attaining release, Hindu traditions also involve a complex variety of rules and regulations regarding social, economic and political life. These rules and regulations are set forth in a group of *smṛti*-texts called *Dharmaśāstra*-s or "law-books." They are also reflected in the two epics, the *Mahābhārata* and the *Rāmāyaṇa* as well as in Kauṭilya's *Arthaśāstra*. Careful study of these texts shows that originally there was a great deal of variation regarding the rules and regulations of social life depending upon the region in which one lived. Eventually, however, certain general principles or categories were devised by way of providing an overview of Indian social life as a whole. These general principles or categories center primarily around three sets of four, namely, (1) the four proper purposes of human life (*puruṣārtha*-s); (2) the four stages of human life (*āśrama*-s); and (3) the four caste-groupings (*varṇa*-s or *jāti*-s). All of these can be taken together as expressing the Hindu's "obligations or duties with respect to stage of life and caste" (*varṇāśrama-dharma*).[65] Closely related to these general principles is the Hindu theory of kingship and statecraft.

The "four proper purposes of life" (*puruṣārtha*-s) refer to certain basic activities that all people can or ought to pursue: (1) *dharma* ("duty," "custom," "law"), the pursuit of one's duty, including all of the general and specific social obligations related to one's place in the family and community; (2) *artha* ("wealth," "work", "governance"), the pursuit of worldly advantage, or, in other words, making a living, pursuing an occupation, including not only everyday life in the family and local community but also the proper political functioning of the kingdom or state; (3) *kāma* ("desire," "pleasure"), the pursuit of one's legitimate erotic and aesthetic activities, including sexuality, play, recreation, the arts, literature, and so forth; and (4) *mokṣa* ("release"), the pursuit of spiritual practices such as ritual performances (*yajña* or *pūjā*), meditation (*yoga*), and devotion (*bhakti*) in order to attain "release" from the continuing round of rebirth and transmigration.

The "four proper purposes of life" are correlated with the "four stages of life" (*āśrama*-s): (1) *brahmacārin* ("pursuing sacred knowledge"), the stage of being a student when a young person lives in the home of the teacher (*guru*) and learns about the tradition; (2) *gṛhastha* ("householder"), the stage of becoming married and raising a family and fulfilling one's basic social responsibilities in the community; (3) *vānaprastha* ("forest-dweller"), the stage of retirement from ordinary family life and social obligations when one begins to think about the ultimate goal of *mokṣa* or spiritual release; and (4) *saṃnyāsin* ("abandoning," "renunciation"), the final stage when one renounces all worldly attachments and becomes a naked, wandering ascetic in pursuit of *mokṣa*. Only a very few pursued the extreme of *saṃnyāsin*, which stage began, interestingly enough, with the ritual performance of one's own funeral rites. It is probably the case that originally these "stages" were simply life-options, that is to say, they did not have to be observed sequentially. Later, in the early centuries of the Common Era, and especially in Manu, they were worked into a sequential series.[66]

Finally, the "four proper purposes of life" and the "four stages of life" are correlated with the "four castes" (*varṇa*-s, *jāti*-s). The word "caste" is from the Portugese word *casta*, meaning "breed," "race," or "kind." The word was first used by the Portugese when they came to India in the sixteenth century in order to describe the peculiar social groupings that they noted among the people of India. There were collections of families or groups of families (*a*) having the same name, (*b*) intermarrying with one another, (*c*) following the same occupations for the most part, (*d*) following certain elaborate rules and restrictions about eating, drinking and exchanging with other groups, and (e) arranging themselves in each area in certain hierarchical orderings. Hindu traditions themselves (in the law-books or *Dharmaśāstra*-s) refer to this "caste" system with two different terms: "*varṇa*," meaning "color," and "*jāti*," meaning "birth-group."[67]

The term *varṇa* or "color" refers to the overall normative valuing or hierarchical arrangements among the many castes in terms of superior or inferior, and this overall valuing is fourfold: (1) *brāhmaṇa*-s ("priests"), the highest castes, made up of those collections of families who were originally responsible for the performance of ritual actions, considered to be the purest and the most learned among the people of India; (2) *kṣatriya*-s ("warriors"), the next highest castes, made up of those collections of families with primary responsibilities in the areas of governance and the maintenance of social order, especially the function of kingship; (3) *vaiśya*-s ("belonging to the people"), those collections of families involved in ordinary economic productivity, including in modern times commerce and business of all kinds; and, finally, (4) *śūdra*-s ("servile"), the lowest castes of servants and those collections of families who serve the higher castes. The highest three castes are referred to as "twice-born" (*dvija*), since they are eligible for initiation into sacred learning, or, in other words, they are sufficiently clean ritually to warrant study of the Veda-s or *śruti*. *Śūdra*-s are not sufficiently clean to warrant exposure to the sacred learning. In addition to this hierarchical fourfold grouping, there is yet another grouping that is even lower than the *śūdra*-s, namely, the so-called "untouchables" (*a-spṛśya*-s). These are collections of families considered to be polluted because they are involved in such activities as cleaning human waste areas, dealing with the dead (both human and animal), tanning, and so forth. Traditionally such untouchables lived in segregated areas outside of a main village or town.

In contrast to the term *varṇa* which is a normative or valuing notion, the other term for caste is descriptive or empirical, namely, *jāti* or "birth-group." The notion of *jāti* refers to the actual "birth-groups" in various parts of India, and they number altogether several thousand. In other words, from the perspective of a descriptive or empirical account of actual social life in India, there are not simply "four" castes but, rather, several thousand. In some areas of the subcontinent, there are almost no *brāhmaṇa*-s, and *jāti*-s other than the *brāhmaṇa* become dominant. The term *jāti*, in other words, is a much more precise, descriptive term regarding the thousands of castes that one actually finds in different parts of the subcontinent. Moreover, hierarchical patterns and rules of exchange differ markedly among the various *jāti*-s in different areas of India. To some extent one can correlate the *varṇa*-system with the *jāti*-system, so that, for example, one might refer to various *jāti*-s as "sub-castes" of *kṣatriya*-s or *vaiśya*-s, and so forth. The

Hindu law-books (the *Dharmaśāstra*-s) also seek to correlate *varṇa* and *jāti*, explaining the many hundreds and thousands of sub-castes to be the result of the mixture of castes in various regions. Overall, however, the correlations are not very precise and in many instances clearly forced, and for a proper understanding of the modern caste system one has to immerse onself in the incredibly complex details of the *jāti*-system in each area of the subcontinent.

As has been pointed out, the caste system is very old in South Asia, and the four *varṇa*-categories are mentioned already in the Ṛg Veda (X.90). It is difficult to know, however, if the system in ancient times resembles the system as it is described in the traditional law-books and in modern field studies. The groupings mentioned in the Veda could possibly be little more than a social division of labor, a kind of ancient class system. What is distinctive about a caste system, in contrast to a class system, is that for the most part one's status is determined by birth rather than by merit and that one's social identity is defined by an elaborate, hierarchical network of ritual exchanges rather than by one's individual economic status. To be sure, the *Dharmaśāstra*-s or law-books of this Indic period, especially perhaps the *Mānava-dharma-śāstra* or "Law-Book of Manu," provide clear evidence that a full blown caste system was operating, but it is not as clear that social life always mirrored the system as articulated in the official texts. There is some reason to believe that over the centuries there has been a good deal more flexibility and mobility among caste groupings in various parts of India than is commonly thought.[68] The more rigid, modern system of caste probably develops during the long centuries (c. 1200–1750) of Muslim dominance in India when Hindu traditions became much more defensive and in-grown for the sake of communal survival.

A similar gap between the ideal and the real is to be noticed with respect to the theory of kingship and statecraft as set forth in the *Law-Book of Manu* and Kauṭilya's *Arthaśāstra* and as reflected in the *Mahābhārata* and the *Rāmāyaṇa*. As was true in the Buddhist traditions already discussed from the Mauryan period (fourth and third centuries B.C.E.), so too in these *smṛti*-texts of the Hindu tradition, some core portions of which are roughly contemporary with the Mauryan period, there is a clear differentiation between the religious domain and the political domain, and the king's position, at least in theory, is a ritually subordinate one. To be sure, Hindu kings are often said to be descended from lineages going back to mythical times. According to the *Matsya-purāṇa*, for example, the ideal kingdom of Rāma (*rāma-rājya*) is in the lineage of the Solar Dynasty traceable back to Īkśvāku, the eldest offspring of the mythical Manu (the Cosmic First Man), and the kings of the *Mahābhārata* (the Kuru-s, Pāṇḍu-s, and so forth) are for the most part in the lineage of the Lunar Dynasty traceable back to Ilā, the youngest offspring of the mythical Manu. Hindu kings are even said to be made up particles from the various gods. In the *Law-Book of Manu* 7.4-8, for example, the king is said to be made up of particles from Indra, Varuṇa, Viṣṇu, and so forth. There is, in other words, some evidence for a tradition of the divine origin of kings.[69]

The king, nevertheless, is often only human in many conceptualizations of kingship, and his function as ruler is clearly differentiated from and subordinated to the function of the priest. Already from Vedic times, the role of the warrior (*rājanya, kṣatriya*) is distinguished from that of the priest. It is the duty of the chieftain or ruler (*rājadharma*) to maintain overall order (*dharma*) between castes and communities and to protect the people. The king or ruler, however, is dependent on the priest for legitimation. It is the priest who performs the sacrifice which enthrones the king. The king in return gives lavish gifts of cattle and land to the priest. As Dumont has shown, power and purity are clearly separated in both the earlier Indo-Brāhmaṇical as well as in the later Hindu ideology of rulership and statecraft. Moreover, power is subordinate or "encompassed" by purity. That is, the king (the embodiment of power) is always dependent on the priest (the embodiment of purity). The king is always in need of his priestly ritual advisor, the *purohita* or the "one who goes before," the *brāhmaṇa* in attendance at the royal household and court.[70]

In fact, of course, there is more than a little evidence that the actual historical situation was quite different from the ideal characterization.[71] In some instances, priests themselves became rulers, and there are many examples of rulers coming from other than priestly or *kṣatriya* groups. Śūdra-s, and even untouchables, came to power at one or another region or time on the subcontinent. Similarly, Kauṭilya's *Arthaśāstra* portrays a largely pragmatic and opportunistic picture of royal behavior that diverges a good deal from the cultural ideal of the king as protector of *dharma*. Nevertheless, it is fair to say that Rāma with his obedient and loyal queen, Sītā, together with the kingdom of Rāma (*rāma-rājya*) as reflected in the *Rāmāyaṇa*, have represented fundamental Hindu ideals throughout the centuries and even down to the present day. To a somewhat lesser degree, the victory of the Pāṇḍava-s in their righteous battle against the usurping Kaurava-s for the sake of maintaining proper order (*dharma*) as reflected in the *Mahābhārata*, also served as fundamental influences regarding authentic governance and the relation between state and society in Hindu sensibilities.

In this Indic period, then, specifically "Hindu" traditions have come into focus: the principal gods and goddesses (Brahmā, Viṣṇu, Śiva, Lakṣmī, Devī, and so forth), the basic patterns of worship (*devapūjā*) and ritual performances among Vaiṣṇavas, Śaivas and Śāktas in the home as well as great public temples (including images and image-worship, devotional songs, great religious festivals, pilgrimage, and so forth), the vast compilations of *smṛti*-literature (the great epics, *Mahābhārata* and *Rāmāyaṇa*, the beloved *Bhagavad-gītā*, the *Purāṇa*-s and the elaborate *Dharmaśāstra*-s), the appearance of the ritual-erotic texts, the *Āgama*-s and *Tantra*-s (among certain Vaiṣṇava, Śaiva and Śākta groups), the formulation of the basic notions of *karman* and rebirth together with the development of the various meditational strategies (types of *yoga*) for overcoming the effects of *karman*, and, finally, an elaborate synthesis of the totality of social life in terms of the four purposes of human life, the four stages of human life, the four castes, and the Hindu conceptualizations of the state and kingship. As mentioned earlier, Hindus themselves sometimes refer to all of this as *sanātana-dharma*, the "eternal law," or as *varṇāśrama-dharma*, the "obligations or duties with respect to stage of life and caste."

Indian Philosophy and the Indic Mendicant Life

Apart from the development of specifically "Hindu" traditions in this Indic period, mention should also be made, at least briefly, of two other closely related cultural traditions, namely, Indian philosophy and Indian monasticism or the Indic mendicant life. They are closely related and deserve to be treated together for two important reasons. First, almost all of the Indian philosophers within this Indic period, as well as those from periods before and after, were deeply concerned about spiritual freedom whether expressed in terms of "release" (*mokṣa*), "final cessation" (*nirodha, nirvāṇa*) or "isolation" (*kaivalya, kevalin*), and, hence, it is hardly an accident that many of these philosophers were *saṃnyāsin*-s ("renouncers"), *bhikṣu*-s (mendicants), *muni*-s ("inspired sages"), *parivrājaka*-s ("wandering ascetics"), and so forth. Most of them were mendicants, monastics or spiritual virtuosos of one kind or another. Already from ancient times there were sages that lived apart from ordinary conventional society in hermitages or *āśrama*-s. Traditions of meditation, religious practice and philosophical reflection were transmitted frequently in one-on-one teacher-student (*guru*-

śiṣya) relationships, referred to as the *guru-paraṃparā* (the authoritative "line of teachers"). Spiritual authority or teaching authority, in other words, was centered not in books, or doctrines, or institutions, but, rather, in living persons, who were perceived to be spiritual masters and who passed on their knowledge and wisdom in one-on-one *guru-śiṣya* encounters. Even in the more highly organized monastic institutions of the Buddhists and Jains, the role of the particular meditation-master or *guru* was central. Moreover, in the larger monastic contexts it was expected that monks would gather together only for certain stated times of the year. Other than those stated times, they would go off and practice the life of meditation as solitary practitioners and wandering ascetics. The ancient Yogins, Mahāvīra, Gautama the Buddha, Nāgārjuna, Vasubandhu, Īśvarakṛṣṇa, Patañjali, Dignāga, Dharmakīrti, Śankara, Rāmānuja, and others, were all linked in one way or another with the mendicant or monastic life. Even the schools of thought that focus on technical problems of logic, epistemology, inferential reasoning and philosophy of language without exception make reference to spiritual wisdom and *mokṣa* or *nirvāṇa* as the final goal of their endeavours.[72]

A second important reason for treating Indian philosophy and Indian monasticism or the Indic mendicant life together is that both cultural traditions provide clear evidence that this Indic period is much more than a "classical Hindu" or "Purāṇic Hindu" period. Clearly Hindu, Buddhist and Jain traditions of philosophizing are in polemical encounter with one another throughout most of the period under review (from the first centuries of the Common Era through the twelfth century), and the institutional environments for these encounters are largely the monasteries of the older Buddhist schools, the Jains, the Mahāyāna Buddhists, the *āśrama*-s and later *maṭha*-s ("monasteries") of the Advaitins, the Viśiṣṭādvaitins, and others. What is emerging in the period, in other words, is not simply a classical "Hindu" philosophizing together with its mendicant or monastic base, but, rather, a much broader "Indic" philosophizing that encompasses Hindu, Buddhist and Jain components along with a variety of monastic institutional environments.

To some extent, of course, we have already referred to Indian philosophizing, at least in its incipient, pre-systematic forms as found in the Indo-Brāhmaṇical Upaniṣadic speculations about *ātman* (the "Self") and Brahman (the "Ultimate" or "Absolute"), or the old Sāṃkhya formulation of *puruṣa* ("pure consciousness") and *prakṛti* ("materiality" or "nature"). Also, we have discussed the old Indo-Śramaṇical Jain speculations about *jīva* ("self") and *ajīva* ("non-self") and the early Buddhist focus on No-Self (*anātman*) and radical transience (*anitya*). We have also noticed the emergence of a number of key philosophical notions such as *karman* ("action"), *saṃsāra* ("transmigration"), *punarjanman* ("rebirth"), *dharma* ("law," "duty" or even "religion"), *mokṣa* ("release"), *nirodha* ("cessation"), *nirvāṇa* ("spiritual quiescence") and perhaps most important of all, *yoga* ("disciplined meditation").

In terms of systematic formulation, it is in the first centuries of the Common Era that the various technical traditions of Indian philosophy begin to take shape, each one centering around a founding figure and a collection of utterances (*sūtra*-s) or verses (*kārikā*-s).[73] The term "*sūtra*" means "string" or "cord" and refers to abbreviated aphorisms composed or compiled by teachers (*guru*-s) for purposes of teaching a particular subject-matter. Most teaching was done orally, and the compilations of *sūtra*-s became the vehicle for memorizing the contours of a subject. The term "*kārikā*" means simply a concise "verse" and like the "*sūtra*" is primarily a vehicle for teaching a particular subject-matter. Followers of these various traditions, or successors in the line of transmission (*guru-paraṃparā* or "the sequence of teachers") would then write elaborate commentaries and subcommentaries on the original *sūtra*-s or *kārikā*-s, and over the centuries a huge technical commentarial tradition developed for each of the systems. What distinguishes this technical philosophizing from older traditions of speculation are (*a*) a concern for specifying at the outset the means of knowing (*pramāṇa*), such as perception, inference, *śruti*, and so forth, of a particular school and for defending those means, (*b*) a concern to define terms precisely and technically, (*c*) a concern that arguments be formulated in a correct manner, (*d*) a fair accounting of the views of other schools together with a polemical attack on those views, and (e) an attempt to present a consistent and clear overall system of thought.

The technical schools of Hindu philosophy are six in number, and all of them appear to have taken shape in the early centuries of the Common Era. They are designated "Hindu" or *āstika* (literally "existent" but really meaning "authentic" or "believing"), since they accept the validity of the Indo-Brāhmaṇical *śruti* (that is, the Veda-s, including the Upaniṣad-s) as a valid means of knowing (*pramāṇa*). Buddhist and Jain traditions of thought are called *nāstika* ("inauthentic" or "nonbelieving"), since they do not accept Indo-Brāhmaṇical *śruti* and rely only on perception and inference as means of knowing (*pramāṇa-s*). There are also references to an old materialist school, called Cārvāka (possibly a proper name for the founder) or Lokāyata (meaning "common" or unrefined or low caste), which is also considered *nāstika* and supposedly accepts only perception as a means of knowing (*pramāṇa*).

The Hindu systems are usually discussed in three pairs, namely, Sāṃkhya and Yoga, Nyāya and Vaiśeṣika, and Mīmāṃsā and Vedānta. The oldest system of technical philosophy in the Hindu tradition is that of the Sāṃkhya, set forth in a text entitled the *Sāṃkhya-kārikā*-s, composed by a certain *parivrājaka* ("wandering ascetic") named Iśvarakṛṣṇa. Closely related is the Yoga system of Patañjali as set forth in the aphorisms he compiled (probably shortly after the *Sāṃkhya-kārikā*-s), entitled the *Yoga-sūtra*-s. The term *sāṃkhya* means "rational enumeration," and the two systems of Sāṃkhya and Yoga deal respectively with the theory and practice of meditation, centering around the old dualist framework of pure consciousness (*puruṣa*) and materiality (*prakṛti*) deriving from the old Upaniṣadic speculations. The next pair, Nyāya and Vaiśeṣika, founded respectively by the sages Gautama (different from Gautama of the Buddhist tradition) and Kaṇāda, together with the two *sūtra*-collections, the *Nyāya-sūtra*-s and the *Vaiśeṣika-sūtra*-s, have to do with logic and what might be called a system of primitive physics. Nyāya ("logic") emphasizes how to argue and how to form correct arguments. Vaiśeṣika ("specific elements") sets forth a naive realism based on a theory of elementary atomic constituents. They represent a pair since Vaiśeṣika accepts the logic of Nyāya and Nyāya accepts the naive realism of Vaiśeṣika. The third pair, Mīmāṃsā and Vedānta, the earliest exponents of which were respectively the sages Jaimini and Bādarāyaṇa and their respective *sūtra* collections, the *Mīmāṃsā-sūtra*-s and the *Brahma-sūtra*-s, have to do with the correct interpretation of the Veda-s and the Upaniṣad-s, that is to say, the correct interpretation of "scripture" (*śruti*). Mīmāṃsā ("measuring" or simply "scriptural exegesis") deals with the ritual portions (*karma-kāṇḍa*) of the Vedic sacrificial system and the elaborate hermeneutical rules for ritual performance. Vedānta ("end of the Veda") deals with the knowledge portions (*jñāna-kāṇḍa*) of the Upaniṣad-s, focusing primarily on the old Upaniṣadic speculations relating to the *ātman*, Prajāpati, *tapas*, and so forth.

In these early centuries of the Common Era, one also sees the development of systematic Buddhist and Jain philosophy. To be sure, both the Buddhist and Jain traditions are a good deal older than the systematic Hindu schools of the first centuries of the Common Era. Buddhist and Jain traditions go back to Gautama the Buddha and Mahāvīra in the sixth century B.C.E. and the canonical writings in Pāli, Prakrit and Sanskrit (the Buddhist Tripiṭaka or "three baskets" and the Jain Āgama-s or "received teachings"). Nevertheless, it is not much before the beginning of the Common Era that Buddhist and Jain thought become systematic in the sense of technical philosophizing along the lines of *pramāṇa*-theory, precise definitions and polemical interaction with other traditions.

If the Sāṃkhya was the first of the Hindu schools to take systematic shape, then for the Jain tradition one would probably point to a work such as Umāsvāti's *Tattvārtha-sūtra* ("Sūtra-s on Jain Truth") in the second century of the Common Era, a work that systematizes Jain thought for the first time, uses the medium of Sanskrit and is in polemical tension with other traditions.[74] On the Buddhist side, one would point to the *Abhidharmakośa* ("Compendium on Abhidharma or Philosophical Matters") and the *Abhidharmakoṣa-bhāṣya* ("Commentary on the Compendium) of Vasubandhu, a Buddhist thinker of the fourth century who discusses the older theories of the School of the Elders in a systematic manner (and specifically those schools known as Sarvāstivāda and Sautrāntika) but who is also a bridge figure to the newly developing Mahāyāna or Great Vehicle Buddhist thought.

Mahāyāna or Great Vehicle Buddhist philosophizing begins in the first centuries of the Common Era with a group of Sanskrit texts called the "Perfection of Wisdom" (*Prajñāpāramitā*), which set forth the new Buddhist ideal of the *bodhisattva* ("enlightenment being" or "being on the way to enlightenment") who extends compassion to all suffering creatures and who cultivates the "perfection of wisdom."[75] Mahāyāna philosophy then develops in three important and innovative directions. First, a second century monk by the name of Nāgārjuna develops a rigorous negative dialectic in a text called the *Mūlamadhyamaka-kārikā*-s ("Verses on the Authentic Middle Way") that criticizes all philosophical views and, as it were, steers a "middle path" between all views (including Buddhist views)—hence, the school's name, "Mādhyamika," or the new "middle way"— and concludes with the radical assertion of the emptiness (*śūnyatā*) and substancelessness (*niḥ-svabhāva*) of all metaphysical constructs and, indeed, of all things. Second, the fourth-century monk Vasubandhu, mentioned above as the author of the *Abhidharmakośa* and *Bhāṣya*, becomes converted to Mahāyāna and helps in developing a new school of Buddhist reflection, which on one level accepts Nāgārjuna's radical notion of "emptiness" but then interprets "emptiness" in terms of a theory of "consciousness-only," a school known as Vijñānavāda (the "Consciousness-Tradition") or Yogācāra (the "Practice of Meditation" as consciousness-only). Third, Mahāyāna thought develops a sophisticated and technical logic and epistemology in the work of the monks Dignāga and Dharmakīrti from the fifth through the seventh century. Through all of these centuries the various Mahāyāna schools are in polemical encounter with one another and with the various Hindu and Jain schools, and, of course, the institutional base for all of these developments is the Buddhist monastery.

Regarding the various Hindu schools, it is fair to say that the Vedānta is without doubt the most important and well-known of all the schools of Hindu philosophy, largely because it was destined to become the primary institutional vehicle for the survival of mainstream Hindu traditions through the long centuries of the Indo-Islamic period, as well as the catalyst for Neo-Hindu renewal during the Indo-Anglian or modern period. Interestingly enough, however, in the early centuries of the Common Era, when the technical schools of Hindu, Buddhist and Jain philosophizing were in their creative first phase, the Vedānta tradition was not especially notable.[76] Bādarāyaṇa's *Brahma-sūtra*-s were for the most part interpreted as a simple devotional theism not unlike the moderate theism of the *Bhagavad-gītā*. This sort of theistic or religious Vedānta was clearly overshadowed by the Mīmāṃsā and other realist schools as well as by the Sāṃkhya and Yoga traditions, not to speak of the many Buddhist schools of philosophy, both Theravāda as well as Mahāyāna (including the Sarvāstivādins, Sautrāntikas, Mādhyamikans and Yogācārins).

By the sixth century, however, the picture begins to change with the more sophisticated Vedānta philosophizing of Gauḍapāda, author of the *Gauḍapādīya-kārikā*-s or *Māṇḍūkya-kārikā*-s, who begins to provide a more rigorous philosophical basis for the old Upaniṣadic speculations about the Self (*ātman*), enriched on one level by the conceptualizations of Sāṃkhya, Yoga and the other Hindu philosophical schools, and enriched on another level by some of the analytical philosophical methods of the Buddhist schools (mainly of Vasubandhu and Nāgārjuna). Gauḍapāda's work in turn then becomes the basis for the great Vedānta philosopher, Śankara (traditional dates, 788–820, but more likely c. 700), who develops the powerful position of Advaita Vedānta or "non-dual Vedānta," a philosophical view stressing that there is only one thing that truly exists, namely, the *ātman* or Brahman, all multiplicity or plurality being ontologically suspect as Māyā and epistemologically deficient by reason of ignorance (*avidyā*). The Advaita Vedānta owes most of its conceptualization and technical terminology to the old Sāṃkhya philosophy and its analytical methodology and critical dialectic to the Buddhist thinkers, Vasubandhu and Nāgārjuna. Śankara wrote elaborate commentaries on the main Upaniṣad-s, the *Brahma-sūtra*-s and the *Bhagavad-gītā*, masterfully synthesizing in his monistic Advaita Vedānta position many of the older philosophical themes from both Hindu as well as Buddhist traditions.

Equally as significant as his philosophical achievement was his reworking or reforming of Hindu monastic and mendicant traditions. The evidence, unfortunately, is not as clear in this area, although tradition is unanimous in ascribing monastic reform and reorganization to the great Śankara.[77] Supposedly Śankara saw the Buddhists and their monastic institutions as great and dangerous rivals to Hindu spirituality and Hindu institutional life. He wanted, therefore, to reorganize the Hindu mendicant life on a firmer institutional base so that it could compete successfully with Buddhist traditions.

The monastic or mendicant life, of course, was known to the Hindu tradition as well as the older Indo-Brāhmaṇical tradition, but it had traditionally been much less organized than Buddhist or Jain monastic life. "Wandering ascetics" (*parivrājaka*-s) were as old as the oldest Upaniṣad-s, and becoming a *saṃnyāsin* or "world renouncer" was as old as the system of *āśrama*-s or "stages of life." As mentioned earlier, this was frequently the institutional mechanism for the transmission of much religious and philosophical reflection in India down through the centuries, that is to say, the ascetic or world-renouncing spiritual leader (*guru*) who passes on his learning in a one-on-one relation with the student (*śiṣya*). Sometimes students would simply go to the home of the *guru* for a period of training. In other instances, small schools or hermitages (*āśrama*-s) would be formed focussed on the *guru* and his students. These could hardly be called "monasteries" (*maṭha*-s), but they were in many instances small mendicant communities. Throughout the epics and Purāṇa-s one can read about *muni*-s or sages who live apart in hermitages or *āśrama*-s. Moreover, it should be noted that even in the more organized Buddhist and Jain monastic environments, in many instances the old tradition of one-on-one learning was maintained. There was a meditation-master who worked individually with members of the community. Regarding organization or institutionalization, there is an old hierarchical ordering of mendicants or monastics in Hindu or Indo-Brāhmaṇical contexts built around a fourfold structure: *kuṭīcaka*-s (those ascetics who live near their families and are supported by them); *bahūdaka*-s (those who gather near pilgrimage places for begging); *haṃsa*-s (those who may stay for only one night in a given place); and *paramahaṃsa*-s (those who must continually roam from place to place).[78]

Śankara, presumably wanting something more carefully structured for Hindu monks, set about the task of founding what came to be known as the Daśanāmi (literally the "ten-named") Orders of Hindu monasticism, made up of four monastic centers in the four regions of the subcontinent: (1) the Śṛṅgeri Maṭha (or monastery) in the South, (2)

Govardhana Maṭha in the East, (3) Śārada Maṭha in the West, and (4) Jyotir Maṭha in the North (or respectively, Śṛṅgeri in the state of Karnataka, Puri in the state of Orissa, Dvāraka in the state of Gujarat and Badrinath in the State of Uttar Pradesh).[79] At the monastery in the South are to be found the Bhāratī, Purī and Sarasvatī Orders. In the East are the Āraṇya and Vāna Orders. In the West are the Tīrtha and Āśrama Orders. And in the North are the Giri, Pārvata and Sāgara Orders. Altogether there are ten orders (hence the name, Daśanāmi), and at the head of each of the four Maṭha-s in the different areas of the subcontinent is a Śankarācārya who is in a line of teachers (*guru-paraṃparā*) going back to the original Śankara. The Daśanāmi system is to a large extent non-sectarian, that is to say, it is neither exclusively Vaiṣṇava nor Śaiva, although overall it is closer to the latter than the former. Institutional rules are relatively unstructured, and there is very little coordination among the various *maṭha*-s (except during great pilgrimage processions like that of the modern Kumbha Melā when the various monks and mendicants follow a traditionally fixed order of march).[80] Also, the Daśanāmi orders are for the most part high caste in orientation with most members coming from the *brāhmaṇa* castes, and, as was mentioned earlier, their lay devotees and supporters are likewise from the high castes and are known as Smārta Hindus.

Śankara's Advaita Vedānta and the Daśanāmi Orders, however, are not the only forms of the Vedānta tradition or organized Hindu monasticism. There is also the tradition of Rāmānuja (c. 1017–1137), the founder of Viśiṣṭādvaita (the "the non-dualism of modified Brahman"), also known as the tradition of Śrī Vaiṣṇavism in the region of Tamil Nadu. In contrast to the strict and uncompromising non-dualism of Advaita, the "modified" non-dualism of Rāmānuja allows for the reality of the individual soul and the world as dimensions or attributes of Brahman, and allows or encourages a rich devotionalism or *bhakti* together with a strong focus on "self-surrender" or *prapatti*. Some two centuries after the founder's death, the tradition broke into two main subdivisions, the so-called Vaḍagalai, a northern school which uses mainly Sanskrit sources and thinks that the devotee must assist God in the process of salvation (just as the young monkey must cling to the neck of its mother), and the Teṅgalai, a southern school which uses mainly Tamil sources and thinks that God needs no help in the process of salvation (just as the cat simply grasps the kitten by the nape of its neck).

The Śrī Vaiṣṇava monks belong to the Rāmānuja-*saṃpradāya* or "monastic group," but there are other Vaiṣṇava "monastic groups" (*saṃpradāya*-s) as well, from the twelfth century onwards, including the

Madhva (c. 1197–1276) *saṃpradāya* (those who follow a form of the dualist Vedānta of the teacher, Madhva), the Nimbārka (c. twelfth century) *saṃpradāya* (those who follow the tradition of *dvaitādvaita* or "both duality and non-duality" Vedānta of the teacher, Nimbārka) and the Vallabha (c. sixteenth century) *saṃpradāya* (those who follow the tradition of *śuddhādvaita* or "purified non-dualism" of the teacher, Vallabha, who equates Brahman, the Ultimate or Absolute, with Lord Kṛṣṇa). There are numerous other Hindu monastic and mendicant orders, for example, the Śaivite Nāth Yogi-s, the later Vaiṣṇava Vairāgī-s, and others, which will be discussed in the sequel, but the Daśanāmi orders and the various orders of the Vaiṣṇava-s are by far the most important in this Indic period.

3

Discontinuity as Continuity (ii): New Indic Formations

> *We must recall that in the Indian subcontinent distinct, self-contained social groups, at different levels of cultural and technological development, survived right into this century. They include hunting and collecting tribes, pastoral nomads, shifting cultivators, traditional settled agriculturalists, modern 'developed' agriculturalists and several levels of urban industrial society, all coexisting and economically interdependent.*
>
> —B. and R. Allchin, *The Rise of Civilization in India and Pakistan*

Each of the first three of the Old Indic formations discussed in the preceding chapter, the Indus Valley, the Indo-Brāhmaṇical and the Indo-Śramaṇical, exhibited particular features that contrasted markedly with one another and developed for the most part quite separately from one another. The fourth formation or layer, however, the Indic, represented an interactive phase in which the various previous formations generated another layer, clearly constituted by components from the older layers but representing as well a variety of new departures. From the perspective of substantive spiritual and intellectual formation, the interactions of the fourth layer are perhaps best illustrated by the lively and polemical exchanges between Hindu, Buddhist and Jain philosophers regarding the nature of the world and human experience. From the perspective of the development of social reality, the interactions of the fourth layer are perhaps most apparent in the political consolidation achieved under the Hindu Gupta kings (c. 320–540 C.E.) together with the accompanying cultural achievements in art, poetry, music, grammar, dance, drama and medicine. Following the Gupta period, there emerges, to use the idiom of Ronald Inden, a series of "imperial formations" along the lines of the older Hindu ideology of kingship as derived from the literature of statecraft (such as Kauṭilya's *Arthaśāstra*) and the great epics, or the even older ideology of the "universal monarch" (*cakravartin*), that is, regional polities interacting and vying with one another, motivated by ambitions for subcontinental hegemony but frequently having to settle for much less.[1] This, then, brings us to the two final layers to be discussed, the New Indic formations of the Indo-Islamic and the Indo-Anglian.

THE INDO-ISLAMIC (C. 1200–1757)

Sometimes this period is called the medieval period in the history of the subcontinent, but it is more accurately characterized by the appearance of a remarkably new cultural force, Islam, and the resulting emergence of yet another layer or level of cultural development on the subcontinent, the Indo-Islamic. Contact with Islamic culture occurred as early as the middle of the seventh century of the Common Era, largely through Arab traders coming to the west coast of India across the Arabian Sea.[2] Some military forays into India by Arab Muslim armies began as early as the eighth century in the region of Sind (present-day Pakistan) and Gujurat, but it was not until the latter part of the tenth century that these intrusions became serious threats to the independence of the subcontinent. When Islamic conquest did begin to occur, however, it was not of the original Arab variety. It came during the period of the 'Abbasid caliphate (750–1258), and more than that, during a late phase of the 'Abbasid dynasty in which a number of independent succession states had emerged, one of which on the far eastern end of the Islamic world, namely, that of the Turko-Afghan Ghaznavid state, was to be the first agent of Islamization on the subcontinent.

By the time of the 'Abbasid caliphate, Islamic culture and civilization had become a cosmopolitan, imperial presence throughout the Middle East and the Mediterranean world, and had indeed become the heir of the heritage of Middle Eastern civilizations. When it entered India, in other words, it brought with it a much richer heritage than the original Arab faith of the founder, Muhammad. Ira M. Lapidus has nicely characterized this heritage in the following:

> Islamic civilization, in both its courtly cosmopolitan and urban religious forms, represented the cultural expression of political and religious elites thrown up by the Arab conquests. Each version also represented a selection and synthesis of the heritage of Middle Eastern civilizations. The ancient world communicated Jewish, Christian, Hellenistic, Byzantine and Sasanian culture. Chrisitan eschatology and theology, neo-Platonic and Hellenistic philosophy, became part of Islamic theology and mysticism. Jewish scriptural, prophetic, ritual and legal precedents were absorbed into Islamic law. Hellenistic science was studied in a continuous tradition. Sasanian and Byzantine court ceremony, art and architecture, administrative precedents, and political concepts were assimilated by the Ummayad and 'Abbasid empires.[3]

This is not at all to suggest that all of this came with the invading forces of Mahmud of Ghazni and Sultan Muhammad of Ghur in the eleventh and twelfth centuries. It was, however, the beginning of a cultural invasion and cultural transformation the likes of which the subcontinent had not experienced in over two thousand years of previous history. Mahmud of Ghazni and Sultan Muhammad of Ghur, in other words, may have appeared to be only two more outside invaders on analogy with so many who had come before. This time, however, there was a profound difference. This time it was not simply an invading force to be absorbed or accomodated, sooner or later, into the dense and rich subcontinental civilization. This time an entire civilization, at least as dense and rich as the subcontinental, was making an appearance, and the encounter and accomodation would be exceedingly fruitful, albeit also deeply frustrating and painful.

From 997 onwards, Mahmud of Ghazni, a Turko-Afghan Muslim from Afghanistan, led his armies in some seventeen bloody attacks, not only in the Punjab region but well into North India as well. A number of important Hindu religious sites were attacked and plundered, including those at Thanesar, Kanauj, Mathura and the famed temple at Somnath. The Ghaznavids, however, made no attempt to hold extensive portions of the subcontinent beyond some areas in the Punjab and Sind. It was over a century later, when Ghazni itself was conquered (1173) by another Central Asian Muslim, Sultan Muhammad of Ghur, that North India became the target for permanent conquest and settlement. As mentioned earlier, in 1192 at the second battle of Tarain the Rajputs under Pṛthivīrāja were completely defeated.

Thereafter most of North India was open to permanent conquest by the Muslim armies. Sultan Muhammand of Ghur himself withdrew from North India and returned to Ghur, leaving the task of the further conquest of North India to his most favored Turkish commander, Qutb ud-Din Aibak, and, as was mentioned above, when Muhammad of Ghur was assassinated in 1206, Qutb ud-Din Aibak claimed the title of Sultan for himself in Delhi and began the series of Turko-Afghan sultanates called simply the Delhi Sultanates (1206–1526). These Sultanates ruled most of North India from the Punjab in the Northwest to the borders of Bengal in the northeast, but they were for the most part simply large regional polities. There were a number of other regional powers during the period, Hindu as well as spin-off Muslim politities, including the Rajput Confederacy (Hindu) in the West (the Rajasthan region), the Bahmani (Muslim) dynasty in the Deccan, the Ilyas Shahi (Muslim) dynasty in Bengal, the Vijayanagara (Hindu) dynasty in the Karnataka region, and so forth.

When yet another Turkish line, the Timurids or Mughals, founded in 1526 by Babar (purportedly a descendent of both Timur on his father's side and the great Chingis Khan on his mother's side), supplanted the last of the Delhi Sultanates (the Lodi dynasty, 1451 - 1526), the battle was not just with the Lodis. The Rajput Confederacy under the Rāṇā Sangā of Mewar (the region of Rajasthan) was at least as formidable as the weakened Lodis. In any case, Babar was finally successful after a series of major encounters in the North with various regional polities. The most important of the Timurid or Mughal rulers included, in addition to Babar himself (ruled 1526–30), his son Humayun (1508–56, ruled from 1530), the great emperor, Akbar (ruled 1556–1605), Jahangir (ruled 1605–27), Shah Jahan (ruled 1628–1707, builder of the Taj Mahal), and Aurangzeb (ruled 1658–1707). Under Akbar, the Mughal dynasty achieved its greatest success and coherence, controlling most of North India from the far Northwest to the far Northeast, although much of the South remained outside of Mughal control. With Aurangzeb the extent of Mughal power covered almost the entirety of the subcontinent (including most of the South), but the control was loose at best and decline was already setting in. By the end of Aurangzeb's rule, the empire was overextended, financially weak, and, therefore, in serious decline, and thereafter the dynasty continued largely in name only until its final representative, Bahadur Shah II, was deposed in 1858 by the British (at the conclusion of the North Indian rebellion, 1857–58).

As mentioned earlier, apart from some early contacts on the western coast by Arab traders, the vehicle for the transmission of Islam into the subcontinent was not the original tradition of the Arabs but, rather, the much more cosmopolitan and sophisticated Islam of the 'Abbasid caliphate. The tradition of the original religious Arab Islam was simply (*a*) that there is only one God (Allah), (*b*) that God is revealed in the sacred text of the Qur'an, (*c*) that Muhammad is the final messenger (*rasul*) or prophet of this God and his revelation, that is to say, the final prophet or "seal of the prophets" in a long line of previous prophets or messengers who brought new revelations leading back through (the Christian) Jesus to the ancient (Hebrew) prophets or messengers, Abraham and Moses, (*d*) that all believers are equal before God and must together excercise total submission (*islam*) to God and have faith (*iman*) in Him, his angels, his revelation, and his lordship over corporate life (that is, all of history, including family, society and state), (*e*) that believers should obey the law (*shari'ah*) as determined by the Qur'an, the traditions of the prophet (*hadith*), the consensus of the community (*ijma'*) and basic custom or "orthodoxy" (*sunnah*), and (*f*) that believers should observe the five "supports of the religion" (*arkan ad-din*), namely, the "witnessing" or credo that there is only one God (*shahadah*), daily "prayer" (*ṣalah*), "fasting" (*ṣawm*) during the month of Ramadan, "almsgiving" (*zakah*), and "pilgrimage" (*hajj*) to the sacred city of Mecca.[4] It was a faith that enabled a broader vision of communal life than the constraints of older Arab tribalisms and that provided a powerful rationale for conquest and proselytization in order to establish a universal "abode of peace" or "house of Islām" (*dar al-islam*).

By the time of the 'Abbasid caliphate (750–1258), the advancing armies of Islam had conquered Syria, Egypt, North Africa, and Spain to the north and west and Iran (the Sasanians), Transoxania, Bukhara and Samarqand to the north and east (up to the Indus River). They threatened the very survival of the Byzantine empire through their attacks on Anatolia and Constantinople, and they very nearly penetrated into the heart of Europe. In any case, as Lapidus points out, these amazing conquests provided a vast "geographical arena for the eventual diffusion of a common culture and a common sociopolitical identity in the name of Islam."[5] The 'Abbasid caliphate truly became the heir of the heritage of Middle Eastern civilizations, including Persian (Iranian), Greek, Roman, Syrian, Egyptian, Jewish, Zoroastrian, Manichaean, and Christian components as well as components from the Turko-Afghan, Inner Asian or Central Asian cultures of Transoxania, Afghanistan, Bukhara and Samarqand, but, of course, all of these components with an Islamic inflection or overlay. Thus, it is no accident that the Islamic culture of the Ghaznavid state of the Turko-Afghan Mahmud of Ghazni, though on one level somewhat crude and rough, should nevertheless have in its midst such highly sophisticated and cosmopolitan figures as the remarkable Arab linguist and scholar, al-Biruni (conversant in Turkish, Persian, Syriac, Hebrew and eventually Sanskrit in addition to Arabic) or the Iranian poet, Firdausi.[6]

One other interesting historical development should also be mentioned which coincides with the appearance of Islamic culture in India, and again, it has to do with the 'Abbasid caliphate. Just as the 'Abbasids provided the"geographical arena for the eventual diffusion of a common culture" as mentioned above, the collapse of that same caliphate in its later phases, after the tenth and eleventh century, provided the occasion for many scholars, artists, intellectuals, and religious leaders in the eastern regions of the learned Islamic world to seek refuge in India. Already in the tenth century, independent succession states began to appear in the faltering 'Abbasid Islamic world—for example, the Ghaznavids, mentioned just above. By the beginning of the thirteenth century with the invasions of the Mongols, beginning in 1220, the situation became desperate. The 'Abbasid caliph was killed by the Mongol leader, Hulagu, a grandson of Chingis Khan, in 1258, and thereafter the glorious Islamic culture that had developed in Iraq, Iran (Persia), Afghanistan and Transoxania went into serious decline.

The subcontinent, fortunately, with the exception of some portions of the Punjab, escaped the Mongol invasions, and the Delhi Sultanates (1206–1526) of North India became a place where Islamic culture could develop in new and intriguing ways. Sunni, Shi'i, and Sufi forms of Islam, all of which had developed into mature traditions by the twelfth century, long before the appearance of Islam as a conquering force in India, underwent a new and vigorous development on the subcontinent.[7]

Sunni Islam was the main "orthodox" tradition. The term "*sunni*" is the adjective derived from the word "*sunnah*," meaning "custom." Sunni Muslims accept the first four caliphs (*khalifah* or "deputy," namely, Abu Bakr, 'Umar, 'Uthman, and 'Ali). They do not ascribe any special spiritual powers to 'Ali (as do Shi'ites and Sufis), and they follow one or the other of the four Sunni schools of law (the *shari'ah*): the Hanafi, Hanbali, Maliki or Shafi'i (representing mainly variant traditions in geographic regions). They accept, of course, the Qur'an and the *hadith* ("authentic traditions" about the Prophet) as authoritative revelation, but Sunni Islam also puts great importance on the notion of the "consensus" (*ijma'*) of the community, either the collective consensus of the legal specialists or learned men of the community (the '*ulama'*) or the corporate Muslim community as a whole (the *umma*). The great majority of all Muslims (well over 80%) through the centuries have been Sunnis. The majority tradition in India has always been Sunni, and Sunni Muslims in India have followed the Hanafite school of law.

Shi'ite Islam represents a minority of about 10% of the Muslim world, and it has three major divisions, the largest of which is Twelve Imam Shi'ism. This latter has had its base primarily in Iran (Persia) and Iraq. There are two other smaller groups, namely, the Five Imam Shi'ites in the Yemen and the Seven Imam Shi'ites or Isma'ilis, largely in India. Shi'ism became an important force in the spin-off (from the Delhi Sultanates) Muslim regional polities in the Deccan in the sixteenth century. Also, Bairam Khan, the guardian and minister of the Mughal emperor, Akbar, was a Shi'ite. The Shi'ites (from the term "shi'ah," meaning "partisan," and more specifically, "shi'at 'Ali," the "party of 'Ali") believe that 'Ali was the first legitimate caliph, since he was in the blood-line of descent (a cousin) of the Prophet. 'Ali was assassinated, and his oldest son, Hasan (through his wife, Fatimah, the daughter of the Prophet), was coerced into abdicating the caliphate to Mu'awiyah, the founder of the Umayyad dynasty in 661. When Hasan finally died, Husayn, 'Ali's second son by Fatimah, proclaimed himself caliph, but Husayn and his small band of followers were ruthlessly massacred on the battlefield of Karbala (in Iraq) in 680 by Yazid, the son of Mu'awiyah. This massacre (commemorated on the 10th day of Muharram in the ritual calendar) is the most important symbolic event for Shi'ism, since it marks the martyrdom and sacrifice of the 'Ali line. Shi'ites believe in a line of spiritually empowered "Imams" in the 'Ali blood-line of descent from the Prophet who preserve and transmit the esoteric or "inner" truth of Islam. It is a messianic form of Islam. The Twelve Imam tradition in Iran and Iraq believes that the last Imam is currently in "occultation" and will return at the end of the age as "*al-Mahdi*" ("the guided one") to restore righteousness and the legitimate caliphate.

Sufism (probably from the term "suf," meaning "rough wool" worn by early Muslim ascetics) represents the mystical tradition within Islam, influenced probably by Neo-Platonism from the Hellenistic tradition and possibly by older traditions of Indic mystical thought from Central Asia (via Buddhism and Iranian Manichaeism). Like Shi'ism it focusses on the "inner" truth of Islam with special emphasis on a living, personal relationship with Allah. Mystical traditions appeared very early in the history of Islam and developed considerably after Islam expanded into Iran or Persia in the late seventh and eighth centuries. Key figures include Abu Yazid al-Bistami of Iran (d. 874) and al-

Junayd of Baghdad (d. 910), and the writings of the great Persian or Iranian poet, Jalal ad-Din ar-Rumi (1207–1273). It received its definitive theological formulation and thereby its solid place within Islamic orthodoxy by the great Persian or Iranian theologian-mystic, Abu Hamid Muhammad al-Ghazali (1058–1111). Sufism focusses on the mystical truth and blessing passed on from Allah to Muhammad and, thence, to either Abu Bakr (the first caliph) or 'Ali (the fourth caliph), and, then, in sequence to "spiritual leaders" (Shaykhs or Pirs) who maintain "lines of transmission" (*silsilah*) and establish "retreat centers" (*khanaqahs* or *tekke*) wherein followers cultivate and follow the mystical "path" (*tariqah*). Some of these "retreat centers" became favored places of pilgrimage after the death of a particularly popular Shaykh or Pir. The inner, spiritual or esoteric mystical path (*tariqah*) parallels the outer, external or exoteric legal way (*shari'ah*). By the time that Islam entered India, Sufism had already become a mature, orthodox tradition. Three Sufi "orders" became especially dominant in India: the Chishti order (founded by Mu'in ad-Din Muhammad Chishti, 1142–1246), strong especially around Delhi, the Suhrawardi order, strong mainly in Sind, and the Firdausi order, strong in the region of Bihar. The Sufis were important in India as a missionizing force, and the obvious parallels between Sufi "retreat centers," "lines of transmission," and popular traditions of pilgrimage, on the one hand, and Hindu-Buddhist-Jain *āśrama*-s ("hermitages"), monasteries, and devotional (*bhakti*) groups, on the other, became important points of contact between Islamic traditions and older Indic traditions.

With the coming of the Mughals in the sixteenth century, and especially the reign of the great Akbar, Indo-Islamic culture emerged as one of the truly sparkling phases in the world-history of Islamic civilization as well as within the history of the older Indic civilization. Indo-Islamic culture was an intriguing combination of the Perso-Arabic (and Hellenized) traditions inherited from the cosmopolitan world of the 'Abbasid era together with the Rajput-Hindu traditions of western and north central India, largely patterned after Iranian or Persian culture and fashioned by migrant Iranians, Persianized Afghans and Turks and, of course, the many converts to Islam in India from peasant agrarian communities (in Kashmir and Bengal), urban artisan groups (in North Central India and in the spin-off Muslim regional polities in the Deccan), various trading groups (on the western coast from Gujarat through Karnataka and down into what is now Kerala), and including, last but not least, the fellow-travelling Rajput clans, some of whom converted to Islam but many of whom remained Hindu, in the Rajasthan region.

The state under Akbar's tutelage became an interesting combination of the traditional Muslim notion of kingship and governance, derived mainly from Iranian sources, with its focus on the maintenance of stability, the enforcement of the Shari'ah, and the general moral uplift of the population through the true practice of Islam, together with older pre-Muslim Persian notions of the majesty and grandeur of the king and of the lavish display of royal patronage in cultural productions and grand public works.[8] Akbar also developed a unique administrative system known as the *mansabdar* system, involving a network of administrative military officers in a hierarchical ordering. The position of the military "office-holder" (*mansab-dar*) in the hierarchy was determined by how many troops he was able to provide in the event of a battle.[9] The administrative military officer was paid in cash or given an estate (*jagir*). The officer would collect revenue and be in charge of a large administrative area. Below him were various local chieftains and regional revenue collectors (*zamindar*-s).

The country overall was divided into provinces (*suba*-s), local districts (*sarkar*-s) and subdistricts (*pargana*-s).[10] Most of the administrative military officers were brought from outside of India, but as many as twenty percent were Hindus (mainly Rajputs and Marathas).[11] Over time elaborate lineage systems of both Muslim and Hindu elites were developed. When the British first established their presence in India, they were quick to see the merits of Akbar's system and to imitate them, especially the overall administrative structure and the symbolic, political value of lavish public displays of power and royal patronage.

On the level of material and political reality, it can be plausibly argued that no great transformations took place during the long centuries of Muslim domination. As Peter Hardy has commented:

> Neither Turk nor Mughal deprived the Hindu cultivator of his holding or settled in closed colonies on the lands of the dispossessed. Both substituted one group of revenue receivers and military chiefs for another, changing the men at the top of the social pyramid without dislodging the pyramid itself.
>
> Neither the Delhi sultanate nor the Mughal empire interfered greatly with the daily life or the religion of its subjects. Except for acts in the heat of battle, violence did not normally characterize the relations of Muslim and Hindu. For the most part the mass of Hindus remained indifferent to their Muslim rulers, rather than antagonistic toward them and their faith.[12]

Muslim rulers accomodated themselves to the larger Hindu culture, if only because they were greatly outnumbered overall and very much in need of Hindu support. Hindus were early along designated "protected peoples" (*dhimmi*-s), and during some periods of Muslim rule—for example, during the reign of Akbar—the "head tax" (*jizya*) for "protected peoples" was waived. For a time under the Emperor Akbar, an open-minded and tolerant attitude towards other religious traditions, including the Hindu, became prevalent, at least among the court elite. Here is where the intriguing blend of Perso-Islamic and Rajput-Hindu traditions became most manifest. Discussions about religion were regularly held in the Hall of Worship with the emperor presiding. Taking part in these discussions were Sunni *'ulama'* ("learned jurists"), Sufi Shaykhs or Pirs, Hindu *paṇḍita*-s, Jains, Parsis and even some Catholic priests (Jesuits) from Portugese Goa. Akbar also devised a new, eclectic religion, later known as the "Divine Faith" (Din-i-Ilahi), a sort of broad-based monotheistic faith that included a variety of religious traditions (mainly Islamic and Hindu). The emperor likewise encouraged the translations of some basic Vedic texts, and the two great epics, the *Mahābhārata* and the *Rāmāyaṇa*, into Persian.[13] He also appointed a Hindi court poet.

Akbar's great grandson, Dara Shikoh (1615–1659), a follower of one of the Sufi mystical orders, was also a student of Hindu philosophy. His brother, Aurangzeb, however, who came to power as Emperor (ruling from 1658–1707) had Dara Shikoh executed in 1659, mainly for political reasons (since Dara Shikoh was a principal claimant to the throne) but with the "religious" excuse that Dara Shikoh had become too influenced by Hindu ideas. In any case, with the coming of Aurangzeb's leadership, the brief period of accomodation between Islamic, Hindu and other religious traditions came to an abrupt halt, and thereafter Islamic orthodoxy was enforced in court circles.

Even during the years of accomodation between Islam and Hindu traditions, however, many of the orthodox *'ulama'* ("learned jurists") were opposed to any close connections between Islamic and Hindu traditions. Even many of the Sufi Shaykhs or Pirs were keen to maintain a distance between Islamic belief and practice and Hindu belief and practice. Shaykh Ahmad Sirhindi (1564–1624), for example, a Sufi of the Naqshbandi order, troubled that the Muslim mystical doctrine of the "unity of existence" (*tauhid-i-wujudi*) might get confused with Hindu notions of monism, argued that the authentic mystic experience is simply "unity of experience" (*tauhid-i-shuhudi*, a subjective sense of the presence of God) and not the "unity of existence" (an objective claim that the mystic and God are one), thereby preserving the absolute transcendence of God and the need for revelation. In a similar fashion, Shah Wali-Ullah (1703–1762), also a Sufi of the Naqshbandi order, during the decline of the Mughal dynasty and before the coming of the British, argued for a clear separation between Islamic and Hindu traditions both spiritually as well as politically. Later in the nineteenth and twentieth centuries, the thought of Shah Wali-Ullah would be used by proponents of Muslim separatism in Pakistan and India.[14]

It appears to be the case overall, then, that any compromise or accomodation between Islamic and Hindu traditions on the learned level during the centuries of Muslim domination hardly went beyond a very small elite in court circles. Generally speaking, with regard to learned or "great tradition" Islamic and Hindu traditions, there has been little more than bare co-existence over the centuries. Mutual hostility and deep suspicion among the respective elites have been the order of the day almost from the beginning of the encounter between the two civilizations, and the hostility and suspicion continued not only until the time of partition in 1947 but is even now, nearly fifty years after partition, still a potent factor between the Hindu and Muslim communities in India as well as throughout the South Asian area.

From the theoretical or theological perspective of the respective elites, of course, the basic reason for the deep suspicion is not difficult to identify. The Muslim belief in one transcendent God who has definitively revealed himself in a cognitively specific revelation (the Qur'an) and who demands absolute submission among all believers who make up one universal community in which all believers are equal is nearly the exact antithesis of the pluralist, plastic, hierarchical and polymorphous spirituality characteristic of Indic (Hindu-Buddhist-Jain) civilization prior to the appearance of Islamic civilization. It is impossible to imagine from a purely theoretical point of view two more contradictory "unique moral visions" or "views of the good life" (to use again Ravinder Kumar's idiom mentioned in chapter 1) than that between the learned Islamic civilization and the learned Indic civilization.

Nevertheless, it must also be noted that there were more than a few accomodations and intermixtures of a non-theoretical or practical kind that occurred on the lower peasant agrarian levels and the urban artisan levels. Sufi pilgrimage places were sometimes visited by Hindu pilgrims as were Hindu shrines by Muslim peasants. It was common in Kashmir for Muslims to visit old Buddhist shrines. This was also the case in Bengal. Muslim peasants in Western India offerred vows to Hindu gods for a good harvest, and Muslim women in Bengal offerred *pūjā* to Sītalā, the Hindu goddess of smallpox. There was also a good deal of intermixture among performers and craftsmen in the areas of music, dance, architecture and painting. Moreover, as Romila Thapar has pointed out, even though Islam accepts the basic equality of all believers and, therefore, in principle rejects the Hindu caste-system, nevertheless, a sort of ersatz caste-system has developed among Muslim communities in India, with "*ashrafs*" ("honorable" ones), that is, the ruling descendants of Turks, Afghans and Persians at the top, followed by Muslim Rajputs, followed by "clean" artisan groups and, finally, "unclean" scavenger-groups.[15]

Regarding developments within the older Indic civilization throughout this Indo-Islamic period, on most levels there was a defensive withdrawal. Buddhist traditions as distinctive and identifiable communities disappeared altogether by the end of the fourteenth century (in the Northwest and Kashmir, in the Northeast and Bengal and throughout most of the South), partly, as has been mentioned, because of the onslaught of the Turko-Afghan Muslim invaders who found Buddhist monks and monasteries to be easy targets, but partly also because much of Buddhist spirituality, especially of the Mahayāna and Tantric variety, was simply absorbed into the larger Hindu framework. Jain traditions somehow survived in certain regional areas such as Gujarat, Rajasthan, northern Maharashtra and Karnataka, partly because of royal favor in certain regional polities and partly because of extensive compromises with the larger Hindu environment.

The basic parameters of the Hindu traditions had been shaped in the preceding pre-Muslim period in terms of the three major kinds or modalities of spirituality: (*a*) sacrificial ritual (*yajña*) much of which became the simple ritual worship (*pūjā*) in the home and public temples, (*b*) ascetic practices or disciplined meditation (the various types of *yoga*) most of which became institutionalized in various monastic orders such as the Daśanāmis, and so forth, and (*c*) devotion (*bhakti*) to a personal god, either in terms of Vaiṣṇava, Śaiva or Śākta devotional groups or in terms of the *pañcāyatana-pūjā* (ritual worship of five symbols or deities: Sūrya, Śiva, Viṣṇu, Devī and Gaṇeśa) of the Smārta (traditional high-caste and Advaita Vedāntin) Hindus. In this Indo-Islamic period, the first two of these three modalities underwent only slight changes, mainly in the direction of greater consolidation and the development of defensive measures against the developing Indo-Islamic civilization.

As mentioned earlier, it is undoubtedly in this period that the caste system began to take on its modern, overly rigid structures, and "orthopractical" ritual behavior became minutely codified and pervaded with this emerging "caste-ism." Furthermore, in this period

Hindus put greater emphasis on vegetarianism, non-violence (*ahiṃsā*) and the veneration of the cow as a symbol of divine benevolence, all of which notions of ritual purity clearly helped to differentiate the Hindu from the Muslim. Vegetarianism, non-violence and cow-veneration are, of course, much older than the Indo-Islamic period, the first two being traceable to the Indo-Śramaṇical traditions of the Jains and Buddhists and the latter (cow-veneration) going back even to Vedic times, but it is in this Indo-Islamic period that these old notions and practices became essential in the increasingly defensive self-understanding of Hindus. The great Śivāji (1627–1680), for example, mentioned earlier as the warrior hero and organizer of the Maratha tribes in Maharashtra who defended Hindu culture and civilization against Muslim encroachment, suggested that the very definition of Hindu tradition involves veneration of the cow, caste and the protection of the priests.[16]

Regarding ascetic practices or disciplined meditation (*yoga*), already back in the eighth century, as mentioned earlier, the great Vedānta philosopher, Śankara, had organized the various Hindu monastic orders into the ten basic groups (the "ten-named" or Daśanāmi-s), and Rāmānuja and the Śrī Vaiṣṇavas (as well as other Vaiṣṇava traditions) developed comparable monastic organizations from the twelfth century onwards. Throughout the Indo-Islamic period these various monastic orders continued to consolidate their traditions and practices. They also developed "militant" orders called *nāga*-s ("naked ascetics" in Hindi), arranged in groups or congregations called *akhāḍa*-s or *akhāṟa*-s (meaning in Hindi an "arena" or "place for wrestling" but coming to mean congregations of militant *sādhu*-s or holy men), groups of Yogins trained in martial arts to defend the monastic institutions against the encroachment of Muslim bands or other, hostile Hindu groups.[17]

Mention should also be made of traditions of Śaiva ascetics, called "Jogī-s," "Nāth Yogī-s," "Kānphaṭa Yogī-s," or "Gorakhnāthī Yogī-s."[18] They were followers of Tantric *yoga* and *haṭha-yoga* ("exertion discipline") and appear to be related to older traditions of both Hindu (Kāpālika and Kālāmukha Śaiva groups) and Buddhist (Vajrayāna or "Diamond Vehicle") Tantric traditions from the preceding Indic period.[19] They are traceable to two founding figures, Matsyendranath and Gorakhnath (in Sanskrit: Gorakṣanātha), who lived somewhere between the ninth and twelfth centuries either in the Punjab or far Northwest region or in the Northeast in the area of Bengal, both of which regions, interestingly, were centers for Tantric traditions. The Nāth Yogī-s are called "Kānphaṭa" ("ear-split" in Hindi) because of the practice of cutting the cartilage in the ears in order to hold the large earrings that the cult followers wear. The focus in these Śaiva ascetic groups is on becoming a "master" (*nātha*), or "perfected" Yogin (*siddha*) by making use of magico-religious rituals (including alchemical, occult and erotic ritual performances) and extreme Yogic exertions of posture and breathing. They were largely low-caste groups and paid little attention to caste rules. They became widely prevalent as magic-workers and healers on a popular level in North and Central India between the twelfth and fifteenth centuries, and they seem to have interacted easily with Sufī Shaykhs and Pirs, possibly because of their low caste status and their general indifference to issues of caste.

Of much greater significance for the development of Hindu traditions in the Indo-Islamic period is the remarkable increase in devotional Hindu spirituality or *bhakti*. Here again the antecedents can be traced back many centuries, to the Indo-Śramaṇical period when hero-cults and local devotional traditions appeared for the first time alongside of the Indo-Brāhmaṇical Vedic system and to such texts as the famous *Bhagavad-gītā* in the Indic period which represented the first major theoretical statement about devotion or *bhakti* as a form of *yoga* (*bhakti-yoga*) within an Indo-Brāhmaṇical context (but also clearly under the influence of Indo-Śramaṇical traditions). Traditions of *bhakti* developed further with the emergence of the Tamil poet-saints of South India, already discussed earlier, both Vaiṣṇava and Śaiva (called Āḷvār-s and Nāyanar-s respectively), whose exuberant devotional piety spreads from the Tamil country to Kannada-speaking Karnataka, thence to Marathi-speaking Maharashtra and finally finds its way to the Gujarati-Hindi, Punjabi and Bengali regions of the Northwest, north central and Northeast regions. These devotional traditions utilize the local regional language rather than Sanskrit, are frequently open to all castes, even low and untouchable groups, avoid excessive ritualism and have for the most part a clear anti-*brāhmaṇa* bias. They represent, in other words, many of the characteristics of the old Indo-Śramaṇical traditions and indeed may be interpreted as the equivalent of those older traditions in the Indo-Islamic period. Mention should perhaps also be made to the Lingāyats ("wearers of the phallic stone," one of the prime symbols of Lord Śiva) or Vīraśaivas (devotees of "Śiva the virile one"), a Hindu group, founded by a certain Basavanna in the twelfth century in what is now Karnataka in South India, with its exuberant devotional poetry to Lord Śiva in the regional language of Kannada. Like their Tamil counterparts, Lingāyats or Vīraśaivas also rejected the caste system, eventually coming to be considered in later times a caste-sect.

These older traditions of devotional spirituality became much more intense all across North India, beginning in the fourteenth and fifteenth centuries and reaching a remarkable crescendo in the sixteenth century.[20] This is unquestionably related in important respects to the growing presence of Islamic traditions, especially Sufi devotional mysticism that was spreading rapidly across North India through the medium of the various regional languages, although it is difficult to determine whether Sufi devotional mysticism influenced Hindu *bhakti* or vice versa. It could well be the case that both Sufi devotionalism and Hindu *bhakti* have a natural affinity for one another (possibly traceable ultimately to Indic influences on original Sufi traditions in Central Asia and eastern Iran) and that, therefore, there was simply a broad-based mutual interaction between these traditions in the fifteenth and sixteenth centuries and after. One might also posit a Weberian elective affinity in the sense that it is hardly an accident that Sufi missionizing was especially effective in areas such as Kashmir, Bengal and those areas of the subcontinent under strong *bhakti* influence, and among low-caste peasants and artisans, areas and groups, in other words, in which the old Indo-Śramaṇical traditions had been especially prevalent.

The devotional songs of Kabir, for example, the poet-saint weaver from the Hindu city of Varanasi, who lived in the late fourteenth or early fifteenth century and who appears to have had some sort of connection with Islam, either in terms of actually having been Muslim or of having been raised in a Hindu family recently converted to Islam, clearly combine Islamic (and probably Sufi) motifs, Hindu *bhakti* as well as Nāth Yogī motifs together with a strong critique of the rigidities of both Islamic and Hindu traditions. According to Hindu traditions, Kabir's guru on the Hindu *bhakti* side was the famed Vaiṣṇava, Rāmānanda, credited with having brought the Rāma cult and the Śrī Vaiṣṇava tradition of Rāmānuja from the South to North India. Rāmānanda settled in the city of Varanasi, supposedly turned away from the high-caste orientation of the southern Śrī Vaiṣṇavas, developed a rich *bhakti* devotionalism centering on the repetition of the name of Rāma, and accepted followers from all walks of life, including low castes, untouchables, women and even Muslims. He taught in the vernacular language (Hindi) and is the supposed founder of the largest Vaiṣṇava ascetic community in North India, the Rāmānandī-s, known as Vairāgī-s ("renouncers"), who down to the present day have many monasteries in Varanasi, Ayodhya and elsewhere all across North India. Whether Kabir was really a Muslim originally or whether Rāmānanda was his guru who taught him to use the vernacular and a *bhakti* devotionalism focusing on the repetition of the name, Rāma, are historical issues that have not yet been satisfactorily settled, but the interesting combination of Islamic (Sufi) motifs, Hindu *bhakti* motifs and Nāth Yogī references are clearly in the poetry regardless of how these traditions came together in Kabir's own life and training.[21]

A somewhat comparable conflation of Hindu, Muslim and Nāth Yogī motifs may be found in the spirituality of Guru Nanak (1469–1539), the founder of the Sikh religion. Clearly the Sikh tradition's focus on one transcendent God and its rejection of the caste system (in theory if not always in practice) owes much to Islamic ideas, while its incorporation of Hindu devotional songs in its sacred scripture (the Ādi Granth, the "Primal Book," or the Guru Granth Sahib, the "Book of the Lord," compiled by Guru Arjan in 1603–04) shows clear influence from the Hindu side. In the final analysis, however, the Sikh tradition is itself a distinct religious tradition that differs from both Islamic and Hindu traditions.[22] Or again, the untouchable shoemaker, Ravidas (c. sixteenth century), like Kabir from the city of Varanasi, represents a form of devotional theism that does not quite fit either Hindu or Islamic patterns completely, but owes much to both. Interestingly, all three poet-saints, that is to say, Kabir, Nanak and Ravidas are considered by tradition to be within the same lineage known as the "*sant*" tradition. The term *sant* (a participle from the root *as*, "to be") comes to mean something like a "truly authentic being," or, in other words, a "good or holy person," and the "*sant*-s" are said to be proponents of *bhakti* or "devotion" to the one transcendent God "without attributes" (*nirguṇa*). God, in other words, cannot be adequately represented in any form or by any particular name.[23]

Other forms of emergent *bhakti* are more identifiably Hindu, although they bear clear family resemblances to the composite Indo-Islamic devotionalism so characteristic of this period. There are, for example, the Hindu poet-saints of Maharashtra, beginning with Jñanadeva and Namdev (c. thirteenth century), continuing through the work of Eknath (c. sixteenth century), reaching a high point in the exuberant devotional poetry of the famous Tukaram (1598 - 1649) and coming down to the present, with their intense devotional songs to the various regional forms of Kṛṣṇa or Viṣṇu in the regional language of Marathi.[24] In the medium of Hindi in North India, there is Surdas (1483–1563) and the woman-saint Mirabai (1498–1546), both devotees of Kṛṣṇa. There is, of course, also in Hindi in North India (in and around the city of Varanasi) the famous devotional poetry of Tulsidas (1532–1623), author of "The Spiritual Lake of the Acts of Rāma," *Rāmcaritmānas*, a Hindi version of the famous old Sanskrit epic, *Rāmāyaṇa*. Most Hindus who are followers of Rāma (and hence also Vaiṣṇavas) are much more familiar with Tulsidas's Hindi version of the

Rāmāyaṇa than they are with the older, elitist Sanskrit version.[25] In the northeast region of Bengal, there is the famous Caitanya (1486–1533), the great exponent of the Gauḍīya Vaiṣṇava tradition (or simply the Bengal Vaiṣṇava tradition), the emotional and expressive devotionalism in the regional language of Bengali (but also utilizing a good deal of Sanskrit as well), focusing on devotion to Kṛṣṇa and his consort, Rādhā. Those followers of *bhakti* who believe that God can be named and represented in a specific form, as, for example, Surdas, Mirabai, Tulsidas, and others, are said to belong to the lineage known as "devotion" (*bhakti*) to the one God "with attributes" (*saguṇa*).

Regarding the overall assessment of the impact of Islam on Indic culture in this period, there have tended to be two seemingly divergent views. On the one hand, there is the view of those who would subscribe to the following comment of Peter Hardy:

> . . . neither educated Muslims nor educated Hindus accepted cultural coexistence as a natural prelude to cultural assimilation. Long before British rule and long before modern political notions of Muslim nationhood, the consensus of the Muslim community in India had rejected the eclecticism of Akbar and Dara Shikoh for the purified Islamic teachings of Shaikh Ahmad of Sirhind and Shah Walī-Ullāh. Cultural apartheid was the dominant ideal in medieval Muslim India, in default of cultural victory.[26]

On the other hand, there are those who would concur with the following assessment of Romila Thapar:

> The argument for the reality of a separate nationality is drawn from the writings of the theologians and court chroniclers, who consciously emphasized the distinctions between Hindus and Muslims because it was in their interests to do so. Sources such as these cannot be accepted uncritically, since their own prejudices are writ large in their attitudes. The fusion of cultures in any case cannot be judged by the writings of a prejudiced minority determined to hold aloof: it can only be judged by the cultural pattern of the society as a whole. From the pattern of society in the Sultanate period it is evident that a synthesis of the two cultures took place, although this synthesis did not occur at every level and with the same intensity.[27]

From the perspective of the historian of religions, of course, both the perspectives of Peter Hardy and Romila Thapar are very much to the point. In other words, what appears to be a case of either-or is really, finally, a case of both-and. As was pointed out earlier, it is perfectly true that the theological or theoretical perspectives of learned Islamic culture and learned Indic culture are nearly exact opposites. There is, finally, an unbridgeable intellectual chasm between a Śankara and a Shah Wali-Ullah. It is likewise perfectly true that an intellectual *modus vivendi* was accomplished between the two learned visions of Indic and Islamic cultures by thoughtful persons such as Akbar and Dara Shikoh. It is also perfectly true that the great regional theologies of the Śaiva and Vaiṣṇava traditions together with their emerging monastic orders or *saṃpradāya*-s, and even more so, the exuberant *bhakti* spirituality of Kabir, Nanak, Mirabai, Tulsidas, and others, together with their sectarian communal formations, are inconceivable apart from the coming and spread of Islamic civilization in South Asia, not only in terms of the mystical and devotional impules within Sufi traditions, but also in terms of Sunni and Shi'a practices that penetrated Indic life in almost every region and on almost all levels of social life, including cultural elites, urban artisans, trading communities and peasant agrarian groups. That this emergent Indo-Islamic cultural tradition was sometimes tense and full of communal resentment and sometimes generous and full of mutual accomodation justifies neither the label of "apartheid" (à la Peter Hardy) nor the label of "synthesis" (à la Romila Thapar). Two great civilizations encountered one another and brought forth over a period of many centuries one of the great cultural periods of humankind, the Indo-Islamic.

The Indo-Anglian (c. 1757–present)

This brings us back to where we started in chapter 2, that is, to the time of Lord Cornwallis and to the coming of the modern civilization of Western Europe as mediated primarily by the British (and to a lesser extent by the Portugese, French and Dutch) and manifesting itself eventually on the subcontinent as Indo-Anglian culture. From one perspective, it should perhaps be pointed out that in an important sense the coming of the British was simply more of the same. That is, to the extent that the Islamic civilization that came to India via the Turko-Afghans of the Delhi Sultanates and the Mughal dynasty was that of the cosmopolitan 'Abbasid caliphate which was itself the heir of the great pre-modern Mediterranean and Middle Eastern civilizations (the heritage, in other words, of the Jewish, Christian, Hellenistic, Byzantine and Sasanian traditions), the coming of the British represented many of those same Mediterranean and Middle Eastern traditions, only now in their incipient modern forms as manifested in the emerging nation-states of western Europe. Apart from the many obvious differences between Islamic civilization and modern Western civilization, there are nevertheless some significant family resemblances in that both civilizations are products of the peculiar marriage in the first millennium of the Common Era of classical Greco-Roman Mediterranean traditions with the great West Asian Jewish, Iranian, Christian and Islamic religious traditions. Put somewhat differently, just as there are important family resemblances between what we have called the Indus Valley, the Indo-Brāhmaṇical, the Indo-Śramaṇical and the Indic, so there are some interesting family resemblances on a deep-structural, valuational level between the Indo-Islamic and the Indo-Anglian.

From another perspective, of course, the profound material and socioeconomic differences between pre-modern Islamic civilization and early (sixteenth, seventeenth and eighteenth century) modern Western European civilization greatly overshadow whatever valuational family resemblances there are between pre-modern and modern social reality. The term "renaissance" (literally "re-birth"), to be sure, stresses perhaps the valuational family resemblance, but the socio-economic, political and ideological transformations that occurred in Europe as a result of the Renaissance, the Protestant Reformation, early industrializing technology, Enlightenment ideology, mercantile trade and colonial exploration brought about fundamental changes that mark a clear departure and radical discontinuity with what had occurred before.

The contrast is clear and striking on the subcontinent. The earlier encounter, beginning in the twelfth and thirteenth centuries, between the older Indic (Hindu-Buddhist-Jain) and the cosmopolitan Islamic had given rise to the Indo-Islamic pre-modern Perso-Arabic-cum-Rajput-Hindu socioeconomic reality and cultural idiom (largely in the medium of Persian) of military force, imperial pretentions to an all-India polity (at least under the Mughals) in a context still largely driven by regional powers and loyalities (for example, the Marathas in the West or the Sikhs in the Punjab), Islamic ideologies of various kinds (both polemic and irenic), largely defensive and reactionary traditional Hindu strategies, and Hindu-cum-Muslim (Sufi) *bhakti* traditions. The modern encounter, in contrast, beginning already to some extent in the seventeenth century and becoming of great importance in the later eighteenth century and after, between the older Indic (Hindu-Buddhist-Jain) and early modern western civilization in its primarily British form gave rise to the Indo-Anglian modern British socioeconomic reality and cultural idiom (largely in the new medium of English) of mercantile trade and investment, improved technology, a much more tightly controlled and bureaucratized pan-Indian social reality, Protestant Christian ideologies of various kinds (both polemic and irenic), and reformist Neo-Hindu traditions. The former (the Indo-Islamic) has been characterized by Peter Hardy as "a partnership between the doctors of the holy law and the sultan in the higher interests of the faith—a partnership between pious professors and pious policemen."[28] The latter (the Indo-Anglian) has been characterized by Eric Stokes as a peculiar partnership of "merchant, manufacturer and missionary."[29]

The encounter in the modern period, however, was not simply between the older Indic (Hindu-Buddhist-Jain) and the Anglian, resulting in the emergence of an Indo-Anglian tradition. There is also the parallel encounter between the Indo-Islamic and the Anglian, resulting in what might be called the Anglo-Islamic. The former (the Indo-Anglian), of course, results finally in the emergence of the modern, "secular" (and pan-Indian) nation-state or civilisation-state of India, and the latter (the Anglo-Islamic) results, finally, in the modern (regional) nation-state, first, of the Islamic Republic of Pakistan (in 1947) and then eventually, in addition, the modern (regional) nation-state of the People's Republic of Bangladesh (in 1971). The former (the Indo-Anglian) can be traced in an intellectual line from Rammohun Roy (1772–1833) and continuing through such reformist figures and movements as Keshub Chunder Sen, Swami Dayananda Sarasvati, Ramakrishna, Vivekananda, the founding of the Indian National Congress (in 1885), M. G. Ranade, Gokhale, Tilak, Savarkar, Rabindranath Tagore, Aurobindo and, finally, the consolidation of the nationalist movement under Gandhi and Nehru (the first prime minister of India). The latter (the Anglo-Islamic) represents an intellectual line, beginning with the founding of the Deoband school (near Delhi) in 1867 and the Anglo-Oriental College at Aligarh in 1877, and traceable also to the important work of the modernist thinker, Sayyid Ahmad Khan (1817–98) and continuing through such figures and movements as Ahmad Riza Khan (founder of the conservative, anti-modernist Barelwi movement), the founding of the Muslim League (in 1906), the Khilafat movement (1919–1924), the founding of the Jami'at al-'ulamā'-i Hind (the "Association of Indian Islamic Scholars," 1919), Muhammad Iqbal (poet and proponent of a separate state for Muslims), Abul Kalam Azad (supporter of the Indian National Congress and proponent of Muslims remaining within India), Muhammad 'Ali Jinnah (the first prime minister of Pakistan), Muhammand Ilyas (founder of the reformist Tablighi Jama'at or "Missionary Society" in 1927) and Sayyid Abul 'Ala Maududi (founder of the conservative Jama'at-i Islami or "Islamic Society" in 1941).

Percival Spear has argued that what he calls the "solution of synthesis," that is, the attempt to synthesize traditional Indian thought (whether Indic or Indo-Islamic) with modern Western thought, in the two lines, as represented primarily in the work of Rammohun Roy on the Indo-Anglian side and the thought of Sayyid Ahman Khan on the Anglo-Islamic side, is the "ideological secret of modern India."[30] Spear also mentions other responses in India to the coming of modernity, in addition to the "solution of synthesis," including an early "military" response (among some of the regional polities), a "reactionary" response (the North Indian rebellion, 1857–58), an "acceptance" response (radical westernizers), and an "orthodox"-renewal response (religious reform and retrenchment). All of these latter, according to Spear, failed, and it was the "solution of synthesis" that won the day, becoming the "ideological secret of modern India."[31] Spear made these comments at the time of independence in the late forties, and he was undoubtedly correct that the "solution of synthesis" was very much in evidence at that time in the emergence of the civilisation-state of modern India. Such, however, was hardly the "ideological secret of modern India," as the decades since independence have revealed. The "solution of synthesis" was the "ideological secret" of only a tiny percentage of the population of modern India, and that in itself would appear to be the true "ideological secret of modern India" in the decades since independence. Only now as India approaches fifty years of independence do we begin to see an "ideological secret of modern India" that is in any way representative of larger segments of the population.

In any case, returning now to our historical discussion, although the Mughal dynasty survived until 1858, in fact, by the middle of the eighteenth century it was a dynasty in name only and proved to be an easy mark for European traders and adventurers (Portugese, Dutch, French and British) who began to appear on the horizons of the subcontinent in the sixteenth and seventeenth centuries. Already in the early decades of the eighteenth century the Mughal empire was breaking up with local "nawabs" or "provincial governors" becoming de facto rulers in their areas, and it was the defeat of one of these, namely, Nawab Siraj-ud-daula of Bengal and his army of fifty thousand troops at the hands of Sir Robert Clive of the British East India Company (a commercial trading company first founded in 1600) with only eight hundred British troops and some two thousand "sepoys" (native recruits) who had better weapons technology and modern military discipline and strategy at the Battle of Plassey in 1757 that is usually cited as the beginning of the modern period in the history of the subcontinent.[32] At first, of course, the British had control of little more than what is now Calcutta and some surrounding regions of Bengal and Bihar and the port areas around Madras and Bombay, and their interest in India was almost completely commercial.

Within a century, however, as a result of certain important military victories together with carefully crafted diplomatic alliances with the leaders of strategic regional polities, the British with only small numbers of troops controlled almost the whole of the subcontinent. Moreover, they fundamentally changed the basic structures of Indian socioeconomic, political and intellectual life. Ravinder Kumar has argued that this shift to British control represents a fundamental material and intellectual discontinuity with all that had gone before on the subcontinent.

> [S]ome of the parameters of Indian civilisation were not drastically altered till the 18th century, when the British established their *imperium* over the subcontinent. . . .
>
> The establishment of the British Empire over India brought about some seminal changes in the political and economic order at the same time as it exposed the professional and the religious intelligentsia to strikingly novel ideas. In the first instance, a variety of experiments in the management of rural society were set in motion by the British with a view to providing a firm underpinning to their rule—among substantial landlords in some regions; and among rich peasants in others—and facilitating the expropriation of the rural surplus. Simultaneously, the commercial economy of the hinterland was transformed and novel economic links were forged between the imperial metropolis and the colonial periphery through the new port cities, which dominated the coastal region, from the 19th century onwards. The momentum for these changes was generated by one of the most advanced administrative systems of the age. The objectives of the colonial bureaucracy, which was qualitatively different in its principles of organisation from the indigenous systems which preceded it, were secured through ensuring that policy initiatives would flow from the apex to the base with facility, at the same time as the tactical appreciations of the officers located at the base could reach out to those perched at the apex. The success with which the British built a novel bureaucratic structure for buttressing their

> rule conferred on the colonial State a strength qualitatively different from that of earlier States in the subcontinent.[33]

There was one attempt towards the end of the first century of British hegemony by Muslim and Hindu nationals to rid the subcontinent of British control by force: the North Indian rebellion of 1857–58 (formerly referred to as the "Indian Mutiny"). The attempt failed, and the powerless Mughal "emperor," Bahadur Shah II, whose name and title was the symbolic rallying cry for the rebels, was exiled to Burma in 1857 (where he died a year later). His sons were all murdered by British officers, thus officially ending the Mughal dynasty in 1858. In addition to the end of the Mughal dynasty, however, the rebellion also brought about the end of the British East India Company. A new Government of India Act was passed in 1858 transferring all power and rights of the East India Company directly to the British crown, and on 1 November 1858 Queen Victoria promulgated an official proclamation indicating that India was now part of the British empire. Lord Canning, heretofore only governor-general, was given the additional title of viceroy.

With the British came, of course, as already mentioned, all of the forces of modernization, including the involvement of the subcontinent in the world economy, new patterns of education (at least in the main urban areas with the introduction of English education after 1835), new bureaucratic and legal structures, new philosophical ideas such as humanism, liberal democracy, and enlightenment rationalism, and new religious ideas through the aggressive work of all sorts of Christian missionaries who were allowed to enter the country after 1813. To some extent the British had great respect for India's rich cultural heritage, and from the eighteenth century onwards a tradition of British Orientalism emerged, beginning with such people as Sir William Jones (1746–1794) and the founding of the College of Fort William in 1800 by Lord Wellesley for training British civil servants, which encouraged serious research into India's cultural heritage and contributed greatly to the renaissance of learning that occurred among Indian intellectuals and artists throughout the nineteenth century and was important as well in encouraging the development of the first modern indigenous political structures in modern India.[34] At the same time, however, others among the British, especially in the early years with people such as Cornwallis, together with the many missionaries that came from Europe and the United States throughout the nineteenth century and into the twentieth, were highly critical of traditional Hindu and Muslim life, especially such practices as the treatment of women generally, widow-burning, child marriage and polygamy, female infanticide and untouchability, all of which practices had developed through the long centuries of Muslim domination and of tense interactions between Hindus and Muslims in which traditional customs on all sides had become in-grown, rigid and defensive.

As would be expected, reactions among Hindus, Muslims and other groups on the subcontinent to the encounters with modernity were complex and multidimensional, and we have already noted Percival Spear's enumeration of five kinds of responses: "military" (early attempts by regional polities to defeat the British on the battlefield), "reactionary" (the North Indian rebellion, 1857–58) "accepting" (the Westernizers), "orthodox" retrenchment and the "solution of synthesis." Among high or forward-caste Hindus, who tended to be either "accepting" (Westernizers) or followers of the "solution of synthesis," there was a rapid and positive response especially in urban centers such as Calcutta, Bombay and Madras to English education, government service and new economic opportunities. A new all-India elite began to emerge, made up largely of these English-speaking "forward" or upper castes in such fields as modern trade, manufacturing, civil service, commercial agriculture and the newly emerging professions of law, journalism and education, and for the most part they readily accepted the new ideas of humanism, liberal democracy and enlightenment rationalism. They also tended to accept the critique of traditional Hindu and Muslim social life and the need for reform articulated by their British rulers and the missionaries. The members of this new elite began to put together the first indigenous political associations as those in Calcutta, Bombay and Madras in the 1840s, the British Indian Association in 1851, the Indian Association of 1876 and the Indian National Congress of 1885. The members of this new elite, in other words, who accepted the notions of humanism, liberal democracy and enlightenment rationalism became the vanguard for the nationalist movement which would eventually turn the new ideas of liberal democracy and enlightenment humanism against the very British rulers who had introduced the ideas in the first place.

In contrast to the positive assimilation of liberal humanism and enlightenment rationalism, there was widespread dislike, even revulsion, against evangelical Christian missionizing. While there was much appreciation for the social work of missionaries in such areas as education and health, and while many of the Neo-Hindu reformist groups, as we shall see, were quick to adopt the methods and techniques of evangelical Protestant Christian missionizing, there was very little positive response to Christian ideas except on the lowest social levels (*śūdras*, untouchables, tribals, and so forth), and even today barely 2.5 percent of the population of India is Christian. Moreover, even among the Christian population, the majority is Roman Catholic rather than evangelical Protestant.

To some extent, of course, older Hindu traditions remained defensive and in-grown as they had been in the preceding Indo-Islamic period. These included such groups as the orthoprax caste-oriented ritual Hindu traditions of those middle and forward castes that did not accept Westernization or the "solution of synthesis," the Yogins, *sādhu*-s or mendicants of the various monastic orders, and the followers of the popular *bhakti* or devotional spirituality of the regional or sectarian varieties of Vaiṣṇava, Śaiva or Śākta traditions. There were also, of course, the many traditional village Hindus (and Muslims) who had little comprehension of or concern with what was happening and simply despised the British and other foreign interlopers as *mleccha*-s (polluted "barbarians") or *feringhee*-s ("foreigners").[35]

Much the same is true for older Muslim traditions. For obvious reasons related to the loss of political power, Muslims from the older, pre-modern elite and landowning classes for the most part did not respond as positively as forward caste Hindu elites to the coming of the British, and, as a result, even Muslims from elite strata never became a dominant voice among the largely Neo-Hindu elites that were emerging and beginning to put together a nationalist political movement. Also, on lower social levels as well, Muslims tended to become even more in-grown, defensive and rigid than comparable Hindu groups. There were, of course, some halting attempts at reform, some, as mentioned earlier, going all the way back to the time of Shaykh Ahmad Sirhindi of the sixteenth century (who protested Mughal accomodation with Hindu traditions) or the important work of Shah Wali-Ullah of Delhi (1703–1762), who also wanted to separate a pure Islamic spirituality from Hindu influences and practices. There was also the work of Sayyid Ahmad (1786–1831) of Rai Bareli (in North India) who sought to reform Hinduized practices around the various Sufi shrines in North India and the Punjab and eventually called for a *jihad* or "holy war" against the Sikhs in the Punjab, and there was the Fara'izi ("duties") movement in Bengal, founded by Shari'at Ullah (1781–1840), an attempt to establish a purified and separatist Islam in Bengal. The failure of all of these came to a symbolic head with the outcome of the "reactionary" North Indian rebellion in 1857–58, perhaps the prime symbol of the defeat of the older Indo-Islamic tradition both politically as well as culturally.[36]

By the early and middle decades of the nineteenth century, however, and thereafter, some significant innovations began to appear among both Muslims and Hindus, and within each of the communities it is possible to discern at least two distinct levels or dimensions. On the Muslim side, there emerges, first of all, a reformist and accommodationist set of movements or organizations as represented primarily by the founding of the Deoband (a town near Delhi) school of *'ulamā'* ("Islamic scholars") in 1867. The Deoband reformers sought to purify those aspects of Islamic spirituality that had become in their view overly Hinduized (for example, certain pilgrimage practices or the worship of local Sufi shrines and saints, and so forth). They wanted a purified, reformed Islam firmly based on the Qur'an but separate from Hindu culture as well as the state. They were willing to work with Hindus in terms of the growing anti-British nationalist movement, and in this sense the Deoband tradition was accommodationist. They wanted an independent Indian state together with their own autonomy within the Indian state. The Deoband reformers encouraged the development of a network of schools—in 1900 there were forty such schools in North India, in 1967 nearly nine thousand—and they used the newly available technology of printing to engage in widespread educational programs in the vernacular.[37] They supported the Khilafat movement (1919-24), an attempt to save the pan-Islamic institution of the caliphate (which failed in 1924 with the abolition of the caliphate in Turkey) and were instrumental in forming the Jami'at al-'ulamā'-i Hind ("The Association of Indian Islamic Scholars," 1919), an organization which for the most part supported the Indian National Congress in the anti-British freedom struggle. The two most well known representatives of the tradition were Hasan Ahmad Madani (1897–1959), principal of the Deoband school during the crucial years of the freedom struggle and the beloved Indian nationalist and Muslim leader, Abul Kalam Azad, both of whom remained with the new state of India after partition from Pakistan.[38]

A second level or dimension on the Muslim side is the modernist and separatist set of movements or organizations as represented primarily by the founding of the Anglo-Oriental College at Aligarh in 1875 by the famous modernist-reformer, Sayyid Ahmad Khan (1817–98). Unlike the Deoband reformers who wanted a purified traditional Islamic spirituality, Sayyid Ahmad Khan argued for a modernized form of Islam that takes seriously Western learning and science. Traditions of modern rationalism need to be employed in order to make Islam relevant to the needs of modern Muslims. At the same time, however, Sayyid Ahmad Khan was not an accommodationist as were the Deoband reformers. He believed that finally Muslims had to be separate from Hindus and Hindu civilization, and it can be plausibly maintained that the so-called "two nations" theory which became the rallying cry for the creation of Pakistan can be traced back to the work of Sayyid Ahmad Khan. The famous poet and Islamic nationalist, Muhammad Iqbal (1873–1938) was in this modernist yet separatist tradition as, of course, finally, was the political organization known as the Muslim League (founded in 1906) and the first prime minister of Pakistan, Muhammad 'Ali Jinnah (1876–1948). Iqbal argued that a pan-Islamic, transnational empire was no longer viable but that it was possible to develop an Islamic nation based on the principles of modernist Islam that could be part of the newly developing nation-state system, and he finally persuaded Jinnah that the formation of such a new nation was essential if South Asian Muslims were ever to be truly free.[39]

Both of these levels or dimensions of Muslim response, namely, the Deoband reformist-accommodationist set of movements and the Aligarh modernist-separatist set of movements are perhaps best referred to as "Anglo-Islamic" and "Neo-Muslim" in the sense that they reflect distinctly new elements being introduced into the older Indo-Islamic traditions as a result of the impact of modernity and the encounter with western civilization. The fact that the Deoband "protestant" Islam coupled its anti-British attitude with its participation in the Indian nationalist freedom movement, and the Aligarh movement coupled "modernist" Islam with its nationalist ideology of a modern but separate Islamic nation-state, clearly separate these traditions from the previous Indo-Islamic traditions, thereby justifying such labels as "Anglo-Islamic" and "Neo-Muslim."[40]

Mention should perhaps also be made here of what might be called "revivalist" Islamic movements, that is to say, to a few movements that are both anti-modernist (contra the Aligarh modernist-separatist Anglo-Islam) as well as anti-nationalist (contra the Deoband "protestant" reformist-accommodationist Anglo-Islam). These would include the anti-modernist and anti-reformist Islam of Ahmad Riza Khan (1856–1921) of Bareilly (in North India), leader of the conservative Barelwis, who wanted to maintain the traditional rituals and customs of the Indo-Islamic era. Also included would be the anti-modernist and transnationalist Islam of Sayyid Abul 'Ala Maududi (1903–79), founder of the conservative Jama'at-i Islami ("Islamic Society"), which rejected the ideology of the nation-state, whether Islamic or non-Islamic. There is also the Tablighi Jama'at (the "Missionary Society"), founded in 1927 by Muhammad Ilyas (1885–1944), an anti-political and pietistic revivalist Islam prominent in the Punjab region in India but popular as well in Pakistan, Southeast

Asia and the Middle East. Finally, there is the messianic and heretical Ahmadiyah movement, founded in the Punjab by Mirza Ghulam Ahmad (1835-1908) who proclaimed himself to be *al-Mahdi* (the "guided one" or messiah) in the last decade of the nineteenth century. The movement has not made much headway among Muslims generally because of the heretical claims of the founder, but it has found a favorable hearing in some parts of Africa and among Black Muslims in the United States. All of these "revivalist" movements have in common that they cannot be called either "Anglo-Islamic" or "Neo-Muslim." They represent one or another attempt to revive an older, largely premodern Indo-Islamic tradition.[41]

Just as there were two distinct levels or dimensions within Anglo-Islamic or Neo-Muslim traditions, namely, the Deoband reformist-accommodationist groups and the Aligarh modernist-separatist groups, so too on the Hindu side there developed two distinct levels or dimensions of Neo-Hindu tradition, first, an early set of reformist and nationalist Neo-Hindu groups focused primarily on the reform and modernization of older Hindu practices and the political development of India into a modern, secular nation-state, and second, coming a bit later in the nineteenth century and gaining considerable prominence in the later decades of the twentieth century, a set of revisionist and internationalist Neo-Hindu groups focused largely on a kind of reverse missionizing, that is, the export of a variety of what Agehananda Bharati has referred to as "yoga-oriented guru-disciple movements" to Western Europe and the United States, especially after the achievement of the independence of India in the middle of the twentieth century. Both levels or dimensions, namely, the reformist and nationalist groups and the revisionist and internationalist groups, can be referred to as Neo-Hindu or Indo-Anglian in the sense that they reflect distinctly new elements being introduced in what we have called classical Hindu or Indic (Hindu-Buddhist-Jain) civilization as a result of the impact of modernity and the encounter with western civilization.

Neo-Hindu Reformist and Nationalist Movements

Under this heading comes a variety of reform movements both before independence (1947) and after, and representing a great variety of political strategies ranging from radical extremism to moderate reformism.[42] The earliest was probably that of Rammohun Roy (1772–1833), a Bengali *brāhmaṇa* with remarkable intellectual and linguistic skills, who founded the Brahmo Sabha ("Society of God," later renamed the Brahmo Samaj) in 1828.[43] He learned English while working for British civil servants, and became deeply influenced by Western ideas. He was especially influenced by Christian notions about God but decided, finally, to remain a Hindu. He focused his attention on the ancient Vedic and Upaniṣadic notion of the oneness of Brahman, which he interpreted as a basic belief in monotheism and which represented a way of overcoming Hindu polytheism without giving up Hindu traditions. He was a thorough-going rationalist as well as an active social reformer, and he argued vigorously that such parochial practices as child marriage, female infanticide and widow-burning had no place in the ancient Vedic texts and ought to have no place in authentic, reformed Hindu tradition. The Brahmo Samaj came to have an extensive following among educated Hindus in Bengal and elsewhere in India as well.[44]

Closely related to the Brahmo Samaj was the Prarthana Samaj ("Prayer Society") of Bombay. Founded in 1867 and inspired by the work of Keshub Chunder Sen, a successor to Rammohun Roy as head of the Brahmo Samaj, the ideas of the "Prayer Society" were very close to those of the Brahmo Samaj, with perhaps a greater focus on devotionalism in the Prarthana Samaj (largely due to the greater influence on Keshub Chunder Sen of Christian devotional notions) in contrast to the heavy focus on rationalism in the Brahmo Samaj.[45] The other significant difference, of course, was the regional base of the two Societies, Calcutta for the Brahmo Samaj and Bombay for the Prarthana Samaj.

A strikingly different reform group was founded by Swami Dayananda Sarasvati (birth-name, Mul Shankar, 1827–1883), a *brāhmaṇa* from Gujarat who pursued the life of a renouncer (*saṃnyāsin*) from an early age. The movement which he established in 1875, known as the Arya Samaj ("Aryan Society") became especially powerful in the Punjab region. Unlike the Brahmo Samaj and the Prarthana Samaj which were for the most part favorably disposed towards Christian traditions, Dayananda's Arya Samaj vigorously rejected Christian and Muslim ideas together with Christian and Muslim missionizing, and asserted that the ancient Hindu Veda is the only authentic scripture. At the same time, however, Dayananda also rejected the caste system (as did all of the reformers and revisionists), idol worship, polytheism and all non-Vedic ritual within Hindu traditions. He also opposed widow-burning, child marriage and female infanticide. Instead, Hindus should believe in one God, follow only the simplest rituals of the Veda, work for social reform and follow strict vegetarianism. He also developed a special "purification" ceremony (*śuddhi)* by means of which Hindus who had been converted to Islam or Christianity could be re-converted or re-admitted into the Hindu tradition.[46]

Perhaps the most famous reformist and nationalist movement in the modern period is the Ramakrishna Mission, established by Swami Vivekananda (birth-name, Narendranath Datta, 1862–1902, from the high or forward clerical caste called *kāyastha*) in Bengal. The Mission was named after the Bengali spiritual teacher Ramakrishna (birth-name, Gadadhar Chatterjee, 1836–86, a Bengali *brāhmaṇa*) who was Vivekananda's *guru*. Ramakrishna himself spent his entire life as a priest in a temple devoted to the goddess, Kālī, in the district of Dakshineshwar near Calcutta. He had a number of extraordinary mystical experiences and over the years attracted a small band of followers, one of whom was Narendranath Datta, later to be given the spiritual name, Vivekananda (meaning "whose bliss is discrimination"). After Ramakrishna's death, Vivekananda made a pilgrimage around India and determined, finally, to propagate the spiritual message of his *guru*. Vivekananda developed and taught a simplified version of monistic Vedānta philosophy and combined those ideas with a program for social action and social reform for modern India. He attended the World Parliament of Religions in 1893 in Chicago as a representative of the Hindu tradition, and his considerable oratorical skills made a deep impression in the popular press and in certain liberal religious intellectual circles. He travelled widely in the United States, made a number of American converts, and in 1897, after his return to India, he established the Ramakrishna Mission in India together with a series of Vedānta Societies outside of India in the United States, Europe and Latin America. He also founded in 1897 the Ramakrishna "Math," the "monastic" wing of the organization. The Ramakrishna Mission in India engages in extensive social work down to the present day, maintaining an elaborate network of high schools, colleges and hospitals throughout the subcontinent, and it is the first and continues to be one of the few Hindu groups in modern India to engage in extensive social work.[47]

Yet another reformist and nationalist figure was the radical Bengali nationalist, Aurobindo Ghose (1872–1950). Aurobindo was educated in England and on his return to India joined the nationalist movement. At first he was a militant extremist, advocating violence if necessary in the freedom struggle against the British. He equated the nationalist struggle for freedom with a profound religious mission. In one of his early speeches he proclaimed: "Nationalism is not a mere political program; Nationalism is a religion that has come from God."[48] During a period of imprisonment for his radical activities in 1909, however, he underwent a deep spiritual conversion, and instead of continuing his political activities, he moved to Pondicherry in South India and established an *āśrama* ("hermitage" or monastery-like community) in order to practice and propagate what is known as Integral Yoga. He had determined that the political regeneration of India first required a spiritual regeneration.[49] One of his earliest disciples was a French lady, Mira Richard, who came to be known as "the Mother," and succeeded Aurobindo as head of the *āśrama* after Aurobindo's death.

The region of Maharashtra in western India was also a center of reformist and nationalist activity. It was the home of such important pre-Gandhian, moderate nationalists as M. G. Ranade (1842–1901) and G. K. Gokhale (1866–1915), as well as the extremist figure, B. G. Tilak (1856–1920).[50] It was also the home of V. D. Savarkar (1883–1966), author of the famous tract, *Hindutva* ("Hindu-ness"), first published in 1923, and president for seven consecutive years of the Hindu Mahasabha ("Great Assembly of Hindus"), a conservative political-cum-religious group first founded in the Punjab in 1907 as a defensive Hindu response to the separatist demands of Muslims. Savarkar's tract *Hindutva* glorified the Hindu motherland and argued for an all-India revitalization of *sanātana-dharma* ("eternal law") as a basis for a new Hindu nationalism. The tract was influential on the thinking of K. B. Hedgewar (1890–1940), also a Maharashtrian and founder in 1925 of the militant RSS (Rashtriya Svayamsevak Sangh, "National Assembly of Volunteers"), a conservative right-wing religious movement which combined a communalist Hindu nationalism with the rigid discipline of the old militant Nāga mendicant orders. Hedgewar led the RSS from 1925–40, and he was succeeded by M. S. Golwalkar, who led the movement from 1940 through 1973. Hedgewar thought that the main problem with modern India was a deep psychological sense of inferiority that could only be cured by careful discipline and an ideology of selfless service to the motherland. He believed in the need for extensive reform of outdated Hindu practices, and he and his organization rejected the inequities of the caste system. He completely disagreed with Gandhi's attitude of non-violence, however, and, indeed, it was a former member of the RSS, N. V. Godse, who assassinated Gandhi in 1948 because of his pro-Muslim, non-violent orientation. Jawaharlal Nehru, India's first prime minister after independence, quickly banned the RSS in 1948 after Gandhi's assassination, but a direct connection between Godse and the RSS was never proved, and the ban was lifted in 1949. The RSS was banned a second time during Indira Gandhi's Emergency (1975–77), and it has often been the object of government censure since independence. The RSS has never been a political movement as such, but it has encouraged the conservative political activities of the Bharatiya Jana Sangh ("Indian People's Party"), founded in 1951 and renamed the Bharatiya Janata Party (BJP and also meaning "Indian

People's Party") after 1979. The RSS together with the BJP and a Hindu cultural organization known as the VHP (the Vishva Hindu Parishad or "World Council of Hindus," founded in 1964) have become prominent in recent years as a conservative religious alternative to India's long-ruling and "secular" Congress's Party. The RSS, BJP and VHP appeal not only to forward or high castes but also to sizable groups of lower- and middle-caste rural and urban Hindus as well as the so-called "Other Backward Classes" or OBCs in the northern Hindi heartland who have been largely ignored (at least until recently) by the leaders of the secular Congress Party.[51]

Finally, mention must also be made of Mohandas Karamchand Gandhi (1869–1948).[52] Born in the region of Gujarat, Gandhi studied law in England (1888–91), practiced law for some twenty-years in South Africa (1893–1914), and then returned to India to lead the nationalist struggle for independence from the British. Gandhi, of course, was primarily a political leader, but his political work was inextricably related with his reformed and nationalist Neo-Hindu vision that stressed (*a*) the validity of all religions, (*b*) the pursuit of non-violent non-cooperation against the British as a political strategy or what he called "truth-force" or "holding firmly to truth" (*satyāgraha*), and (*c*) the cultivation of non-violence (*ahiṃsā*) in all conflict situations. Like the other reformist groups already mentioned, he disliked the inequities of the caste system, especially untouchability, and he thought that the spiritual life was essential to political life. Although he never founded a religious group as such, it can be said that he mobilized the entire nation to his Neo-Hindu vision of reform and nationalism. Gandhi's own approach differed, on the one hand, from the older liberal, democratic, highly westernized approach of earlier nationalist leaders (such as Ranade or Gokhale), and also, on the other hand, from the more radical postures, such as the Marxian internationalism of an M. N. Roy (1887–1954), the militant extremism of a Subhas Chandra Bose (1897–1945), or the democratic socialist approach of a Jawaharlal Nehru (1889–1964).[53] Gandhi's great genius was his ability to bring the liberal Westernizers and the radical socialists together with the large landowners, industrialists, and the great rural masses of India into a grand coalition based on a reformed Neo-Hindu ideology of "holding firmly to truth" (*satyāgraha*) and "non-violence" (*ahiṃsā*), and it is fair enough to argue that without the Neo-Hindu component such a coalition would never have been realized.

In any case, the common features of all of these Neo-Hindu reformist and nationalist movements, in spite of their varying political orientations and strategies, were and are (1) a primary focus on developing among the people of India a self-confident national awareness that will provide a solid foundation for India as a modern nation-state; (2) the reform of outdated, parochial and superstitious Hindu practices; (3) the rejection or radical reform of the caste system; (4) female emancipation; (5) the improvement of social conditions for the poor; (6) economic progress for the entire nation (*sarvodaya* or the "uplift of all"); and (7) the development of techniques of communication and propagation borrowed largely from Protestant Christian models. Regarding the last feature, it is striking to note that although Neo-Hindu reformist and nationalist groups overwhelmingly rejected Protestant Christian beliefs, they nevertheless at the very same time overwhelmingly accepted missionary methods. J. N. Farquhar noticed this many years ago, and his observations are still important. He points out that the traditional South Asian methods of dissemination in terms of priestly schools, wandering mendicants, wandering *bhakti* singers and vernacular poet-saints, wandering monks with their interpretations of the *Vedānta-sūtra*-s, and so forth, are nearly totally absent in the Neo-Hindu reformist and nationalist movements.[54] Farquhar then goes on simply to list the manner in which missionary methods were employed.

> We shall merely give a list of the more notable of the methods copied, and leave readers to carry the inquiry farther themselves. The modes of congregational worship, the educated ministry, preaching, lecturing, pastoral work, prayer meetings, itinerancy, conferences, make the first group. Sunday schools, Bible classes, Young People's Societies, Bands of Hope, social gatherings and other forms of work for young people make another. . . . All forms of medical work, and also the Christian leper asylum, have been copied. . . . Every movement has copied the Y.M.C.A., and a few have tried to reproduce the Salvation Army. The very names used by Christians are adopted and used by non-Christians . . . *revival*; . . . Hindu Ārya or Muslim *missionaries*; . . . the title *Reverend* is conferred; . . . *mission* . . . *classes* . . . *Prayer Meetings* . . . *Young Men's* Hindu . . . *Associations*.[55]

More recently Kenneth W. Jones has also noted the same phenomenon and has gone so far as to call it a process of "Protestantization" among Neo-Hindu reformist and nationalist movements.

> Printing, translation, and literacy combined to create a framework, in many ways parallel to the Protestant Reformation in Europe with its abandonment of classical Latin, its proliferation

> of translations and religious writings, and its insistence that the devout read scriptures as an essential part of their search for salvation. As in Protestantism, many of the socio-religious movements of South Asia taught that truth lay in the text, and that it was the duty of their adherents to study these writings in order to find within them a key to a proper, moral and spiritual life.[56]

Whether or not one wishes to refer to these Neo-Hindu groups in terms of "protestantization," it is nevertheless true that the present-day existence of India as a modern nation-state is inconceivable apart from the important contributions that these Neo-Hindu reformist and nationalist groups provided. The great tragedy, of course, was that the Muslims in South Asia fully recognized that all of these movements, together with the Gandhian nationalist movement itself, were finally incorrigibly Neo-Hindu, thereby creating a profound alienation and a deep suspicion that would ultimately issue in the great fissure of partition. Gandhi's greatest success, in other words, was at one and the same time his greatest failure, and that devastating historical paradox has continued to haunt South Asia ever since.

Neo-Hindu Revisionist and Internationalist Movements

But there is a second level or dimension of the Indo-Anglian and Neo-Hindu trajectory, namely, a set of movements which can be characterized as revisionist and internationalist. By the terms "revisionist" and "internationalist" is meant some new ideas and practices that have clear antecedents in older patterns of Hindu or Indic (Hindu-Buddhist-Jain) spirituality but represent new directions and emphases and, most of all, are designed to appeal not only in South Asian environments but to a broad-based international audience as well.

It is important to note, first of all, that at least two of the groups already mentioned as Neo-Hindu reformist and nationalist movements, namely, the Ramakrishna Mission and the Aurobindo Integral Yoga tradition, also fit into this second set of Neo-Hindu revisionist and internationalist movements, and thus may be considered "swing" groups or "both-and" groups. Clearly on one level Vivekananda was a reformist and nationalist leader as can be seen in his representing and defending Hindu traditions at the World Parliament of Religions in 1893 and in his continuing attempts to raise the social conscience of the people of modern India. On another level, however, he was intrigued by the international implications of Vedānta and the manner in which the life and teachings of Ramakrishna could be brought to non-Indian audiences, especially in the United States. Towards the end of his life he focused increasingly on the development of Vedānta Societies outside of India, and it is no accident that Vedānta Societies exist all across the United States today (in such places as Hollywood, Santa Barbara, New York City, Chicago, St. Louis, and so forth). It is also important to observe that the Vedānta movement tends to deify not only Ramakrishna, the founding *guru*, but Vivekananda and others as well, and, as we shall see, this is one of the common characteristics among all of the Neo-Hindu revisionist and internationalist movements.

Likewise, Aurobindo clearly was originally a reformist and nationalist leader and saw the nationalist movement as a religious mission. After his prison conversion, however, he proceeded to develop an international Integral Yoga tradition at his *āśrama* in Pondicherry and maintained the claim that Integral Yoga is the spiritual technique for the higher evolution of all mankind. Moreover, Aurobindo as *guru* together with the Mother as divine power or *śakti* have become objects of devotion by their followers. Thus, there would appear to be a good case for claiming the Ramakrishna Mission and Aurobindo's Integral Yoga for both types of Neo-Hindu tradition.

Other groups are more narrowly within the Neo-Hindu revisionist and internationalist category, and they continue to emerge down to the present day. They cannot all be mentioned in this context, but some of the more well-known may be briefly characterized as follows (roughly in chronological order):[57]

1. Swami Sahajananda (1781–1830), also called Swaminarayana ("Lord of the Universe") and founder of the Swaminarayana movement in the state of Gujarat. It is a highly visible movement in Gujarat and has been carried throughout the world by emigrating Gujaratis with especially large communities in the United States, Great Britain and East Africa. It is basically a Vaiṣṇava *bhakti* movement, focusing on Kṛṣṇa, Rādhā (Kṛṣṇa's consort) and the interacting male and female cosmic forces. Both Swami Sahajananda and his chief disciple, Gunatitananda, are deified in the movement.[58]
2. Swami Shiv Dayal (1818–1878), also known as Soamiji Maharaj, founder of the Radhasoami Satsang ("Association of Radhasoamis") in 1861 in the city of Agra in North India. The movement is a blend of Hindu and Sikh elements, focusing on the interplay between Rādhā (Kṛṣṇa's consort, but also symbolizing the soul) and the "master" ("Soami" or "Swami," symbolizing God). A special *yoga* or meditation is followed by the group, focusing on sacred sound (called *shabad*, from the Sanskrit, *śabda*) or a universal sound current (*surat*-

shabad-yoga) that is heard only by the mind. The group believes in a monotheistic God and gets many of its theological ideas from Sikh traditions and other *sant* traditions (see above under the Indo-Islamic period) and many of its practices from older North Indian *bhakti* traditions. A schism in the group has led to the development of two distinct centers in India, an original group still in the region of Agra (south of Delhi) and a second group in Beas (in the state of Punjab near Amritsar). The latter group has more affinities with Sikh traditions, although most Sikhs are not sympathetic to the Radhasoamis, mainly because of the incorporation of too many Hindu motifs in the Radhasoami Satsang. There are a number of American followers of the group, especially in California.[59]

3. Paramahamsa Yogananda (birth-name, Mukunda Lal Ghosh, 1893–1952), a Bengali *sādhu* or "holy man" and founder of the Self-Realization Fellowship in Los Angeles and San Diego. Yogananda first came to the United States to attend a conference in Boston in 1920 and then remained in the United States to establish his Self-Realization Fellowship in the same year. He was keen to reconcile Hindu traditions and Christian traditions. He taught various kinds of Yoga and published his life's story in his well-known *Autobiography of a Yogi*, first published in 1946.[60]
4. Meher Baba (birth-name, Merwan Irani, 1894–1969), founder of the Meher Baba Mandali ("Father of Love Society") with centers around the United States, especially on the West Coast. Born of Iranian parents who were Zoroastrian Parsis, Meher Baba's group is a peculiar combination of Zoroastrian, Sufi and Hindu notions, emphasizing interreligious discussion and simple meditation techniques. Meher Baba himself took a vow of silence in 1925.[61]
5. A. C. Bhaktivedanta Prabhupada (birth-name, Abhay Charan De, 1896–1977), a Bengali businessman from Calcutta who became a Vaiṣṇava monk and founded the International Society for Krishna Consciousness (ISKCON) in the 1960s. It is also known as the Hare Krishna movement, and its followers have been seen on street-corners in many American and European cities, chanting "Hare Krishna, Hare Rama," the basic *mantra* of the group. Unlike some of the groups that have only shallow roots in traditional Hindu culture, the Hare Krishna movement is an authentic offshoot of the Bengal Vaiṣṇava tradition of the sixteenth-century Vaiṣṇava saint and devotee of Kṛṣṇa, Caitanya (and see above under the Indo-Islamic period). The focus of the movement is on exuberant *bhakti* or devotion to Kṛṣṇa. The movement retains a strong base in India in Vrindavan in the Mathura district of Uttar Pradesh in North India, the

sacred grove in which Kṛṣṇa danced with young maiden-devotees. The movement is widely known and respected in India.[62]

6. Swami (Baba) Muktananda (1908–1982), founder of the Siddha Yoga ("discipline of spiritual fulfillment") movement, currently based at an *āśrama* in India at Ganeshpuri in the state of Maharashtra (near Bombay) and at an *āśrama* in South Fallsburg, New York. Since the death of the founder in 1982, the movement has been led mainly by a young woman, Gurumayi Chidvilasananda. The movement is a blend of classical and Tantric *yoga* practices, emphasizing the importance of *śakti* ("power" or divine energy). Followers believe that "power" can descend suddenly (a process called *śaktipāt* or "the falling down or infusing with power") into a devotee by the mere presence or touch of the *guru*. Gurumayi is deified as are Baba Muktananda and other preceding *gurus*. The movement traces its roots back to old traditions of Śaiva meditation from Kashmir. In addition to the two main *āśrama*-s in Ganeshpuri and South Fallsburg, the movement has meditation centers throughout the United States and around the world.[63]
7. Maharishi Mahesh Yogi (birth-name, Mahesh Prasad Varma, 1911–), founder of the Spiritual Regeneration Movement or Transcendental Meditation in the 1960s. TM centers are found throughout the United States and Europe. The international headquarters of the movement is in Switzerland. The Maharishi teaches a simple technique of sound-meditation. The devotee is given a sacred *mantra* or sound and then told to meditate one-half hour to an hour every day. The technique is designed to bring about a relaxed state of mind and to purify one's awareness. Popular in the 1960s, the movement currently has lost many of its followers, and it has never been highly regarded in India.[64]
8. Satya Sai Baba (birth-name, Satya Narayan, 1926–), a spiritual teacher and healer from Puttaparthi in the state of Andhra Pradesh in South India. At the age of fourteen he declared himself to be a reincarnation of the Shirdi Sai Baba, a holy man from the state of Maharashtra who had died in 1918. Purported to be a great healer, he is supposedly able to produce ashes in his hands at will (called *vibhūti*-s or occult spiritual powers) as well as other "miracles" (*siddhi*-s), especially miracles of healing. He has a purported following in India of two to three million. Worldwide he supposedly has a following of ten million, including a significant number of Americans.[65]

There are, of course, many more movements which could be mentioned, but perhaps enough has been said to provide at least some flavor of these Neo-Hindu revisionist and internationalist movements. Although all of these movements have some connection with traditional Hindu spirituality, some with deep roots in India—for example, the Hare Krishna movement of Bhaktivedanta and the Siddha Yoga tradition of Muktananda and Gurumayi—and others with only shallow connections—for example, Paramahamsa Yogananda's Self-Realization Fellowship and the TM movement of Maharishi Mahesh Yogi—all have clearly moved away from an exclusively Indian identity. These are all international movements with sizable followings throughout the world. The common features of all of these "export" brands of Neo-Hindu revisionist and internationalist movements were and are (1) devotion to a deified *guru* or teacher; (2) total obedience to the will of the *guru* or teacher; (3) the practice of one or another type of *yoga* or disciplined meditation; (4) the claim that all religions are basically valid; (5) the claim that one's ethnic identity has no bearing on the practice of the particular Neo-Hindu tradition, so long as the devotee has been properly initiated; and (6) a tendency to deemphasize social work and secular political or ideological involvement of any kind. In striking contrast to the other level or dimension of Neo-Hindu development, that is, the reformist and nationalist, discussed earlier, while these revisionist and internationalist movements make full use of modern technology and means of communication, there is a clearly marked move away from the "protestant" "missionizing" methodology of the reformist and nationalist groups and a clearly marked hearkening back to the notion of a deified or highly venerated "true teacher" (*satguru*, *siddha*, *buddha*, *jina*, and so forth) who exemplifies enlightenment in his or her presence or being and is fully empowered to teach *yoga* or disciplined meditation and, more than that, is fully able to exhibit and transmit truth and insight simply by being perceived or seen (*darśana*).

It may seem somewhat odd to use the expression "Neo-Hindu" for both the reformist and nationalist movements as well as the revisionist and internationalist movements, but it does appear to be the case that these seemingly disparate traditions have much more in common with each other than they do with older, pre-modern Hindu traditions. Both sets of movements have in common (1) the use of English as a primary medium of discourse, (2) a reliance on modern methods of education in contrast to traditional methods, (3) a rejection of the ritual-based hierarchies of the traditional caste system, (4) a self-confident assertion of the value and global importance of certain fundamental Hindu notions such as a broadly pluralistic notion of *dharma*, the practice of meditation of one kind or another, and the need for an exemplary spiritual guide or *guru*, and (5) the utilization of modern means of communication, including newspapers, pamphlets, tracts, film and public broadcasting of all kinds.

Perhaps also worth noting, finally, in regard to comparing and contrasting the two levels or dimensions of Neo-Hindu spirituality, is that whereas the Neo-Hindu reformist and nationalist groups tend to come from the high or forward castes and to have a deep commitment to the legitimation of India as a modern nation-state, the Neo-Hindu revisionist and internationalist groups tend to have a much broader social base and to be detached from issues of political ideology or governance. The two levels or dimensions, in other words, tend to be modern reformulations of the two dominant strains that have fashioned Indic civilization almost from the beginning, that is, the Indo-Brāhmaṇical and the Indo-Śramaṇical.

This, then, brings to a conclusion our tracing of the continuity of India through her discontinuities: (*a*) the Indus Valley with its archaic, chthonic spirituality of village and city, (*b*) the Indo-Brāhmaṇical with its sacrificial, hieratic spirituality of purity and power, (*c*) the Indo-Śramaṇical with its itinerant, mendicant quest for inner truth together with its rejection of external authority, (*d*) the Indic (Hindu-Buddhist-Jain) with its massive synthesis of caste and family, regional polity and pan-Indian vision of the "eternal dharma" (*sanātana-dharma*) that appears to absorb everything around it but, in fact, permits a complex fabric of diversity and interaction, (*e*) the Indo-Islamic with its components of other civilizations and alternative religious visions that will not abide the Indic synthesis in a context of tension that nevertheless generates exuberant devotion that breaks the bounds of all traditions, and, finally, (*f*) the Indo-Anglian, with its subset of the Anglo-Islamic, with its embrace of modernity together with its critique of and separation from its older heritage, but with a final and painful recognition that the older heritage will not, indeed, cannot be denied, generating clashes of loyalty and betrayal and confusion that tear the fabric of everything that has gone before and yet also issue in the emergence of the modern nation-states of India (with a dominant Indo-Anglian heritage but with a vulnerable Anglo-Islamic heritage to be protected) and Pakistan (with a dominant Anglo-Islamic heritage but with its own Indo-Anglian heritage).

Moreover, through the torturous centuries of cultural discontinuities that have shaken the subcontinent time and time again, there have only been five brief times when the parochial loyalties of family, caste and region have been transcended by a larger pan-Indian vision of what a united India might be, namely, (1) the Mauryan vision under the great Aśoka (third century B.C.E.) with its largely Buddhist or Indo-Śramaṇical legitimation; (2) the Gupta vision under Candra Gupta II (fourth and early fifth century C.E.) with its largely Indic (Hindu-Buddhist-Jain) legitimation; (3) the Mughal vision under the great Akbar (sixteenth century) with its largely Indo-Islamic legitimation; (4) the British imperial vision (mid-nineteenth and first half of the twentieth century) with its largely Indo-Anglian legitimation; and, finally, (5) India as a "sovereign, socialist, secular, democratic republic" (1947 or 1950 to the present) with its unique "secular" (Neo-Hindu) legitimation. One is reminded again of Percival Spear's observation: "There has been a constant striving for unity without the power of achieving it."[66] A strong pan-Indian state is clearly not a noticeable feature throughout the history of the subcontinent. Regional polities in interaction with one another represent the more typical pattern. Even under the occasional strong pan-Indian polities, that is, under Akbar's or Aurangzeb's Mughal hegemony, under the British *imperium* or under the modern Indian nation-state since independence, regional rivalries and tensions continuously threaten the pan-Indian power structure.

The story is much the same in terms of the history of religions through the centuries. There are, of course, pan-Indian patterns of belief and practice among Hindu, Buddhist, Jain and Muslim traditions and a pan-Indian network of communities and castes, but overall one is struck by the great discontinuities that continually contend with one another between, within and among the many religious formations in each of the layers that we have discussed. In the religious realm as well as in the political realm one can say with Spear that there is a "constant striving for unity without the power of achieving it." In India, though the many religious formations would promise knowledge, unity, release and peace, on more than a few occasions, and especially now in these last decades of the twentieth century, they have brought instead the agony of ignorance, alienation and violence.

4

The Minority as Majority

> *Western notions of religious organization and communication, including popular and academic ideas on the subject, reflect conceptualizations based upon Christian patterns of hierarchical bureaucratic organization, compartmentalization of sects, congregational worship, and division between spiritual and temporal spheres of life. In contrast, South Asian religions lack some or all of these features.*
> —Paul Brass, *Religion and Politics in North India*

> *Unfortunately, one is disappointed in trying to find theoretical significance in the recent sociology of religion. . . . [C]ompared to Weber's and Durkheim's view of religion as the key to the understanding of society, the state of theory in the recent sociology of religion is, in the main, regressive.*
> —Thomas Luckmann, *The Invisible Religion*

The Problem of Coherence in Indian History and Civilization

In chapters 2 and 3 it was suggested that whatever continuity one finds in Indian history and culture is directly related to India's basic discontinuities. Another way of putting the same point is to say that there is nothing like an abstract "essence" of Indian civilization. There are, to be sure, distinctive cultural presuppositions operating in each of the six historical periods (the Indus Valley, the Indo-Brāhmaṇical, the Indo-Śramaṇical, the Indic, the Indo-Islamic and the Indo-Anglian) that we have examined. But there are no common features or presuppositions that hold overall. What emerges, instead, by way of continuity is a certain distinctive kind of on-going conversation or cluster of conversations about the salience of certain diverse, even contradictory, cultural values and who or what are the basic warrants or authorities for those cultural values. How is it possible to maintain a reasonably stable community over time in a context of mutually contested values? Who are the appropriate authorities and what are the means, both ideological and sociopolitical, for prioritizing and thereby ranking the contested values? Of comparable importance is a distinctive kind of on-going conversation or cluster of conversations about how to frame the terms and categories of the cultural debate. What are the important distinctions in framing questions for intellectual analysis and debate? Or, to use the discourse of our two metaphors, what are the important fault lines for assessing the on-going stability of the cultural environment, or again, what are the crucial secondary trunks together with the primary trunk that enable the banyan tree to continue to grow? Also of comparable importance is a certain kind of distinctive and on-going conversation or cluster of conversations about the character and modalities of the spiritual life and the manner in which the spiritual life relates to the larger cultural context. To what extent is the spiritual life coterminous with ordinary cultural life? To what extent is the spiritual life a powerful critique of ordinary culture?

Such a distinctive conversation or cluster of conversations recurs again and again over time throughout the history of the subcontinent and comes to be shaped in each particular cultural period by the idioms, persons and cultural artifacts of the given period. The coherence, however, is not to be found in the specific contents of a given historical period or the authoritative utterances of this or that particular group. The deep and substantive coherence in Indian history and civilization is in the on-going conversation itself that cuts across or spills over the boundaries of periods and groups and provides, finally, an unfolding all-India dialogue, or perhaps better, a "multi-logue," that extends from the archaic cultural productions of the Indus Valley civilization in the third millenium B.C.E. to the most recent cultural debates in the latter decade of the twentieth century.

In attempting to frame the texture of this conversation or cluster of conversations, it is important to keep in mind that many of the conventional dichotomies in comparative discussions do not quite hold in the South Asian context. For example, the dichotomies of ancient and modern, indigenous and foreign, or East and West can be seriously misleading when discussing the conversation or cluster of conversations that provides the coherence in Indian history and civilization. As was mentioned in chapter 1, it can be argued cogently that as many as 400 million "Hindus" in present day India follow a form of archaic spirituality that is as old or older than the Indus Valley period of the third millenium B.C.E. The enclaves of modernity are, of course, clearly present all over India and are greatly increasing, especially in modern urban centers and in the organized areas of the country's economy, but it must always be remembered that in India the ancient is never past. The ancient past is very much the present substance of India, demographically as well as culturally. The distinctive conversation in South Asia, in other words, is always at one and the same time diachronic and synchronic. Likewise regarding the dichotomy of indigenous and foreign. As was pointed out in chapter 2, much of the cultural content of every historical period, even that of the Indus Valley period, can be shown to have come somehow from the "outside." In India the indigenous is sometimes the foreign, and the foreign is sometimes the indigenous.

Finally, the dichotomy of East and West is seldom helpful—except, of course, for important, albeit relatively superficial, matters of historical genesis—and is little more than a variation on the dichotomy of indigenous and foreign. Classical Western influences from the Mediterranean world and the ancient Near East have been present on the subcontinent since the first millenium B.C.E. Christian, Jewish and Muslim communities are almost as old in India as they are in their original cultural contexts. Likewise the presence of modern Western notions and institutions, including modern philosophy, modern socioeconomic theorizing, industrial organization, socialist and capitalist economic structures, and so forth, have been present in India since the middle of the eighteenth century, or, in other words, almost as long as they have been characteristic of the emerging nation-states of Western Europe and fully as long as they have been operative in North, Central and Latin America. In other words, the terms "East" and "West," very much like the terms "indigenous" and "foreign," are really synonyms, or even identities, in the South Asian context, in the sense that such perspectives or orientations are fully Indian or intracultural. There is no pristine, pure India "essence" over and above so-called "extraneous" or "outside" forces or influences. There is only the continuing conversation or cluster of conversations regarding the manner in which the many peoples and institutions belonging to the contested (and contesting) value systems interact with another and negotiate their place in the larger context of the overall civilisation-state that is India.

Putting the matter somewhat differently and more concretely, in any attempt to identify the distinctive conversation or cluster of conversations that provides the basic coherence in Indian history and civilization, full account must be taken of all six of the historical and intracultural periods that we have discussed in chapters 2 and 3. All are important intracultural components, and more than that, authoritative voices in the on-going conversation regarding the fashioning of the world-class civilisation-state that is India. Each of the voices has something profound to contribute to the ongoing conversation, and it is in the interactions and interrelations between the various conversation partners that the deep and substantive coherence that is India begins to show itself.

It is impossible, of course, to provide an exhaustive account of such a conversation or cluster of conversations within the limits of the present monograph, but it is useful and necessary to provide at least a preliminary sketch of the quality or texture of that conversation by way of clarifying the great overarching themes and notions that polemically encounter and interact with one another within the civilisation-state of India. Such a preliminary sketch can provide, at least provisionally, two perspectives that can assist us in the sequel when we turn to a discussion of current issues relating to religion and the state. The first perspective involves an appreciation for some important frameworks of meaning or, if you prefer a more technical characterization, some important semantic fields within South Asian thought and culture. The second perspective can provide some sense of how the frameworks of meaning interact with one another, or, in some instances, fail to interact with one another, over time and in contemporary debates in present-day India.

Moreover, in constructing a preliminary sketch of India's ongoing conversation, I want to make use of Wittgenstein's notion of "family resemblance."[1] I have stressed above that the coherence in Indian history and civilization is not to be construed in terms of some sort of abstract "essence," no pristine or pure conceptualization that provides for an unambiguous and determinate definition of India or Indian culture. It is clear enough, however, that there are a great number of approximate similarities in Indian civilization or a great number of common features that overlap with one another, not all of which similarities or features appear in any one example but are widely enough distributed over a set of examples to warrant the recognition of an obvious similarity, very much like the "family resemblance" features that manifest themselves in kinship groups. Such a notion of "family resemblance" enables one to analyze varieties of common features and similarities without falling into the trap of essentialism. It is admittedly a somewhat messy procedure in that a "family resemblance" is never a clear-cut, unambiguous and exclusive certainty, but it does allow for a broad discussion of comparative data that is not totally enslaved to empiricism.

Furthermore, in constructing a preliminary sketch of India's ongoing conversation, I want to make use of a piece of Indian philosophical methodology, namely, the notion of analytic "absences" (*abhāva*-s).[2] Indian philosophy, at least from the time of Vācaspatimiśra (ninth or tenth century C.E.) and probably earlier, and mainly in the traditions of Nyāya (the school of Indian logic), Navya-Nyāya (the "New Logic" school), Sāṃkhya (the old, speculative dualist school) and Yoga (the school of meditation), identifies four specific kinds of absences or *abhāva*-s, namely, (1) "prior absence" (*prāg-abhāva*), (2) "absolute absence" (*atyanta-abhāva*), (3) "mutual absence" (*anyonya-abhāva*), and (4) "subsequent" or "consequent absence" (*pradhvaṃsa-abhāva*).[3] "Prior absence" refers to the sort of absence or non-existence that characterizes a thing before its appearance or construction—for example, a jar prior to its being constructed by a potter. The jar before its construction is characterized by "prior absence." "Absolute absence" refers to the material absence of relation between two things, either in terms of unexampled classes or untenable classes—for example, the son of a barren woman. In our sort of world there are such things as "sons," and there are such things as "barren women;" but there is an "absolute absence" or a material absence of relation between "sons" and "barren women." There can be no such thing, in other words, as the "son of a barren woman." Such a relation is logically as well as materially or ontologically unwarranted. "Mutual absence," the third type of absence, refers to the logical absence of identity between two things—for example, a jar and a cloth, or a chair and a table. They are characterized by "mutual negation" or "mutual absence." There is an ontological absence of relation, or, in other words, a fundamental difference or separation between two things. Finally, "subsequent" or "consequent absence" refers to the sort of absence that characterizes a thing after it has been destroyed—for example, the jar after it has been smashed is characterized by "subsequent" or "consequent absence." Sometimes the four types of absences are reduced to two. "Prior absence," "absolute absence," and "subsequent absence" are all taken to be instances of a single "absence of relation" (*saṃsarga-abhāva*), that is, a material "absence of relation," whereas "mutual absence" (*anyonya-abhāva*) is a separate or second type referring to the logical absence of identity.[4]

Each of these four kinds of absence represents a form of infinite absence, and what is interesting regarding the analytic discourse about absences is the way that it enables one to speak about an object, or to tease out what an object is, in terms of what it is not. The device is somewhat like the *via negativa* in Western philosophizing, the difference being mainly that the *via negativa* was used to characterize things that simply cannot be characterized positively—for example, God—whereas in Indian philosophy the method of analytic absences was used widely in order to speak precisely and to highlight in innovative ways aspects of even very commonplace things like jars, and so forth. In any case, I want to make use of this negative analytic device in classical Indian thought in trying to formulate my preliminary sketch of the ongoing conversation or cluster of conversations that provides the fundamental coherence in Indian history and civilization.

Frameworks of Meaning in Conversation (Old Indic and New Indic)

As already mentioned in passing in chapters 2 and 3, there are certain clear "family resemblances" among the historical and cultural periods that we have discussed: (1) the Indus Valley, (2) the Indo-Brāhmaṇical, (3) the Indo-Śramaṇical, (4) the Indic, (5) the Indo-Islamic, and (6) the Indo-Anglian. The Indic period is largely a conflation of the streams flowing into it from the Indo-Śramaṇical and the Indo-Brāhmaṇical, and to the extent that the Indo-Brāhmaṇical and the Indo-Śramaṇical resonate and assimilate many of the archaic rituals and beliefs of the subcontinent that are as old and older than the Indus Valley period, it is not unreasonable to see a set of "family resemblances" or rather obvious cultural "kinship patterns" among and between periods (1) through (4), namely, the Indus Valley, the Indo-Brāhmaṇical, the Indo-Śramaṇical and the Indic. For convenience we have been referring to these simply as "Old Indic" formations.

A quite different set of "family resemblances" shows itself among and between periods (5) and (6), namely, the Indo-Islamic and the Indo-Anglian. As pointed out earlier, the form of Islam that finally became dominant on the Indian subcontinent was not at all the original tradition of the Arabs but, rather, the much more cosmopolitan tradition of the 'Abbasid caliphate which itself was a grand synthesis of the heritage of the great Middle Eastern civilizations. As Lapidus has cogently suggested, 'Abbasid Islam was a remarkable synthesis of the older Mediterranean and Middle Eastern civilizations, including assimilated components from the simple faith of Arab Islam, Christian theological notions, Neo-Platonic and Hellenistic philosophy, traditions of Jewish exegetical, prophetic and ritual literature, Hellenistic science, and Byzantine and Iranian art and ritual traditions. Inasmuch as the coming of the British, from one important perspective, represents a modernized update of many of those same Mediterranean and Middle Eastern civilizations, there is also a rather obvious "family resemblance" between the Indo-Islamic and the Indo-Anglian. As was stressed in chapter 3, although there are, of course, profound differences between Islamic civilization and modern western civilization, perhaps the most important being the fundamental structural changes brought about by industrialization, the rise of a modern economy and the incipient emergence of the modern nation-state system, nevertheless, there is also an interesting deep-structural or valuational "family resemblance" between Islamic and western civilization to the extent that both civilizations are products of that remarkable coming together in the first millennium C.E. of classical Greco-Roman Mediterranean traditions with the West Asian Jewish, Iranian, Christian and Islamic religious traditions.[5] For convenience we have been referring to the Indo-Islamic and the Indo-Anglian simply as "New Indic" formations.

But let me turn now from identifying the sets of family resemblances and attempt to formulate the basic frameworks of meaning within each of the formations. This, of course, is an exceedingly difficult undertaking, and, as indicated earlier, I only wish to offer in this context a preliminary sketch, but one, I hope, that will prove useful, at least heuristically, as I seek to address the basic issues of religion and the state in the South Asian context in the sequel. Also as already indicated, in setting forth this preliminary sketch, I shall make use of the notion of analytic "absences," especially "mutual absence" or the absence of identity.[6]

1. *In the Old Indic formations (the Indus Valley, the Indo-Brāhmaṇical, the Indo-Śramaṇical and the Indic), there is for the most part the absence of an ontological separation between mind and body or between thought and extension, whereas in the New Indic formations (the Indo-Islamic and the Indo-Anglian) a basic separation between mind and body or between thought and extension is frequently taken for granted.* The Old Indic tradtitions, of course, are fully able to distinguish mind and body or thought and extension, but they never view such a distinction as having the force of an ontological separation between a pure realm of thought and a pure realm of matter. S. Schayer has put the matter as follows:

> In this connection it must be strongly emphasized that the concept of a non-spatial Being, especially the hypostasis of a psychic,

> non-extended reality which has been current in Occidental philosophy since Descartes, remained foreign to the Indian systems.[9]

E. H. Johnston offers a similar observation.

> Early Indian thought, as exemplified for instance by Sāṃkhya, drew no clear line of demarcation between the material, mental and psychical phenomena of the individual. . . . All classes of phenomena are looked on alike as having a material basis, the difference resting merely on the degree of subtlety attributed to the basis.[8]

In Western philosophical traditions, of course, as represented in the New Indic traditions of the Indo-Islamic and the Indo-Anglian, the recognition of a separate and pure realm of ideas is as old as Pythagoras and Plato, and the precise nature of the ontological distinction between the realm of ideas (or the pure mind of God), on the one hand, and the realm of matter or stuff, on the other, has been an important and recurring philosophical problem.

That the Old Indic traditions do not make an ontological separation between mind and body or thought and extension leads to the interesting (and admittedly puzzling) observation that Old Indic thought appears to be tending towards what modern philosophy of mind calls physicalism or reductive materialism, that is, that the realm of ideas or mind is simply a manifestation of a kind of subtle matter. The old systems of Sāṃkhya and Yoga philosophy, for example, clearly assert that *citta* or "mind-stuff" or *antaḥkaraṇa* (the internal "mental" organ made up of intellect, ego and mind), are products of primordial materiality (*prakṛti*).[9] Likewise, in Nyāya and Vaiśeṣika, mind is construed to be an atomic form of "substance" (*dravya*). To some extent , then, there is some validity to the claim that these Old Indic traditions are physicalist, at least regarding conventional discussions of mind-body and thought-extension.

It must be immediately pointed out, however, that the Old Indic systems then go on to make another kind of separation. They posit a separation between the mind-body realm of determinate manifestation or being, on the one hand, and a qualityless (*nirguṇa*), contentless or indeterminate realm of pure consciousness (*puruṣa, ātman, Brahman*, and so forth), on the other. This latter realm of indeterminate ultimacy is the ultimate goal of the spiritual life. It is spiritual "release" or "salvation" (*mokṣa* or *nirvāṇa*). The Old Indic systems, of course, express this basic separation in a great variety of ways, and there was much polemic through the centuries about the manner in which this indeterminate ultimacy should be explained.

Sāṃkhya and Yoga directly posit two separate realms of "pure contentless consciousness" (*puruṣa*), on the one hand, and "primoridial materiality" or the mind-body realm (*prakṛti*, including "mind-stuff" or *citta*), on the other. The traditions of Vedānta posit a "qualityless" (*nirguṇa*) realm of *Brahman* or *ātman* and a "qualified" (*saguṇa*) realm of mind-body or manifest reality, and the various schools interpret the relation between the former and the latter in terms of pure monism (whereby the *saguṇa* realm of mind-body is, finally, an inexplicable illusion), modified monism or one or another kind of dualist interpretation. The Buddhists and the Jains of the Indo-Śramaṇical traditions likewise accept a similar separation between a determinate mind-body realm (known as the realm of becoming or dependent origination by the early Buddhists and the realm of "non-self" or *ajīva* by the early Jains) and a realm of indeterminate ultimacy (*nirvāṇa, kevala*), on the other.

What is important to recognize, however, is the basic difference in ontology which shows itself between the Old Indic and the New Indic. The New Indic with its separate realm of ideas and mind (either in terms of Plato's ideas, the theological mind of God or modern notions of the realm of pure thought) and its separate realm of extended matter tends to see being and truth and ultimate value in terms of the determinate formulation of a pattern of intelligible ideas, or theologically as the determinate formulation of the mind and will of God as made known in some sort of determinate revelation. The Old Indic, on the contrary, combines the determinate realms of mind and body or thought and extension into one determinate (*saguṇa*) realm of primordial materiality or manifest becoming (in terms of *prakṛti, māyā, pratītyasamutpāda*, and so forth) but then posits an indeterminate (*nirguṇa*), contentless ultimate (*puruṣa, ātman, nirvāṇa, kevala*, and so forth) that is finally uncharacterizable precisely because of its indeterminacy.[10] For the New Indic, what truly is and what is truly valuable is always the determinate. For the Old Indic, what truly is and what is truly valuable is always the indeterminate.

2. *In the Old Indic formations (the Indus Valley, the Indo-Brāhmaṇical, the Indo-Śramaṇical, and the Indic), there is for the most part the absence of an epistemological separation between reason and experience, whereas in the New Indic formations (the Indo-Islamic and the Indo-Anglian) a basic separation between reason and experience is frequently taken for granted.* Again, the

Old Indic traditions, of course, are fully able to distinguish between the epistemological realms of reason and experience, but there is little if any inclination to make a hard separation between the two. J. N. Mohanty has put the matter well.

> [L]et us note an important difference in locution, which, however, is not a mere matter of locution, but points to deep substantive issues. In the Western philosophical tradition, it was usual, until recent times, to ask: does knowledge arise from reason or from experience? The rationalists and empiricists differed in their answers. These answers, in their various formulations, determined the course of Western philosophy. In the Sanskrit philosophical vocabulary, the words "reason" and "experience" have no exact synonyms, and the epistemological issue was never formulated in such general terms.[11]

There is no separate realm of reason, no pure rationalism, no pure realm of ideas, no pure possibilities and no transcendent "mind of God," Mohanty suggests.[12] To some extent this is like our earlier ontological discussion about the lack of an ontological separation between mind and body or thought and extension, but here the point has to do with the crucial epistemological issue of certainty. The New Indic traditions as represented by the Indo-Islamic and the Indo-Anglian have focused largely on the quest for determinate certainty, whether that certainty derives from the pure realm of reason (Plato's ideas), the Word or Logos of God in determinate revelation as Torah, Qur'an or New Testament, or from one or another tradition of modern rationalism, empiricism or scientific realism.

In the Old Indic traditions there is no privileged realm of knowing of a purely rational kind or of a purely experiential kind that guarantees reliable knowledge. Even general inferential knowledge (*anumāna*) always has an empirical instantiation and is itself a material operation. Karl Potter comments as follows:

> [T]here is a general failure on the part of Indian philosophers to distinguish such opposites as *a priori* and *a posteriori*, analytic and synthetic, formal logic and empirical reasoning. No need seems to have been felt for any such distinctions.[13]

Regarding issues of logic, S. Chatterjee makes the following observation.

> In Indian logic an inference is a combined deductive-inductive reasoning consisting of at least three categorical propositions. All inferences are thus pure syllogisms of the categorical type which are at once formally and materially valid.[13]

The Old Indic traditions, rather than separating reason and experience, tend to deal with the epistemological issue in terms of what might be called cognitive frustration. The first part of the first verse of Īśvarakṛṣṇa's *Sāṃkhyakārikā*, for example, asserts that the desire to know arises directly out of the "threefold (psychological, social and theological) frustration" of the human condition ("*duḥkha-traya-abhighātāj jijñāsā*"), and most other Old Indic traditions (including the Buddhist and Jain Indo-Śramaṇical traditions) would concur in such a formulation of the epistemological problem.[15] Epistemology has to do with the various means of knowing (*pramāṇa*), including perception, inference, reliable authority, and so forth, and the various Old Indic traditions debated both the number and the nature of the *pramāṇa*-s. Generalized notions of "reason" or "experience" are simply cognitive episodes within the unfolding flow of human awareness, and there is no privileged realm of knowing of a purely rational kind or of a purely experiential kind that guarantees reliable knowledge or certainty. The determinate realm, rather, is fraught with uncertainty. The determinate realm of mind-body or manifest reality is largely a realm of ignorance and non-discrimination (*avidyā, aviveka*). Some ordinary awarenesses, to be sure, are conducive to liberation in that they point to what truly is, namely, that indeterminate ultimacy which is pure unqualified and contentless consciousness or quiescence.

As was true in the earlier discussion of ontology, so here too in the area of epistemology, it is important to see the substantive contrast between the Old Indic and the New Indic traditions. The New Indic posits a realm of determinate certainty, either in terms of a realm of pure ideas, a determinate revelation of the mind and will of God, or some form of pure rationalism or scientific realism. The Old Indic traditions, on the other hand, are deeply suspicious of the determinate realm, whether rational or experiential, and look, rather, for epistemological clues within the determinate that lead away from the determinate to the indeterminate, or that lead away, finally, from the cognitive frustration of ordinary human existence to a quiescent contentlessness that transcends ordinary determinate knowing.

3. *In the Old Indic formations (the Indus Valley, the Indo-Brāhmaṇical, the Indo-Śramaṇical, and the Indic), there is for the most part the absence of a psychological separation between birth and rebirth, whereas in the New Indic*

formations (the Indo-Islamic and the Indo-Anglian) each human organism is distinct from all others. Again, it is to be indicated that the Old Indic traditions certainly recognize that one life is to be distinguished from another, but there is a great reluctance in the Old Indic traditions to limit the notion of human being to a single lifetime. The Old Indic traditions posit, rather, what might be called a psychology of intrapersonal plurality or a diachronic ontogeny of more than one life. They posit, in other words, a greatly expanded notion of selfhood encompassing more than one life.

The New Indic traditions, on the contrary, in terms either of the Indo-Islamic stress on the importance of the transcendent creator God who creates all of reality and every person as a distinct creature, or in terms of the Indo-Anglian, post-Reformation or modern notion of every human organism as a unique "individual," focus on a single lifetime together with the rights and responsibilities that pertain to that single lifetime (before the judgment throne of God in the case of Indo-Islamic traditions, or in the light of the common law, citizenship, freedom of conscience and rational self-interest in the case of the Indo-Anglian).[16] There are, to be sure, examples of traditions in the Mediterranean world and the Middle East that accepted belief in reincarnation in one form or another—Plato himself is said to have believed in reincarnation—but for the most part the belief never became a mainstream cultural notion as it did in South Asian traditions.[17]

In Old Indic traditions the person is much more than the genetic heritage of father and mother. Father and mother contribute only the gross physical constituents of the person. The deeper identity is a transmigrating "subtle body" (*sūkṣma-śarīra*) which enlivens the gross physical embryo at or shortly after the time of conception. According to the old Sāṃkhya philosophy, the subtle body is made up of the threefold internal mental organ (of intellect, ego and mind) together with sense capacities, action capacities and a subtle material substratum that is capable of linking up with a gross physical embryo. The subtle body is "marked" by certain fundamental "predispositions" (*saṃskāra*-s) and "traces" (*vāsanā*-s) that have been accumulated as a result of the karmic residues from preceding rebirths. In other words, any given human organism (and for that matter, any sentient creature within any species) is to be understood in terms of a series of recycling identities unfolding over time (*saṃsāra*)—hence, the expressions "psychology of intrapersonal plurality" or a "diachronic ontogeny of more than one life," mentioned above. The quality of a given person's life is, thus, a composite of accumulated *karman* and the trajectories of previous rebirths (*punarjanman*).[18] There are, of course, many other explanations of *karman* and rebirth in the various Old Indic traditions besides that of the Sāṃkhya, but the Sāṃkhya interpretation is reasonably representative. Fundamental to all interpretations, however, is the basic belief that personal psychology involves an intrapersonal plurality that stretches over many lives and through myriads of unfolding cycles of time. Even in Buddhist traditions which reject the Upaniṣadic notion of selfhood together with the notion of a transmigrating self in the sense that Hindu traditions speak about transmigration, there is still the fundamental axiomatic belief in a trajectory of rebirths in terms of karmic trajectories that encompass a series of successive embodiments.[19]

As in ontology and epistemology, so, too, in psychology there would, thus, appear to be deep and substantive contrasts between Old Indic and New Indic traditions. Notions such as *karman*, rebirth (*punarjanman*), long periods of recurrent becoming (*saṃsāra*), predispositions (*saṃskāra*-s), and traces (*vāsanā*-s) are fundamental to the Old Indic group or cluster, and, hence, the notion of personal identity and issues of personal psychology are construed in radically different ways. For Old Indic thought the human species is only one among many in which there may be ongoing exchanges and in which the identity of any particular sentient being is a rich composite of intrapersonal components stretching backwards and forwards through continuing cycles of birth and rebirth. The perspective of the Old Indic group or cluster is breathtaking in its evolutionary scope, an ancient psychology of intrapersonal plurality involving nothing less than the ecology of the universe itself.

4. *In the Old Indic formations (the Indus Valley, the Indo-Brāhmaṇical, the Indo-Śramaṇical and the Indic), there is for the most part an absence of a sociological or social anthropological separation between person and person or self and other, whereas in the New Indic formations (the Indo-Islamic and the Indo-Anglian) a basic separation between persons in community is frequently taken for granted.* If the preceding point about the distinctive psychology of the Old Indic traditions could be expressed in terms of a psychology of intrapersonal plurality and a diachronic ontogeny of more than one life, then a parallel characterization about the sociology or social anthropology of the Old Indic traditions might be something like a social anthropology of interpersonal plasticity and a synchronic phylogeny of hierarchical ranking. Here, of course, I have in mind the many studies of social stratification and the caste system within the Old Indic traditions and the manner in which this older social anthropology of interpersonal plasticity and hierarchical ranking differs from the New Indic emphases on the equality of all believers in the "abode of

peace" or "house of Islam" (*dar al-islam*)(in Indo-Islamic traditions) and on the notions of citizenship, personal freedom and individual rights (in Indo-Anglian traditions). For the New Indic traditions (both Indo-Islamic as well as Indo-Anglian) there is a clearcut distinction between persons and a strong sense of the integrity of individuality. The pre-modern or traditional Indo-Islamic notion of individuality within a larger believing community (*umma*), of course, is strikingly different from modern Indo-Anglian ideological notions of the abstract "individual" as citizen and free agent, but there is an obvious family resemblance between the two which is strikingly divergent from Old Indic notions.[20]

The social anthropological work of Louis Dumont and McKim Marriott has been especially helpful in highlighting the distinctive social reality or "ethno-sociology" of the Old Indic traditions, and in showing how many of the Old Indic notions are still operative in present-day India. According to Dumont, the key to understanding the social anthropology of these Old Indic traditions is the notion of "hierarchy" together with the related notions of separation, interdependence (or holism), and the twofold polarities of purity-pollution and purity-power, most of which notions derive from the Indo-Brāhmaṇical tradition and provide the basis for the ordering of law and society (*dharma*) as well as caste (*varṇa)* and "birth-group"(*jāti*) in South Asia. The Indo-Śramaṇical traditions (the Buddhists, Jains, and so forth), to be sure, never accepted notions of caste and frequently disputed the Indo-Brāhmaṇical interpretations of the ordering of law and society (*dharma*), but Indo-Śramaṇical traditions, if for no other reason than their mostly minority status throughout the subcontinent, early along developed functional equivalents to caste, de facto accommodations to caste, and, of course, institutional substitutions for ordinary caste society, that is, the monastic communities. More to the point, although Indo-Śramaṇical groups were critical of Indo-Brāhmaṇical notions of *dharma* (custom or "law") and *varṇa* or *jāti* (caste), debates about law and society and social reality nevertheless unfolded within the idiom of the Indo-Brāhmaṇical discourse.

Hierarchical ranking, according to Dumont, is determined by the degree of purity. Groups that engage in impure or polluting activities (involving, for example, bodily contact with dirt, death, blood, and so forth) are ranked according to the amounts of pollution involved. All groups continually interact with one another, performing services as mutually needed, but with clearly established ritualized rules for maintaining dominant and subordinate roles based on the degree of purity and pollution.[21] Furthermore, according to Dumont, in these Old Indic traditions not only is purity related to pollution by way of establishing hierarchical ranking, it is also superior to, or "encompasses" power. In the Old Indic traditions, the *brāhmaṇa* priests, or in Buddhist environments the Buddhist monks, are basically superior in rank to those who perform the ruling function, namely, the *kṣatriya*-s or rulers. There is a basic separation between the purity function (in terms of priests or sacred figures) and the power function (in terms of political functioning), but it is always understood that purity encompasses power, or, in other words, sacred purity ranks higher than secular power. There is, thus, a separation between sacred and profane, or "religion" and the "state" in these Old Indic traditions, but the relation is always hierarchical with sacred purity at the apex.[22]

Finally, in these Old Indic traditions, according to Dumont, there is nothing like the egalitarian ideological notion of "individualism" of modern social reality, and in this sense the Old Indic traditions are the exact antithesis of modernity. There is, interestingly enough, a somewhat unusual notion of "individual" in the Old Indic traditions, according to Dumont, not the "individualism" of modern social reality but, rather, the "individualism" of the ascetic (*saṃnyāsin, sādhu*) who opts out of social reality in order to pursue *mokṣa* or *nirvāṇa*. In terms of ordinary social life, however, the notion of the "individual" is totally absent. The human organism is simply part of a larger, holistic and plastic social reality with its elaborate ritualized rules for exchange and on-going interaction.[23]

McKim Marriott's work focuses on developing an "ethno-sociology" based on the particularities of the South Asian traditions and, thus, his work is quite different in theoretical flavor from Dumont's primary interest in comparative social anthropology. His work nicely complements Dumont's work, however, with respect to focusing on holism, transactional exchange and what Marriott calls the "fluidarity" in Old Indic notions of the ordering of law and society (*dharma*) and caste and birth-group (*varṇa, jāti*). Rather than using the term "individual," says Marriott, it is better to think of persons in the Old Indic traditions as "dividual," that is, caught up in elaborate networks of the patterned ritual exchange—often referred to as the *jajmānī* or *yajamānī* system, literally the "ritual exchange or performance" system—of things, services, and bodily substance which maintain a basic flow or "fluidarity" or a fundamental interpersonal plasticity in given social environments. In Old Indic traditions, according to Marriott, "dividual" persons continually interact and transact with one another on a great variety of levels and according to elaborate sets of rules that establish the manner in which dominant and subordinate groups relate, in terms, for example, of giving and taking food, performing services, and arranging marriages. This broadly based continuous flow or "fluidarity" of transactions involves giving and receiving both of a symmetrical as well as of an asymmetrical kind.[24] The obligations of customary law (*dharma*), caste (*varṇa, jāti*), stage of life (*āśrama*), and so forth, are rich and varied. There are a few obligations that hold for all, referred to as *sādhāraṇa-dharma* or "general obligations" (such as personal virtues like steadfastness, forgiveness, cleanliness, restraint of anger, and so forth), but for the most part *dharma* differs from group to group, caste to caste, family to family and even in terms of the different stages of a single person's life. There is a remarkable interpersonal plasticity or "fluidarity" operating in the system as a whole. There is no one law to be observed by all "individuals." There is only the multivalent *dharma* of hierarchical interpersonal transactions.

It must be stressed, however, that this "fluidarity" or interpersonal plasticity is not to be construed in terms of historical development but, rather, unfolds in a context of timelessness. The Old Indic focus on the basic ordering of law and society (*dharma*) with its patterned transactions relating to the proper purposes of life (*puruṣārtha*-s), the stages of life (*āśrama*-s), and the various "birth-groups" (*jāti*-s) and caste valuations (*varṇa*-s), oftentimes summarized overall by the general expression "the eternal law" (*sanatana dharma*) or the "obligations or duties with respect to stage of life and caste" (*varṇa-āśrama-dharma*) has a thoroughly timeless or ahistorical quality about it. Madhav Deshpande has characterized the timeless *dharma* or *sanātana-dharma* as follows:

> Thus there was no history in a real sense. All forms always existed. . . . The classical Indian tradition looked upon the Sanskrit language and the Sanskritic culture as eternal entities. . . .
>
> We certainly do not know the real cause of Manu's failure to take note of the facts of Indian history as our modern historians perceive it. However, the historical impact of this 'unhistoric history' has been quite significant. By failing to recognize the foreign and racially different origins of the different peoples in India, and by focusing on their synchronic socio-religious positions, rights and duties, the classical Indian tradition brought about a wonderful racial and cultural synthesis of Indian peoples. . . .
>
> The synchronic feeling of socio-religious unity was more important than the historical fact of diverse origins, and therefore, to serve a synchronic purpose, the synchronic unity had to be projected back into history to the first acts of creation.[25]

The "eternal law" (*sanātana-dharma*) is, thus, a kind of synchronic phylogeny wherein all sorts and conditions of people are encompassed in a holistic, hierarchically ranked, dynamic system of patterned and ritualized exchange, and just as there is a personal psychology of intrapersonal plurality encompassing more than one life diachronically, so, too, there is a social anthropology of interpersonal plasticity encompassing the larger social reality synchronically. As with ontology, epistemology and psychology, so, too, in this fourth area of social anthropology, the Old Indic provides a fascinating and provocative contrast with the the New Indic.

5. *Finally, in the Old Indic formations (the Indus Valley, the Indo-Brāhmaṇical, the Indo-Śramaṇical, and the Indic), there is for the most part an absence of a theological separation between the divine and human, whereas in the New Indic formations (the Indo-Islamic and the Indo-Anglian) a basic separation between the divine and human is frequently taken for granted.* To the extent that the Old Indic systems even accept a notion of god or gods, and, of course, many of them do not (for example, Sāṃkhya, Mīmāṃsā, many Buddhists and Jains, and so forth), the divine in Old Indic traditions is never "wholly other" (to use Rudolf Otto's idiom) or transcendent in the sense of the Jewish, Christian and Islamic monotheist systems. The divine in the Old Indic traditions is polymorphous and plastic. There is nothing like a *creatio ex nihilo* or a willful mind of God in the Old Indic formations. To be sure, there are some references—for example, *Ṛg Veda X.129, Chāndogya Upaniṣad VI*, and so forth—which suggest that there was an early tradition of thought that argued that something can come from nothing or that there may be a primordial condition that precedes both being and non-being or order and chaos, but early along this was rejected in favor of the basic axiom that something does not come from nothing and something does not become nothing.[26] Old Indic theological reflection tends towards what might be called a cosmo-theology of polymorphic multiplicity which parallels in interesting ways its psychology of intrapersonal plurality and its social anthropology of interpersonal plasticity. Again, Marriott's notion of "fluidarity" comes to mind. The hierarchies of ranked, sentient life, ranging from the highest levels of the divine to the lowest hells is one, continuous interactive macrocosm, and through disciplined meditation (*yoga*), strategic karmic praxis and the process of rebirth, one can successively move to different levels of life or speciation, including divine levels.

The old Sāṃkhya philosophy, for example, which, as mentioned above is on one level basically atheistic in the sense of rejecting a notion of a high or principal God (*īśvara*)—and in this regard, of course, it is close to the old Buddhist and Jain traditions—nevertheless, accepts the various old gods (*deva*-s) of the Indo-Brāhmaṇical tradition. In terms of the mind-body or thought-extension realm of primoridial materiality (*prakṛti*), according to the old Sāṃkhya philosophy, there are three constituent processes (called *guṇa*-s or constituent "strands"), namely, the thinking or cognizing strand (*sattva*), an energizing or activating strand (*rajas*) and an objectivating strand (*tamas*).[27] All sentient beings are combinations of these three constituent strands or material processes, and, interestingly enough, the "gods" or *deva*-s have more *sattva* than other sentient beings but are not qualitatively different from, say, ordinary human beings, who have less *sattva* and more *rajas*, and so on. The point is that it is quite possible within such a metaphysical framework to move from one form of life to another form of life, including movement into the divine realms.

Hence, in these Old Indic traditions, for a divine being to become human (*avatāra* or "descending") is not at all an extraordinary occurrence. A Kṛṣṇa or a Rāma is always a possibility. Any chosen *guru* or spiritual teacher may embody the divine in this polymorphic sense, and believers take "*darśana*," or, in other words, an actual visual contact with divinity by coming into perceptual contact with their Bhagavān or Lord. By the same token it is hardly surprising that the Buddhists or the Jains might be "atheistic" in the sense that their own human founders, namely, Gautama or Mahāvīra, may, indeed, through their meditation, attain levels of awareness quite superior to that of the conventional gods!

To return to the old Sāṃkhya philosophy, it must always be remembered that the realm of primordial materiality (*prakṛti*), which includes the *deva*-s as predominantly *sattva*-beings, is to be distinguished from pure, contentless consciousness (*puruṣa*) or what we have called earlier an "indeterminate ultimacy." Finally, the attainment of authentic salvation or "release" (*mokṣa*) is the realization of a level of being quite beyond God or the gods.[28] Similarly in traditions of Vedānta, the level of God is the level of determinate or "qualified" (*saguṇa*) being, the mind-body or thought-extension realm of manifest, determinate experience. Salvation or "release" (*mokṣa*) entails moving to a higher level of "indeterminate ultimacy," the contentless or qualityless (*nirguṇa*) Brahman.

As has been pointed out at length in the preceding chapter, there are, of course, numerous devotional (*bhakti*) traditions that focus on the "grace" and "devotion" (*anugraha, praṇidhāna*) of Lord Viṣṇu, Lord Śiva, the Great Goddess (Devī, Kālī, and so forth), and many, many other forms of the divine including the *grāma-devatā*-s or "village goddesses" present in every village and hamlet. Many of these devotional traditions are undoubtedly as old as the Indus Valley and earlier, but in all of them, at least prior to contact with Islamic, Jewish and Christian traditions, there appears to be an ease of access, a spontaneous emotional rapport, an absence of a separation in kind from the polymorphous divine that is strikingly different from the God of Abraham, Isaac, Jacob, Moses, Jesus and Muhammad who came to be known in India through the Indo-Islamic tradition and through the post-Reformation, Protestant but secularized Indo-Anglian tradition. Here again the contrast between Old Indic and New Indic is dramatic and fundamental.

By way of summary, let me pull together a simple chart (table 4.1) of the preceding discussion, and let me then proceed to comment briefly on what, finally, might be said about the overall coherence in Indian history and civilization.

Throughout the preceding discussion, I have carefully qualified these various analytic descriptions with the expressions "for the most part" and "frequently" in order to make clear that I have been attempting only a preliminary sketch of the various frameworks of meaning in the South Asian context. There are many exceptions, subtle nuances, clarifications and qualifications that would need to be made if a more detailed and exhaustive treatment were attempted. Also, the boundaries between what I have been calling the Old Indic and the New Indic are obviously not as clearcut as the constraint of a necessarily brief discussion has perhaps suggested. Especially the Indo-Islamic period is one requiring much more detailed treatment than I have been able to provide in this overview sketch. In the Indo-Islamic period, stretching from the thirteenth to the middle of the eighteenth centuries, much overlapping occurred between what I have called the Old Indic and the New Indic, especially in those frameworks of meaning relating to social anthropology and theology.

Overall, however, I would want to argue that this preliminary sketch has at least highlighted many of the more important frameworks of meaning operating in the civilisation-state that is India. Furthermore, presenting the preliminary sketch in the format of negative "absences" has had, I would hope, the effect of exhibiting the sorts of substantive conceptualizations and values that have been and are currently being contested in India together with some of the basic choices that are available in the on-going cultural debates. The negative always presupposes the positive—the old Indian philosophers referred to this implicit positive as the counterpositive or *pratiyogin*[29]—and by calling attention to the "absence of a separation" in Old Indic traditions, we

TABLE 4.1
Indic Frameworks of Meaning

Old Indic	*New Indic*
1. Ontology:	
—no separation of mind-body, thought-extension	—separation of mind-body thought-extension
—indeterminate ultimacy (*nirguṇa*)	—determinate ultimacy (*saguṇa*)
2. Epistemology:	
—no separation of reason and experience	—separation of reason and experience
—cognitive frustration	—cognitive certainty
3. Psychology:	
—no separation of birth and rebirth	—separation of birth and death
—intrapersonal plurality	—individual person or believer
—diachronic ontogeny of more than one life	—single life experience
4. Social Anthropology:	
—no separation of person and person	—separation of person from person
—interpersonal plasticity	—individual person in community
—synchronic phylogeny of hierarchical ranking	—historical existence
5. Theology:	
—no separation of divine and human	—separation of divine and human
—cosmo-theology of polymorphic multiplicity	—theology of monomorphic unity and certainty

were able to focus on the positive equivalents in Old Indic traditions vis-à-vis New Indic traditions. Deep and substantive differences emerged between the Old Indic and the New Indic in terms of basic conceptualizations and values relating to ontology, epistemology, psychology, social anthropology and theology.

One immediate result of our preliminary sketch is to document the need for greater clarification in our various discourses about India and South Asia. For example, older European interpreters that referred to Indian philosophy as being largely "idealist" or comparable to certain traditions of German idealism—one thinks of the endless articles and books on "Śankara and Bradley," or "Śankara and Hegel," and so forth—were obviously using New Indic frameworks of meaning for discussing Old Indic notions in which the New Indic distinctions were simply absent! To speak about Indian philosophy in terms of "idealism" is to do European philosophizing, not Indian philosophizing. There is no such thing as "idealism" in the European sense in any tradition of Old Indic philosophizing. An even better example in this regard is the tradition of Indology and Orientalism in many of its varieties. It is often little more than a New Indic rewrite of the Old Indic. It has simply translated and appropriated the Old Indic for the New Indic, an innocent and understandable enough procedure on one level, so long as it does not claim that it has properly assimilated and understood the Old Indic.

But let me come now to my basic point about the coherence of the civilisation-state that is India. There is no "essence" of the Old Indic or the New Indic. There are only, finally, the sets of family resemblances between the various cultural traditions interacting with one another over long periods of time. Old Indic traditions are very much alive and well in the modern civilisation-state of India, and they need to take their full authoritative place in the ongoing conversation regarding the nature and future of India as a civilisation-state. But just as there is no "essence" to the Old Indic but only a collection of cultural family resemblances, so the Old Indic itself ought not to be construed as the "essence" of India or as having a privileged or favored place in the continuing conversation about the future of India. The Old Indic is simply a series of similar cultural conceptualizations and values, no more or less valuable than any other sets of conceptualizations and values.

In a similar fashion, the New Indic ought not to be construed as the "essence" of a new, modern India. New Indic traditions have been present on the subcontinent for centuries, and though from the perspective of the millennia of the existence of subcontinental civilization, they are somewhat late-comers to the stage of the unfolding drama of India, and indeed initially came from the outside as "foreign" and "other" in a blatant, strident manner, they are nevertheless now and have been for some centuries fully Indian. Like the Old Indic traditions (also in origin "foreign" and "other" in a blatant, strident manner), they deserve a full authoritative place in the conversation regarding the nature and future of India as a civilisation-state, but also like the Old Indic traditions, they ought not to be privileged or favored any more than the Old Indic should be privileged or favored. That the New Indic traditions in their Indo-Anglian forms are "modern" or representatives of "modernity," in contrast to the Old Indic and the Indo-Islamic that are supposedly "traditional," is neither an advantage nor a compliment. If post-modernism has taught us anything, it is that the term "modern" is a loaded notion that, on a superficial level, passes itself off as a universal claim but, in fact, on a deeper level, is an historically derived ideology of self-interest among relatively small cultural elites.

The coherence, finally, in Indian history and civilization, or perhaps better, in the civilisation-state of India, is the on-going great conversation occurring among and between its many constituent peoples with their varying frameworks of meaning and their contesting sets of values. Coherence, in other words, need not be thought of as a thing, or an entity or an abstraction. It is best thought of as a process unfolding over time, a struggle for meaning and purpose and integrity. Sometimes the conversation is exhilarating, creative and unifying. Sometimes it is dull, tedious and boring. Sometimes it is aggressive, polemical and disruptive. What is important in the final analysis is the attempt to communicate, to negotiate, to understand and to keep faith with all of the conversation partners. The word "coherence" is from the Latin *co-haerere*, "to adhere," "to stick together." A rough Sanskrit equivalent would be a "disciplined holding together," or, in other words, the old word "*yoga*."

The Problem of "Religion" in Indian History and Civilization

In our historical discussion in chapters 2 and 3 as well as in our immediately preceding discussion of coherence, it has become increasingly clear that the various cultural periods and the various frameworks of meaning in the civilisation-state of India are inextricably related to the many religious visions that have developed throughout the history of the subcontinent. Even the notion of the secular state in the modern period is inconceivable and unintelligible apart from the many religious traditions, as our discussions of Neo-Hindu and Neo-Muslim reform movements have indicated. An understanding of religion is fundamental and basic to an understanding of the civilisation-state of India. This was already indicated early along in chapter 1, but a full discussion of the theoretical significance of the notion of "religion" was deferred to this fourth chapter.

In chapter 1 a brief survey of the the various "world religions" in India was provided (in terms of Hinduism, Buddhism, Jainism, Christianity, Islam, Sikhism, Parsiism, Judaism, and tribal traditions), but it was suggested that such a characterization of "religion" in terms of the so-called "world religions" was hardly adequate for a proper understanding of the significance of religion in South Asia. Peter Hardy's wry comment was mentioned—"that Islam in South Asia has been united only by a few common rituals and by the aspirations of its scholars"—as was Frykenberg's observation that the lame attempts to define Hinduism "has led this concept into trackless deserts of nonsense."[30] Neither "Islam" nor "Hinduism" as proper names seem to mean very much, according to Hardy and Frykenberg, much less the term "religion."

The discussions of W. C. Smith and Frits Staal were also cited, the former showing how the great "-isms" (Hindu-ism, Buddh-ism, and so forth) are little more than the reifying constructs of Enlightenment European scholarship,[31] and the latter showing how the term "religion" itself has been derived largely from the Western monotheist traditions of Judaism, Christianity and Islam and then improperly applied to other traditions. Staal's point is that the term "religion" for the most part is a "naming" rather than a general or generic notion. That is, it is a proper name derived from the western monotheist traditions and then extrapolated and improperly utilized as a general notion outside of its proper framework of reference.[32] Both W. C. Smith and Staal recommend that we stop using the term "religion" and attempt to find a more precise and accurate terminology.

As may be recalled, I took issue to some extent with both W. C. Smith and Staal in terms of their recommendation that we stop using the term "religion." Because a term has been used by a group of scholars in a reifying manner or as a naming term, it does not follow that it should no longer be used. It is quite possible that a given term has a general significance but has been wrongly formulated up to now, and it may well be the case that a term can be given a proper general characterization, thereby clarifying older provincial and improper usages and advancing our understanding of the matter under consideration. Such, it seems to me, is the case with the term "religion." Although it may have been treated for the most part in a provincial, naming manner (derived from Jewish, Christian and Islamic paradigms) and then employed in a largely non-theoretical manner as a way of identifying a set of things called "world religions" (Hindu-ism, Buddh-ism, and so forth), the term nevertheless does point to something much more central and general in human culture and understanding.

It is, of course, not the purpose of this monograph to come up with a complete theory of religion for the field of religious studies, but the rich complexity and density of the Indian material demands at least some attention to the theoretical problem if for no other reason than that of properly understanding the Indian context. In other words, the theoretical problem of "religion" must be addressed at least to the extent of making clear what is at issue in the Indian context. If what follows also contributes to general issues in theorizing about religion outside of the Indian context, so much the better, but the primary purpose of the following discussion is to clarify the problem of "religion" within the South Asian context. Moreover, as was true in the earlier discussion of coherence and the basic frameworks of meaning in the civilisation-state of India, I shall attempt only a preliminary sketch of a theory of religion for South Asia but one that, I hope, will prove useful in the sequel. I shall proceed, first of all, to propose a definition of the term "religion" that adequately encompasses South Asian traditions, and then, secondly, I shall propose a typology of religions designed to highlight the variety of forms of religion found in South Asia.[33]

The Term "Religion"

The notion of religion, I would like to suggest, involves three basic relations, namely, (1) first, the relation between the human organism and culture (enculturation), (2) second, the relation between the human organism and society (socialization), and (3) third, the relation between culture and society, on the one hand, and the internalization or reflexive awareness of the human organism, on the other (individuation). Religion, in other words, while involving culture (enculturation), society (socialization) and personal development (individuation), cannot be reduced to any one of these factors, but represents, rather, the manner in which these three factors come together in a "normal" or "acculturated" person's life.[34] Furthermore, in contrast to other cultural and social dimensions of human development (for example, the development of other unique human traits such as language, law, art, and so forth), religion has to do with the development of comprehensive interpretive frameworks regarding the meaning and significance of human existence-as-such (together, of course, with an accompanying behavioral life-style in terms of rituals, normative patterns of behavior, and so forth), or, put somewhat differently, the development of a comprehensive interpretive framework that renders human existence meaningful, significant and practically workable.[35]

By the expressions "comprehensive interpretive framework" or "comprehensive world-view" I have in mind something like Feuerbach's "species-notion" (*Gattungs-begriff*), that is, comprehensive explanations and interpretations of the meaning of the human species-as-such.[36] Such comprehensive interpretive frameworks may range from highly sophisticated and ramified theological frameworks to relatively simple and direct agnostic, skeptical, atheistic or nihilistic frameworks. They may be reflective of traditional and pre-modern belief-systems of a Christian, Muslim or Jewish kind, or they may be reflective of the most current trends in post-structuralist and post-modernist thought. They may be broadly accepted by large numbers of persons or limited to very small numbers. In most instances the comprehensive interpretive frameworks will closely correlate with the levels of material wealth and the structures of education and social reality in which they operate. What makes them religious is their capacity to provide an overall sense of the meaning and significance of the human venture for normal persons.

Religion-formation is itself a process over and above enculturation, socialization and individuation. The process by means of which the human organism assimilates or coordinates the three relations of enculturation, socialization and individuation into a comprehensive interpretive framework or a comprehensive worldview (together with an accompanying behavioral life-style), thereby becoming a mature and normal person within a given social reality, may be said to be the process of religionization. That which emerges as a result of what has been assimilated or coordinated by the process of religionization may be said to be the person's religion. Religion, therefore, though not by any means the only component in the development of a normal person, is nevertheless a fundamental and unique aspect of human development.

I am suggesting, in other words, a broadly anthropological notion of religion and religionization which makes the religious dimension along with such other dimensions as language, law, art, and so forth, an important component in any normal human life. Obviously such a broad view of religion goes beyond the traditional so-called "world religions." Many people are attracted, of course, to the large-scale comprehensive interpretive frameworks and institutional structures of traditional Christian or Islamic traditions, but not by any means all. Many prefer, rather, small-scale frameworks and intimate institutional contexts not much larger than the family or a local *āśrama*. Many prefer interpretive frameworks totally detached from the traditional "world religions," interpretive frameworks that are secular ideologies or simple pragmatic strategies for survival in complex modern societies. All such comprehensive frameworks are nevertheless religious in the sense that I am suggesting. The religious dimension or the process of religionization is not this or that substantive interpretation, but, rather, the meaning-conferring dimension of human maturation and development, the manner in which a mature, normal person comes to terms with the human condition and is enabled thereby to continue to live.

But let me clarify a bit more how I am using the terms "enculturation," "socialization," and "individuation," and what is meant by the relations between them.

1. The relation between the *human organism* and *culture (enculturation)*. The notions of culture and enculturation have been usefully characterized by Melford E. Spiro as follows:

> "culture" designates a cognitive system, that is, a set of "propositions," both descriptive (e.g., "the planet earth sits on the back of a turtle") and normative (e.g., "it is wrong to kill"), about nature, man and society that are more or less embedded in interlocking higher-order networks and configurations. Cultural and non-cultural propositions differ in two important dimensions. First, cultural propositions are *traditional*, that is, they are developed in the historical experience of social groups, and as a social heritage, they are acquired by social actors through various processes of social transmission (enculturation) rather than constructed by them from their private experiences. Second, cultural propositions are encoded in *collective*, rather than private, signs (indices and icons, to employ Pierce's distinctions, as well as symbols).[37]

Spiro quickly adds,

> This is not to say that cultural statements, rules, values, norms, and the like are always stated in propositional form, for clearly they are not, but that they are susceptible of statement in that form.[38]

The important point about culture and enculturation, as Spiro has stressed, is that they relate primarily to the cognitive side of human development, and especially those cognitive components that are traditional and collective, that is, handed down and "discoverable . . . in collective representations of social groups."[39] Regarding the cognitive dimension of our discussion of religion in the South Asian context, however, it is important to note that the cognitive systems are most often polymorphous or plastic (at least in the Old Indic traditions) and cannot be formulated in a clearcut, direct manner. Hence, "world religions" discourse can be very misleading from the perspective of traditional Hindu and Buddhist traditions. A "world religion" such as Christianity or Islam has a fairly specific and identifiable body of determinate beliefs together with a determinate revelation in terms of a sacred person or a sacred book (or both) that can be articulated in a general way. Few such determinate formulations are found in the environments of Hindu and Buddhist traditions, not because these traditions failed somehow to consolidate their belief-systems but, rather, because these traditions argue that ultimate truth is in principle indeterminate. Cognitive certainty or determinacy is not possible on the highest levels of the spiritual life, according to many of the the Old Indic formations.

2. The relation between the *human organism* and *society (socialization)*. Here again Spiro's treatment is helpful.

> If "culture" refers to traditional propositions about nature, man and society, then "society," as I am using that term, refers to traditional forms of social relations, in which "social" refers to a range extending from a dyad to a nation-state.
>
> Cultural acquisition begins in childhood, and children acquire culture from persons who are their "significant others," that is, persons—usually parents or parent surrogates—with whom they have a powerful emotional involvement, both positive and negative. . . .
>
> [I]n their modes of socialization and enculturation, not only do parents intentionally transmit the meanings or messages *of* cultural propositions to their children, but they also unintentionally transmit another set of messages to them: messages about the kinds of persons they (the parents) are, the conditions under which they offer and withhold love, and punishment, and the like.[40]

In terms of our treatment of religon, it is important to stress Spiro's focus on "society" and "socialization" as referring to a "range extending from a dyad to a nation-state." This again is a basic weakness of "world religions" discourse as well as the many discussions of religion in terms of institutional forms such as "churches" or "denominations." The tendency is to think of religion in terms of macro-communities instead of micro-communities. In the South Asian context, however, the vehicle for socialization is sometimes little more than the *guru-śiṣya* relation (the dyadic relation between "teacher" and "student") or a small *āśrama* community consisting of little more than the teacher's residence or hermitage and a few pupils. Family and caste are somewhat larger institutional settings as are the regional monastic communities of the Buddhists, Jains and later Hindu *saṃnyāsa* communities. Overall, however, in the South Asian context, there is an absence of large institutional frameworks like "churches," "denominations," or large bureaucratic organizations of any kind beyond caste and regional associations. Religious socialization, at least in many of the Old Indic formations, is frequently micro-communal, the most prevalent structure being that of the dyadic relation of *guru* and student.

3. The relation between *culture* and *society*, on the one hand, and the *internalization* or reflexive awareness of the human organism, on the other (*individuation*). Regarding the issue of individuation, the work of the sociologist of knowledge, Thomas Luckmann, is helpful. He points out at the outset that individuation is not a matter of subjectivity. Says Luckmann,

> Subjective experience considered in isolation is restricted to mere actuality and is void of meaning. Meaning is not an inherent quality of subjective processes but is bestowed on it in interpretive acts. In such acts a subjective process is grasped retrospectively and located in an interpretive scheme.[41]

Individuation arises, rather, out of the intersubjective encounters with others and requires a reflexive distancing or stepping back from the flow of immediacy, that "permits the construction of interpretive schemes" and "systems of meaning."[42] Through the development of "interpretive schemes," "systems of meaning" and "symbol systems," the process of individuation allows the human organism to rise above its purely biological nature, and, according to Luckmann, this process of becoming a civilized person is inextricably linked with the concept of religion.

> Religion is rooted in a basic anthropological fact: the transcendence of biological nature by human organisms. The individual human potential for transcendence is realized, originally, in social processes that rest on the reciprocity of face-to-face situations. These processes lead to the construction of objective world views, the articulation of sacred universes and, under certain circumstances, to institutional specialization of religion. The social forms of religion are thus based on what is, in a sense, an individid-

> ual religious phenomenon: the individuation of consciousness and conscience in the matrix of human intersubjectivity.[43]

Luckmann goes on to point out, of course, as did Spiro mentioned above, that empirically each human organism does not construct its own symbolic universe of meaning. People, rather, are born into frameworks of meaning, and they internalize the historically derived frameworks of meaning as they grow and mature.[44] Individuation, thus, is a social process whereby culture (through enculturation) and society (through socialization) become internalized, and, as it were, create "subjectivity" (as well as an "objective" and moral world in which one can be a self or person in some sense). Individuation is that dimension of religionization having to do with the manner in which the human organism comes to be internally aware of the relation between culture and society, on the one hand, and his or her own identity as a normal person, on the other. Since individuation is itself a social process dependent upon the related processes of enculturation and socialization which greatly vary from culture to culture and over time, it is to be expected that there will be a great variety of "normal person" types, ranging in an area such as South Asia from the hierarchical, "dividual" and polymorphous notions of a normal person in Old Indic formations to modern notions of the abstract, isolated "individual" in New Indic formations.

By way of summary, then, the notion of religion has to do with three basic factors (culture, society and the human organism) in relation with one another (through the processes of enculturation, socialization and individuation). Religion-formation has to do with a unique process known as religionization, a process over and above enculturation, socialization and individuation. Religionization is that process whereby the human organism becomes a mature, normal person through the assimilation and coordination of enculturation, socialization and individuation into a comprehensive interpretive framework (together with an accompanying behavioral life-style) that renders human existence meaningful and significant.

Towards a Typology of Religions

Thus far "religion" and "religionization" have been discussed largely as a set of abstract relations, and little attempt has been made to provide any empirical content whatever beyond a few broad comparative comments. This has been by design. The great fault in most theoretical discussions of religion is to move too quickly to the level of substance and content, thereby establishing a substantive bias at the outset of any analysis, a bias that then becomes an integral component of the analysis and from which the analysis can never be methodologically distinguished. A better approach, as we have attempted above, is to identify certain crucial relational features of religion and religionization regardless of the synchronic or diachronic features of this or that substantive religious tradition. In this way it becomes possible to construct a theoretical model that enables one to analyze any manifestation of religious content in a comparative and critical manner.

The three relational features that have been identified (enculturation, socialization and individuation), which provide the basis for the process of religionization, correspond approximately to the cognitive, the communal and the personal. While it is not possible to give a single definition to each of these, it is possible to point to a continuum or range of meanings which have been given to the cognitive (enculturation), the communal (socialization) and the personal (individuation).

The *cognitive (enculturation) continuum* or range moves from a limit of total cognitive determinacy on one end of the continuum to total cognitive indeterminacy on the other end. The former limit anticipates the possibility of an unequivocal and specific account of what is the case. The latter limit anticipates the possibility of a radical indeterminacy or incommersurability regarding cognitive matters.[45] To use a Sanskrit idiom, the former would be *saguṇa* or the claim that truth can be given a determinate formulation. The latter would be *nirguṇa* or the claim that truth, finally, is radically indeterminate, "without qualities," or contentless.

The *communal (socialization) continuum* or range moves from a limit of macro-communal formulation (global, transnational, multinational or national communal structures) on one end of the continuum to a limit of micro-communal formulation (family, caste, village, local monastic community, or *guru-śiṣya* structures) on the other end. The former limit anticipates the possibility of large-scale meaningful communities, possibly of global or species-wide extension. The latter limit anticipates the possibility of small-scale meaningful communities, as small possibly as the one-to-one dyadic *guru-śiṣya* relationship.

Finally, the *personal (individuation) continuum* or range moves from a limit of the completely contextualized, polymorphous and hierarchical individual (in Dumont's sense, or what Marriott calls the "dividual"), characteristic largely of pre-modern societies on one end of the continuum to a limit of the full modern notion of the independent citizen or the abstract, isolated individual (in Dumont's sense) on the other end. The former limit anticipates such traditional notions as hierarchy, exchange, inequality, ascribed status (in contrast to merited status) and holism as a measure of individuation. The latter limit anticipates such modern notions as equality, individual liberty, merited status (in contrast to ascribed status) and the discrete monadic individual as the measure of individuation.

These three relational features may then be charted as follows:

THE COGNITIVE CONTINUUM:	
Cognitive determinacy	Cognitive indeterminacy
THE COMMUNAL CONTINUUM:	
Macro-communal	Micro-communal
THE INDIVIDUATION CONTINUUM:	
Individuality (hierarchical)	Individuality (abstractive or isolative)

The three continuums with their six limits then yield eight possible combinations or types which may be charted as follows:

1. Cognitive determinacy Macro-communal Individuality (hierarchical)	5. Cognitive indeterminacy Macro-communal Individuality (hierarchical)
2. Cognitive determinacy Macro-communal Individuality (abstractive)	6. Cognitive indeterminacy Macro-communal Individuality (abstractive)
3. Cognitive determinacy Micro-communal Individuality (hierarchical)	7. Cognitive indeterminacy Micro-communal Individuality (hierarchical)
4. Cognitive determinacy Micro-communal Individuality (abstractive)	8. Cognitive indeterminacy Micro-communal Individuality (abstractive)

At least three aspects of the relations among the eight types are especially worth noting. First, the types on the left of the chart (types 1–4) have in common the feature of cognitive determinacy, whereas the types on the right (types 5–8) have in common the feature of cognitive indeterminacy.[46] Second, the types on the upper half of the chart (types 1–2 and 5–6) all have in common the feature of being macro-communal, whereas the types on the lower half of the chart (types 3–4 and 7–8) have in common the feature of being micro-communal. Third, the eight types appear to form four common pairs (types 1 and 5, types 2 and 6, types 3 and 7 and types 4 and 8) in the sense that these pairs all share at least two of the three variables, differing only in terms of the variable cognitive determinacy versus cognitive indeterminacy.

Using such a relational typology, and keeping in mind that our notion of religion is especially sensitive to the three main relations of enculturation (the cognitive), socialization (the communal) and individuation (the personal), we should be able to identify, at least by way of rough approximation, eight distinct types of religion. The expression "by way of rough approximation," however, is an important qualification, inasmuch as the structure of the typology is largely formal or abstract and any empirical exemplification can only more or less coincide with the ideal type. Moreover, it must be remembered that we are dealing with the notion of a continuum rather than hard and fast distinctions, and, hence, again, the empirical exemplifications only more or less coincide with a particular place on the continuum. There may indeed be many more than simply eight types (depending upon how much one wishes to refine the typological model), taking note, for example, of various median or mediating traditions that would fall somewhat in the middle of a given continuum. Overall, however, the typology has the merit of moving in the direction of increasing specification in our discussion of types of religion. There may be many types of religion, but there are at least these eight typological possibilities in terms of the three variables we have identified.

By way of exemplifying and identifying eight basic types of religion, I would offer a preliminary framework (table 4.2). I am especially interested in identifying South Asian traditions, but I include, of course, exemplifications outside of South Asia in order to provide an appropriate comparative framework.

The pair of types identified as "tradition-oriented, 'pre-modern' religions" (types 1 and 5) refers to those religious traditions that emerged during what Anthony Giddens has called the period of "traditional states," "imperial states" and "absolutist states," that is, the centuries prior to the development of the modern nation-state system.[47] The pair of types identified as "polity-oriented, 'nation-state' religions" (types 2 and 6) refers to modern religious traditions that have clear affinities with the modern nation-state system.[48] The remaining two pairs of types, namely, "experience-oriented, 'shamanic-ecstatic' reli-

TABLE 4.2
Types of Religion

Type 1.	Cognitive Determinacy Macro-communal Individuality (hierarchical) **[*tradition-oriented,* *'pre-modern' religions*]** —Zorastrian Reform —Hebrew Israelite —Pre-Reformation Roman Catholic —Tridentine Roman Catholic —Eastern Orthodox —Confucian (State and Neo-) —Sunni and Shi'a Islamic	Type 5.	Cognitive Indeterminacy Macro-communal Individuality (hierarchical) **[*tradition-oriented,* *'pre-modern' religions*]** —Old Iranian —Brāhmaṇical Vedic —Jain (non-monastic) and Buddhist (non-monastic) —Vaiṣṇava Hindu (Bhakti) and Śaiva Hindu (Bhakti) —Smārta Hindu —Non-'Khalistani' Sikh
Type 2.	Cognitive Determinacy Macro-communal Individuality (abstractive) **[*polity-oriented,* *'nation-state' religions*]** —Islamic Republic of Iran —Islamic Republic of Pakistan —People's Republic of China —Zionist Israel —Hindu RSS-VHP-BJP —Arya Samaj —'Khalistani' Sikh	Type 6.	Cognitive Indeterminacy Macro-communal Individuality (abstractive) **[*polity-oriented,* *'nation-state' religions*]** —American civil religion (biblical-cum-secular) —Indic civil religion (Gandhian-Nehruvian) —Church of England (Anglican) —Japanese civil religion
Type 3.	Cognitive Determinacy Micro-communal Individuality (hierarchical) **[*experience-oriented,* *'shamanic-ecstatic' religions*]** —Evangelical-Pentecostal- Charismatic ("born-again") —Millenialist-Fundamentalist Protestant —Sufi, Hasidic	Type 7.	Cognitive Indeterminacy Micro-communal Individuality (hierarchical) **[*experience-oriented,* *'shamanic-ecstatic' religions*]** —Village Hindu —Tribal (Indic, *et al.*) —Taoist —Hindu and Buddhist Tantra —Siddha Yoga, ISKCON, Satya Sai Baba —New Age
Type 4.	Cognitive Determinacy Micro-communal Individuality (abstractive) **[*askesis-oriented,* *'ascetic-enstatic' religions*]** —Catholic and Orthodox monastic —Lutheran and Reformed Protestant —Orthodox, Conservative and Reform Judaic —Islamic and Catholic modernist —Brahmo Samaj, Ramakrishna Mission, Aurobindo	Type 8.	Cognitive Indeterminacy Micro-communal Individuality (abstractive) **[*askesis-oriented,* *'ascetic-enstatic' religions*]** —Sāṃnyāsa Yoga —Sāṃkhya-yoga —Jain monastic —Buddhist monastic —Mādhyamika-Yogācara —Vedānta Monastic (Daśanāmi, Vaiṣṇava —Intinerant Hindu-Buddhist (*pratyeka-buddha, sādhu*)

gions" (types 3 and 7) and "askesis-oriented, 'ascetic-enstatic' religions" (types 4 and 8) refer to religious traditions, whether traditional or modern, that deemphasize macro-communal formulation, even though in some instances they represent sizable numbers of adherents, and focus, rather, on largely personal religious experience, with the 'shamanic-ecstatic' placing a strong emphasis on an expressive religious experience within an intense and close-knit micro-communal setting, and the 'ascetic-enstatic' placing a strong emphasis on introspective, internal spiritual experience in terms of inner-worldly or other-worldly asceticism.[49]

What distinguishes the pairs internally is the matter of cognitive determinacy versus cognitive indeterminacy, and South Asian religions for the most part clearly come out on the side of cognitive indeterminacy. On the cognitive determinacy side are those traditions that have clear-cut belief-systems together with the accompanying conviction that ultimate truth can be given a determinate formulation. To use one of the common interpretive devices from Indian philosophy, one might well say that religions that focus on cognitive determinacy in terms of rational theology or determinate revelation can be called religions "having determinate qualities," or, in other words, *saguṇa*-religions. On the cognitive indeterminacy side are those traditions that allow for great diversity or a rich cognitive pluralism, including what S. C. Dube has called "minimal cognitive participation," together with the accompanying conviction that ultimate truth is finally indeterminate, or "without determinate qualities," or, in other words, *nirguṇa*-religions.[50]

Although South Asian religions are clearly on the *nirguṇa* side for the most part, there are some interesting exceptions. The Hindu RSS-VHP-BJP, for example, or the Arya Samaj, appear to have close affinities with such cognitively determinate, polity-oriented, 'nation-state' traditions as the Islamic Republic of Iran or the Islamic Republic of Pakistan. Or again, there appears to be an interesting affinity between the Brahmo Samaj or the Ramakrishna Mission and such cognitively determinate, askesis-oriented, 'ascetic-enstatic' traditions as one or another Reformed Protestant or Christian monastic tradition. By the same token, Christian traditions, which for the most part appear on the cognitive determinacy side of the typology, also show some interesting exceptions. American civil religion or the Church of England, for example, with their traditions of a broad-based, rather pragmatic cognitive pluralism appear to have definite affinities with religions of cognitive indeterminacy.

It is also interesting to note that the typology helps to differentiate religions with definite political inclinations versus religions that are for the most part non-political or a-political. The types in the upper half of the typology are all macro-communal, thereby becoming involved, willy nilly, in issues of statecraft, governance and political allegiance, either in terms of traditional, pre-modern regional polities (types 1 and 5) or in terms of the modern system of nation-states (types 2 and 6). The types in the lower half of the typology are all micro-communal, thereby frequently eschewing political entanglements or involvement in the large institutional structures of the conventional world, at least in theory, for the sake of pursuing intensely personal religious experience.

In this regard the typology helps us to locate the various Neo-Hindu formations discussed in the last chapter. The Arya Samaj and the Hindu RSS-VHP-BJP, for example, were and are highly motivated politically and have had aspirations to attain all-India macro-communal status. The Gandhian-Nehruvian Neo-Hindu nationalist movement, which I have referred to in the typology simply as "Indic civil religion (Gandhian-Nehruvian)," has also been highly motivated politically and has, indeed, been the basic power-base for the modern Indian nation-state since independence (and will be the primary focus of our discussion in the next chapter). On the other hand, the traditions of Siddha Yoga, Satya Sai Baba, the Brahmo Samaj, the Ramakrishna Mission, and others, have tended towards a non-political or a-political orientation. It should perhaps be remarked, of course, that just because a tradition is in theory non-political or a-political, it does not necessarily follow that it will not become involved politically from time to time, sometimes deeply so. The Lutheran "state" churches, for example, have tended towards "nation-state" status, even though in theory Lutheran traditions more naturally appear to belong in type 4. Overall, however, it appears to be clearly the case that some religions have definite affinities towards politicization by reason of their attaining macro-communal status vis-à-vis the other two variables of enculturation and individuation.

The basic reason for introducing the typology is to provide a preliminary theoretical device for identifying religious traditions in a much more specific manner than the conventional categories of "world religions" discourse. One can certainly quarrel with this or that aspect of the typological placement of traditions, and one might well argue for a much broader set of variables beyond those of enculturation, socialization and individuation. Furthermore, it is clearly the case that a complete typology and taxonomy of religions would require a much fuller treatment than the limits of this particular monograph permit. Overall, however, even with this fairly elementary and provisional attempt at a typology, it becomes immediately clear that the singular abstraction "Hinduism" is really a complex, pluralistic network of religions, including Vaiṣṇava, Śaiva, Smārta, Village Hindu, Tribal, Sāṃnyāsa

Yoga, Vedānta, RSS, Brahmo Samaj, Siddha Yoga, Ramakrishna Mission, Satya Sai Baba traditions, and many others as well. Precisely the same can be said about the singular abstractions of "Islam," "Christianity," "Sikhism," and so forth. Moreover, the typology opens up a much broader conceptual field for the analysis and taxonomy of religions. One is no longer tied to pre-modern, conventional labels such as "Christian," "Muslim," "Hindu," and so forth, nor is religion limited to pre-modern or traditional belief-systems of one kind or another. One can begin to trace what I have called the process of "religionization" in a great variety of cultural and social environments and into a great variety of movements and traditions that do not appear to be "religious" in the pre-theoretical, conventional sense but, in fact, are profoundly "religious" in a critical, theoretical sense. Put somewhat differently, the typology has hopefully shown that to say that 83% of the present population of India is "Hindu," 11% "Muslim," and so forth, is to say next to nothing at all. The typology exhibits twenty or more distinct religious traditions in a great variety of social configurations all coming under the umbrella in some sense of the word "Hindu" or "Neo-Hindu." The diversity is not so extreme perhaps within "Muslim" traditions, but there is nothing like a monolithic Islam in India any more than there is a monolithic "Hinduism."

Let me close this chapter with the words of the social critic, Rajni Kothari, who makes a similar point, not simply with respect to religions, but with respect to the overall social reality of modern India.

> [O]ne must recognize that . . . there has been a set of problems which has today brought us to a point of crisis in respect of this very relationship between the Hindu 'majority' and the various minorities. By minorities I don't only mean Muslims and Sikhs and Christians but also the great diversity of tribals and large parts of Hindu society itself, *viz.*, its various peripheries such as the Dalits and various other socially depressed and 'backward' castes and communities. They are all minorities. In fact, one way to think about India is *as a people and a land made up of a series of minorities.* For Hindu society itself is internally highly structured and diverse and pluralistic. There are castes and sub-castes and clans and all manner of groupings and sub-groupings. You go in any region and you will immediately be told that there is this caste and that caste, this grouping and that grouping, this ethnic identity and that ethnic identity—*it is all really a set of minorities.* It is thus wrong to think of Hindus as a 'majority' except that it is being thought like that of late and that is what is causing the problems.[51]

5

The Secular as Religion and the Community as Citizen

[W]hat has been established in the past half a century is the upper caste Hindu raj, depriving the backwards and the minorities. . . . Q. But aren't we a secular nation? *A. That's just gloss. But in various forms the political system has reacted against the upper caste Hindu raj. . . . The reaction arises because they [the backward groups] are not party to the operations of power. . . .* Q. Is the structure not delivering what Gandhi and Nehru wanted? *A. An iniquitous social structure has produced an iniquitous power structure.*

—V. P. Singh, *From India Today*

The contradiction in India's concept of secularism was its simultaneous commitment to communities and to equal citizenship.

—Lloyd and Susanne Rudolph, *In Pursuit of Lakshmi*

India's Hybrid Discourse of Modernity

In some ways India is simply one among a number of other, modern nation-states, and it is possible to treat India in the same general manner that one would treat other states. Thus, one can set forth the social and cultural reality of contemporary India, the history of India, and the philosophical and religious traditions of India in a direct, conventional manner, and the preceding chapters can be read on one level as precisely that sort of undertaking. In many other ways, however, India is remarkably different from other nation-states, not simply by reason of the sheer antiquity and continuity of its civilization but more by reason of the complex density of traditions that exist side by side on the subcontinent, ranging from archaic traditions to the most sophisticated developments in the late-twentieth-century high-tech arena. The preceding chapters, it is to be hoped, can also be read as laying out the remarkably idiosyncratic texture, the sheer "otherness," of the history and culture of India.

Recalling once again our two suggested metaphors for India, namely, the geological metaphor of layers or tectonic plates or the metaphor of the "down-grower" (*nyagrodha*) or banyan tree, the same sort of paradoxical juxtaposition shows itself. From the perspective of the geological metaphor, while it is true enough that the various discrete layers or tectonic plates maintain a balance that provides a basic stability that permits India to survive over centuries, indeed millennia, there are nevertheless deep fault lines among and between the layers or plates wherein pressures build up over long periods of time issuing, finally, in periodic upheavals that tear open the fabric of the entire cultural terrain. Or, from the perspective of the metaphor of the banyan tree, while it is true enough that India is simply one more tree in the great forest of nation-states, India is not just any tree but, rather, the dramatically twisted and fascinating banyan tree with its secondary trunks reaching out in every direction and its tendrils "growing down" into new areas, assimilating and absorbing the ground all around it, driven by an inner impulse continuously to replicate itself in embodiment after embodiment.

A similar kind of *double entendre* operates when looking at India as a "secular state." D. E. Smith has defined the notion of a "secular state" in a general manner as follows:

> The secular state is a state which guarantees individual and corporate freedom of religion, deals with the individual as a citizen irrespective of his religion, is not constitutionally connected to a particular religion nor does it seek either to promote or interfere with religion.[1]

The secular state, D. E. Smith continues, involves

> . . . three distinct but interrelated sets of relationships concerning the state, religion and the individual. The three sets of relations are:

> 1. religion and the individual (freedom of religion),
> 2. the state and the individual (citizenship),
> 3. the state and religion (separation of state and religion).
>
> It may help to visualize a triangle in which the two angles at the base represent religion and the state; the apex represents the individual. The sides and base of the triangle represent the three sets of relationships mentioned above.[2]

From such a general, analytic perspective, moreover, as D. E. Smith has persuasively argued, it is legitimate to identify modern India as a "secular state." At the conclusion of his excellent study, Smith poses the basic question and offers his own final assessment:

> Is India a secular state? My answer is a qualified "Yes." It is meaningful to speak of India as a secular state. . . . India is a secular state in the same sense in which one can say that India is a democracy. Despite various undemocratic features of Indian politics and government, parliamentary democracy is functioning, and with considerable vigor. Similarly, the secular state; the ideal is clearly embodied in the Constitution. . . . The question must be answered in terms of a dynamic state which has inherited some difficult problems and is struggling hard to overcome them along generally sound lines.[3]

From the perspective of substantive content, however, the picture has not been as clear and straightforward. Anomalies, discrepancies and equivocations have appeared again and again all along the way. Thus, for example, when discussing notions of "state formation," the "secular state," and the concept of the "nation," we found that Ravinder Kumar's formulation of the idea of a multinational "civilisation-state" came closer to an adequate characterization of what India is than the usual discourse about nations and nation-states. Likewise when discussing notions of the modern "individual" and the concept of the "citizen," we found that in modern India there are not only these "New Indic" notions of the "individual" and the "citizen" but a great variety of "Old Indic" notions of hierarchy, "dividuality," and communal identity that are as strong and, in many instances, stronger than the modern notions. So, too, when discussing notions of "religion," we found, of course, conventional characterizations in terms of the "world religions" together with an attempt to fit Hindu, Buddhist and Jain traditions into a comparable mold, but we also found that in India, both with respect to the history of religions and with respect to contemporary sociocultural reality, conventional characterizations in terms of "-isms" or in terms of large institutional structures and determinate belief-systems fit only a very few instances of religion and that we had, therefore, to reformulate the notion of "religion" to accommodate the much richer texture of the spiritual life in India.

Putting the matter somewhat differently, it is, of course, possible in modern India to use the terms "secular," "nation," "state," "individual," "citizen," and "religion" in quite the same way as one would use such terms in a discussion of any modern polity in any number of nation-states. The problem, however, is that one is then speaking about only a surface level or layer of discourse in India. Just below the surface are a whole host of other conceptualizations that are also operating and playing distinctive parts in what is happening in modern India in terms of the discourse about the "secular," the "nation," the "state," the "individual," and "religion." At the very beginning of this monograph reference was made to W. H. Morris-Jones's comment about a "play within the play" in Indian politics and to his remark that "nothing is ever quite what it seems or what it presents itself as being."[4]

The metaphor of a "play within the play," however, probably does not go far enough. Closer perhaps is an analogy from linguistics: the notion of a hybrid language. For a long time in South Asian studies it was noted that a class of Mahāyāna Buddhist texts (for example, the well-known "Lotus Sūtra" or *Saddharmapuṇḍarīka*) was composed in what was apparently a form of classical Sanskrit but containing what appeared to be numerous grammatical errors. The usual explanation offered to account for the errors was that early Mahāyāna monks did not know their classical Sanskrit very well. The Yale Sanskritist Franklin Edgerton, however, discovered that much more was involved in these texts than poor grammatical construction. There was, rather, a different language being used, a peculiar combination of classical Sanskrit and various Prakrits or Middle Indic languages. Edgerton then set about the task of writing a grammar of the language together with a lexicon, which scholars of South Asia now routinely use, and the new language came to be known as "Buddhist Hybrid Sanskrit."[5] The point is that what appeared initially as an incorrect use of one language was, instead, a quite different, albeit related, language.

I want to argue in this chapter that in many ways the discourse about "religion" and the "state" or "nation" in modern India is very much a "hybrid" discourse in this sense and that it is important to understand the significant differences and subtle nuances that separate this "hybrid" discourse of India from other discourses about "religion" and the "state." To be sure, the words tend to look and sound the same—for example, "secular state," "nation," "individudal," "citizen," "religion," and so forth—but the usages and meanings of the words tend to diverge rather significantly from their usage and meaning in the conventional discourse of modern social science. To follow through with our linguistic analogy, whereas the phonology of the discourse about religion and the state in modern India is the same as in other contexts, the syntax and semantic are interestingly different. There is, in other words, not only a "play within the play" operating, some sort of subplot or distraction that a sophisticated observer must catch, but much more than that, an intriguing new language or discourse with a syntax and semantic all its own.

The "Secular" as "Religion"

The Tragic Creation-Narrative: Partition

In any attempt to decipher or comprehend India's "hybrid" discourse of modernity, it is important to understand that in August of 1947, the old British Raj did not give birth to one but, rather, two independent Dominions, namely, India and Pakistan. India became a "Sovereign Democratic Republic" when its Constitution came into effect on 26 January 1950, following adoption of its draft Constitution by its Constituent Assembly on 26 November 1949, and Pakistan became the "Islamic Republic of Pakistan" when its first Constitution came into effect on 23 March 1956, following adoption of its draft Constitution by its Constituent Assembly on 29 February 1956. Partition was the defining event of modern, independent India and Pakistan, and it is hardly an exaggeration to assert that partition continues to be the defining event of modern India and Pakistan even now after fifty years of independence. Partition, moreover, I wish to argue, was and is a profoundly *religious* event for both sides, namely, Neo-Muslim Pakistan as well as so-called "secular" India, and most of the agony over religion throughout the South Asian region is to a large extent traceable to it. Partition is at the heart not only of the great regional conflicts of the Northwest region, namely, the conflict with the Sikhs in the state of Punjab and the continuing warfare and strife in the state of Jammu and Kashmir. It is also an important component or factor in a whole series of religous-cum-political conflicts reaching down to the present time, including (*a*) the secession of Pakistan's Eastern Province and the founding of the People's Republic of Bangladesh in 1971, (*b*) the deep suspicions about Muslims in India as a pampered and alien community, symbolized by the furor among Muslim and Neo-Muslim groups over the Shah Bano case and the even greater furor among Hindu and Neo-Hindu groups over the passage of the Muslim Women (Protection of Rights on Divorce) Bill of 1986, (*c*) the social unrest in modern India generated by resentment of the "socially and educationally backward classes," symbolized by the famous Mandal Commission Report of 1980 calling for just under fifty percent (49.5%) of compensatory discrimination for OBCs or "other backward classes," and, finally, (*d*) the well-known Babri Masjid-Ramjanmabhoomi controversy in Ayodhya in the state of Uttar Pradesh. To be sure, partition as a defining *religious* event is not by any means the only event or condition for an appropriate analysis and explanation of these great religious controversies currently tearing the fabric of India's cultural life, but I would argue that it is, indeed, one of the necessary and central events or conditions for understanding India's current agony over religion. In many ways it is the core plot in the unfolding narrative of modern, independent India.

Interestingly enough, the genesis of the idea of partition is little more than a century old, a product of what we have called the Indo-Anglian period, and specifically, that period in the later decades of the nineteenth and the early decades of the twentieth century when Neo-Hindu and Neo-Muslim groups were first encountering one another. It may be recalled from chapter 3 that the Neo-Hindu and Neo Muslim (Anglo-Islamic) traditions were of two types on either side.[6] That is to say, on the Neo-Hindu side, there were both "Neo-Hindu reformist and nationalist movements" (including such figures and movements as Rammohun Roy, the Brahmo Samaj, the Arya Samaj, the Ramakrishna-Vivekananda movement, Aurobindo Ghose, V. D. Savarkar, M. K. Gandhi, and others) as well as "Neo-Hindu revisionist and internationalist movements" (including such figures and movements as Paramahamsa Yogananda, Meher Baba, Satya Sai Baba, the Swaminarayana movement, and others). Similarly on the Neo-Muslim (or Anglo-Islamic) side, there were both the "Neo-Muslim reformist and accommodationist movements" (including such figures and movements as the Deoband school of 'ulama', the Jami'at al-'ulama'-i Hind, Hasan Ahmed Madani, and Abul Kalam Azad) and the "Neo-Muslim modernist and separatist movements" (including such figures and movements as the modernist Anglo-Oriental College at Aligarh, Sayyid Ahmad Khan, Muhammad Iqbal, the Muslim League, and Muhammad 'Ali Jinnah).

The idea of partition or two-nation separatism had its base primarily in the "Neo-Muslim modernist and separatist" tradition of Aligarh modernism, and, as was mentioned in chapter 2, its first clear spokesperson was Sayyid Ahmad Khan (1817–98). This tradition itself, of course, was in many respects a direct response to the "Neo-Hindu reformist and nationalist" traditions which had been building throughout the nineteenth century and had reached an important watershed with the founding of the Indian National Congress in 1885.[7] Sayyid Ahmad Khan was suspicious of the very idea of an Indian National Congress that could speak for India in its entirety. Such a view, he believed, was either naive or a cover for Hindu hegemony or both. Says Sayyid Ahmad Khan,

> Friends, in India there live two prominent nations which are distinguished by the names of Hindus and Mussulmans. Just as a man has some principal organs, similarly these two nations are like the principal limbs of India.[8]

In 1888 he comments as follows about the Indian National Congress:

> The aims and objects of the Indian National Congress are based upon an ignorance of history and present-day realities; they do not take into consideration that India is inhabited by different nationalities; they presuppose that the Muslims, the Marathas, the Brahmins, the Kshatriyas, the Banias, the Sudras, the Sikhs, the Bengalis, the Madrasis, and the Pesawaris can all be treated alike and all of them belong to the same nation. The Congress thinks that they profess the same religion, that they speak the same language, that their way of life and customs are the same.... I consider the experiment which the Indian National Congress wants to make fraught with dangers and suffering for all the nationalities of India, specially for the Muslims.[9]

Sayyid Ahmad Khan's view was not at the time a widespread view, and many Neo-Muslims (especially among the Deoband "reformist and accomodationist" traditions) were sympathetic to the Indian National Congress movement. This early phase of the nationalist movement was hardly radical, and the Indian National Congress was broadly inclusive of a great variety of groups, including, for example, at its meeting in 1887, some 965 Hindus, 221 Muslims and 62 "others" (European Christians, Indian Christians, Jains, Jews, Parsis, Sikhs, and so forth).[10] It largely accepted the liberal-democratic principles of British parliamentary democracy and looked upon British rule as basically benevolent. Recalling our earlier reference to Percival Spear's identifying five types of response to the coming of the British (namely, the "military," the "reactionary," the "acceptance" or westernizing, the "orthodox-renewal" and the "solution of synthesis"), clearly the early Indian National Congress represented the "acceptance" or Westernizing mode.

This was to change, however, in the first decade of the twentieth century when the British partition of Bengal in 1905—ostensibly a purely administrative move by the viceroy, Lord Curzon, to make the administration of the overly large region of Bengal more workable by creating a largely Muslim East Bengal and Assam and a largely Hindu West Bengal, Bihar and Orissa, an administrative change that was finally rescinded in 1911–12 when the capital of the Raj was shifted from Calcutta to New Delhi—coincided with the emergence of a more radical and extremist nationalist movement (deeply resentful of the partition but also angry about a variety of other issues as well in the northwest region of the Punjab and in the western region of Maharashtra) led by such Neo-Hindu figures as Aurobindo Ghose (1872-1950) and Bankim Chandra Chatterjee (1838–1894) in Bengal, B. G. Tilak (1856-1920) in Maharashtra, and Lala Lajpat Rai (1865–1928) (an Arya Samaj leader) in Punjab. Aurobindo, Chatterjee, Tilak, Rai, and other extremists tended to use Hindu religious imagery in their fiery rhetoric which had the (perhaps unintended) effect of driving away Muslim supporters who had been all along somewhat suspicious of the dominantly Neo-Hindu nationalist movement. It was not long afterward, specifically 1906, that a group of Neo-Muslims from Aligarh and Dacca (in Bengal) first approached the viceroy about a possible separate electorate for the Muslim community in India, and it was also in 1906 that the All-India Muslim League was founded in Dacca.

The extremists in the Indian National Congress eventually lost their influence, and more moderate national leaders came to the fore again in the second decade of the twentieth century, culminating, of course, in Gandhi's taking over the leadership of the nationalist movement in 1920 after the death of M. G. Ranade (in 1901), G. K. Gokhale (in 1915) and B. G. Tilak (in 1920). By this time, however, the Indian National Congress had moved from its earlier "acceptance" or Westernizing mode of response and was basically set on a course of seeking independence from British rule. The key task was one of devising a nationalist strategy that would mobilize the country politically. For a time the developing nationalist movement was broadly inclusive as can be seen, for example, in the cooperation of the Muslim League with the Congress in the Lucknow Pact of 1916 (providing for balanced representation by Muslim League members and Congress members in provincial assemblies) and Congress's and Gandhi's vigorous support of the Muslim effort (the so-called Khilafat movement that continued from 1919 to 1924) to save the pan-Islamic institution of the caliphate, which, as was mentioned in chapter 2, finally failed when the caliphate was abolished by Ataturk in Turkey in 1924.

More and more, however, the nationalist movement took a Neo-Hindu turn, and Muslims in general, and many Neo-Muslims in the modernist Aligarh tradition in particular, became increasingly alienated. The Neo-Muslim alienation had a responsive echo on the Neo-Hindu side with the growing radicalism of the older Arya Samaj (especially in the Punjab region) and with the emergence of the conservative Hindu Mahasabha (a communal "Great Assembly of Hindus" political organization), politically active after 1923 and led by the conservative Neo-Hindu reformer Pandit Madan Mohan Malaviya (1861–1946), partly in response to the founding of the separatist Muslim League some years earlier but also partly as a pressure group to keep the Neo-Hindu nationalist movement on its basically Hindu track without unnecessary concessions to the various Muslim and Neo-Muslim groups.

This tendency towards separatism was exacerbated by many of the electoral reforms brought about by the British Raj, including the Morley-Minto Reforms of 1909, the Montagu-Chelmsford Reforms of 1919, and the Government of India Act of 1935. To be sure, all were important steps towards eventual self-government in India, but all also established a growing pattern of separate electorates. At first (1909) it was only separate electorates for Muslims. The 1919 reforms increased the system of separate electorates to include Sikhs, Anglo-Indians, Indian Christians and Europeans. Finally, by 1935 separate electorates were provided for Muslims, Sikhs, Indian Christians, Anglo-Indians, Europeans and the so-called Depressed Classes (later to be called Scheduled Castes and Scheduled Tribes).

At every step in the process of developing communal or group-electorates, great regrets were expressed as in the following comments quoted by D. E. Smith from the Montagu-Chelmsford Report of 1918:

> Division by creeds and classes means the creation of political camps organized against each other, and teaches men to think as partisans and not as citizens. . . . We regard any system of communal electorates, therefore, as a very serious hindrance to the development of the self-governing principle.[11]

Nevertheless, the system was allowed to continue, providing more than a little ammunition for those who maintain that the British did not hesitate to use "divide and rule" tactics whenever that suited their imperial purposes. Whether British policy was in any sense a cause of communalism in India is, of course, quite another matter.[12] My own view, as the present essay is hopefully beginning to make clear, is that the causes of modern communalism in India to some extent clearly lie in Neo-Muslim contexts (of the modernist Aligarh variety), and to at least an equal extent in Neo-Hindu contexts (of the reformist and nationalist variety). That the British took advantage of the emerging communalism is, of course, clearly evident throughout the history of the nationalist movement, although this was more true of conservative politicians such as Winston Churchill than it was of liberal leaders.

It should perhaps be mentioned here that Gandhi was successful in bringing about one important change in the 1935 system of separate electorates. Originally, Bhim Rao Ambedkar (1891-1956), the untouchable leader (from the Mahar community in Maharashtra, and eventually to be independent India's first law minister as well as chair of the drafting committee of India's Constituent Assembly), wanted separate electorates for the Depressed Classes (the so-called "untouchables" or Scheduled Castes, renamed by Gandhi "*harijan*-s" or "children of God" and nowadays usually called simply "Dalits," meaning "ground down" or "oppressed"), but Gandhi vigorously opposed such a move, realizing that it would be a serious threat to the integrity of the Hindu community. Gandhi began a "fast-unto-death" against separate electorates for untouchables, and finally Ambedkar reached a compromise with Gandhi on the issue in 1932.[13] The compromise involved a generous allotment of "reserved seats" for untouchables but no separate electorates. The compromise was accepted by the British government. Interestingly, when India became independent and its Constitution came into effect in 1950, separate electorates were abolished but the principle of "reserved seats" for Scheduled Castes (some 15%) and Scheduled Tribes (some 7.5%) was retained. In any case, those sympathetic to the Gandhian cause see his opposition to separate electorates for the Scheduled Castes as part of Gandhi's larger project of emancipating the untouchables. Ambedkar and others not especially sympathetic to the Gandhian cause see Gandhi's position as an example of his incorrigible "caste-ism," but more on this later.

Eventually, what had only been an intellectual worry by Sayyid Ahmad Khan and his Neo-Muslim cohorts at Aligarh about the dangers of a possible Hindu hegemony by the early Indian National Congress was becoming a more prevalent point of view, inclining more and more Neo-Muslims to turn away from the accommodationist attitude of the Deoband tradition and to embrace the defensive and separatist tradition of the Aligarh modernists. Many Muslims and Neo-Muslims, of course, stayed with the nationalist Congress movement, perhaps the most famous being Maulana Abul Kalam Azad (1888–1958) (who actually became Congress president from 1940–45). By the end of the third decade of the twentieth century, when the Gandhian consolidation of the nationalist movement was a decade old, some Neo-Muslim leaders began to think seriously about an independent status for the Muslim majority areas of the subcontinent (in the far northwest region of the Punjab and the Indus Valley and the eastern region of Bengal). Muhammand Iqbal (1877–1938), the prominent writer, speaking at the annual meeting of the Muslim League in 1930, called for

> the formation of a consolidated North-West Indian Muslim state . . . the final destiny of the Muslims, at least of North-West India. . . . We are seventy million and far more homogeneous than any other people in India. Indeed the Muslims of India are the only Indian people who can fitly be described as a nation in the modern sense of the word.[14]

Stanley Wolpert points out that Iqbal's characterization of such a northwest state, including Punjab, Sind, Baluchistan, and the Northwest Frontier, was, somewhat prophetically, almost exactly the same as the post-1947 boundary of West Pakistan (except for the eastern half of Punjab which was awarded to India) and all of Pakistan after its Eastern Province broke away in 1971 to become the People's Republic of Bangladesh.[15] Again, just as the older Neo-Muslim formation of the Muslim League had had its echo in the Neo-Hindu Arya Samaj and the founding of the Neo-Hindu Mahasabha, so Iqbal's prophetic words were to find their echo at the annual meeting of the Hindu Mahasabha in 1937 in the following words of V. D. Savarkar (1883-1966), author of the famous tract, *Hindutva*, and president for seven years of the Mahasabha:

> India cannot be assumed today to be a unitarian and homogeneous nation, but on the contrary there are two nations in the main; the Hindus and the Muslims.... There are two antagonistic nations living side by side in India.[16]

D. E. Smith makes the following wry observation about Savarkar's comment: "M. A. Jinnah could have constructed his two-nation theory, which led to the demand for Pakistan, on the basis of Savarkar's speech!"[17]

In fact, Jinnah's speech calling for partition at the annual meeting of the Muslim League at Lahore in March 1940 was more than a call for two nations or states. It was a declaration of two separate civilizations. Said Jinnah:

> If the British government are really in earnest and sincere to secure the peace and happiness of the people of the subcontinent, the only course open to us all is to allow the major nations separate homelands by dividing India into "autonomous national states."...
>
> It is extremely difficult to appreciate why our Hindu friends fail to understand the real nature of Islam and Hinduism. They are not religions in the strict sense of the word, but are, in fact, different and distinct social orders, and it is a dream that the Hindus and Muslims can ever evolve a common nationality, and this misconception of one Indian nation has gone far beyond the limits and is the cause of most of your troubles and will lead India to destruction if we fail to revise our notions in time. The Hindus and Muslims belong to two different religious philosophies, social customs, literatures. They neither intermarry nor interdine together and, indeed, they belong to two different civilizations which are based mainly on conflicting ideas and conceptions.[18]

Gandhi, of course, was vigorously opposed to partition, and he reacted strongly to Jinnah's call for partition in 1940. "Partition means a patent untruth," he commented.

> My whole soul rebels against the idea that Hinduism and Islam represent two antagonistic cultures and doctrines. To assent to such a doctrine is for me denial of God. For I believe with my whole soul that the God of the Koran is also the God of the Gita, and that we are all, no matter what name designated, children of the same God.[19]

Furthermore, Gandhi refused to accept a two-nation theory. Said Gandhi: "The vast majority of Muslims of India are converts to Islam or are descendents of converts. They did not become a separate nation as soon as they became converts."[20] The debate started by Jinnah and Gandhi was to continue for the next seven years with many taking sides one way or the other. Says Wolpert: "Intellectually, India thus became a land divided by advocates of the one-nation and two-nation theories long before the subcontinent's partition in 1947.[21]

There is no need to rehearse the details of what finally came to be accepted by all concerned as the inevitable outcome. The political, economic and psychological exhaustion of World War II brought about Great Britain's desire to leave India with alacrity. Churchhill's Tory government was succeeded by the Labor government of Clement Atlee, and Atlee appointed Lord Louis Mountbatten (1900–1979) as the new viceroy in 1947 charged with the responsibility of transferring power to the new Dominion of India by June of 1948. All efforts to avoid partition failed. Jinnah was adamant, and the impasse between Congress and the Muslim League was complete. Violence erupted throughout the Punjab and in Bihar and Bengal, the major areas of sizable Muslim populations.

In many ways the situation in the Northwest and the Punjab was much more volatile than in the Bengal area, since in the Punjab there was not only the presence of yet a third religious community deeply caught up in the mounting communal tragedy, namely, the Sikhs, but also an especially complex religious-cum-political problem in the princely state of Kashmir in which an overwhelming Muslim majority of Kashmiris was ruled by a Hindu Maharaja together with an elitist, minority *brāhmaṇa* community known as Pandits (from which community, of course, came the family of "Pandit" Nehru, the first prime minister of independent India). As pressure built for Pakistan, Master Tara Singh, a militant leader of the Sikhs, wanted a Sikhistan, or, in other words, an independent Sikh nation. The Maharaja of Kashmir was also understandably worried about the prospects of uniting either with Pakistan or India, and likewise toyed with the idea of maintaining an independent state of Kashmir. Interestingly, both separatist impulses, that is, for an independent Sikhistan or "Khalistan" and for an independent Kashmir continue down to the present day.

Finally, the time of the holocaust drew near. By order of the House of Commons in London, two independent dominions were to be created in India between 15 July and 15 August of 1947, with 82.5 percent of wealth and territory going to India and 17.5 percent to Pakistan. Millions of Hindus, Muslims and Sikhs—estimates run as high as ten million—felt constrained to change lands because of the partition. Possibly as many as a million never reached their destination.[22] Wolpert concludes:

> A totally inadequate boundary force of fifty thousand troops, most of them infected with communal fever, had been assembled

> in the Punjab to help make the transition a peaceful one. For the most part they stayed in their barracks, cleaning their weapons and boots, while trainloads of Sikh refugees moving east were slaughtered by Muslims in Pakistan and Muslims headed west were butchered by Sikhs and Hindus in India. The stream became a flood, the flood a holocaust of pain, looting, rape and murder.[23]

It was a creation-narrative, an epic founding myth, of sheer agony over religion!

The "Secular" as "Neo-Hindu"

D. E. Smith is surely right when he notices that the rhetoric surrounding the notions of "secular" and "secularism" has a somewhat unusual twist or nuance of meaning within the context of the communal hatreds exhibited with partition in 1947. Says Smith,

> "Communalism" is the term used in India to describe the political functioning of individuals or groups for the selfish interests of particular religious communities or castes. Today the antithesis of communalism is secularism, the principle of the secular state and the kind of political life which is in consonance with it. Before 1947 the term "secularism" was rarely used in this context; the antithesis of communalism was "nationalism."[24]

In other words, in independent India the terms "secular" or "secularism" are roughly synonymous with the terms "nationalist" and "nationalism," and both "secular" and "national" are construed to be the opposite of "communal." It is not unusual to encounter interpretations of modern India since independence as the "communal" "bad guys" (read "rigid" Muslims, or even better, these days, "fundamentalist" Muslims, or "right-wing," "fascist" Hindus) versus the "secular" "good guys" (read the "courageous" and "modern" supporters of the Congress and other mainstream "secular" political forces fighting for the integrity of the nation in order to overcome "fissiparous" tendencies). Such Manichaean rhetoric is perhaps recognized by most thoughtful persons for what it is: either the political propaganda of those in power or the exaggerated discourse of popular journalism rushing to meet its deadlines. A closer reading of the context, however, shows quite a different picture, a picture involving a dense religious complexity that calls into serious question our usual penchant for identifying "bad guys" and "good guys", "winners" and "losers," and so forth. A closer reading provides again, in other words, what W. H. Morris-Jones has warned us about in the Indian political arena: "nothing is ever quite what it seems or what it presents itself as being."

One way of getting at this dense religious complexity that provides the context in which the terms "secular," "national," and "communal" come to be used in independent India is to call attention to the following observation of W. Norman Brown.

> In his own major purpose Gandhi may be considered to have failed. His aim was the religious regeneration of India and Indians. As success for nationalism became step by step more likely, the politicians slipped out more and more from his control. They had no faith in the ultimate value of his religious purpose, as he had none in the ultimate worth of any purely secular end. He had said that he made a religious use of politics; many a politician of the time, if frank, would have admitted that he, in his turn, was making a political use of religion. . . .
>
> Even more, though Gandhi abhorred Hindu-Muslim communalism and partition, he nevertheless contributed to them. He could not in his time have become the political leader of the majority group in India, fortified by mass support, without being religious, he could not be religious without being Hindu. He could not be Hindu without being suspect to the Muslim community. . . .[25]

Whether or not one agrees that Gandhi failed in achieving his religious goal, there is no denying that his great achievement was the creation of a mass political movement that provided, at least ostensibly, an all-India national identity for the people of the subcontinent in their struggle against British rule. He was able to articulate and, more than that, to exhibit in his own person a masterful combination of the "Old Indic" and the "New Indic." He was a kind of yogin and *sādhu*, but he was also a competent attorney. He was a devotee of Rāma, but he was also a shrewd political organizer. He could spend long periods in quiet meditation and prayer, but he could also lead massive non-violent noncooperation protest movements (*satyāgraha* or "firmness in the truth" campaigns) as he did in the early years of the 1920s, the 1930s and the 1940s. He could relate well with rural peasants and the urban poor, but he could also interact with wealthy landowners, entrepreneurial business people and the new industrialists. Perhaps most important of all, he was able to mediate between the small elite (between 2% and 3%) of

English-speaking and "forward caste" leaders of the emerging independent India and the great mass of rural and urban poor.

His was a thoroughly Neo-Hindu reformist and nationalist vision, influenced by the older Neo-Hindu traditions stretching from Rammohun Roy and the Brahmo Samaj in the early nineteenth century through Keshub Chunder Sen, Dayananda Sarasvati and the Arya Samaj, Ramakrishna, Vivekananda, Aurobindo, and others, but influenced also by English education, liberal democratic ideas, enlightenment rationalism, liberal humanism, socialist ideology, the practice of parliamentary democracy, and, of course, Christian missionary activities of one kind or another. As noticed earlier in chapter 3, what unites the various Neo-Hindu "reformist and nationalist" traditions are their common commitments to (1) developing a self-confident national identity, (2) reforming outdated, parochial and superstitious Hindu practices, (3) reforming or rejecting the caste system, (4) emancipating women, (5) encouraging the economic progress of all sections of the population (which Gandhi designated as *sarvodaya*, the "uplift of all"), and (6) utilizing techniques of modern communication and propagation derived for the most part from Protestant missionary models. Clearly Gandhi's nationalist movement fits easily in this Neo-Hindu mold.

In terms of Gandhi's own inflection of his Neo-Hindu religious vision, two well-known passages from his own autobiography are sufficient by way of summarizing its basic features. Says Gandhi:

> What I want to achieve—what I have been striving and pining to achieve these thirty years—is self-realization, to see God face to face, to attain Moksha. I live and move and have my being in pursuit of this goal. . . . But as I have all along believed that what is possible for one is possible for all, my experiments have not been conducted in the closet, but in the open. . . . The experiments I am about to relate are... spiritual, or rather moral; for the essence of religion is morality. . . .
>
> But for me, truth is the sovereign principle, which includes numerous other principles. This truth is not only truthfulness in word, but truthfulness in thought also, and not only the relative truth of our conception, but the Absolute Truth, the Eternal Principle, that is God. There are innumerable definitions of God. . . . But I worship God as Truth only. . . .[26]
>
> My uniform experience has convinced me that there is no other God than Truth. And if every page of these chapters does not proclaim to the reader that the only means for the realization

> of Truth is Ahimsa (non-violence), I shall deem all my labour in writing these chapters to have been in vain. . . .
>
> To see the universal and all-pervading Spirit of Truth face to face one must be able to love the meanest of creation as oneself. And a man who aspires after that cannot afford to keep out of any field of life. That is why my devotion to Truth has drawn me into the field of politics; and I can say without the slightest hesitation, and yet in all humility, that those who say that religion has nothing to do with politics do not know what religion means.[27]

Jawaharlal Nehru (1889–1964), aristocrat, British-educated high-caste Kashmiri *brāhmaṇa*, democratic (Fabian) socialist and independent India's first prime minister, first got to know Gandhi at the Lucknow meeting of the Indian National Congress in 1916 and eventually became Gandhi's most well-known follower. Gandhi himself finally designated Nehru not only as his successor in the leadership of the nationalist movement but also as the person most suitable to be independent India's first prime minister. Nehru comments as follows about Gandhi's Neo-Hindu vision and example:

> And then Gandhi came. He was like a powerful current of fresh air that made us stretch ourselves and take deep breaths, like a beam of light that pierced the darkness and removed the scales from our eyes, like a whirlwind that upset many things but most of all the working of people's minds. He did not descend from the top; he seemed to emerge from the millions of India, speaking their language and incessantly drawing attention to them and their appalling condition. Get off the backs of these peasants and workers, he told us, all you who live by their exploitation; get rid of the system that produces this poverty and misery.[28]

Regarding Gandhi's broad-based appeal and his ability to mediate, Nehru comments:

> It is not surprising that this astonishingly vital man, full of self-confidence and an unusual kind of power, standing for equality and freedom for each individual, but measuring all this in terms of the poorest, fascinated the masses of India and attracted them like a magnet. He seemed to them to link up the past with the future and to make the dismal present appear just as a stepping-stone to that future of life and hope. And not the masses only, but

> intellectuals and others also. . . .[29]

But Nehru is especially insightful when characterizing the religious dimension of Gandhi.

> Gandhi was essentially a man of religion, a Hindu to the innermost depths of his being, and yet his conception of religion had nothing to do with any dogma or custom or ritual. It was basically concerned with his firm belief in the moral law, which he calls the Law of Truth or Love. Truth and nonviolence appear to him to be the same thing or different aspects of one and the same thing, and he uses these words almost interchangeably.[30]

In a footnote to the above passage, Nehru amplifies his remark that Gandhi's Neo-Hindu vision had little to do with dogmas or rituals.

> Gandhi told the Federation of International Fellowships in January 1928 that "after long study and experience I have come to these conclusions, that: (1) all religions are true, (2) all religions have some error in them, (3) all religions are almost as dear to me as my own Hinduism. My veneration for other faiths is the same as for my own faith. Consequently, the thought of conversion is impossible. . . ."[31]

Elsewhere, Nehru comments still further.

> Proud of his Hindu inheritance as he was, he tried to give to Hinduism a kind of universal attire and included all religions within the fold of truth. He refused to narrow his cultural inheritance. "Indian culture," he wrote, "is neither Hindu, Islamic nor any other, wholly. It is a fusion of all." Again he said: "I want the culture of all lands to be blown about my house as freely as possible. But I refuse to be blown off my feet by any. I refuse to live in other people's houses as an interloper, a beggar or a slave." Influenced by modern thought currents, he never let go of his roots and clung to them tenaciously.[32]

It is hardly surprising, therefore, that Gandhi was always opposed to any kind of establishment of any of the traditional religions, which would clearly undercut the universalism of his Neo-Hindu vision. Said Gandhi,

> We have suffered enough from state-aided religion and a state church. A society or a group which depends partly or wholly on state aid for the existence of its religion does not deserve, or better still, does not have any religion worth the name.[33]

Nehru himself, as is well known, claimed to be something of an agnostic, but one has a sense that beneath the urbane, sophisticated exterior of independent India's first Prime Minister there was at least a nostalgia for a Neo-Hindu vision almost as strong as Gandhi's own.

> Religion, as I saw it practiced, and accepted even by thinking minds, whether it was Hinduism or Islam or Buddhism or Christianity, did not attract me. It seemed to be closely associated with superstitious practices and dogmatic beliefs, and behind it lay a method of approach to life's problems which was certainly not that of science. There was an element of magic about it, an uncritical credulousness, a reliance on the supernatural.[34]

When the notion of religion became separated from the "-isms" of the pre-modern traditional religions (Hindu-ism, Buddh-ism, and so forth), however, and became associated instead with the Neo-Hindu universalism of a Gandhi, Nehru's attitude changed markedly.

> I have always hesitated to read books of religion. The totalitarian claims made on their behalf did not appeal to me. . . . Yet I had to drift to these books, for ignorance of them was not a virtue and was often a severe drawback. . . .[B]ut the sheer beauty of some passages would hold me. And then a phrase or a sentence would suddenly leap up and electrify me and make me feel the presence of the really great. Some words of the Buddha or of Christ would shine out with deep meaning and seem to me applicable as much today as when they were uttered two thousand or more years ago. There was a compelling reality about them, a permanence which time and space could not touch.[35]

This "presence of the really great" Nehru obviously found in Gandhi and his Neo-Hindu universalism.

> Gandhiji was continually laying stress on the religious and spiritual side of the movement. His religion was not dogmatic, but it did mean a definitely religious outlook on life, and the whole

> movement was strongly influenced by this and took on a revivalist character so far as the masses were concerned.[36]

Nehru concludes,

> What I admired was the moral and ethical side of our movement and of satyagraha. I did not give an absolute allegiance to the doctrine of non-violence or accept it forever, but it attracted me more and more, and the belief grew upon me that, situated as we were in India and with our background and traditions, it was the right policy for us. The spiritualization of politics, using the word not in its narrow religious sense, seemed to me a fine idea. A worthy end should have worthy means leading up to it.[37]

D. E. Smith has pointed out that it was Dr. Sarvepalli Radhakrishnan, the second president of India (1962) and a philosopher and apologist for the Neo-Hindu view of life who explicitly related this Gandhian universalism to the notion of the secular state. He quotes Radhakrishnan as follows:

> It may appear somewhat strange that our government should be a secular one while our culture is rooted in spiritual values. Secularism here does not mean irreligion or atheism or even stress on material comforts. It proclaims that it lays stress on the universality of spiritual values which may be attained in a variety of ways.... This is the meaning of a secular conception of the state though it is not generally understood.[38]

Nehru, of course, was somewhat more explicit and simply assumed that any modern, democratic state would be "secular" and all-inclusive.

> Do we believe in a national state which includes people of all religions and shades of opinion and is essentially secular as a state, or do we believe in the religious, theocratic conception of a state which considers people of other faiths as something beyond the pale? That is an odd question to ask, for the idea of a religious or theocratic state was given up by the world some centuries ago and has no place in the mind of the modern man. And yet the question has to be put in India today, for many of us have tried to jump back to a past age.[39]

D. E. Smith then goes on to comment himself as follows:

> Hindu tolerance is far more than an intellectual abstraction expounded by Radhakrishnan and Gandhi. It is indeed a living tradition which has contributed vitally to the establishment of a secular democratic state in India. There is the doctrinal assertion of the essential oneness of all religions, to which many educated Indians (and not only Hindus) subscribe as a self-evident truth. More important, however, is the general attitude of "live and let live" toward all manifestations of religious diversity. When questioned about the theoretical basis of India's secular state, a large majority of the Indian leaders of all persuasions will immediately relate it to the Hindu tradition of tolerance.[40]

"Neo-Hindu" as Gandhian-Nehruvian Indic Civil Religion

Whereas Gandhi and Radhakrishnan clearly represent a positive and explicit Neo-Hindu conceptualization of the nationalist movement, it is not always recognized that Nehru's view is likewise Neo-Hindu to the core. Here our analysis in the preceding chapter of the notion of religion and our discussion of a typology of religions is very much to the point wherein we suggested that both Hindu and Neo-Hindu traditions in South Asia are largely praxis-oriented, cognitively indeterminate (*nirguṇa*) traditions.[41] As S. C. Dube has put it, as we already noticed earlier in chapter 2: "Hinduism, such as it is, is a loosely structured federation of faiths rather than a faith. . . . Birth and minimal cognitive participation are enough to identify one as belonging to the Hindu faith."[42] Gandhi's and Radhakrishnan's view that all religions are true, and Nehru's agnostic view that the ultimate truth of all religions cannot be determined but can be tolerated within a broad-based democratic polity are both within the boundaries of a Hindu or a Neo-Hindu interpretation of religion. They are simply two sides of the same Neo-Hindu coin of a broadly tolerant universalism. One is almost tempted to suggest that Nehru was to Gandhi what the apostle Paul was to Jesus of Nazareth, or perhaps better, to keep the analogy within a modern South Asian frame, Nehru was to Gandhi what Vivekananda was to Ramakrishna. That is, there was an initial, creative charismatic figure who articulated and embodied a new spiritual vision followed by a sustaining and organizing charismatic genius able to consolidate, routinize and internationalize the movement. In the case of Jesus and Paul it was the consolidation and internationalization of the early Christian movement. In the case of Ramakrishna and Vivekananda, it was the consolidation and internationalization of the Ramakrishna Mission and Math. And, of course, in the case of Gandhi and Nehru, it was the consolidation and internationalization of what V. P. Singh (in the epigraph at the top of the present chapter) has called a "Hindu raj," or perhaps better, to use our own idiom as it has been developed in the course of this monograph, a Neo-Hindu multi-national civilisation-state.

Just as Gandhi had successfully created a mass political movement based on a Neo-Hindu vision of universalism, "firmness in the truth" (*satyāgraha*) and non-violence (*ahiṃsā*) in pre-partition India, so Nehru successfully created a comparable mass political movement based on a translation, or perhaps better, a kind of "demythologization," of that same Neo-Hindu vision in terms of "secularism," "socialism," "a mixed economy," "democracy," and "non-alignment" in post-partition India.[43] This is not to say that the translation or demythologization was an exact one-to-one rendering. There were, of course, some important differences between the two visions. If Gandhi's vision represented what might be called the "religionization of the political," that is, the transformation of issues regarding governance and the distribution of power into issues directly related to the ultimate meaning and significance of human existence, then Nehru's translation or demythologization (much like Muhammad 'Ali Jinnah's and Liaquat 'Ali Khan's in Neo-Muslim Pakistan) represented in many ways what might be called the "politicization of the religious," that is, the transformation of the search for ultimate meaning and significance into the immediate tasks of political mobilization and the acquisition of power. Similarly, Gandhi's vision had been one of decentralization, village autonomy (the so-called *pañcayati raj* or local "village councils of five") and the "uplift of all" (*sarvodaya*) from the bottom up, whereas Nehru's vision was one of a strong Centre, rapid industrialization and a mixed economy with the government making the fundamental economic decisions from the "commanding heights." It is surely no accident that the Gandhian "from the bottom up" theory has a clear affinity with Gandhi's own *bania*-caste origins in Gujarat—Gandhi family members, though *bania* and, hence, of the "merchant" or "trading" castes, nevertheless were deeply involved in the endless transactions of local grass-roots politics—whereas the Nehruvian "commanding heights" theory has an obvious affinity with Nehru's own Kashmiri *brāhmaṇa* elitism.

These important differences notwithstanding, many of the basic valuations, the dynamics, and equally important, the ruling ideas of the pre-partition and the post-partition nationalist movements were remarkably similar: (*a*) an all-India (Neo-Hindu or "secular") nationalist stance, contra "communalism," (*b*) a focus (at least rhetorically) on self-reliance, non-violence, and detachment in personal life and in the life of the nation (non-alignment), (*c*) the recognition of the right of any and all religions and minorities to maintain their religious, linguistic and cultural identities within the larger *de facto* if not *de jure* Neo-Hindu superstructure, (*d*) a reliance upon an elite cohort of 2% to 3% of "forward caste" or high-caste English-educated and English-speaking managers, administrators and professionals, (*e*) an alliance with private industrialists, landlords and other monied groups under a theory of economic protectionism (import substitution) and trusteeship—the wealthy can be tolerated because they hold their wealth in "trust" for the entire nation—and (*f*) an electoral compromise with the lowest, minority segments of the society (Scheduled Castes, Scheduled Tribes, and "other backward classes" including not only low castes but minority groups such as Muslims, Christians, and so forth) through the *quid pro quo* of "reserved seats" for Scheduled Castes and Tribes, various special benefits for "other backward classes" through compensatory discrimination, and the maintenance of separate "personal laws" for distinct minority groups such as Muslims, Parsis, and so forth. Gandhi, of course, was the charismatic figure and exemplary prophet of the pre-partition Neo-Hindu nationalist movement as was Nehru the charismatic figure and exemplary prophet of the post-partition demythologized Neo-Hindu (or "secular") "civilisation-state" of India.

What begins to emerge, in other words, by way of characterizing India's "hybrid" discourse of modernity is that such terms and expressions as "nation-state," "persistent centrism," "secularism," "socialism," "non-alignment" and "democracy" must be understood from within the framework of a broadly based Neo-Hindu multinational civilisation-state, created by the extraordinary vision and person of Gandhi (the creator), sustained by the sophisticated touch and person of Nehru (the sustainer), but brought into being by the terrible violence and destruction of partition (the destroyer). It is almost as if the high gods of the old Indic heritage, namely, Brāhma the creator, Viṣṇu the preserver, and Śiva the destroyer were having a last cosmic laugh over the emergence of India as a modern, "secular" nation-state; and, to follow the analogy one step further, one might well be inclined to say that the lurking tragedy for India as a modern, secular nation-state some fifty years after independence is that whereas the creativity of the Gandhian vision seems to have waned and the sustaining hand of the Nehruvian touch has all but disappeared, the violent and destructive spectre of partition is still alive and well on the subcontinent!

Let me hasten to comment that to characterize the modern Indian nation-state as a Neo-Hindu, multinational civilisation-state is not at all to offer a negative criticism of modern India nor is it to claim that it is somehow illegitimate to refer to modern India as a "socialist," "secular," and "democratic" state. It is only to specify and to make clear that the terms are being used somewhat differently in the Indian context, and that when one begins to "hear" and "understand" the in-house hybrid discourse of modernity in contemporary India, one begins to get a much better sense of what has been and what is at stake in the religious and political struggles unfolding in India since independence. What is somewhat surprising is that Gandhi himself never saw how thoroughly Neo-Hindu the nationalist movement had become. Nehru and other nationalist leaders likewise were not as sensitive to the importance of the Neo-Hindu component as one might have expected, although they at least finally came to accept the inevitability of partition and by their acquiescence exhibited at least some recognition of their own Neo-Hindu contribution to the religious conflagration.

But the Gandhian-Nehruvian Neo-Hindu multinational civilisation-state is not just a political or national entity. I am inclined to think that it is also important to realize that it is a religious entity as well, a religious entity that might be called simply the Gandhian-Nehruvian Indic civil religion. In other words, the hybrid discourse of modernity in India is not simply a political idiom wherein such notions as "secular state," "socialism," "persistent centrism," "non-alignment," and "democracy" have a strong Neo-Hindu coloring and provenance. The hybrid discourse of modernity in India is also symptomatic of a new kind of religion.

I have in mind here, of course, the notion of a "civil religion" along the lines set forth by Robert N. Bellah in his seminal article "Civil Religion in America" in the journal *Daedalus* in 1967. The actual expression "civil religion" derives from Rousseau (1712–78) and refers to a sort of generalized religion that Rousseau identified (in chapter 8, book 4 of *The Social Contract*) as being typical of late-eighteenth-century civil society in France and including such generalized beliefs as the existence of God, belief in an afterlife, retribution for good and evil deeds and the need for tolerance.[44] Bellah then applies the notion to American culture, and his basic thesis is set forth in the opening sentences in his article:

> . . . few have realized that there actually exists alongside of and rather clearly differentiated from the churches an elaborate and well-institutionalized civil religion in America. This article argues

> not only that there is such a thing, but also that this religion—or perhaps better, this religious dimension—has its own seriousness and integrity and requires the same care in understanding that any other religion does.[45]

The general "civil religion" exists alongside the various particular religious traditions in the United States, says Bellah. It is neither any particular Christian or Jewish religious tradition nor is it simply the general notion of religion as such. It is something in between. It is, as it were, the "American way of life" as well as the "religion of the Republic," and it has some general beliefs, various ritual or cultic performances and a definite community base. In terms of belief, the American civil religion is a peculiar combination of the biblical notions of exodus, a new promised land, election, sacrifice, redemption and covenant together with certain Enlightenment notions of reason, science and progress. In terms of ritual or cult, it is founded on the creation-narratives of the American Revolution and the Civil War with such epic heroes as George Washington and Abraham Lincoln and with such sacred holidays as Thanksgiving Day and the Fourth of July. In terms of community, it is, of course, the American people as the "chosen people" and the democratic and republican American nation over and above all particular traditions.[46]

The specific content of the American civil religion need not detain us, but the idea of a civil religion is, I would argue, important for understanding the hybrid discourse of modernity in independent India. There is, in other words, I wish to argue, a Gandhian-Nehruvian Indic civil religion that exists in India alongside the various particular religious traditions. Its cognitive base or belief system is the loose conglomeration of Neo-Hindu notions and liberal-democratic-cum-socialist ideas already discussed above. Its creation-narrative is partition, as celebrated on Independence Day, 15 August, and its sustaining myth is the fashioning of the all-inclusive Neo-Hindu "socialist" and "secular state," as celebrated on Republic Day, 26 January. Its exemplary prophets are Gandhi and Nehru, and in good Neo-Hindu fashion it recognizes and celebrates with national holidays the founders of all the great religions of the world (Gautama the Buddha, Mahāvīra, Jesus, Muhammad, Guru Nanak, and others) as well as such Hindu figures as Kṛṣṇa, Rāma, and so forth. *Mutatis mutandis*, when Indians speak about their respect for all religions and their "secular" traditions of tolerance, non-violence, non-attachment (non-alignment), self-reliance, commitment to the life of the nation, abhorence of "communalism," and their desire to share the spiritual riches of the Indic heritage with the ("materialist") West, it is not unlike Americans speaking about the "American way of life" and the "religion of the Republic" or about America as the promised land and the American people as a chosen people with a special "mission" in the world. In both instances one is dealing with much more than rhetoric or a political idiom with a religious tint. One is also dealing with the religious idiom of an institutionalized civil religion.

Critiques of the Gandhian-Nehruvian Indic Civil Religion

It was not only the Neo-Muslim Aligarh modernists, of course, who were fully aware of the Hindu or Neo-Hindu identity of the developing nationalist movement. A number of other important national figures also were aware of the Neo-Hindu influence and were quick to criticize. On the far left, for example, was the Marxian thinker (later to become simply a radical humanist), Manabendra Nath Roy (1887–1954) who commented:

> The most commonly agreed form of India's world message is Gandhism. Not only does it dominate the nationalist ideology: it has found some echo outside of India. It is as the moralizing mysticism of Gandhi that Indian thought makes any appeal to the Western mind. . . .
>
> But Gandhism is not a coordinated system of thought. There is little of philosophy in it. In the midst of a mass of platitudes and hopeless self-contradictions, it harps on one constant note—a conception of morality based upon dogmatic faith. But what Gandhi preaches is primarily a religion: the faith in God is the only reliable guide in life.
>
> . . . The masses pay their homage to a Mahātmā—a source of revealed wisdom and agency of supernatural power. The social basis of Gandhism is cultural backwardness; its intellectual mainstay, superstition. . . .[47]

Even more critical were the comments of the great untouchable leader, already referred to above, Bhim Rao Ambedkar:

> The first special feature of Gandhism is that its philosophy helps those who want to keep what they have and to prevent those who have not from getting what they have a right to get. No one who examines the Gandhian attitude to strikes, the Gandhian reverence for caste and Gandhian doctrine of Trusteeship by the rich for the benefit of the poor can deny that this is an upshot of Gand-

> hism. . . . Gandhism is the philosophy of the well-to-do and the leisure class.
>
> The second feature of Gandhism is to delude people into accepting their misfortunes by presenting them as best of good fortunes. . . .[48]

Regarding the implications of Gandhism for the untouchables, Ambedkar continues:

> What hope can Gandhism offer to the Untouchables? To the Untouchables, Hinduism is a veritable chamber of horrors. The sanctity and infallibility of the Vedas, Smritis and Shastras, the iron law of caste, the heartless law of *karma* and the senseless law of status by birth are to the Untouchables veritable instruments of torture which Hinduism has forged against the Untouchables. These very instruments which have mutilated, blasted and blighted the life of the Untouchables are to be found intact and untarnished in the bosom of Gandhism.[49]

Finally, to those who argued that Gandhi's views regarding caste changed in the later stages of his career and the nationalist movement, Ambedkar comments:

> Gandhists may say that what I have stated applies to the old type of Gandhism. There is a new Gandhism, Gandhism without caste. This has reference to the recent statement of Mr. Gandhi that caste is an anachronism. . . . But is this really a matter for jubilation? . . . [A]ll that Mr. Gandhi has said is that caste is an anachronism. He does not say it is an evil. He does not say it is anathema. Mr. Gandhi may be taken to be not in favour of caste. But Mr. Gandhi does not say that he is against the *Varna* system. And what is Mr. Gandhi's *Varna* system? It is simply a new name for the caste system. . . .
>
> The declaration of Mr. Gandhi cannot be taken to mean any fundamental change in Gandhism.... The Untouchables will still have ground to say: "Good God! Is this man Gandhi our Saviour?"[50]

Though Ambedkar was to serve as chair of the drafting committee of the Constituent Assembly and to be independent India's first law minister, thereby helping to formulate the Nehruvian demythologized version of the Neo-Hindu state, he nevertheless came to realize what he saw as the incorrigible nature of the Neo-Hindu Raj, even in its demythologized Nehruvian form, first, by resigning from the Government in 1951 (over controversy related to the Hindu Code Bill), and, then, by publicly converting to Buddhism in October of 1956, taking some half a million of Untouchable Mahars from Maharashtra with him from their traditional Hindu identity into a modernist, Neo-Buddhist identity, a mass conversion which eventually numbered over four million among Untouchables in Maharashtra and elsewhere.[51]

Two other critiques from the other side of the political spectrum should also be mentioned by way of rounding out this emerging picture of the overall religio-ideological environment in which the Neo-Hindu multinational civilisation-state of modern India with its Gandhian-Nehruvian Indic civil religion functioned or interacted. The first is that of the radical militarist, Subhas Chandra Bose (1897–1945), the fiery Bengali Neo-Hindu nationalist who became attracted to the European fascist movements of the 1930s and eventually put together (with the blessings and support of Hitler and Tojo) the famed Indian National Army (the INA) in 1943, an army that would supposedly free India from the British Raj when the Japanese were successful in their conquest of Asia. The INA made little military progress in South Asia, however, and surrendered in Rangoon in May of 1945. Subhas Chandra Bose himself managed to escape from imprisonment but was killed in a plane crash on Formosa in August of 1945. Although his movement had little long-range political or military significance, it had great popular symbolic visibility as an extremist, activist alternative to the more passive Gandhian-Nehruvian Neo-Hindu nationalist movement. Already in 1928, Subhas Chandra Bose was critical of both Gandhi (whose base at the time was at Sabarmati in Gujarat) and Aurobindo (who had by this time given up his political extremism and had founded an *āśrama* in Pondicherry in South India):

> As I look around me today, I am struck by two movements or two schools of thought about which . . . it is my duty to speak out openly and fearlessly. I am referring to the two schools of thought, which have their centers at Sabarmati [Gandhi] and Pondicherry [Aurobindo]. . . . The actual effect of the propaganda carried on by the Sabarmati School of thought is to create a feeling and an impression that modernism is bad. . . .
>
> It is the passivism, not philosophic but actual, inculcated by these schools of thought against which I protest. In this holy land of ours, Ashramas are not new institutions and ascetics and Yogis are not novel phenomena. They have held and they will continue

> to hold an honored place in society. But it is not their lead we shall have to follow if we are to create a new India at once free, happy, and great. . . .
>
> In India we want today a philosophy of activism. We must be inspired by robust optimism.[52]

The other critique was from another conservative source, namely, Vinayak Damodar Savarkar (1883–1966), already mentioned earlier as author of the tract, *Hindutva*, president for seven years of the conservative Hindu Mahasabha and a proponent on the Neo-Hindu side of Muslims and Hindus as "two nations." As was discussed in chapter 3, he was not only deeply involved in the conservative Hindu Mahasabha but was also in many ways the intellectual father of the conservative Neo-Hindu movement founded in 1925 by K. B. Hedgewar (1890–1940), the Rashtriya Svayamsevak Sangh (RSS). Moreover, both Savarkar and the RSS are in a direct line of development with the emergence of the conservative Neo-Hindu political party, the Bharatiya Jana Sangh (founded in 1951), later (in 1979) renamed the Bharatiya Janata Party (the BJP or "Indian People's Party") and the more recent conservative Neo-Hindu religious revival movement known as the Vishva Hindu Parishad (the VHP) or "World Council of Hindus" founded in 1964. Savarkar was critical of the Indian National Congress and Gandhi's leadership from the time of the Khilafat movement (1919–1924). He comments in a speech to the Hindu Mahasabha in 1939:

> I have no space here nor the inclination to frame a charge-sheet against the Congress, enumerating the grievous errors it has been committing under the dictatorship of Gandhiji and the leaders of his persuasion ever since the Khilafat agitation. . . . It is not their motive but their judgment and in a couple of cases a monomaniac incompetence which were responsible for the erroneous policy they persisted in which has done incalculable harm to the Hindu cause and which if not checkmated is likely to jeopardize not only the legitimate interests of Hindudom far more dangerously than in the past but even the vital interests of the "Indian Nation" too as the Congress itself understands it and loves so well.[53]

His criticism is also directed at all the nationalist Neo-Hindu leaders who were overly inclined, in his view, to concede too much to the Muslims.

> Well, gentlemen, I am not referring to these few details in any light mood. I want you to realize the mentality and the ideology of these Hindu leaders who happen to be at the helm of the Congress. Neither Gandhiji or Pandit Nehru, nay, not even Subhas Babu or Mr. Roy who, although they do not contribute in any way to some of the above vagaries of the Gandhist school, are still votaries—I call it victims—of the school of thought which says in so many words, "Give to the Moslems so much that they could not wish to ask for anything more." They may sincerely believe that to be the crux of nationalism and wisdom. But do you, who do not wish to see Hindudom humiliated and browbeaten into servility, believe it to be so?[54]

Overall, then, we see a variety of religious orientations and traditions interacting with one another in these formative years before and after partition: Neo-Muslim Aligarh modernists and separatists (Sayyid Ahmad Khan, the Muslim League, Muhammad Iqbal, M. A. Jinnah, and others), Neo-Muslim Deoband reformists and accommodationists (Hasan Ahmad Madani, and others), Neo-Hindu reformists and nationalists with an aggressive (militant) and exclusivist orientation (the Arya Samaj, the Hindu Mahasabha, the early Aurobindo, B. G. Tilak, V. D. Savarkar, Hedgewar and the RSS, Subhas Chandra Bose and his INA, and so on), and Neo-Hindu reformists and nationalists with a passive aggressive (non-violent non-cooperation, *satyāgraha*) and inclusivist orientation (the Brahmo Samaj, the Ramakrishna Mission, the Indian National Congress, the later Aurobindo, the Gandhian *sarvodaya* movement, and so on). There were also, of course, the purely Westernizing or European orientations of liberal democratic pluralism (in such early moderate leaders as M. G. Ranade and G. K. Gokhale) deriving from the intellectual traditions of the Western European nation-states, of the Nehruvian socialists and of radical socialist and communist theorizing (M. N. Roy, and others) growing out of the Russian revolution and its aftermath. The Westernizing orientations, however, hardly had an independent social base and were finally absorbed for the most part in the Neo-Muslim (mainly among Aligarh modernists) and Neo-Hindu traditions (mainly in the Gandhian-Nehruvian Congress ideology). One should perhaps also mention Ambedkar's Neo-Buddhist movement, largely among the Mahars in Maharashtra but also appealing to untouchables or Scheduled Castes elsewhere as well.

All of these traditions, it should be noted, except for Ambedkar's Neo-Buddhist movement, which does not get started, in any case, until nearly a decade after partition, were thoroughly elitist, involving not more than 2% to 3% of the general population, who were overwhelmingly from the "forward castes" (among the Neo-Hindu groups) or high-status Muslim families (among the Neo-Muslims), English-educated and English-speaking, and largely urban-based professionals (in such new fields as government service and administration, law, education, journalism, and so forth). The Gandhian-Nehruvian movement, to be sure, addressed itself to the rural and urban poor and succeeded in achieving mass mobilization, but, nevertheless, its leadership was as elitist as the other traditions in the nationalist struggle, both before partition and even more so afterwards. To put the matter directly, the freedom movements in South Asia, both for the Republic of Pakistan as well as for the Republic of India, were very much products of the "commanding heights."

The Community as Citizen

Thus far we have dealt with only one part of the hybrid discourse of modernity in India, namely, the religious discourse of the "secular," the Neo-Hindu "secular state," and what I have called the the Gandhian-Nehruvian Indic civil religion. There is, however, an equally important second part or half in deciphering India's hybrid discourse, and that is the unusual juxtaposition of "community" and "citizen." Communities have a special place in modern India unlike in almost all other modern polities, and the notion of the individual citizen is, thus, interestingly different in many instances. In the epigraph at the head of this present chapter, in addition to V. P. Singh's observation about the "Hindu raj," which we have discussed thus far in terms of our own idiom of a "Neo-Hindu Raj," a comment from the Rudolphs was also cited: "The contradiction in India's concept of secularism was its simultaneous commitment to communities and to equal citizenship."[55]

The term "contradiction" is undoubtedly too strong in this context, but it cannot be denied that the relation between community and citizen in independent India is an incredibly complex and intriguing interpretive problem. In chapter 1 reference was made to the first report of the "People of India" project of the Anthropological Survey of India in which it was estimated that there are some 4,599 separate communities in India with as many as 325 languages and dialects in 12 distinct language families and some 24 separate scripts.[56] The sheer magnitiude of what might be called the "communities"-issue is staggering in its scope and diversity. The communities-issue, it should be noted, of course, is not the same as the so-called communalism-issue, or putting the matter somewhat differently, the communalism-issue is only one component of the much larger communities-issue. "Communalism" refers to the self-serving political behavior of individuals and groups in terms of the narrow interests of their own specific religious communities and castes. It is for the most part, as we have seen, a normative notion of condemnation and is contrasted with the Neo-Hindu nationalism and "secularism" of the Gandhian-Nehruvian variety. The communities-issue, on the other hand, is largely a descriptive notion and refers to the bewildering complexity of India's multiple communities.

At the time of partition, for example, in terms of political communities, in addition to the areas under the direct control of the British Raj, there were between 550 and 600 princely communities (the so-called "Indian States" some 28 of which had populations of over half a million) that had to be integrated into the new dominions of India and Pakistan.[57] In terms of regional linguistic communities, quite apart from the figure of 325 quoted above which includes all sorts of local languages and dialects, there were at least fifteen major languages representing major regional or national cultures (e.g., Hindi, Telugu, Tamil, Bengali, Marathi, Gujarati, Kashmiri, Punjabi, and others.). In terms of caste communities, at the low end of the caste hierarchy there were the Scheduled Castes and Scheduled Tribes, making up hundreds of separate communities and totalling nearly a quarter (22.5%) of the population of the subcontinent.[58] At the other end of the caste hierarchy there were the so-called forward castes or high castes (Brahmins, Bhumihars, Rajputs, Marathas, Jats, Vaishya-Banias, Kayasthas, and so forth) making up just under eighteen percent (17.58%) of the population. Just above the Scheduled Castes and Scheduled Tribes were the so-called "Other Backward Classes," estimates for which range from 25% of the total population to as high as 52% and, again, involving hundreds, possibly several thousand, separate communities depending upon the manner in which the various caste groups are classified.[59] In terms of religion, as we have discussed at some length already, in addition to the many Hindu caste communities, monastic *sampradāya*-s, regional *bhakti* communities, and numerous Neo-Hindu communities, there were varieties of separate communities for Muslims, Sikhs, Jains, Buddhists, Christians, Parsis, and Jews. And finally, in terms of law among the various religious communities, there were various traditions of "personal law" (in contrast to territorial law) regarding marriage, inheritance, succession, and so forth, for Hindus, Muslims, Parsis, Jews and Christians.

There were and are, in other words, communities within communities within communities, and when it is remembered, as was pointed out in chapter 1, that even now in the last decade of the twentieth century only a minority of the total population can be considered part of the modern economy in which notions of "equality before the law," "class," "citizenship," and so forth, are fully understood and have their full modern meaning, one can begin to get a sense that here in the area of the relation between community and citizen, "nothing is ever quite what it seems or what it presents itself as being," to use W. H. Morris-Jones's idiom once again. Like the discourse regarding the "secular" and "religion," so, too, with the discourse regarding "community" and "citizen," India's hybrid discourse of modernity continues to have its own eccentric syntax and semantic.

Perhaps the most striking manifestation of the matter can be seen in the Gandhian-Nehruvian ruling class itself in comparison with the population as a whole. The Neo-Hindu Raj and its Gandhian-Nehruvian Indic civil religion with its purported universal tolerance and inclusiveness, its rhetorical concern for *sarvodaya* (the "uplift of all") and its commitment to "socialism" and "secularism" has given rise to the following rather grim statistics, summarized by Khushwant Singh.

> During British rule, the largest proportion of government jobs (40%) was held by Kayasthas. Today their figure has dropped to 7%. Next came the Muslims who were given special privileges by the British. They had 35% of jobs in 1935. In free India their representation has dropped to 3.5%. Christians, likewise favoured by the English, had 15%; their figure has dropped to 1%. Scheduled castes, tribes and backward classes, who had hardly any government jobs, have achieved a representation of 9%. But the most striking contrast is in the employment of Brahmins. Under the British, they had 3%—fractionally less than the proportion of their 3.5% of the population. Today they hold as much as 70% of government jobs. . . . In the senior echelons of the civil service from the rank of deputy secretaries upwards, out of 500, there are 310 Brahmins, i.e., 63%; of the 26 state chief secretaries, 19 are Brahmins; of the 27 Governors and Lt. Governors 13 are Brahmins; of the 16 Supreme Court judges, 9 are Brahmins; of the 330 judges of High Courts, 166 are Brahmins; of 140 ambassadors, 58

> are Brahmins; of 98 vice-chancellors 50 are Brahmins; of 438 district magistrates, 250 are Brahmins; of the total of 3,300 IAS officers [the elite Indian Administrative Service], 2,376 are Brahmins. They do equally well in electoral posts. Of the 530 Lok Sabha members, 190 are Brahmins. Of 244 in the Rajya Sabha 89 are Brahmins. These statistics clearly prove that this 3.5% of the Brahmin community of India holds between 36% to 63% of all the plum jobs available in the country.[60]

These statistics are not from 1950 or even 1970, but from the 1980s, nearly half a century after partition. Not only is there a "forward caste" hold on the distribution of power within government administration, but, indeed, a concentration in the hands of Brahmins, very much reminiscent of the old Indo-Brāhmaṇical and Indic structures of brahmanical hegemony. Reasons for this preponderance of Brahmins in "plum jobs" include not only such obvious factors as privileged social status and ease of access to modern education but also simple nepotism and jobbery. The picture becomes even more grim, moreover, when the above statistics are compared with the following findings of the report of the United Nations Development Program in 1991, summarized by Barbara Crossette in her new book, *India Facing the Twenty-First Century*.

> [T]he United Nations Development Program in 1991 ranked India 123rd among 160 Third World nations on a Human Development Index measured by longevity, access to knowledge, and reasonably decent living standards. For quality of life, India trailed behind all of Latin America (except Haiti), most of Asia . . . and some Sub-Saharan African nations. In India, the report found, 370 million people had no access to clean water and more than 400 million lived below a locally computed poverty line. . . . About 30 percent of babies were born with low birth weights (compared with 12 percent in Thailand or 17 percent in Ghana). India spent less than one percent of its gross national product on health care (compared with 2.4 percent in Brazil or 2.8 percent in Jamaica). . . . India, which calls itself a socialist republic, has no social security system or comprehensive national health service.[61]

In chapter 1 reference was made to Dipesh Chakrabarty's claim that there are two kinds of political "languages" operating in modern India, a modern idiom of individual freedom, "citizenship" and "nation-building," which pertains to only a small elite, and an older pre-colonial idiom of community power, which pertains to the overwhelming majority of the people of India.[62] Chakrabarty then comments further:

> the language of class in India overlaps with the *language of citizen-politics* only in a minority of instances. For the greater part of our daily experience, class relations express themselves in that other language of politics, which is *the politics of a nation without 'citizens.'* It is in this realm that notions of hierarchy, domination and subordination work themselves out, as do the traditions of resistance to domination and deference towards the dominant.[63]

The fundamental issue, however, is not simply an historical dichotomy between pre-modern notions of hierarchical community and modern notions of citizenship and individuality, important as that dichotomy is. There is, rather, an even more basic structural issue, as the Rudolphs have rightly noted, and that is the "simultaneous commitment to communities and to equal citizenship" *even in the modern context*. That is, there appears to be a peculiar parity between community-rights and citizen-rights in India's hybrid discourse of modernity, requiring almost a neologism along the lines of a term such as "community-ship" to parallel the more well-known notion of "citizen-ship." Moreover, this issue of "community-ship" like the earlier issues of partition and the emergence of the "secular state" is, I would argue, an important *religious* issue in modern India in the sense that social organization and stratification in terms of the ranked status of interacting castes and religious minorities has always been a fundamental component in determining religious identity in India, either within the multiple communities of the Hindu system or over against the Hindu system (in terms of Buddhists, Jains, individual *sādhu*-s, and so forth). Furthermore, it might well be said that just as the Nehruvian post-partition Neo-Hindu multinational civilisation-state is a demythologized version of the pre-partition Gandhian Neo-Hindu nationalist movement, so in many ways India's "simultaneous commitment to communities and equal citizenship" in its Constitution and in its continuing maintenance of traditions of community-based "personal law" represents to a large extent a Neo-Hindu demythologized version of the older pre-partition hierarchical caste system. Put somewhat differently, it could be said that both visions of society, pre-partition as well as post-partition, are thoroughly discriminatory, the former representing discrimination in terms of hierarchical ranking with a bias in favor of forward or high castes, the latter representing discrimination in terms of hierarchical ranking with a bias in favor of compensatory remediation with respect to Scheduled Castes, Scheduled Tribes and Other Backward Classes. In both instances, however, hierarchical, group-oriented "community-ship" plays a significant role in public policy and social theory as strong or stronger than any commitment to equal citizenship.

Some of the "community-ship" matters were successfully resolved early along after independence and partition. The matter of the princely communities (the "Indian States"), for example, was for the most part solved at the outset of independence by the masterful work of the powerful and authoritarian nationalist leader, Sardar Vallabhbhai Patel, independent India's first deputy prime minister.[64] If Nehru with his radical socialist ideology was always on the left side of Gandhi and the nationalist movement, then Patel with his solid, conservative and traditional Hindu orientation was always emphatically on the right side. That Gandhi could hold together two such divergent characters in one united political movement is no little tribute to his mediating skills and personal charisma. In any case, Patel took a no-nonsense approach to the problem of the princely states, as did Lord Mountbatten, the last viceroy and the first governor general of the Dominion of India, and almost all of the princely states quickly acceded. There were a few exceptions, including Junagadh, which acceded under pressure in December of 1948, and Hyderabad, which after being invaded finally acceded on 26 January 1950. The glaring exception, of course, was Kashmir. The Maharaja of Kashmir acceded on 26 October 1947, but since the population of Kashmir was overwhelmingly Muslim, the accession was made conditional upon holding a plebiscite by way of final confirmation. Because of continuing hostilities between India and Pakistan, both diplomatic and military, a plebiscite has yet to be held, but more on that later.

Likewise the matter of large cultural and linguistic communities was solved fairly early along. Disputes over the recognition of various languages and the autonomy of the various cultural regions led to the formation of a States Reorganization Commission in 1955 which in 1956 issued in a complete redrawing of the map of the Republic of India based for the most part on the large linguistic and cultural regions, Andhra Pradesh (for Telugu language and culture), Tamil Nadu (for Tamil), Kerala (for Malayalam), and so forth. Two regions proved to be problems, the first, Bombay, a region made up of both Marathi and Gujarati speakers, and the second, Punjab, made up of both Hindi and Punjabi speakers, but more to the point, made up of a myriad of Hindu and Neo-Hindu groups alongside the minority religious community of the Sikhs. The problem of Bombay was solved by adding the region to Maharashtra in 1960. The problem of the state of Punjab was not resolved until 1966, since for some years the linguistic issue was overshadowed by the religious issue of Sikh separatist demands, but again more on that later. The political scientist Paul Brass has noted, interestingly, that there appears to be a *de facto* set of four rules or tests that have been used by the Government of India in responding to demands for linguistic and cultural regional autonomy: (*a*) the demands must not include secession, (*b*) the demands must be expressed primarily on linguistic and cultural grounds and never explicitly on religious grounds, (*c*) there must be broad community support for the demands in the region, and (*d*) there must be some support for the demands, some recognition of the legitimacy of the demands, even from different linguistic groups in the region.[65]

In terms of other "community-ship" matters, including untouchable castes (Scheduled Castes or Dalits), tribal communities (Scheduled Tribes), Other Backward Classes (OBCs), religious minorities, and "personal law" communities (Hindu, Muslim, Parsi, and Christian), the Constitution of India walks a fine line between its "simultaneous commitment" to "community-ship" and "citizen-ship," and it is instructive to see how the commitments interweave with one another in certain crucial passages. For example, Articles 14 and 15 assure equality before the law for all citizens and prohibit any discrimination on the basis of religion, race, caste, and so forth, but language is also included which allows for certain hierarchical "community-ship" rights in favor of Scheduled Castes, Scheduled Tribes and Other Backward Classes.

> Article 14
> The State shall not deny to any person equality before the law or the equal protection of the laws within the territory of India.
> Article 15
> (1) The State shall not discriminate against any citizen on grounds only of religion, race, caste, sex, place of birth or any of them.
> (2) No citizen shall, on grounds of religion, race, caste, sex, place of birth or any of them, be subject to any disability, liability, restriction or condition with regard to
> (a) access to shops, public restaurants, hotels and places of public entertainment; or
> (b) the use of wells, tanks, bathing ghats, roads and places of public resort maintained wholly or partly out of State funds or dedicated to the use of the general public.
> (3) Nothing in this article shall prevent the State from making any special provision for women and children.

> (4) Nothing in this article or in clause (2) of article 29 shall prevent the State from making any special provision for the advancement of any socially and educationally backward classes of citizens or for the Scheduled Castes and the Schedule Tribes.[66]

A crucial word in Article 15 (1), appearing also in Article 16 (2), Article 29 (2) and Article 325 (and see below), is the term "only," for it can be read to mean that it *is* possible to discriminate if there are grounds *in addition* to the items listed (for example, compensatory discrimination in favor of the advancement of certain specified groups); and, indeed, Indian courts have on occasion permitted discrimination on the basis of the word "only" in Article 15 (1).[67] The Calcutta High Court, for example, in *Anjali* v. *The State of West Bengal*, commented about 15(1) as follows:

> Of paramount importance in clause (1) are the words "discrimination" and "only". . . . The discrimination which is forbidden is only such discrimination as is based solely on the ground that a person belongs to a particular race or caste or professes a particular religion or was born at a particular place or is of a particular sex and on no other ground. A discrimination based on one or more of these grounds and also on other grounds is not hit by the article.[68]

Similarly, Article 16, which guarantees equality of opportunity for all citizens in matters of public employment, also provides for compensatory discrimination in favor of certain designated communities.

> Article 16
> (1) There shall be equality of opportunity for all citizens in matters relating to employment or appointment to any office under the State.
> (2) No citizen shall, on grounds only of religion, race, caste, sex, descent, place of birth, residence or any of them, be ineligible for, or discriminated against in respect of, any employment or office under the State.
> . . . .
> (4) Nothing in this article shall prevent the State from making any provision for the reservation of appointments or posts in favour of any backward class of citizens which, in the opinion of the State, is not adequately represented in the services under the State.[69]

Article 17 then proceeds to abolish Untouchability "and its practice in any form" after having just provided for special provisions for untouchables (Scheduled Castes), explicitly in Article 15 and implicitly in Article 16. The intent would appear to be the elimination of all noxious practices relating to the traditional low ranking status of untouchable groups, even though special provisions have been made for such groups in 15(4) and 16(4). In other words, a sort of "both-and" logic is operating. Untouchability is both abolished (in terms of ranking) and yet provided for (in terms of compensatory remediation).

> Article 17
> "Untouchability" is abolished and its practice in any form forbidden. The enforcement of any disability arising out of "Untouchability" shall be an offense punishable in accordance with law.[70]

A similar dual commitment to "community-ship" and "citizenship" is evident in Articles 25 to 30 having to do with freedom of religion and the rights of minorities. Articles 25 to 30 likewise give a great deal of authority to yet another community, namely, the state itself, by way of regulating, reforming and in some cases administering religious communities and institutions. Clearly the state is differentiated or separated from religious communities and permits all persons "freedom of conscience and the right freely to profess, practise and propagate religion," but there is no Jeffersonian "wall of separation" in the Constitution of India. As C. H. Alexandrowicz, D. E. Smith, Ved Prakash Luthera, and others, have documented at great length, the state interferes in religious matters with alacrity in post-partition India, and while there is certainly no "establishment" and overall "no preference" in matters relating to conflicts between religious communities or between believers, thereby making the state legitimately "secular" or "neutral" in many instances, there is nevertheless a heavy Neo-Hindu "invisible hand" operating from the "commanding heights" on a great variety of levels, suggesting what Luthera has called a "jurisdictionalist" or Erastian pattern as a better way of describing the interaction of religion and the state in modern India than the more conventional description of India as a "secular state."[71] C. H. Alexandrowicz and D. E. Smith to the contrary argue that it is possible to refer to post-partition India as a "secular state" so long as one makes adequate allowance for the more-than-usual interference of the state in religious matters in India in comparison with other "secular states." Here again a "both-and" logic appears to be operating, and it is worth quoting the relevant provisions from the Constitution.

Article 25

(l) Subject to public order, morality and health and to the other provisions of this Part, all persons are equally entitled to freedom of conscience and the right freely to profess, practise and propagate religion.

(2) Nothing in this article shall affect the operation of any existing law or prevent the State from making any law—

(a) regulating or restricting any economic, financial, political or other secular activity which may be associated with religious practice;

(b) providing for social welfare and reform or the throwing open of Hindu religious institutions of a public character to all classes and sections of Hindus.

Explanation I—The wearing and carrying of kirpans [daggers] shall be deemed to be included in the profession of the Sikh religion.

Explanation II—In sub-clause (b) of clause (2), the reference to Hindus shall be construed as including a reference to persons professing the Sikh, Jain, or Buddhist religion, and the reference to Hindu religious institutions shall be construed accordingly.

Article 26

Subject to public order, morality and health, every religious denomination or any section thereof shall have the right—

(a) to establish and maintain institutions for religious and charitable purposes;

(b) to manage its own affairs in matters of religion;

(c) to own and acquire movable and immovable property; and

(d) to administer such property in accordance with law.

Article 27

No person shall be compelled to pay any taxes, the proceeds of which are specifically appropriated in payment of expenses for the promotion or maintenance of any particular relgion or religious denomination.

Article 28

(1) No religious instruction shall be provided in any educational institution wholly maintained out of State funds.

(2) Nothing in clause (l) shall apply to an educational institution which is administered by the State but has been established under any endowment or trust which requires that religious instruction shall be imparted in such institution.

(3) No person attending any educational institution recognised by the State or receiving aid out of State funds shall be required to take part in any religious instruction that may be imparted in such institution or to attend any religious worship that may be conducted in such institution or in any premises attached thereto unless such person, or if such person is a minor, his guardian has given his consent thereto.
Article 29
(1) Any section of the citizens residing in the territory of India or any part thereof having a distinct language, script or culture of its own shall have the right to conserve the same.
(2) No citizen shall be denied admission into any educational institution maintained by the State or receiving aid out of State funds on grounds only of religion, race, caste, language or any of them.
Article 30
(1) All minorities whether based on religion or language, shall have the right to establish and administer educational institutions of their choice.
(2) The State shall not, in granting aid to educational institutions, discriminate against any educational institution on the ground that it is under the management of a minority, whether based on religion or language.[72]

All of the above articles come under the section entitled "Fundamental Rights" in the Constitution of India, and this section is immediately followed by a section entitled "Directive Principles of State Policy." The latter are distinguished from the former as follows: "The provisions contained in this Part [that is, the Directive Principles] shall not be enforceable by any court, but the principles therein laid down are nevertheless fundamental in the governance of the country and it shall be the duty of the State to apply these principles in making laws."[73] Again, in this section the "simultaneous commitment" to "community-ship" and "citizen-ship" is striking, especially in Articles 38, 44 and 46. Article 38 sets the overall tone for the section with a focus on both communities and citizens.

Article 38
(1) The State shall strive to promote the welfare of people by securing and protecting as effectively as it may a social order in which justice, social, economic and political, shall inform all the institutions of the national life.

> (2) The State shall, in particular, strive to minimise the inequalities of income, and endeavour to eliminate inequalities in status, facilities and opportunities, not only amongst individuals but also amongst groups of people residing in different areas or engaged in different vocations.[74]

Article 44 calls for the fashioning of a uniform civil code thereby recognizing the existence and validity of the "personal law" for distinct religious groups in India.

> Article 44
> The State shall endeavour to secure for the citizens a uniform civil code throughout the territory of India.[75]

The criminal law in India had been long codified by the British Raj with the passing of the Code of Civil Procedure (1859), the Penal Code (1860) and the Code of Criminal Procedure (1861), but the British held back from codifying the so-called "personal law" (involving marriage, dowry, dissolution of marriage, parentage and legitimacy, guardianship, maintenance, gifts, wills, inheritance, succession, and so forth) of Hindus and Muslims, since these matters were in the judgment of the British administrators and legal experts inextricably intertwined with the customs and laws of specific religious communities.[76] J. D. M. Derrett quotes a passage from the Privy Council in 1871 which nicely characterizes this notion of "personal law":

> While Brahmin, Buddhist, Christian, Mahomedan, Parsee, and Sikh are one nation, enjoying equal political rights and having perfect equality before the Tribunals, they co-exist as separate and very distinct communities, having distinct laws affecting every relation of life. The law of Husband and Wife, parent and child, the descent, devolution, and disposition of property are all different, depending, in each case, on the body to which the individual is deemed to belong; and the difference of religion pervades and governs all domestic usages and social relations.[77]

Derrett goes on to comment:

> The personal law goes with him, within the territories where it is part of the law of the land, and he is entitled to have it applied and not the law which would be applied in respect of the local land, or other property within the jurisdiction, to persons professing some

> other personal law, or subject to the residual law (if any), or even that same personal law as declared by a court other than the court of his domicile. Shortly, there is no *lex loci* in India with regard to the topics for which personal law provides.[78]

The Hindu traditions of law were based on the old *smṛti* literature, especially the *Dharmaśāstra*-s, and such later digests as the eleventh century compilation by Vijñāneśvara, called *Mitākṣarā* (meaning "well crafted"), which came to be authoritative regarding issues of inheritance in south India and much of north India as well, and the compilation of the fourteenth century writer, Jımūtavāhana, called *Dharmaratna* and with a section on the law of inheritance known as *Dāyabhāga* (meaning "portions for inheritance") which came to be authoritative in the region of Bengal.[79] The Muslim traditions of law were dominantly Sunni and of the Hanafite type, that is, followers of the tradition founded by Abu Hanifa.[80] For both Hindu and Muslim traditions, however, there was great variance depending upon region and local custom. Moreover, the traditions of Hindu *dharma* and the traditions of Muslim *Shari'ah* were totalistic, covering all aspects of life and making little differentiation between moral, customary and legal matters. Most important of all, these traditional systems of custom and law had little if anything resembling the notion of equality before the law. Hence, Muslim and Hindu communities, at least with respect to what we identify as civil law, operated quite separately from one another from region to region and with respect to different status groups, and even during centuries of Muslim control, so long as Hindus paid the required taxes, they were permitted to be ruled by their own local customs and personal laws.

When the British first came to the subcontinent they did not concern themselves with local or regional law, and it was not until 1772 that the East India Company decided to "stand forth as Diwan" (that is, as "civil administrators").[81] Warren Hastings introduced a uniform criminal law (based largely on Muslim criminal law) together with the notion of equality before the law for both Hindus and Muslims, but he also provided that "in all suits regarding marriage, inheritance, the laws of the Koran with respect to Mohammedans, and those of the Shastras with respect to Gentus (Hindus) shall be invariably adhered to."[82] Thereafter *brāhmaṇa* pandits and Muslim jurists were regularly appointed and consulted by way of administering and developing the Anglo-Hindu and Anglo-Islamic "personal law."

A first attempt at the development of a uniform civil code came shortly after independence in 1948 with the introduction of the Hindu

Code Bill, a bill designed to codify the myriad of regional Hindu customs and laws as a first step towards a uniform civil code for all. There was much Hindu opposition, and the bill was set aside without passage in 1951, thereby triggering the resignation of the distinguished law minister and untouchable leader, B. R. Ambedkar, who had led the fight for the bill.[83] The Hindu Code Bill was later introduced piecemeal in the mid-1950s and passed as the Hindu Marriage Act (1955), the Hindu Succession Act (1956), the Hindu Minority and Guardianship Act (1956), and the Hindu Adoptions and Mainenance Act (1956). No further attempts have been made to implement Article 44 of the Constitution, since it is widely feared that any such attempt to establish a uniform civil code would lead to communal violence. There is perhaps no more powerful symbol of India's "simultaneous commitment" to "community-ship" and "citizen-ship" than this continuing absence of a uniform civil code.

Article 46 calls upon the State to take an active role in helping "weaker sections," especially Scheduled Castes.

> Article 46
> The State shall promote with special care the educational and economic interests of the weaker sections of the people, and in particular, of the Scheduled Castes and Scheduled Tribes, and shall protect them from social injustice and all forms of exploitation.[84]

Finally, in the sections of the Constitution of India dealing with "Elections" and "Special Provisions Relating to Certain Classes," specific instructions are provided for a single electorate, "reserved seats" for Scheduled Castes and Tribes, the duration of reservation, and the appointment of a special officer to oversee implementation of state procedures. Also, provision is made for appointing a special commission to examine the situation of the backward classes to assist the President and the Houses of Parliament in dealing with these community issues. Article 325 sets forth a provision for a single "electoral roll" thereby doing away with the multiple electorates which had been in operation prior to independence.

> Article 325
> There shall be one general electoral roll for every territorial constituency for election to either House of Parliament or to the House or either House of the Legislature of a State and no person shall be ineligible for inclusion in any such roll or claim to be

> included in any special electoral roll for any such constituency on grounds only of religion, race, caste, sex or any of them.[85]

The provisions for reservation are as follows:

> Article 330
> (1) Seats shall be reserved in the House of the People [the Lok Sabha] for (a) the Scheduled Castes; (b) the Scheduled Tribes
> (2) The number of seats reserved in any State or Union Territory for the Scheduled Castes or the Scheduled Tribes under clause (l) shall bear, as nearly as may be, the same proportion to the total number of seats alloted to that State or Union territory in the House of the People as the population of the Scheduled Castes in the State or Union territory or of the Scheduled Tribes in the State or Union territory or part of the State or Union territory, as the case may be, in respect of which seats are so reserved, bears to the total population of the State or Union territory.[86]
> Article 332
> (l) Seats shall be reserved for the Scheduled Castes and the Scheduled Tribes in the Legislative Assembly of every State.
> (2) The number of seats reserved . . . shall bear . . . the same proportion . . . as the case may be, in respect of which seats are so reserved, bears to the total population of the State.
> Article 334
> Notwithstanding anything in the foregoing provisions of this Part, the provisions of this Constitution relating to . . . the reservation of seats for the Scheduled Castes and the Schedule Tribes in the House of the People and in the Legislative Assemblies of the States . . . shall cease to have effect on the expiration of a period of fifty years from the commencement of this Constitution.[87]

Regarding Article 334, it should be noted that in the original draft of the Constitution, reservation was only to be for ten years. In 1960, 1970, 1980 and 1990 the time limit has been routinely extended for an additional ten years.

> Article 338
> (1) There shall be a Special Officer for the Scheduled Castes and Scheduled Tribes to be appointed by the President.
> (2) It shall be the duty of the Special Officer to investigate all matters relating to the safeguards for the Scheduled Castes and

> Scheduled Tribes under this Constitution and report to the President. . . .[88]
> Article 340
> (1) The President may by order appoint a Commission consisting of such persons as he thinks fit to investigate the conditions of socially and educationally backward classes within the territory of India and the difficulties under which they labour and to make recommendations as to the steps that should be taken by the Union or any State to remove such difficulties and to improve their condition and as to the grants that should be made for the purpose by the Union or any State and the conditions subject to which such grants should be made, and the order appointing such Commission shall define the procedure to be followed by the Commission.
> (2) A Commission so appointed shall investigate the matters referred to them and present to the President a report setting out the facts as found by them and making such recommendations as they think proper.
> (3) The President shall cause a copy of the report so presented together with a memorandum explaining the action taken thereon to be laid before each House of Parliament.[89]

With respect to Article 340, two such commissions have been appointed, the Kalelkar Commission which reported in 1955 and the Mandal Commission which reported in 1980. The recommendations of the Kalelkar Commission were never implemented. The recommendations of the Mandal Commission were finally implemented, at least in part, by Prime Minister V. P. Singh in August of 1990 and became a major factor in the fall of his government three months later in November. We will return to this matter a bit later in the discussion.

In trying to understand precisely how the older hierarchical caste system has been demythologized into the Neo-Hindu post-partition "simultaneous commitment" to "community-ship" and "citizen-ship," the work of Marc Galanter is very much to the point.[90] He has been studying Indian social reality for the past several decades and has tried to trace how notions of caste have changed over time. He argues that there are at least four conceptualizations of caste that can be formulated: (1) a "sacral view of caste," (2) a "sectarian view of caste," (3) an "associational view of caste", and (4) an "organic view of caste."[91] The "sacral" perspective, of course, is the old hierarchical ranking system, based on purity and ritual exchange, with appropriate high and low status in interacting frameworks of dominance and submission, still very much in existence in hundreds, even thousands, of caste communities, especially in rural India. The "sectarian" perspective has to do with the development of a community as a separate, isolated sectarian group, a "self-contained religious unit, dissociated from any larger religious order," including, for example, such regional sectarian groups as the Vīra Śaivas or Lingayats in Karnataka. The "associational" perspective refers to large caste clusters, nowadays found in all sections of India, both rural and urban, which are organized not for ranking or sectarian purposes but rather for certain general interests largely of a political or economic kind. Finally, the "organic" perspective refers to caste groups which combine low status without, however, a "sacral" or "sectarian" orientation, but rather with an "associational" orientation, the prime example of which, Galanter suggests, are the various "Other Backward Classes" (OBCs) which the Rudolphs, as may be recalled from chapter 1, refer to as "bullock capitalists."

According to Galanter, the Constitution of India exhibits three basic principles in terms of its reworking of the caste system, namely, (*a*) the substitution of voluntary belonging for ascribed status, (*b*) the protection of the autonomy of castes and communities, and (*c*) the non-recognition of rank ordering among caste groups.[92] Says Galanter,

> The Constitution can be read as the 'disestablishment' of the sacral view of caste—the courts can give no recognition to the integrative hierarchical principle; yet it recognizes the religious claims of the component parts. Claims based on the sacral order are foreclosed (in personal law reform, temply-entry, abolition of untouchability, de-recognition of exclusionary rights), but claims based on sectarian distinctiveness or group autonomy are not.[93]

In other words, although the "sacral" perspective is no longer countenanced, the "sectarian," the "associational," and the "organic" are recognized and approved. Thus, there is clearly a compromise, a both-and accomodation of the old and the new.

Galanter has also studied in great detail the issue of "compensatory discrimination" and the manner in which it has been employed in terms of reservations for Scheduled Castes, Scheduled Tribes and Other Backward Classes, and he expresses the basic issue in the following terms.

> If secularism is defined in terms of the elimination of India's compartmental group structure in favor of a compact and unitary society, then the compensatory discrimination policy may indeed

> have impeded secularism. But one may instead visualize not the disappearance of communal groups but their transformation into components of a pluralistic society in which invidious hierarchy is discarded while diversity is accomodated. In this view compensatory discrimination policy contributes to secularism by reducing group disparities and blunting hierarchic distinctions.[94]

In terms of final assessment, Galanter concludes,

> The Indian example is instructive: India has managed to pursue a commitment to substantive justice without allowing that commitment to dissolve competing commitments to formal equality that make law viable in a diverse society with limited consensus. The Indian experience displays a principled eclecticism that avoids suppressing the altruistic fraternal impulse that animates compensatory policies, but that also avoids being enslaved by it. From afar it reflects to us a tempered legalism—one which we find more congenial in practice than in theory.[95]

Galanter also quotes the following passage from Granville Austin, author of *The Indian Constitution: Cornerstone of a Nation* (Oxford, 1966):

> India's original contributions to constitution-making [include] . . . accommodation...the ability to reconcile, to harmonize, and to make work without changing their content, apparently incompatible concepts. . . . Indians can accomodate such apparently conflicting principles by seeing them at different levels of value, or, if you will, in compartments not watertight, but sufficiently separate so that a concept can operate freely within its own sphere and not conflict with another operating in a separate sphere. . . . With accommodation, concepts and viewpoints, although seemingly incompatible, stand intact. They are not whittled away by compromise but are worked simultaneously.[96]

What is intriguing, of course, in terms of my own analysis in this monograph, are the expressions "principled eclecticism," "tempered legalism," "more congenial in practice than in theory," "accommodation," "different levels of value," "concepts and viewpoints . . . worked simultaneously," in the idiom of both Galanter and Austin. Both are struggling to give expression to notions about "community-ship" and "citizen-ship" in independent India which are interestingly different from the ordinary use of the terms "community" and "citizen." They are struggling, in other words, to get at the meaning of what I have been calling India's hybrid discourse of modernity. To one familiar with the many frameworks of meaning operating in South Asian thought, both Old Indic and New Indic, expressions such as "principled eclecticism," "tempered legalism," "accommodation," "different levels of value," and "more congenial in practice than in theory," sound very much like demythologized rewrites or recastings of one of the most abiding notions in South Asia, namely, the notion of *dharma*.

Here again, however, as I also cautioned earlier in my discussion of the "secular state" as basically a Neo-Hindu state, let me hasten to add that this is in no way meant as a negative criticism of independent India's "simultaneous commitment" to "community-ship" and "citizen-ship." It is only to clarify and make clear how words and notions relating to "community" and "citizen" are being used in India's hybrid discourse of modernity. That caste and the closely related notion of *dharma* should have no place in modern India and be dismissed as "caste-ism" reminds one of Rajni Kothari's comment that "...those in India who complain of 'casteism' in politics are really looking for a sort of politics which has no basis in society."[97] By the same token it may well be said that those who complain of "communalism" and "caste-ism" from the perspective of an ideological secularism totally divorced from the frameworks of meaning and social reality of South Asian civilization have completely misunderstood not only the genius and promise of India, but more to the point, the serious dangers and threats that exist to the very survival of India as a viable civilisation-state.

Five Current Crises

Let me turn now in this next and final section of the chapter to relating the preceding conceptual analysis to some of the more salient religious crises currently unfolding in India. I am somewhat reluctant to move in this direction, it should be noted, for I recognize that to do so is to cross a boundary line from the realm of scholarly discourse and debate of an historical, philosophical and analytic kind to the realm of current events in which emotions run high, political commitments matter, and outcomes are impossible to predict or determine. Moreover, it is to cross a boundary line from a realm in which there are reasonably reliable sources and materials deriving from many years of patient scholarly work by professional researchers to a realm in which evidence is seldom complete, impressions are often distorted and exaggerated, and the difference between the trivial and the substantive has not yet become clear.[100] The scholar, of course, has every right, perhaps even a responsibility, along with all other interested observers, to comment on the events of the present, so long as it is remembered that the privileged authority that the scholar exercises within his or her own realm of expertise does not necessarily carry over into the realm of current events.

There are, of course, many crises of a religious kind in contemporary India, but five in particular appear to be especially representative, in my judgment, of what I would call "India's agony over religion," namely, (1) the crisis over Sikh separatist demands in the state of Punjab, (2) the crisis over Kashmiri Muslim demands for autonomy in the State of Jammu and Kashmir, (3) the crisis regarding "personal law" and the difficulties of developing a uniform civil code as exhibited in the Shah Bano Begum case and the Muslim Women (Protection of Rights on Divorce) Bill of 1986, (4) the crisis regarding the notion of compensatory discrimination and its extension to the Other Backward Classes (OBCs) as a result of the recommendations of the Report of the Backward Classes Commission (The Mandal Report) and their partial implementation by the V. P. Singh government in 1990, and (5) the crisis in Ayodhya arising out of the destruction in December of 1992 of an old Muslim mosque (Babri Masjid), purportedly located on the precise birthplace of the Hindu Rāma, and the attempt by conservative Neo Hindu groups to rebuild a temple to Rāma on that sacred site (the so-called "Ramjanmabhoomi" or "place of the birth of Rāma").

What I would like to accomplish in briefly treating these five current crises is to show the manner in which a more precise understanding of what I have been calling the syntax and semantic of India's hybrid discourse of modernity may help to clarify what is at stake in each of these situations. As mentioned earlier, far from being a Manichaean struggle in each instance between the enlightened followers of a liberal, democratic "secular state," on the one hand, and the dark forces of "communalism," "fundamentalism," and "terrorism," on the other, I am inclined to see, rather, a much more complicated network of problems, both religious and political, whose origins derive in each instance from unresolved problems stemming from the holocaust of partition, a network of problems in which there appears to be some measure of good will and at the same time an equal measure of malfeasance and bad faith, on all sides.

Before turning to the various crises, however, let me first quickly survey some of the more important historical and political developments in India since partition by way of filling in the background for understanding the contemporary context in which the current religious crises have emerged.[99] The Republic of India has had nine prime ministers since independence in the following order: Jawaharlal Nehru (1947–64), Lal Bahadur Shastri (1964–66), Indira Gandhi (1966–77), Morarji Desai (1977–79), Charan Singh (1979–80), Indira Gandhi for a second time (1980–84), Rajiv Gandhi (1984–89), Viswanath Pratap Singh or simply V. P. Singh (1989–90), Chandra Shekhar (1990–91) and P. V. Narasimha Rao (1991–present). This gives the somewhat misleading picture of a great variety of leaders since independence, when, in fact, there have really been primarily only two, namely, Nehru, for seventeen years, and his daughter, Indira Gandhi, for sixteen years, both of whom were from the Indian National Congress, or simply the Congress party. As might be ancticipated from the earlier statistics mentioned by Khushwant Singh, most of the prime ministers have been Brahmins.

Jawaharlal Nehru, as has been discussed already, guided the newly independent nation through the formative years of constitutional consolidation, the integration of the princely states, states reorganization, and the fashioning of a centrist consensus based on "socialism," "secularism," and non-alignment. With M. K. Gandhi's assassination in 1948 and the deaths of Subhas Chandra Bose in 1945 and Vallabhbhai Patel in 1950, the leading voices for alternative models for the newly emerging state—that is, Gandhi's notion of decentralized *pañcayati raj*, Bose's fascistic notion of authoritarian control by a great leader, and Vallabhbhai Patel's preference for a centralized and authoritarian Hindu state—had been silenced, and Nehru was thus largely free to develop his own ideas and to fashion his own consensus.[100] He was prime minister during the first Indo-Pakistani war over Kashmir (1947–49) and during the Chinese military incursion into Indian territory, also in the Kashmir region, in 1962. Lal Bahadur Shastri, Nehru's successor and also a member of the Congress party, served for only two years and died suddenly of a heart attack in 1966 while negotiating the end of the second Indo-Pakistani war over Kashmir which had begun in 1965. Shastri was succeeded in 1966 by Nehru's daughter, Indira Gandhi, who was selected mainly because she was perceived at the time as a weak interim figure who could serve until Congress party leaders could resolve their various quarrels regarding a stronger successor.

Mrs. Gandhi, however, slowly began to consolidate political power, won the elections of 1967 with only a slim margin, took on the party bosses directly in 1969, split the party and formed her own subsection known as Congress (I) ("I" for Indira) without the old party bosses, and proceeded to win the election in 1971 on a platform of

"Eliminate poverty!" ("garībī haṭao!") with some 43.7% of the vote and a sizable majority of 352 seats in the Lok Sabha or House of the People.[101] Her impressive victory in 1971 was soon followed by another major success, also in 1971, namely, her decisive victory over Pakistan in the third Indo-Pakistani war which issued in the secession and partition of East Pakistan from West Pakistan and the creation of the new state of Bangladesh. Under her leadership the reorganization of the Punjab took place on 1 November 1966 creating the state of Haryana in the southeastern region of the territory with a Hindi-speaking Hindu majority and the state of Punjab in the northwestern region with a Punjabi-speaking Sikh majority, and transferring yet some additional territory to Himachal Pradesh. She negotiated a Treaty of Peace, Friendship and Cooperation with the Soviet Union in August of 1971, and in negotiating the final settlement with Pakistan over Bangladesh she also negotiated the so-called Simla Agreement, signed in 1972, whereby Pakistan and India agreed to the "line of actual control" between Pakistan and India in Kashmir and agreed that further negotiations over Kashmir would be handled bilaterally (or, in other words, not involving outside agencies such as the United Nations).

By the mid-1970s Mrs. Gandhi became increasingly concerned with her own personal power and set about transforming both party and governmental structures from independently functioning agencies into highly personalized fiefdoms based on personal loyalties.[102] She was attacked by political opponents from various sides for alleged election frauds and, finally, on 26 June 1975 called upon the President of India to proclaim an Emergency, setting aside democratic procedures and giving special authoritarian powers to the prime minister. The Emergency was eventually lifted on 18 January 1977 and new elections called. Other political parties, both from the moderate left (but with the exception of the two Commmunist parties) and from the right, then united to form the new Janata Party ("People's" party) in oppostion to Indira Gandhi's Congress (I), and in March of 1977 for the first time since independence the Congress party was thoroughly defeated in a general election. Morarji Desai became the new prime minister under the banner of the new Janata coalition.

The Janata coalition, however, was exceedingly unstable, inasmuch as it combined an utterly unworkable congeries of political positions, ranging from the moderate left (various socialist parties for laborers, farmers and so forth) to the conservative right (the Swatantra, an "Independent" party of big business interests and landowners, and the Bharatiya Jana Sangh, an "Indian People's Party" founded in 1951 and representing conservative Hindu elements from the old Hindu

Mahasabha and the RSS). Quarreling began almost immediately, and in little more than two years, following a brief interim prime ministership for Charan Singh for a few months after July of 1979, Mrs. Gandhi returned to power in January of 1980 with some 42.7 percent of the vote and a comfortable parliamentary majority of 353 seats.[103] Interestingly, it was in these years when she was out of power that Mrs. Gandhi sought support from various regional areas, in the south of India and in the region of the Punjab. In the Punjab she needed a power base apart from the Akali Dal (the "eternal party," the main political organization of the Sikhs in the Punjab region), which had vigorously opposed her Emergency. She and some of her supporters in the Congress (I) then encouraged a young charismatic Punjabi Sikh leader to develop a political base in the Punjab separate from the Akali Dal in the hope that eventually Congress (I) could use such a base to build an alliance against the Akali Dal. The young Sikh leader's name was Jarnail Singh Bhindranwale.[104]

Within a few years Bhindranwale developed his own power base quite apart from the Congress (I) and began to emerge as the key figure in the Sikh separatist movement that was demanding a new independent state for Sikhs in the Punjab, an independent state to be known as "Khalistan" (the "Land of the Khalsā" or the "Land of the Pure"). He and his followers took control of the Sikh Golden Temple and the Akal Takht (the "Eternal Tower"), the central shrine and symbol of the Sikh faith, in Amritsar early in 1984, stockpiling huge caches of weapons and apparently preparing for armed insurrection. In June of 1984 Mrs. Gandhi responded by unleashing the Indian Army against the Golden Temple in Amritsar, under the code name, Operation Blue Star, a bloody encounter in which thousands of Sikhs were killed within the temple grounds, including Bhindranwale. The Sikhs were furious over the destruction of their sacred precinct, and some months later a group of angry Sikhs took their vengeance, persuading two of Indira Gandhi's bodyguards to assassinate Mrs. Gandhi on 31 October 1984. India erupted in fury after the assassination, especially in Delhi. At least a thousand Sikhs were murdered by angry Hindus, and some 50,000 became refugees.

Mrs. Gandhi was succeeded by her son, Rajiv Gandhi, thus continuing the Nehru "dynastic" line. Rajiv had been an Indian Airlines pilot and for the most part uninterested in politics. His younger brother, Sanjay, had been heavily involved in politics, especially during the Emergency period in 1975–77, but he had died suddenly in an airplane accident, and Indira Gandhi was eventually successful in persuading Rajiv to leave Indian Airlines and join her in the political arena. When Mrs. Gandhi was assassinated, Rajiv was immediately sworn in as successor and shortly afterwards in the general elections in December of 1984 received a huge wave of support with some 48.1 percent percent of the popular vote and an overwhelming 415 seats in the House of the People.[105] December of 1984, however, was to bring yet one more major tragedy for India, the famous Union Carbide accident at Bhopal in the State of Madhya Pradesh, killing at least 2,000 and injuring thousands more.

On the political front Rajiv was at first successful in negotiating a settlement with a key leader of the Sikhs in the Punjab, Sant Harchand Singh Longowal, a settlement known as the Punjab Accord and signed in July of 1985. One month later, however, Longowal was assassinated by Sikh extremists. Elections were nevertheless held in the state of Punjab, and Longowal's wing of the Akali Dal, the main Sikh political party, came into power under the chief ministership of Surjit Singh Barnala, a disciple of Longowal. By May of 1987, however, factional squabbling, extremist violence and the failure of Rajiv Gandhi's government to follow through on the agreements of the Punjab Accord led to the dismissal of the Barnala government and the imposition of President's Rule from Delhi. Elections were held again in February 1992 with Congress winning most of the seats largely because the elections were universally boycotted by the Sikh majority.

There was also separatist trouble with Kashmir, as we shall see in the sequel, as well as in the tribal regions in the Northeast (Assam and Mizoram). A separatist problem was also developing in Sri Lanka where some four million Tamil Indians in the north of the island were feeling increasingly alienated from the majority Sinhalese Buddhist population. An armed guerilla movement, known as the LTTE (Liberation Tigers of Tamil Elam), was pushing for the development of an independent Tamil nation on the island. Rajiv Gandhi negotiated what came to be known as the Indo–Sri Lanka Peace Agreement in July of 1987 in Colombo with President J. R. Jayewardene, the leader of Sri Lanka, involving greater autonomy for Tamil areas in Sri Lanka but mainly involving an agreement to send some 15,000 Indian Army troops (later to be increased to some 40,000) into Sri Lanka (the so-called IPKF or Indian Peace Keeping Force) to disarm the Tigers. The effort was a huge failure, and eventually, after sizable casualities on all sides, Indian troops were withdrawn. Just as Mrs. Gandhi paid the price of assassination for her intrusion into the Golden Temple, so Rajiv Gandhi was to pay the price of assassination for his actions against the Tigers, for it is evidently the case that the group responsible for the assassination of Rajiv Gandhi on 21 May 1991 at Sriperumbudur, some twenty miles outside of Madras in the state of Tamil Nadu, had direct links with the Tamil Liberation Tigers.

Rajiv Gandhi was prime minister from 1984 to 1989. He was welcomed initially for his fresh ideas in such areas as high-tech development and liberalization of the economy and for his expressed desire to bring new faces into the political process. He also enjoyed widespread support out of sympathy for the tragic assassination of his mother and for his willingness to carry on the Nehru "dynasty." By 1989, however, his popularity had greatly slipped. A number of scandals developed, including disclosures that large industrialists were not paying taxes and the discovery of a wide-ranging kickback scheme among government officials (and possibly including the prime minister's office) over the procurement of military hardware from a Swedish armaments company named Bofors, a kickback scheme involving huge sums of money.

In October of 1987, V. P. Singh, a political figure from Allahabad in the state of Uttar Pradesh and former finance and defense minister in the cabinet of Rajiv Gandhi, after having been forced to resign from his cabinet posts and having been expelled from the Congress (I), mainly for having called attention to the growing corruption in the Congress (I), formed a Jan Morcha (a "people's movement") in opposition to the Congress (I). The Jan Morcha eventually united with the Janata Dal ("People's Party") and other opposition groups to oppose Rajiv Gandhi and the Congress (I) in the general elections of 1989. Rajiv Gandhi and his Congress (I) were defeated, and V. P. Singh became prime minister in December of 1989 under the banner of the National Front, an electoral alliance of opposition parties, including the Janata Dal ("People's Party"), the Dravida Munnetra Kazhagam or DMK, a Tamil nationalist party, the Telugu Desam (from the State of Andhra Pradesh or the "Telugu Regional" party), and the Asom Gana Parishad or AGP, an Assamese party from the Northeast.

Unfortunately, the V. P. Singh alliance controlled only 145 seats and had to form a minority coalition government. On the left, V. P. Singh made an alliance with both Communist parties, that is, the CPI, the Communist Party of India, a party closely related to the so-called Moscow line, and the CPM (M for Marxist), a more indigenous Communist movement which has been in power in the State of West Bengal since 1977 and is a close rival with Congress in the state of Kerala. On the right, V. P. Singh formed an alliance with the BJP, the Bharatiya Janata Party, formed after 1979 (from followers of the older Bharatiya Jana Sangh, originally founded in 1951), a conservative Hindu party, closely related to the conservative Hindu RSS, the Rashtriya Swayamsevak Sangh or the "National Assembly of Volunteers" (first founded back in 1925), and the VHP, the Vishva Hindu Parishad or the "World Council of Hindus" (founded in 1964). Congress (I) became, of course, the opposition party, and Rajiv Gandhi, the leader of the opposition.

As might well be imagined, such a coalition had difficulties almost from the beginning, and by November of 1990, just eleven months after taking office, V. P. Singh's government was defeated with a no-confidence vote of 356–151 in the House of the People (or Lok Sabha). The primary reason for the defeat was the withdrawal of support for V. P. Singh by the conservative BJP. In addition to the continuing separatist problems in the states of Punjab and Jammu and Kashmir, the V. P. Singh government also had become entangled in two other major cultural and religious crises, the crisis related to V. P. Singh's decision to implement some of the recommendations of the Mandal Commission regarding job reservations for Other Backward Classes in central government posts (in August of 1990) and the emerging crisis at Ayodhya in the State of Uttar Pradesh concerning a Muslim mosque (the Babri Masjid) on the site of the sacred birthplace of the Hindu Rāma (the Ramjanmabhoomi or "birth-place of Rāma").

The V. P. Singh coalition was followed by an even more unstable coalition put together by Chandra Shekhar in November of 1990 and lasting only until March of 1991. Thereafter new elections were called, and in the middle of the election campaigning on 21 May 1991 Rajiv Gandhi was assassinated in Sriperumbudur, as already mentioned. The elections were finally resumed and in June of 1991 the Congress (I) returned to power, undoubtedly helped by the sympathy vote created as a result of the tragic assassination. Yet again, however, a coalition was required, since Congress (I) only won some 213 seats although by 1994, by reason of political realignments, it became a majority government. P. V. Narasimha Rao, a loyal Congress (I) supporter from the Dravidian south (the state of Andhra Pradesh) who had served as chief minister in Andhra Pradesh (1962–77) and then minister of external affairs (1980–84 and again 1988–89) and defense minister (1984-85) on the national level under both Mrs. Gandhi and Rajiv Gandhi, was sworn in as India's ninth prime minister on 21 June 1991, and he has continued in office. Some measure of stability has been achieved under Rao's leadership, although the destruction of the Babri Masjid by Hindu militants in December of 1992 nearly brought down his government. It is generally agreed, however, that even though all of the separatist troubles and cultural crises remain unresolved, conditions in India under Rao's leadership are somewhat less volatile, and it could possibly be the case that he will be able to finish his five-year term.

1. The crisis with the Sikh community in the state of Punjab. The origin of the Sikh tradition in the fifteenth century under Guru Nanak (1469–1539) and its transformation under the tenth Guru, Gobind Singh (1666–1708) into a militant spiritual-cum-political movement has already been briefly sketched in chapter 1, and the relation of the movement to other religious traditions within the Indo-Islamic context was briefly discussed in chapter 3. After the long and painful struggle of the Sikhs against the Mughals (especially Aurangzeb) in the seventeenth century, the eighteenth century was a period of growing Sikh political power in local areas of the Punjab, culminating in the emergence of a major Sikh kingdom towards the end of the eighteenth century under the remarkable Maharaja Ranjit Singh, who ruled over most of the Punjab region from 1799–1839, or, in other words, almost to the time of the annexation of the Punjab by the British in 1849. The Sikhs remained loyal during the 1857–58 North Indian rebellion (the so-called "Mutiny") and were a great help to the British in putting down the rebellion, thereafter becoming a favored group for recruitment into the Indian military under the British Raj.[106]

From the beginnings of the tradition in the fifteenth century, as a small minority religious tradition that was neither Muslim nor Hindu, though nevertheless influenced by both traditions, the key issue for the Sikh community has been one of maintaining a distinct identity, to avoid, on the one hand, the power of the Muslims (both political and military), and, on the other hand, absorption or assimilation by the huge Hindu population that surrounds the community on all sides. The formation of the Khālsā (the "pure" or "distinct" community) and its code of conduct (known as the *Rahit*), the so-called "five K-s" (unshorn hair, comb, steel bangle, dagger and special undergarment), the special rituals of initiation, the centrality of the *gurdwara* or "temple" for group worship and devotional singing, the separate Sikh scripture known as the Ādi Granth or the Guru Granth Sahib ("The Book of the Lord") in a unique script called Gurmukhi (which differs from the Arabic-Persian-Urdu script of Muslims and the Devanagari script of Hindus), the common meal from the "kitchen" (*langar*) in the *gurdwara* in which all partake regardless of caste, and so forth, are all obvious and apparent symbolic markings designed to set Sikhs apart from other traditions, especially Hindu traditions.[107]

At the same time, however, Sikh religious literature and poetry appear to conflate both Hindu (*bhakti*) and Muslim (mainly Sufi) motifs and not all followers of the Sikh tradition are "baptized" or "initiated" (*amrit-dhārī* or "taking the nectar"), becoming *Kes-dhārī*-s ("wearing unshorn hair") or full members of the Khālsā. Many remain simply *Sahaj-dhārī*-s or "non-Khālsā Sikhs" or "not yet committed." These latter are loyal to the teachings of Guru Nanak and the Sikh way generally, but they do not wear unshorn hair and frequently consider themselves very close to Hindus. In addition, there are a great variety of splinter groups, sectarian offshoots and one or another kind of "heretical" (in the opinion of Khālsā Sikhs) sub-groups, including Nirankaris, Udasis, and others. There are also accepted traditions of intermarriage and interdining in the Punjab between some Hindu and Sikh families. Thus, although on one level there is a distinct and definite Sikh identity that is deliberately cultivated, there is also nevertheless a significant subset of members constantly tending to be absorbed or assimilated into the larger Hindu environment. There is no one monolithic Sikh tradition, in other words, despite the rhetorical claims of the Khālsā Sikhs to the contrary. There are, rather, various kinds of Sikh tradition, although the Khālsā tradition is certainly the most dominant and apparent.

In the twentieth century there have been primarily four periods in which the relations between the Sikh community and the state have reached crisis proportions: (*a*) the period 1920–25, in which the Khālsā Sikh community finally succeeded in establishing clear spiritual and institutional control over the network of *gurdwara*-s in the Punjab region, culminating in the consolidation of the authority of the Shiromani Gurdwara Prabandhak Committee (the SGPC), the "Supreme Temple Management Committee," and the emergence of the Akali Dal as the primary spiritual-cum-political vehicle for articulating Sikh concerns; (*b*) the period 1946–1966, in which the Sikh community actively sought either a separate state (at the time of partition) or at least a distinct linguistic cultural region, the so-called "Punjabi *suba*" or "Punjabi state," which was finally granted under Indira Gandhi in 1966; (*c*) the period 1973–1984, in which the Sikh community sought to implement the Anandpur Sahib Resolution of October of 1973, which included, among other items, securing the city of Chandigarh as the capital of the state of Punjab, greater autonomy within the Indian nation-state, institutional control of all *gurdwara*-s in India, and so forth, culminating in the tragedy of Operation Blue Star and its aftermath; and (*d*) the period 1985–present, in which continuing efforts have been pursued to implement the provisions of the Punjab Accord (signed in 1985 but never implemented) and to reestablish full Sikh participation in the politics of the state of Punjab and in the nation generally.[108]

The crisis of the first period (1919–25) coincided with the earliest phase of the nationalist movement under Gandhi's leadership, a period in which Gandhi was forging a broad consensus by supporting Muslim causes (as, for example, the Khilafat movement, as already discussed) and by supporting the demands of the Sikh community for representation in the Punjab legislative councils and for control over their *gurdwara-s* or temples in the Punjab. In terms of the nationalist movement overall, not only in the decade of the 1920s but up through the attainment of independence as well, the Sikh community for the most part supported Gandhi and the Indian National Congress and its strategy of non-violent non-cooperation, although the community always kept one eye on its own specific concerns.[109] On the local regional level, the Sikh community was primarily concerned about consolidating its own identity and establishing control over its own institutional structures. For some time many of the Sikh *gurdwara*-s had come under the hereditary control of local priests or *mahant*-s, most of whom were *Sahajdhārī*-s or "non-Khālsā" Sikhs. There was a great deal of financial abuse and general corruption, but, worst of all, a careless disregard for the Sikh traditions and the introduction of many Hindu idols and rituals that had no place in a Sikh *gurdwara*, at least in the opinion of many Khālsā Sikhs.[110] The Sikh agitation against the *mahant*-s was led by a group of reformers who began to become prominent from 1920 onwards and who took the name of an old ascetic group within the Sikh tradition going back to the time of Gobind Singh, namely, the "Akalis," which means something like the "eternally vigilant ones."[111] In many ways the Akalis were the twentieth century successors of the nineteenth century reformist group known as the Singh Sabha and its radical wing known as the Tat ("true") Khālsā.[112]

The strategy employed for the agitation was the Gandhian one of non-violent occupation of the various *gurdwara*-s. At first the British administrators of the Punjab government, though officially neutral, were largely unsympathetic to the Akali cause and took the side of the *mahant*-s as having legitimate property rights to the *gurdwara*-s. After repeated demonstrations and occupations, however, including the violent massacre of some 130 Sikhs by Muslim mercenaries at a *gurdwara* in Nankana in 1921 and a number of other ugly incidents, the Akali demands were finally conceded in 1925 with the passage of the Sikh Gurdwaras and Shrines Act which placed all *gurdwara*-s under the control of the elected Shiromani Gurdwara Prabandhak Committee (the SGPC or Supreme Temple Management Committee), a group that had been founded in 1920 at about the same time as the emergence of the Akali movement.[113] The SGPC was largely under the leadership of the Akalis who now called themselves the Akali Dal (the "eternal party"), a spiritual-cum-political party which has continued to be the main vehicle for Sikh community action down to the present day. The passage of the 1925 act assured that the dominant and controlling voice in the Sikh movement would be the *Kes-dhārī* or Khālsā Sikhs. The *Sahaj-dhārī* or non-Khālsā Sikhs and other sectarian sub-groups would thereafter have to conform with the strict definitions of the Khālsā conceptualization of the Sikh Panth (the Sikh "community").[114]

The SGPC was to have over 150 members, just over 120 of which were to be elected for a five-year term, the rest nominated or appointed to represent various other constituencies. The five chief priests of the main *gurdwara*-s were members, including the chief priest of the Golden Temple in Amritsar. All adult male and female Sikhs within the Punjab were eligible to vote in elections to the SGPC, and the elections were administered through the electoral machinery of the Punjab state. It was a powerful religious organization which quickly gained control over the finances and leadership for all *gurdwara*-s in the Punjab.[115] It, therefore, also controlled enormous patronage power in terms of schools, missionaries, publications and countless jobs for managers, servants, and so forth. Little of significance could occur in the Sikh community after 1925 without the approval of the SGPC. Moreover, the Akali Dal had been a powerful, driving force in the Sikh community from this early period, and it continues to be the dominant voice within the SGPC. Both organizations, of course, have undergone many changes through the years as a result of many amendments to the original enabling act of 1925 and the development of various factions and wings within the Akali Dal. The consolidation achieved in 1925, however, was fundamental in shaping the Sikh community.[116]

If the crisis of the first period was centered largely on developing a cohesive spiritual and institutional identity for the community, then it can be said that the crisis of the second period (1946–66) was to center on then determining the manner in which the Sikh community would locate itself over against other communities in the Punjab region and within the newly independent Republic of India. As partition became ever more likely, the Sikhs felt ever more isolated and ignored. On one side Muslims were calling for Pakistan. On another side Sikhs were continually being absorbed into the older amorphous Hindu environment. On yet another side militant Neo-Hindus of the Arya Samaj variety were pursuing active campaigns of re-conversion and performing "purification"-ceremonies (*śuddhi*) among Indian Muslims, Christians and Sikhs for readmission into a reformed Neo-Hindu fold.[117] And, of course, there was the continuous pressure for conversion from the ever-present Protestant evangelical missionaries. The Sikhs, indeed, had good reason to think that their survival as a distinct religious community was seriously threatened.

The Sikh Panth (community) did not want partition, for they realized that that would seriously divide their communities in the Punjab. In order to head off the partition proposal, the Akali Dal first presented a counter-proposal to create an "Azad Punjab," a "Free Punjab," made up of carefully balanced groups of Hindus, Muslims and Sikhs with no one community having a majority.[118] The proposal was largely ignored by Indian political leaders. In 1946 Master Tara Singh (1885–1967), leader of the Sikh Panth, then wrote a memorandum, arguing against partition because it would seriously divide the Sikh community, but then saying that if partition were to be implemented, there should also be provision for a separate Sikh state which would have the right to federate with either India or Pakistan.[119] Finally, in March 1946 the executive committee of the Akali Dal passed the following resolution:

> Whereas the Sikhs being attached to the Punjab by intimate bonds of holy shrines, property, language, traditions, and history claim it as their homeland and holy land . . . and whereas the entity of the Sikhs is being threatened on account of the persistent demand for Pakistan by the Muslims on the one hand and of danger of absorption by the Hindus on the other . . . [the] Executive Committee of the Shiromani Akali Dal demands, for the preservation and protection of the religious, cultural and economic rights of the Sikh nation, the creation of a Sikh state.[120]

The demand for a "Sikhistan" or "Khalistan" was ignored, and, thus, just as partition was the tragic creation-narrative for both India and Pakistan, so it was for the Sikh community, except that in the case of the Sikh community partition was even more wrenching, inasmuch as no appropriate place was provided for what was being created, no special provision was made for an autonomous status of any kind, yet the community was forced to undergo a cultural upheaval and trauma as great or greater than that for Hindu India or Muslim Pakistan.[121]

Even though no special status or place emerged because of partition, the political situation for the Sikhs in terms of demography and representation was greatly altered as a result of the community migrations. Before partition Punjab had been 26 percent Hindu and 13 percent Sikh. After partition Punjab was to be 60 percent Hindu and 35 percent Sikh, a tremendous increase in the presence of Sikhs. Almost immediately, then, Master Tara Singh and his chief lieutenant, Sant Fateh Singh, together with the Akali Dal, began to push for greater regional autonomy, and, under the states reorganization plan, for the creation of a Punjabi-speaking linguistic-cultural region (or, in other words, a "Punjabi *suba*") on analogy with other linguistic-cultural regions coming into existence in the mid-1950s such as Tamil Nadu, Kerala, and so forth. The effort was fully justified under the provisions of the new Constitution which allowed for the protection, preservation and autonomy of religious and linguistic minorities. Nehru, however, was unsympathetic and considered the Sikh demands religious and "communal" instead of simply linguistic and cultural, and the report of the States Reorganization Commission in 1955, undoubtedly under Nehru's influence, recommended that Punjab remain bilingual (both Punjabi-speaking and Hindi-speaking). Akali agitations continued, however, for a "Punjabi *suba*" (an "entity" or "state"), until finally under Indira Gandhi in 1966, partly as a reward for Sikh support in the second Indo-Pakistani war in 1965, two new states were created, a Hindi-speaking and Hindu-majority state of Haryana and a Punjabi-speaking and Sikh-majority (originally 54%, but in more recent years, 60%) state of Punjab.[122] The city of Chandigarh was to serve initially as the capital of both states but would eventually become, according to an alleged promise made by Mrs. Gandhi, the capital of the state of Punjab. The Sikh community had finally achieved one of its important goals, a region, a "Punjabi *suba*" in which they could have an autonomous, majority status.

The third and fourth periods, namely, 1973–1984 and 1985–present, are best treated together, since they represent a twenty-year continuing process of deterioration and alienation between the Sikh community and the Neo-Hindu civilisation-state characterized by cynical political maneuvering, extremist rhetoric, strident hostility and excessive violence on both sides. Neither the Neo-Hindu Republic of India nor the Sikh community can be proud of the events of the past twenty years. The Golden Temple and the Akal Takht, proud symbols of a great religious heritage, were occupied and desecrated by armed religious extremists and thugs led by a young Sikh preacher, Jarnail Singh Bhindranwale, and then nearly destroyed by the tanks and troops of Operation Blue Star. The prime minister of India, Indira Gandhi, was ruthlessly assassinated. Thousands of innocent Sikhs were slaughtered in the resulting Hindu rage, a rage at least partly orchestrated by Congress (I) leaders. Sikh assassins have attacked public officials and innocent civilians with impunity throughout the Punjab and even outside the Punjab, in the city of Delhi and elsewhere. Indian Army troops, police and paramilitary forces in retaliation have turned much of the state of Punjab into an occupied territory in which civil liberties have been set aside with alacrity. People on all sides have suffered, and worst of all, even now after twenty years of brutal conflict and violence, and even though elections have been held and there is a great weariness over the continuing agony on all sides, there is very little interaction, let alone understanding, between the Punjabi Sikhs and the Neo-Hindu state.

The basic problem appears to be that even with a "Punjabi suba" after 1966, the Khālsā Sikhs of the Akali Dal and the SGPC continued to be unable to establish an uncontested political and religious dominance in the new State of Punjab. There was still a sizable Hindu population (nearly 40%), and the Akali Dal could only put together governments in coalition with other non-Sikh forces, ironically enough, with the conservative Hindu Bharatiya Jana Sangh and the Communist party.[123] Congress (I) continued to have support not only among Hindu and Neo-Hindu groups but also among many Sikhs, both Khālsā and non-Khālsā, which supports the point made earlier that the Sikh tradition in the Punjab is not at all a monolithic one but represents, rather, a whole range of political and religious views. Finally, in 1972 because of factional disputes and general disorder, the Akali Dal was defeated in provincial elections and a Congress (I) government came into power in the state of Punjab. The frustration over this defeat together with the continuing conviction that the Centre (meaning Indira Gandhi's Congress [I]) was undercutting the Akali Dal and cyncially delaying all attempts to deal with the various grievances of the Sikh community triggered a major gathering of Akali Dal leaders at Anandpur Sahib, the place where the tenth Guru had first formed the Khālsā, and on 17 October 1973 the Anandpur Sahib Resolution was approved, proclaiming the Shiromani Akali Dal as the very embodiment of the Sikh community and hence its authentic representative, and demanding, among other things, the city of Chandigarh as the capital of the state of Punjab, greater autonomy for the Sikh community in the Punjab beyond that allowed for other regional areas in the Constitution of India, an all-India *gurdwara* act so that all Sikh temples in India would come under control of the SGPC, and so forth.[124] This was followed some years later on 8 September 1981 with a Charter of Akali Grievances.[125] The resolution and the charter, which together contain a variety of religious, political and economic grievances, are usually cited as the basis for Sikh complaints down to the present time. Some claim that the documents are secessionist and represent a demand, finally, for a separate Sikh state. Others contend that the documents can be read as wanting only clear and unambiguous autonomy for the Sikh community within the framework of the Constitution of India.

In 1975, as already discussed, Indira Gandhi proclaimed her Emergency, which the Akali Dal vigorously opposed, and when the Emergency was lifted and elections called in 1977, Mrs. Gandhi and the Congress (I) were overwhelmingly defeated by a coalition of opposition parties known as the Janata party. The Janata party formed a government at the Centre (under Morarji Desai) and also joined with the Akali Dal in the state of Punjab to form a provincial coalition government there. Also, as mentioned earlier, it was in this period when she was out of power that Mrs. Gandhi and her supporters (mainly her son, Sanjay, and the former Congress chief minister of Punjab and later president of India, Giani Zail Singh) tried to develop a power base within the Sikh community apart from the Akali Dal and began to encourage a young, charismatic preacher from a seminary school (known as the Dam dama Taxal) near Amritsar, a young preacher named Jarnail Singh Bhindranwale.[126] The idea was to develop a base within the Khālsā Sikh community apart from the Akali Dal with which Congress (I) could eventually align itself and thereby regain and maintain political power in the state.

By 1979 the Janata party coalition had come apart, and by January 1980 Mrs. Gandhi and the Congress (I) had come back into power at the Centre. Also in the provincial assembly election in Punjab, Congress (I) won 54 percent of the seats and formed a new Congress government in the state of Punjab. By 1980 the Akali Dal was breaking up into two factions, a larger moderate faction led by Sant Harchand Singh Longowal (1928–85) and a lesser faction led by Jagdev Singh Talwandi.[127] Moreover, Jarnail Singh Bhindranwale was developing his own independent power base and rapidly coming to be perceived as the key leader of the radical wing of the Sikh community wanting total autonomy from India.[128] Mrs. Gandhi continued to negotiate with the Sikh community regarding their various demands, but little progress was made, partly because of the contradictory demands among the various Sikh factions and partly because of what appears to have been a strategy of cynical delay on the part of Mrs. Gandhi and the Centre. In the meanwhile terrorist acts of violence and police repression were greatly increasing. After two and one half years of continuing negotiation, little of significance was resolved in terms of Chandigarh, greater regional autonomy, an all-India *gurdwara* act and a host of other concerns.[129]As was described earlier, by 1984 Bhindranwale had occupied the Golden Temple and the Akal Takht, Operation Blue Star was implemented (in June) , Mrs. Gandhi was assassinated (31 October 1984), and relations between the Sikh community and the Neo-Hindu state had descended into terrorist attacks, massive government repression and massive violence.

Some hope for compromise and the restoration of order appeared in 1985. Harchand Singh Longowal was again the chief spokesman for the Akali Dal and proposed a "peace offensive."[130] This was to issue in the Punjab Accord agreed to by Rajiv Gandhi, the new prime minister, and Longowal on 23 July 1985, calling for the transfer of Chandigarh to Punjab by 26 January 1986, greater autonomy for the Sikh community in the state of Punjab but within the framework of the Constitution, consideration of an all-India *gurdwara* act, a commission to be formed to study the issue of water rights, and a host of other compromise agreements.[131] Reaction in the Punjab to the accord was mixed, some calling it a "sellout" and others supporting it, but, unfortunately, just as Longowal was making progress in gaining support for the accord, he was assassinated on 20 August 1985. In spite of the assassination, Rajiv Gandhi pushed ahead with the new elections that had been called for in the accord, and the Akali Dal won a decisive victory. Surjit Singh Barnala, a close follower of Longowal, became chief minister in the new government. Rajiv Gandhi, however, was not successful in delivering on his promises regarding Chandigarh, greater autonomy and most other aspects of the accord, and the Barnala government soon lost support in the Punjab. In May 1987 Barnala was dismissed and President's Rule established in the state together with a growing and massive military presence. Throughout 1988 and 1989 various efforts were made to negotiate with Sikh militant radicals, including an attempt to work with the militant leader, Jasbir Singh Rode, and more recently with Simranjit Singh Mann.[132] The V. P. Singh government in 1989–90 tried to ease the crisis in the Punjab but largely failed as did the short-lived efforts of the Chandra Shekhar government in 1990–91. Under the present prime minister, P. V. Narasimha Rao, who came into power in June of 1991 after the assassination of Rajiv Gandhi, elections in the Punjab were finally held in February of 1992, and a Congress (I) government installed with Beant Singh as chief minister, but, unfortunately, all of the factions of the Akali Dal and related organizations boycotted the voting. Thus, the new government had hardly any support from the Akali Dal, the SGPC or the Khālsā Sikh community generally. Since February of 1992 the level of violence has subsided considerably, and Beant Singh has lasted much longer than anyone had supposed.[133] There is still deep alienation and lack of understanding between the Sikh community and the Neo-Hindu state, however, and the grisly narrative of violent confrontation may well have additional chapters. In April of 1994 various factions of the Akali Dal joined forces and put forth the Amritsar Declaration, a call for a special status for the state of Punjab within a new Indian "confederation." If a special status is not granted, the groups reserve the right to begin a new struggle for an independent state.

From the perspective of the present book, certain points are worth noting. First, there are a variety of religious players, as it were, in the unfolding crisis: Khālsā Sikhs, non-Khālsā Sikhs, caste Hindus, Arya Samaj Neo-Hindus, conservative Bharatiya Jana Sangh and more recently BJP Neo-Hindus, and, of course, the Neo-Hindu state itself. To the extent that Nehru suspected that the Sikh demands for linguistic and cultural autonomy were a cover for a hidden religious agenda for independent status and possibly even secession, to the same extent the Sikh community has always suspected that the so-called "secular state" is little more than a cover for a repressive Neo-Hindu state and its hidden agenda for absorption and assimilation. Rhetoric aside, both suspicions have more than a little validity. There are, in other words, fundamental religious issues in the Punjab crisis that need to be carefully sorted out and analyzed.

Second, the trauma of partition is fundamental for understanding the crisis in the Punjab, and it can well be argued that much of the problem has to do with unresolved issues stemming from partition. There can be no doubt but that Sikhs were dealt with in a high-handed and unfair manner by both Hindu India and Muslim Pakistan. That Sikhs should continue to be deeply disturbed about their self-identity and their autonomy is hardly surprising.

Third, the trauma of partition was compounded by Nehru's continuing refusal to support a Punjabi-speaking linguistic and cultural area on analogy with the other cultural areas that were emerging in the mid-fifties during the states reorganization process. That the Sikhs had to wait another decade (until 1966) for attaining some kind of "Punjabi *suba*" was a clear denial of Sikh rights under the provisions of the Constitution of India. Delays regarding not only autonomy but a host of other issues as well greatly increased the frustration and anger of the Sikh community and contributed in no small measure to the growing radicalization of Sikh demands.

Fourth, while the actions and delays of the Centre have been a major, and possibly even the major factor, in the crisis in the Punjab, it cannot be overlooked that the Sikhs themselves bear a good deal of responsibility for the chaos and disorder. Through 1966 the Sikh demands were for the most part reasonable and workable, although even in the earlier years the Khālsā Sikhs of the Akali Dal and the SGPC claimed a hegemony over the Sikh cultural heritage and a monopoly of the very definition of what it is to be Sikh that is hardly reflective of the broad, pluralistic heritage going back to Guru Nanak. One has the sense that legitimate concerns regarding identity and autonomy tended to become all too quickly an uptight defensiveness and rigidified provincialism. Moreover, after 1966 the ambiguous claims by squabbling Sikh leaders for autonomy that clearly bordered on secession and insurrection together with the SGPC's and Akali Dal's acquiescence in random acts of violence and guerilla terrorism were totally unwarranted and counterproductive and had the fully predictable result of bringing down the full power of the police and military on their own Sikh communities as well as the surrounding Hindu communities. By 1984 one can only describe the behavior of Khālsā Sikh leaders in terms of mindless communal suicide. Longowal finally realized this in 1985, and it is a great tragedy that he was not able to follow through with his "peace offensive." In any case, as I have suggested earlier, there is no Manichaean good versus evil in the Punjab situation. There is plenty of blame for all concerned and a desperate need for all to step back and to try to understand where the mistakes were made so that new trajectories can be pursued away from the tragic path of death and violence. Possibly the recent respite from violence under Beant Singh's chief ministership may prove to a welcome opportunity to rebuild lines of communication between the Sikh community and the Government of India.

2. *The crisis over Kashmiri Muslim demands for autonomy in the state of Jammu and Kashmir.* The basic background surrounding the crisis in Kashmir is somewhat simpler than the long and complex Sikh story, but the overall crisis is no less fundamental and tragic.[134] Since the time of Aśoka (third century B.C.E.) Kashmir had been ruled either by Buddhist or Hindu rulers and it was not until the fourteenth century that it came under Muslim dominance. Kashmir became part of the Mughal Empire under Akbar in 1586, was for a time under Afghan rule from 1756 onwards, and was finally annexed to Ranjit Singh's Sikh Empire in the Punjab in 1819. In 1820 Ranjit Singh transferred the area of Jammu to Raja Gulab Singh, a Hindu ruler of Dogra (Rajput) ancestry, and in 1846 under the Treaty of Amritsar the Kashmir Valley also came under the control of Gulab Singh and the Dogras. In these years, of course, the British presence was greatly expanding, and British supremacy was rapidly being recognized and would continue to be recognized until the time of independence in 1947.

Before partition, the princely state of Kashmir was the largest in land area as well as the most populous among the princely states. Following partition, it came to be known as the state of Jammu and Kashmir. It included not only the Kashmir Valley itself, a relatively small area some 85 miles across from east to west and some 20 to 25 miles from north to south (making up about 10% of the total region), but also the Jammu region to the south (making up about 15% of the total region), the vast Ladakh region to the east (making up over 50% of the area), and the mountainous area to the far north, including Gilgit, Baltistan, and so forth.[135] The Kashmir Valley, though the smallest region in area, has the largest population with some four million Kashmiri Muslims (about two-thirds of the entire population of the state), who were and are mainly peasants, service workers and artisans, and a very small but influential percentage of Hindu Kashmiri Brahmins known as "Pandits" (from which latter group, as has been mentioned, the Nehru family derives), who were a learned and educated elite community of administrators, educators and managers.[136] The main languages in the Valley are Urdu and Kashmiri, and the Valley's most important city, Srinagar, serves as the summer capital of the state. The Jammu region in the south is the homeland of the Hindu Dogra (Rajput) ruling family and a mainly Hindu population of under 2 million. The main languages in Jammu are Dogri and Punjabi, and the most important city, Jammu, is the winter capital of the State. The remaining regions of the state are sparsely populated. In addition to the majority Muslims and the smaller Hindu community, the state also has some 130,000 Sikhs and some 70,000 Tibetan Buddhists. The state of Jammu and Kashmir is the only Muslim majority state in the Indian Union.

The struggle for freedom and a distinct identity for Kashmiri Muslims was a problem long before partition during the extended period when Kashmiri Muslims were controlled by the minority Hindu Dogra dynasty and by the numerically small but remarkably influential Kashmiri Brahmin Pandits. Moreover, in earlier times as well, before the nineteenth century, Kashmiri Muslims had seldom been trusted by earlier rulers for any sort of political or administrative leadership. Even in Mughal times, Kabuli Muslims (from Afghanistan) and Punjabi Muslims were brought into the Kashmir Valley to govern the Kashmiri Muslims.[137] Even then, members from the small Kashmiri Brahmin community were regularly utilized for key leadership roles. Likewise during the periods of Afghan and Sikh rule, outsiders were regularly brought into the valley for purposes of administration and combined with Kashmiri Brahmins. Thus, the Kashmiri Muslims have always been a neglected, rather isolated and distinct Muslim community, largely under Sufi influence, distinct not only from Hindu traditions but from other traditions of Islam as well. Kashmiri Muslims, in other words, are in language, culture and religion a unique and unusual community in South Asia.[138]

The first stirring of cultural and political awakening occurred in the early 1930s with the emergence of one of the most remarkable characters of twentieth century South Asian history, Sheikh Muhammad Abdullah (1905–1982), who eventually came to be known as the "Lion of Kashmir."[139] Sheikh Abdullah took a science degree from the Anglo-Oriental College at Aligarh (the place, it may be recalled, for the emergence of modernist yet separatist Neo-Muslim sentiment) and after returning to the valley formed a political movement in 1932 called the All-Jammu and Kashmir Muslim Conference, the name of which by 1939 was changed to the All-Jammu and Kashmir National Conference, or simply the National Conference.[140] The original purpose of the movement was to improve the situation of Kashmiri Muslims, but very quickly it became the symbolic rallying point for a variety of dissident groups, including Hindus, Sikhs, Buddhists, and so forth, all of whom were becoming increasingly dissatisfied with the autocratic Hindu Dogra Maharaja. Sheikh Abdullah was a vigorous opponent of Maharaja Hari Singh whom he considered to be not only high-handed and dictatorial but utterly illegitimate in view of the overwhelming Muslim majority in the region.

Early along, Jawaharlal Nehru, who was more than a little interested in developments in the valley because of his Kashmiri ancestry, came to appreciate Sheikh Abdullah's efforts against the Maharaja and involved the Sheikh in the larger freedom movement of the Indian National Congress. Sheikh Abdullah and Nehru became close friends, and the friendship endured throughout the lives of both men, even though Nehru would in later years have the Sheikh arrested and imprisoned for years on end. In any case, in 1946 as partition and independence were approaching, Sheikh Abdullah mounted a "Quit Kashmir" movement against Hari Singh, the Dogra Maharaja, and the Maharaja responded by having Sheikh Abdullah arrested and imprisoned.[141]

This created a double-bind problem for Maharaja Hari Singh at the time of partition in August of 1947. On the one hand, as a Hindu monarch ruling over a Muslim majority population, the prospect of acceding to Pakistan was obviously not attractive. Similarly, however, especially with Sheikh Abdullah, Nehru's good friend, currently in jail, the prospect of acceding to India was hardly more attractive. Hari

Singh was inclined to push for independence from both Pakistan and India, but Lord Mountbatten made it clear that independence was not an option. Hari Singh's only immediate alternative other than accession either to India or Pakistan was to arrange a "standstill" agreement, that is, a period of delay. By the end of September Hari Singh finally released Sheikh Abdullah from jail, and shortly thereafter Nehru invited Sheikh Abdullah to Delhi for a visit.

By the middle of October, Hari Singh was unable to delay a decision any longer. Armed Pathan tribesmen with the tacit approval and apparent support of Pakistan had launched an assault to take Kashmir for Pakistan on 22 October 1947, and by 24 October were within fifty miles of Srinagar.[142] Hari Singh fled from Srinagar to Jammu and immediately indicated a willingness to accede to India. Accession to India was finally negotiated and an instrument of accession signed on 26 October 1947 with the understanding that Sheikh Abdullah would be put at the head of a new state administration (eventually to become interim prime minister). Moreover, accession was to be only in the areas of defense, foreign affairs and communications with the remainder of government functions to be left in the hands of the Kashmiris. Most important of all, accession was to be conditional upon a plebiscite being held in which the population would confirm the accession to India. Nehru commented as follows during an address on All-India Radio on 2 November.

> I want to speak to you tonight about Kashmir. . . . It was on the night of October 24 that for the first time a request was made to us on behalf of Kashmir state for accession and military help. . . . We received urgent messages for aid not only from the Maharaja's government but from representatives of the people, notably the great leader of Kashmir, Sheikh Mohammad Abdullah, the president of the National Conference. . . . We decided to accept this accession and to send troops by air, but we made a condition that the accession would have to be considered by the people of Kashmir later when peace and order were established. . . . And let me make it clear that it has been our policy all along that where there is a dispute about the accession of a state to either dominion, the decision must be made by the people of that state. It was in accordance with this policy that we added a proviso to the instrument of accession of Kashmir.[143]

It should be noted, as M. J. Akbar has pointed out, that at the time of accession the reason for the provision of a plebiscite had nothing to do with any worries over what the people of Kashmir would choose. The Kashmiri Muslim population under the leadership of Sheikh Abdullah and the National Conference together with the smaller Hindu population would have overwhelmingly supported accession to India with proper safeguards. The provision of a plebiscite, rather, was to make clear to the Maharaja that accession could not be granted solely on the basis of his (the Maharaja's) decision apart from the will of the people.[144]

The attack by the Pathan tribesmen, sponsored by Pakistan and destined to become the first Indo-Pakistani war, continued even after accession, and the soldiers of a "peace brigade" sponsored by the National Conference under Sheikh Abdullah's leadership together with the Indian Army were finally able to turn the tide in favor of India against Pakistan. In the meantime Nehru took the issue to the United Nations on 31 December 1947, hoping to put pressure on Pakistan to force the Pathan tribesmen to withdraw from Kashmir.[145] Finally, after the war dragged on for almost fifteen months, a ceasefire was negotiated by the UN in January 1949. A "line of actual control" between the forces of India and Pakistan was established, in effect partitioning Kashmir, with some 60% of the old princely state, including the Kashmir Valley, Jammu, and most of Ladakh together with some 75% of the total population remaining with India, the remaining portions, mainly farther to the north and representing some 40% of the old state and some 25% of the population, to be under the control of Pakistan and known as "Azad Kashmir" or Free Kashmir.[146]

Over the years the United Nations has attempted to get both Pakistan and India to withdraw all forces from the Kashmir region and to establish a "neutral" interim government for a period of time, with the understanding that shortly thereafter a plebiscite would be held in the region under international supervision. Such a plebiscite has never taken place. As has been mentioned earlier, there was a second Indo-Pakistani war over Kashmir in 1965 which failed to resolve the impasse between Pakistan and India. Moreover, a third Indo-Pakistani war in 1971 (mainly over East Pakistan or Bangladesh) also to some extent touched upon the Kashmir issue in the sense that in the final settlement of that third war, the ceasefire line agreed to on 17 December 1971 in Kashmir became the new "line of actual control" in the region between Pakistan and India. Furthermore, in the July 1972 Simla Agreement between Mrs. Gandhi and Zulfikar Ali Bhutto it was determined that future conflicts over Kashmir would be handled through bilateral peaceful negotiations between India and Pakistan, which India has chosen to interpret as thereby excluding third-party international agencies such as the United Nations.

Kashmir also became an issue in yet another international dispute, this time between India and the People's Republic of China, involving a desolate piece of land known as the Aksai Chin in the eastern region of Ladakh in what India considered to be part of Kashmir. In the late 1950s when China was taking Tibet, a road was built by the Chinese across the Aksai Chin in order to maintain ease of access to Tibet from south China. When this was disputed by India, the Chinese attacked and occupied the region in 1962, badly bludgeoning the Indian troops in the area. The region continues to be disputed between the two countries to the present day.[147]

To return, however, to the internal situation of the state of Jammu and Kashmir, following accession in October 1947, Sheikh Abdullah returned to Srinagar as head of the new interim administration. As just mentioned, his first task was to defeat the pro-Pakistani tribal incursion. With that finally resolved by the UN ceasefire of January 1949, Sheikh Abdullah then set about the task of governing, which involved both setting up a new government and consolidating the precise terms on which the accession of the state of Jammu and Kashmir to India would be finalized. He instituted a number of reforms, including a popular land reform program known as "land to the tiller."[148] Regarding accession to India, he tried to mediate the various positions in the region. There was some minor support among some Muslim groups for accession to Pakistan. There was some support among other groups for total independence. There was other support, largely among Hindus, Buddhists and Sikhs in Jammu and other places outside the valley, for total integration into India under India's new Constitution. Sheikh Abdullah and his National Conference opted for a compromise position, rejecting, on the one hand, either accession to Pakistan or independence, but also, on the other hand, rejecting total integration into India. The National Conference under Sheikh Abdullah's guidance decided to agree with accession to India precisely as the original instrument of accession drawn up by the Maharaja had stipulated, that is to say, only in areas of defense, foreign affairs and communications, with the remainder of legislative powers belonging to the State. Moreover, Sheikh Abdullah took the position that a final settlement would have to be worked out by a soon to be appointed Constituent Assembly. In the interim before a Constituent Assembly could finish its work, a compromise was worked out between India and the state of Jammu and Kashmir whereby the state would have a special status within the Indian Union unlike any of the other former princely states. This special status is spelled out in Article 370 of the Constitution of India and includes the right of the state of Jammu and Kashmir to have its own constitution.[149]

In 1951 the Constituent Assembly was formed but by that time Sheikh Abdullah was already beginning to waver in his attitude towards the emerging Neo-Hindu state. He trusted Nehru, but he began to worry about what would happen to the Kashmiri Muslim majority after Nehru. He began to worry about the heavy hand of the developing Neo-Hindu state and the emergence of conservative Hindu and Neo-Hindu forces such as the Bharatiya Jana Sangh (founded in 1951).[150] He was not in favor of complete independence for Jammu and Kashmir, which he thought would be unworkable, but he did begin to favor some degree of independent status for Jammu and Kashmir within the Indian Union. He began to advocate a theory of confederation between India, Pakistan and Kashmir that would allow a loose federation between the three states in a framework of basic independence for all three.[151]

Sheikh Abdullah informed the Constituent Assembly in 1953 that it had three options, that is, (*a*) accession to Pakistan, (*b*) accession to India, or (*c*) independence. By this time officials in India, including Nehru, were becoming impatient and irritated with what appeared to be dangerous vacillation on the part of Sheikh Abdullah and the National Conference. Sheikh Abdullah was accused of backsliding, tilting towards Pakistan and betraying India's good faith. Nehru was at first supportive of his old friend but then slowly and reluctantly came to be persuaded that Sheikh Abdullah was a serious obstacle to final resolution of Kashmir's accession. Finally, in August of 1953 Sheikh Abdullah was arrested and imprisoned, and he was to remain in jail for many of the next eleven years.[152]

With Sheikh Abdullah out of the picture, India invited Bakshi Gulam Mohammad to form a second interim government in 1953. A former associate of Sheikh Abdullah, he continued the reforms that had been set in motion, but he was also more willing than the Sheikh had been to compromise with India over the accession arrangement. By 1956 the new state constitution was adopted, and while it still clearly articulated a special status for the state of Jammu and Kashmir in the Indian Union in keeping with Article 370 of the Constitution of India, it also declared directly: "The State of Jammu and Kashmir is and shall be an integral part of the Indian Union."[153] The new constitution for the state of Jammu and Kashmir came into effect on 26 January 1957, and shortly thereafter Bakshi Gulam Mohammad was sworn in as the state's first chief minister. Many, however, including Sheikh Abdullah, were deeply dissatisfied with what appeared to be a contrived and coerced settlement and with the failure to follow through on the promised plebiscite. A "Plebiscite Front" was formed by dissident Kashmiri Muslims in order to press the demand for a general plebiscite. Sheikh Abdullah never joined the front, but many of the dissidents looked to him for inspiration.[154]

The government of Bakshi Gulam Mohammad was succeeded in 1963 by the more enlightened one of G. M. Sadiq, a socialist intellectual and reformer, and shortly thereafter Sheikh Abdullah was released from prison. His return to Srinagar was greeted with mass demonstrations of support. He was in touch with his old friend Nehru, and he travelled to Delhi at Nehru's invitation in order to plan yet another compromise over the Kashmir issue. He and Nehru discussed the old idea of confederation. Sheikh Abdullah was also invited to visit Pakistan, and Nehru encouraged him to go and try out the idea of confederation on the Pakistanis. Ayub Khan, Pakistan's prime minister, was uninterested in the idea of confederation, but there evidently was some willingness to discuss the issue of Kashmir. Unfortunately, however, while Sheikh Abdullah was in Pakistan in May 1964 visiting Pakistan-controlled "Azad Kashmir," Nehru suddenly died, and any plan for further compromise or accommodation was no longer possible.[155] Later in the same year, much to the consternation of the Government of India, Sheikh Abdullah also met with the Chinese leader, Zhou Enlai, and articulated his hopes for Kashmiri self-determination. His continuing dissident behavior infuriated officials in Delhi, and yet again Sheikh Abdullah was arrested and imprisoned.

The year 1965 brought the second (and largely indecisive) Indo-Pakistani war over Kashmir, as has already been mentioned, and even the third war in 1971, though immediately about East Pakistan and Bangladesh, did also involve renegotiating the "line of actual control" in Kashmir in December of 1971 and the Simla Agreement of 1972. In 1968 Sheikh Abdullah was once again released from jail, and by 1972, Indira Gandhi, greatly strengthened because of her significant election victory in 1971 together with her decisive defeat of Pakistan over Bangladesh, decided to try once again to settle the Kashmir issue. She negotiated with Sheikh Abdullah the Kashmir Accord, the text of which was announced in parliament on 24 February 1975, providing that Jammu and Kashmir would be a "constituent unit of the Union of India" governed under the terms of Article 370 of the Constitution, that Jammu and Kashmir would have powers of legislation for its own welfare and development but that all matters of territorial integrity would be controlled by the legislative power of parliament.[156] As a result of the accord, on 25 February 1975 Sheikh Abdullah was sworn in as chief minister of the state of Jammu and Kashmir, and he remained in that position until his death on 8 September 1982.

Sheikh Abdullah supported Mrs. Gandhi during the Emergency period (1975–77) and supported her again in her return to power against the Janata coalition in the 1980 elections. He continued to vacillate, however, regarding the status of Jammu and Kashmir in the Indian Union, as did his son and successor, Farooq Abdullah, who took over leadership of the National Conference after the death of his father in 1982. There was still much resentment in the valley that a plebiscite had not yet been held together with a growing suspicion that a plebiscite would probably never be held. There was growing resentment over what was perceived to be the increasingly heavy hand of the Hindu (or Neo-Hindu) state along with growing resentment against the elite Kashmiri Brahmin Hindu minority. There were also Kashmiri Muslim dissident groups of one kind or another, some wanting complete independence from India or Pakistan, some wanting some sort of linkage with Pakistan. In later years there were widespread complaints about corruption and ineptitude directed against Sheikh Abdullah, and, of course, as was true in the Punjab in the same period, there was a continuing rivalry between local political parties (for example, the National Conference and various Muslim political groups) and Congress (I) in the state.

Shortly after Mrs. Gandhi took action against the Sikhs in the state of Punjab with Operation Blue Star in June of 1984, she also moved against Farooq Abdullah's National Conference government in the state of Jammu and Kashmir in July of the same year. In both cases she was convinced that dissidents were becoming too strong, that the Centre was losing control and that outside forces (most of all, Pakistan) were meddling in the internal affairs of the country. In the state of Jammu and Kashmir she engineered the fall of the government of Farooq Abdullah by instructing her appointed governor, Jagmohan, to dismiss Abdullah and to install, instead, G. M. Shah, as chief minister.[157] She acted with almost total disregard to ordinary due process and the various special provisions in place for the state of Jammu and Kashmir under Article 370. People throughout the state exploded in protest as did many in other parts of India as well. Police and paramilitary forces from the outside had to be brought in to control the rioting and resulting disorder.[158]

A few years later in 1987, after Mrs. Gandhi's assassination and under the new Congress (I) government of Rajiv Gandhi, Farooq Abdullah was allowed to return to power with an electoral alliance between the National Conference and the Congress (I). Unfortunately, in the interim all of the opposition Muslim parties and other dissidents had joined forces to form a new Muslim United Front, and it was anticipated on all sides in the state of Jammu and Kashmir that the dissidents would easily win.[159] The election, however, was evidently not a fair one. Charges of widespread manipulation and outright fraud were levelled, so that the Farooq Abdullah National Conference-Congress (I) "victory" was altogether hollow and unconvincing to the entire population of the state. Demonstrations began almost immediately, and Kashmiri Muslim dissident groups began to grow and gain prominence. Two in particular came to be especially prominent: the Jammu and Kashmir Liberation Front (the JKLF), which seeks total independence for Jammu and Kashmir apart from India or Pakistan, and the Hizb-ul-Mujahadin, a Neo-Muslim dissident group wanting to establish linkage with Pakistan.[160] Both groups have become increasingly violent since 1987, making use of aggressive street demonstrations, kidnappings, assassinations and a variety of other guerilla tactics throughout the valley.

In December of 1989, when the new V. P. Singh government had just come into power at the Centre, Kashmiri Muslim militants kidnapped the daughter of Mufti Mohammad Sayeed, himself a Kashmiri and recently appointed home minister in V. P. Singh's cabinet. As ransom for her release, the militants demanded that their jailed activist colleagues be released. The V. P. Singh government acquiesced in the ransom demand. The activists were released from jail, and the daughter of the home minister was set free.[161] Shortly thereafter, however, in January of 1990 in order to send a signal that the new government was not acting out of weakness, the hard-line and intensely disliked Hindu administrator and former governor, Jagmohan, was sent to the state again as the new governor. Farooq Abdullah, who had been desperately trying to hold the situation together in the state and remembered only too well his previous experience with Jagmohan, immediately resigned as chief minister.[162] Jagmohan thereafter dismissed the state legislature, imposed strict curfews, instituted house-to-house searches and ordered thousands of dissidents arrested. It is estimated by the U.S. State Department that some 2,293 people lost their lives in the state during 1990. As many or more have been killed in 1991 and 1992 with the carnage continuing down to the present day. V. P. Singh finally dismissed Jagmohan in May of 1990 and replaced him with G. C. Saxena, a much more moderate figure. In July of 1990 President's Rule was established in the state, and the state has been ruled with a heavy military hand from the Center ever since. The current governor of the state is retired General K. V. Krishna Rao.[163] Human rights abuses have been common, and hundreds of those arrested have been tortured and executed, according to the reports of human rights organizations such as Asia Watch and Physicians for Human Rights.[164] Like the state of Punjab, the state of Jammu and Kashmir is for all intents and purposes an occupied territory. Unlike the Punjab, however, where there are at least some forces for moderation and compromise, in Jammu and Kashmir the Kashmiri Muslims of the valley are overwhelmingly opposed to the Indian state. In October 1993 a group of some forty militant Muslims took over Srinagar's Hazratbal Mosque, a particularly sacred area because it preserves, according to Kashmiri Muslim tradition, a hair of the Prophet, Muhammad. The area was immediately surrounded by police and military forces, and many anticipated a replay of Operation Blue Star. Fortunately, the Government of India was able to negotiate a peaceful solution in November of 1993. Possibly this is a hopeful portent of a more enlightened approach to the Kashmir crisis in the months and years to come.[165]

From the perspective of the present book, the story of the Kashmir crisis is in many ways similar to the story of the Punjab crisis. Here again is a crisis involving a number of distinct religious players: the Neo-Muslim reformist and moderately separatist National Conference of Sheikh Abdullah, the Neo-Muslim JKLF seeking independence for Jammu and Kashmir, the Neo-Muslim reformist and separatist Hizb-ul-Mujahadin, the Sufi-oriented Kashmiri Muslim tradition which is interestingly different from almost all other sorts of Muslim tradition in India, the traditional Hindu Kashmiri Brahmin Pandit community, the Gandhian-Nehruvian Neo-Hindu state, the conservative Bharatiya Jana Sangh and more recently the Bharatiya Janata Party, Sikhs, Tibetan Buddhists, and so forth. To describe the crisis simply in terms of secular India against communal Kashmir, or simply in terms of Hindus against Muslims, or again, simply in terms of the Neo-Hindu Centre against the regional community is to miss the complex texture and multilayered density of the crisis that involves all of these factors and much more. Kashmir, to be sure, has always been something of an anomaly in the region. That it was a majority Muslim area remaining with India gave to the emerging Neo-Hindu state of India a much needed aura of secular inclusiveness. That it was a majority Muslim area choosing not to be part of Pakistan called into question the basic *raison d'être* of the Islamic Republic of Pakistan, that is, that a Muslim community could not find a satisfactory political home outside of an explicitly Muslim state. Both India and Pakistan, in other words, had important ideological and religious reasons for wanting Kashmir. Interestingly, both Sheikh Abdullah as well as Nehru were quick to claim the title "secular" for themselves, but finally they both came to realize that they were taking part in institutions and structures that had deep religious overtones. The only thing that transcended their cultural and religious differences finally was their personal friendship that somehow miraculously survived the years of conflict and alienation, but then it was always the case that there was a special personal bond between the Kashmiri Muslim and the Kashmiri Hindu Pandit.

Second, here as in the Punjab is a crisis that has its origins primarily in the trauma of partition and its unresolved problems but with the interesting twist that it was the only area in which there was a Hindu-ruling minority among an overwhelming Muslim majority. That Sheikh Abdullah and the followers of the National Conference would opt basically for India for as long as they did and continue to carry Kashmiri Muslim support generally for as long as they did is truly remarkable. It suggests that at least initially what Kashmiri Muslims really wanted was partition from Hari Singh and illegitimate Hindu Dogra rule. It also suggests that their identity as Muslims had little to do with any universal and monolithic sense of Islam. They thought of themselves in much more specific terms as Kashmiri Muslims.

Third, as was the case in the Punjab, inordinate delay played a key role in exacerbating the separatist crisis. That India did not move immediately to a plebiscite by way of confirming the early commitment of the Kashmiri Muslim community to India is more than a little surprising. India dithered and delayed time and time again until the tide began to turn and Kashmiri Muslims came more and more to want a greater degree of independence. Now India is in the unenviable and completely untenable position of having to force the Kashmiri Muslims to remain with India by the sheer force of military arms and occupation. A denied plebiscite to avoid literal partition has generated a much more troublesome partition, a deep psychological partition of resentment, hatred and total alienation.

Finally, however, it must also be said that Sheikh Abdullah and his followers in the National Conference bear some degree of responsibility for the current impasse. It cannot be denied that the Kashmiri Muslims played India off against Pakistan on more than one occasion for the sake of maintaining their own special status. Sheikh Abdullah, moreover, vacillated time and time again, and one can well understand the growing impatience and irritation of India, including the impatience and irritation of his old friend Nehru. Furthermore, when Sheikh Abdullah in 1964, just after the death of Nehru and not long after India's international reputation had been wounded by the People's Republic of China in 1962, took it upon himself to talk with Zhou Enlai about Kashmiri self-determination, it must surely have occurred to the Sheikh that this would not go over well with India's new prime minister, Lal Bahadur Shastri. Likewise, Farooq Abdullah's acquiescence if not participation in what appears to have been an obviously rigged election in 1987 can only be understood to have been a cynical and opportunistic ploy that would inevitably lead to massive suffering and death among his own fellow Kashmiri Muslims. There is here again, in other words, more than enough blame on all sides in India's continuing agony over religion.

3. The crisis regarding "personal law" and the difficulties of developing a uniform civil code as exhibited in the Shah Bano Begum case and the Muslim Women's (Protection of Rights on Divorce) Bill of 1986. This third crisis also involves the issue of community identity or what we called earlier "community-ship," only in this instance it is the antithesis of region or territory and has to do, rather, with the issue of "personal law" or, in other words, the community identity that a person carries regardless of the region or territory in which a person happens to reside. As we noticed earlier, Article 44 of the Directive Principles of State Policy of the Constitution of India states: "The State shall endeavour to secure for the citizens a uniform civil code throughout the territory of India." As a directive principle, such a provision "shall not be enforceable by any court," but such a provision shall be "fundamental in the governance of the country and it shall be the duty of the State to apply these principles in making laws" (Article 37). There has been a uniform criminal code and procedure in India since the middle of the nineteenth century, but there is even now in modern India no uniform civil code regarding such matters as marriage, divorce, inheritance, and so forth. Some first steps were taken in the direction of a uniform civil code with the passage of the various parts of the Hindu Code Bill in the mid 1950s which had the effect of codifying and making personal law uniform for most Hindus in the territory of India, but since that time no other steps have been taken towards implementing Article 44 for all citizens.

The issue of a conflict between personal law and a uniform civil code became something of a crisis in the mid-1980s in connection with a Muslim divorce case in the city of Indore in the state of Madhya Pradesh between Mohammad Ahmed Khan and his wife, Shah Bano Begum. The two were married in 1932, and in 1975 after 43 years of marriage Mohammad Ahmed Khan "drove her out of the matrimonial home."[166] Three years later he officially divorced (*talaq*) Shah Bano Begum. In April 1978 Shah Bano Begum brought charges against her former husband under the Criminal Procedure Code (Sections 125 and

127(3)(b) concerning vagrancy and destitution and the obligation of former husbands to support divorced wives if they are destitute), claiming that she was destitute and asking for maintenance in the amount of Rs. 500 per month (at the time, about $50 per month). Mohammad Ahmed Khan, her former husband, defended himself by arguing that he had more than fulfilled his obligations of support under Muslim personal law, which requires only that the original, contracted dowry (*mahr*) be retained by the divorced woman and that the divorced woman be supported during a required "period of waiting" (*'iddah*), a period of three months during which a woman may not be remarried.[167] Since 1975, Mohammad Ahmed Khan argued, he had already supported Shah Bano Begum at Rs. 200 per month for over two years. Moreover, he further argued, he had deposited a sum of Rs. 3,000 in court by way of providing the requisite dowry (*mahr*). Under the terms of Muslim personal law, he, therefore, had no further obligations to his former wife.

The magistrate found in Shah Bano Begum's favor but ordered a maintenance payment of only Rs. 25 (about $2) per month. Shah Bano Begum then appealed the amount to the High Court in Madhya Pradesh in 1979, and the High Court raised the maintenance amount to Rs. 179.20 (or to about $18 per month) in its decision dated 1 July 1980. Mohammad Ahmed Khan then appealed the decision of the High Court to the Supreme Court in 1981, and the Supreme Court issued its decision on 23 April 1985. The Supreme Court decision was written by Chief Justice Y. V. Chandrachud. The Court found in favor of Shah Bano Begum, rejecting the appeal of her former husband and confirming the judgment of the High Court. The Court also commented that "it would be open to the respondent to make an application under Section 127(1) of the Code for increasing the allowance of maintenance granted to her on proof of a change in the circumstances as envisaged by that section."[168]

In sustaining the right to maintenance for Shah Bano Begum under the Criminal Procedure Code, Chief Justice Chandrachud argued that it is not necessarily the case that the Muslim personal law and the criminal code are in conflict. That maintenance is to continue only during a "period of waiting" (*'iddah*) is only for those cases in which a divorced woman is not destitute or unable to support herself following the waiting period. In the latter case of destitution, however, both the Muslim personal law and the criminal code provide grounds for justifying some sort of maintenance. Regarding the issue of the dowry or *mahr* as a "payment on divorce" or "payable on divorce," this is a misunderstanding of the notion of *mahr*, according to the chief justice. The notion of *mahr* is a payment at the time of marriage "as a mark of respect for the wife" and cannot be interpreted to be the equivalent of a "payment on divorce" as is intended by the criminal code. In other words, the *mahr* is not an appropriate substitute for proper maintenance under the criminal code. The chief justice quotes a variety of sources regarding Muslim personal law to support his basic argument that the personal law does not conflict with the criminal law.

Chief Justice Chandrachud shows a good deal of impatience and even exasperation over the matter of personal law towards the end of his judgment when he comments:

> It is a matter of deep regret that some of the interveners who supported the appellant [that is, the former husband], took up an extreme position by displaying an unwarranted zeal to defeat the right to maintenance of women who are unable to maintain themselves. The written submissions of the All India Muslim Personal Law Board have gone to the length of asserting that it is irrelevant to inquire as to how a Muslim divorcee should maintain herself. The facile answer of the Board is that the Personal Law has devised the system of Mahr to meet the requirements of women and if a woman is indigent, she must look to her relations, including nephews and cousins, to support her. This is a most unreasonable view of law as well as life.

Moreover, in the very next section of his judgment he also goes on to express more than a little irritation at the failure to address the issue of a uniform civil code.

> It is also a matter of regret that Article 44 of our Constitution has remained a dead letter. . . . There is no evidence of any official activity for framing a common civil code for the country. A belief seems to have gained ground that it is for the Muslim community to take a lead in the matter of reforms of their personal law. A common Civil Code will help the cause of national integration by removing disparate loyalties to laws which have conflicting ideologies. No community is likely to bell the cat by making gratuitous concessions on this issue. It is the State which is charged with the duty of securing a uniform civil code for the citizens of the country and, unquestionably, it has the legislative competence to do so. A counsel in the case whispered, somewhat audibly, that legislative competence is one thing, the political courage to use that competence is quite another. We understand the diffi-

culties involved in bringing persons of different faiths and persuasions on a common platform. But, a beginning has to be made if the Constitution is to have any meaning.[169]

Reactions among Hindu communities to the Supreme Court ruling were overwhelmingly positive as was the initial reaction of the Rajiv Gandhi government. Reactions among Muslim communities in India, however, were overwhelmingly negative. Violent protests broke out in Bombay and elsewhere, and the issue rapidly became a major national crisis.[170] The issue was obsessively discussed in the Indian media as well as in parliament. Many Muslims felt that the ruling was a direct attack upon their minority status and their identity as Muslims. For a Hindu judge to make negative comments about the Muslim personal law or about the All India Muslim Personal Law Board was insulting and altogether unacceptable. An attack on the Muslim personal law, many Muslims thought, was nothing less than an attack on Islam itself. Moreover, for a Hindu judge to take it upon himself to interpret the Muslim personal law was high-handed and utterly gratuitous, quite apart from the inaccuracy and ineptitude of his reasoning.[171]

The Rajiv Gandhi Congress (I) government soon began to realize that it had a potentially serious crisis with respect to the minority Muslim communities, and it began to back away from its support for the Supreme Court ruling in the Shah Bano Begum case. This case along with other growing tensions in various parts of India between Hindu and Muslim communities over issues of conversion, unfair employment practices and other types of perceived discrimination were threatening to erode what generally had been reasonably strong and reliable Muslim support for Congress (I) candidates, programs and policies. Some local elections at the time in which Congress (I) candidates were rejected by Muslim constituencies seemed to document the threat.[172]

In an attempt to counteract Muslim loss of support and to calm fears in the Muslim communities of what appeared to be obtrusive Hindu meddling in the Muslim personal law, the government introduced in parliament the Muslim Women (Protection of Rights on Divorce) Bill. Regarding Section 125 of the Criminal Procedure Code, the new bill provided that the provision regarding support for divorced women would not apply to Muslim women. Instead, Muslim women would be protected under the Muslim personal law. Indigent divorced Muslim women would be supported, mainly, by their family and relatives. If family support were not possible, then indigent Muslim women could apply to the local *waqf* ("endowment") boards, endowed trusts in various communities for charitable purposes of one kind or another.[173] The bill became law on 6 May 1986, and somewhat predictably, public opinion which had been polarized in one direction quickly reversed itself. Conservative Muslim forces reacted favorably while Hindu and Neo-Hindu groups characterized the bill as one more example of pampering the minorities and catering to Muslim obscurantism and separatism. The Muslim intelligentsia (lawyers, teachers, intellectuals, and so forth) also opposed the new bill. Embree comments: "The government's public defense of its case was remarkably poor, consisting largely of the reiteration by the law minister and others that one had to give the minorities what they demanded."[174] The Rudolphs have commented: "The Rajiv Gandhi government had reverted to a version of secularism implied by the Congress party's informal 'rule,' observed in the Constituent Assembly, that no act directly affecting a particular (religious) community should be taken without support of an extraordinary majority in that community."[175] This also calls to mind the Rudolphs' comment at the outset of this chapter: "The contradiction in India's concept of secularism was its simultaneous commitment to communities and to equal citizenship."[176]

Quite apart from the issue of "secularism," a debate about which in this context is utterly useless given the massive equivocations regarding the term, the truly extraordinary dimension of the crisis is the bill's clear and unequivocal violation of both the letter and spirit of Article 44 of the Constitution. Gratuitous or not, Chief Justice Chandrachud was very much on the mark when he commented (see above): "It is also a matter of regret that Article 44 of our Constitution has remained a dead letter. . . . There is no evidence of any official activity for framing a common civil code for the country." To the contrary, the Muslim Women (Protection of Rights on Divorce) Bill of 1986 is evidence of official activity in precisely the opposite direction.[177]

One quick final comment before proceeding further. As is generally admitted, there is precious little empirical evidence regarding public opinion among Muslims in India. There was, however, one public opinion survey in Tirupati in the state of Andhra Pradesh involving some 800 Muslim households and some 422 interviews (234 with males and 188 with females) regarding the Shah Bano Begum case and the desirability of developing a uniform civil code. The polling and interviewing involved three distinct groups: illiterate groups, moderately educated and highly educated. Regarding the Shah Bano Begum case, 75 percent of all Muslims supported Shah Bano Begum, both male and female, and nearly 100 percent of Muslim women supported her.

Regarding the development of a uniform civil code, Muslim men are divided about half and half in terms of supporting the idea, but, interestingly, 60 percent of young unmarried males support a uniform civil code. Among Muslim women, 63 percent support a uniform civil code and 37 percent are opposed. The author of the survey concludes simply: "It appears that a minority of the minority community is standing in the way of the majority of the minority community."[178] Further empirical evidence of a more recent kind in support of the increasing diversity of views within the Muslim communities in India together with a much more open attitude towards a uniform civil code is summarized in a recent cover story in *India Today*, entitled "Young Muslims: Forging a New Identity."[179]

4. The crisis regarding the notion of compensatory discrimination and its extension to the Other Backward Classes (OBCs) as a result of the recommendations of the Report of the Backward Classes Commission (the Mandal Report) and their partial implementation by the V. P. Singh government in 1990. Article 340 of The Constitution of India recognizes the need for a commission "to investigate the conditions of the socially and educationally backward classes," "to remove . . . difficulties" of those classes, and to take the necessary steps "to improve their condition."[180] A first commission, under the chairmanship of K. Kalelkar, did its work between January of 1953 through 1955. Its recommendations, however, were not accepted for a variety of reasons, largely because there were inconsistencies in the collection of data and proper objective interpretation coupled with a great deal of dissension among commission members, including the dissent, finally, of the chairman himself. A second commission was appointed by Prime Minister Morarji Desai on 21 March 1979 with B. P. Mandal as chairman of the commission. Following two extensions, the report was finally submitted in December of 1980 when Indira Gandhi had returned to power as prime minister.[181] The Mandal Report established criteria for identifying OBCs, argued that caste could legitimately be used as one factor in identifying backward classes, clearly separated economic backwardness from social and educational backwardness thereby denying that the problems of the backward classes were only economic rather than social or educational, and made a number of recommendations, including a job reservation quota of 27 percent for OBCs in central government jobs and schools, special educational facilities for OBCs and a variety of special programs and financial grants and loans for OBCs.

Although the commission determined that the percentage of OBCs is probably as high as 52 percent of the population of India, over and above the 22.5 percent made up of Scheduled Castes and Scheduled Tribes, the commission recommended only 27 percent reservation for OBCs so that the combined total of reservations would not exceed 50 percent of the population, that is to say, 22.5 percent for Scheduled Castes and Scheduled Tribes and 27 percent for OBCs making a total of 49.5 percent for reservations overall. The 50 percent limit was in keeping with previously established guidelines in various High Court and Supreme Court decisions.[182]

Mrs. Gandhi's government received the Mandal Report in 1980 but did not proceed immediately to implement it, although Congress (I) and most other political parties indicated support for the commission's findings and recommendations. Finally, some ten years later, on 7 August 1990, Prime Minister V. P. Singh issued a Government Order implementing one part of the Mandal Report recommendations, namely, that portion establishing a job reservation quota of 27 percent for central government jobs. This triggered a major political explosion, not so much in the South which had had reservations on the state level in much higher percentages for years, but primarily in the so-called Hindi heartland in the North (the states of Uttar Pradesh, Bihar, Haryana, Madhya Pradesh and Rajasthan). Violent demonstrations broke out in various places together with a series of bizarre self-immolations by distraught "forward caste" young people, and it was this strong reaction against the implementation of the Mandal Report along with the controversy in Ayodhya (to be discussed later) that brought down the V. P. Singh government in less than a year. Under the current prime minister, P. V. Narasimha Rao, a subsequent Government Order was issued on 25 September 1991, supplanting the previous Government Order and raising the total percentage of reservation to a full 60 percent, including 22.5 percent for Scheduled Castes and Scheduled Tribes, 27 percent for OBCs, and now an additional 10 percent for economically backward forward castes and classes. Also, in the new Government Order an economic criterion is introduced overall in the reservation system to insure that only the truly backward (socially, educationally and economically) classes receive preferential treatment rather than those groups on whatever level that have become economically advanced.

The main thrust of the Mandal Report is the claim that social and educational backwardness in India is not simply or even primarily a matter of economic inequity or disparity, although economic factors may well be symptomatic of backwardness. The main factor in understanding backwardness is the heritage of a hierarchical social order built largely on a religious understanding of caste whereby groups of people were systematically discriminated against on grounds of ritual impurity and rendered incapable of competing or functioning in a fair and equitable manner. Says the report,

> The real triumph of the caste system lies not in upholding the supremacy of the Brahmin, but in conditioning the consciousness of the lower castes in accepting their inferior status in the ritual hierarchy as a part of the natural order of things. In India the caste system has endured for over 3,000 years and even today there appear to be no symptoms of its early demise.[183]

The massive social inequity in India, in other words, has an ancient and profoundly religious base and must be understood as being deep-seated and structural. Simple economic engineering, industrialization, free markets or even planned economic development will never be sufficient to change the structural realities of India.

> [W]e have shown . . . how the lower and impure castes in the Hindu caste hierarchy were permanently assigned menial tasks and refused any access to all avenues for a better life. It was the all pervasive tyranny of this caste system which kept the lower castes socially backward and economically poor. The poverty of these castes stemmed from their social discrimination and they did not become socially backward because of their poverty. In view of this, historical and sociological evidence does not support the view that, in the ultimate analysis, social backwardness is the "result of poverty to a very large extent." In fact, it is just the other way round.[184]

Furthermore, the modern democratic polity with its stress on equality and political mobilization has had, ironically enough, the opposite effect in many instances of increasing the salience of caste in modern India.

> Inevitably, the Constitutional commitment to establish a casteless and egalitarian society and, particularly, the introduction of adult franchise, has unleashed the strongest forces to which the caste system has been exposed so far. But, characteristically, here also this wily institution, emulating the example of Hindu Avatars [periodic divine 'incarnations"], is assuming new forms without showing much loss of its original vitality. In fact, several

> observers feel that the logic of democratic politics and mass mobilisation has brought caste to the centre of the stage. . . .[185]
>
> [D]espite the resolve of our Constitution-makers to establish a casteless society, the importance of caste has increased in some of the most important spheres of our national life. As electoral politics is primarily a numbers game, this development was implicit in the very scheme of things. . . . [186]
>
> [A]s pointed out by Rajni Kothari, the institution of caste has played a useful role by providing ready-made traditional channels of mobilisation and articulation. . . . [M]any political observers have pointed to the importance attached to caste by all political parties in the selection of candidates for elections to the Parliament and the State legislatures. And this phenomenon surfaced soon after Independence when the stalwarts of the freedom movement were still dominating the national scene. . . .[187]
>
> The size and area of activity of . . . caste associations operating in India today is truly enormous. Most of the leading castes like Rajputs, Thakurs, Kayasthas, Yadavas, Jats, etc., have forged countrywide links amongst similar caste-clusters. Other important regional castes like Kamas, Reddis, Vokkaligas, Lingayats, Nadars, Ezhavas, Mahars, Marathas, etc., are having strong regional organizations and pressure groups.[188]

Given the fact that caste is so all-pervasive in Indian life even after decades of independence and given the fact that very little progress has been made in correcting the massive inequity of social, educational and economic backwardness, only a massive commitment to reservation and compensatory discrimination can realistically begin to address the enormity of India's social problems.

By way of identifying the Other Backward Classes, the Mandal Report constructed an outline of "indicators (criteria) for social and educational backwardness" as follows:

> A. Social
>
> —castes/classes considered as socially backward by others.
>
> —castes/classes dependent mainly on manual labor.
>
> —castes/classes where at least 25% females and 10% males above the state average get married at an age below 17 in rurual areas and at least l0% females and 5% males do so in urban areas.

—castes/classes where participation of females in work is at least 25% above the state average.

B. Educational

—castes/classes where the number of children in the age group of 5-15 years who never attend school is at least 25% above the State average.

—castes/classes where the rate of student drop-out in the age group of 5-15 years is at least 25% above the State average.

—castes/classes amongst whom the proportion of matriculates is at least 25% below the state average.

C. Economic

—castes/classes where the average value of family assets is at least 25% below the state average.

—castes/classes where the number of families living in Kuccha houses [grass huts] is at least 25% above the State average.

—castes/classes where the source of drinking water is beyond half a kilometer for more than 50% of the households.

—castes/classes where the number of households having taken consumption loans is at least 25% above the State average.[189]

The report then gives a weighted numerical rating to each category depending on its importance. Social criteria are each given a rating of 3 points, educational criteria a rating of 2 points, and economic criteria a rating of 1 point. A total score of "backwardness" would then be 22, and the commission determined that any caste/class with a total score of 11 or more should be classified as an Other Backward Class or OBC. This involves, of course, hundreds of castes in present-day India.

A major problem, of course, is that there is very little systematic, reliable data about caste and caste-clusters in contemporary India, since the Census of India has not kept caste statistics since the census of 1931. The Mandal Commission was largely dependent on State lists, dated census reports and more than a little anecdotal information derived from interviews and selective site visits around India. The report's final estimate, therefore, that OBCs make up just over half (52 percent) of the population of India, over and above the 22.5 percent comprising the Scheduled Castes and Scheduled Tribes, for a mind-boggling total of 72.5 percent in need of compensatory discrimination, is at best a ball-park figure. It is, nevertheless, at least some concrete measure of the enormity of India's problems in the area of what I have been calling issues of "community-ship" and compensatory discrimination.

When one combines earlier issues of community separatism (as with the Sikhs in the Punjab and the Kashmiri Muslims in Jammu and Kashmir) and issues of "personal law" for non-Hindu communities with this most recent call for massive reservation up to 50 percent for Other Backward Classes, one can perhaps begin to understand the growing conviction among Hindu and Neo-Hindu "forward caste" groups that they are somehow being overlooked in the modern scheme of things. To be sure, the forward caste elite Brahmin who is English-speaking and English-educated still occupies a privileged place in the modern Neo-Hindu civilisation-state, as the Khushwant Singh statistics mentioned earlier in this Chapter indicate. Those Hindu and Neo-Hindu forward caste groups, however, just below the top, who speak a vernacular Indian language and only a smattering of English, who live in urban centers in the great Hindi heartland and who occupy lesser jobs in middle management and below are becoming increasingly frustrated and angry. It is hardly surprising that they have a strong sense of being a minority in their own country because, of course, in fact, that is precisely what they are!

5. The crisis in Ayodhya culminating in the destruction in December of 1992 of an old Muslim mosque (Babri Masjid), purportedly located on the precise birthplace of the Hindu Lord Rāma, and the attempt by conservative Neo-Hindu groups to rebuild a temple to Lord Rāma on that sacred site (the "Ramjanmabhoomi" or "place of the birth of Lord Rāma"). Conservative Neo-Hindu groups claim that in the year 1528 in the city of Ayodhya in what is now the state of Uttar Pradesh in North India, a certain Mir Baqi, a lieutenant of the first Mughal emperor, Babar, tore down a temple that marked the birthplace of Rāma (hence, the expression "Ramjanmabhoomi" or "birth-place of Rāma") and built in its place a mosque in honor of the Emperor Babar (hence, the expression "Babri Masjid" or "the mosque of Babar"). There is very little evidence prior to the nineteenth century to support this particular claim.[190] There is, of course, evidence of Muslim armies destroying Hindu temples in Mughal times as well as earlier, and it is undoubtedly the case that in some instances mosques were built from the ruins of older Hindu temples. There is also considerable evidence of Hindu temples having been built from the ruins of older Buddhist and Jain temples in various parts of India.[191] Whether or not the Babri Masjid itself, however, was built from the ruins of an original Hindu temple to Rāma and whether or not this particular place in ancient times was considered the birth-place of

Rāma (Ramjanmabhoomi) are matters impossible to determine. Inconclusive "evidence" can be and has been cited on both sides of the controversy.

Very little is known about the city of Ayodhya in ancient times, even whether there was such a place in the fabled "time" of Rāma.[192] Bakker has conjectured that Ayodhya was originally the fictional city of the epic hero and heroine, Rāma and Sītā, and only later became identified with a specific geographical place.[193] The specific geographical place with which Ayodhya became associated was the city of Saketa on the Saryu (or Sarayu) river in the region of Kosala in north India, a city and a region that had been sacred not only to Hindus, but to Buddhists, Jains and Ādivāsis (the "original or first inhabitants" or, in other words, the tribals) as well. A portion of the site is also known as "Sītā kī rasoi" (meaning something like "Sita's kitchen") suggesting that the original site may have been the center of some sort of chthonic vegetation or fertility ritual.[194] In any case, by the fifth century of the Common Era, Ayodhya or Saketa had become the capital of the Hindu Gupta dynasty and was associated with the revival of the Indo-Brāhmaṇical and the emergence of Indic ("Hindu") traditions after centuries of Indo-Śramaṇical (mainly Jain and Buddhist) hegemony. It was probably in this period that the cult of Rāma as an "incarnation" (*avatāra*) of the high god, Viṣṇu, was getting started.[195] It was not until many centuries later, however, probably some time in the tenth century, that Ayodhya became a major center for Vaiṣṇava spirituality; and it was even later, towards the end of the seventeenth century and thereafter, following the advent of Islamic civilization and the interaction between Sufi traditions with exuberant Hindu *bhakti* traditions, when Vaiṣṇava Rāmānandi ascetics, known as Vairāgī-s (or Bairāgī-s), popularized the cult of Rāma, as it is known and practiced today all across North India, and focused their activities in such sacred places as Varanasi and Ayodhya.[196] At the time, interestingly enough, Śaiva traditions (and probably Nāth Yogī traditions) were dominant, and the Rāmānandī-s had to take Ayodhya by force.

> During the eighteenth century a struggle continued between the 'Shaiva' *Sanyasis* and Vaishnava *Bairagis* over the possession of religious places in Ayodhya. Shaivas were dominant in Ayodhya and elsewhere. . . . The '*Sanyasis*' were a militant group and the *Bairagis* could only take over by waging a bloody war. There is evidence that Raja Naval Rai, a Rāma *bhakta*, encouraged the building of several Rāma temples in Ayodhya. The *Bairagis*

> received encouragement and political backing to win away the places of worship from the *Sanyasis*.[197]

This was also the period of the oppressive rule of the Mughal, Aurangzeb (ruled 1658–1707), and it could well have been in this period and after, that is, the eighteenth and nineteenth centuries, when North Indian Hindu traditions were reacting defensively not only against the older oppressive order of Muslim rule (especially that of Aurangzeb) but also against the new oppressive order of the British, that the Babri Masjid–Ramjanmabhoomi story as we know it today got started.

However one wishes to interpret the ancient evidence, it is nevertheless the case that by the nineteenth century many believed that the location of the Babri Masjid was on the site of the Ramjanmabhoomi. Armed conflict between Hindus and Muslims regarding the site occurred in 1853, again in 1855 and during and after the North Indian rebellion of 1857. The British quickly realized that both religious communities had to be accommodated. A compromise was, therefore, worked out whereby both religious groups could worship at the site of the mosque, with Hindus using a raised platform (*chabutarā*) for their *pūjā* in the outer enclosure of the mosque by the eastern gate or entry to the site, and with Muslims continuing to use the interior of the mosque but only by entering through the northern gate of the site.

Tensions of one kind or another continued over the next decades, but it was not until shortly after partition in 1947 that a major conflict was to arise. On the night of 22–23 December 1949 Rāma and Sītā idols "appeared" inside the mosque. According to Hindu accounts, the appearance was a miracle. According to Muslim accounts, a Hindu mendicant had gotten inside the mosque and deposited the idols. According to the only police report, by early morning of 23 December a group of fifty or sixty Vaiṣṇava Hindus had broken into the mosque, had deposited the idols, and were already singing devotional songs when the police arrived.[198] The district magistrate, K. K. Nayar, immediately notified higher authorities about the incident, and he was instructed to have the idols removed immediately. He refrained from having the idols removed, however, claiming that the removal would cause needless violence. Instead, he had the area declared "disturbed," ordered the Imam to leave the mosque and had the mosque locked. Hindus, however, were allowed to continue to offer *pūjā* outside the locked structure.[199] Thus, in effect, the mosque had been turned into a Hindu temple, for it obviously could no longer be used by Muslims for worship, locked or not.

Later, on 29 December 1949 the district magistrate put the mosque into receivership under the supervision of the chairman of the municipal board, Mr. Priya Datt Ram. Concerned Muslims in Ayodhya then sent a delegation to Prime Minister Nehru in New Delhi asking that the idols be removed from the locked mosque, and Nehru requested the state government of Uttar Pradesh to remove the statues. In the interim, however, a civil suit was filed (on 16 January 1950) asking for a declaration of a right to worship by Hindus, and on 3 March 1951 a civil judge ordered that the idols not be removed and that worship be permitted.[200]

The situation remained the same until the early 1980s, a time, it may be recalled, when separatist and minority problems (as in the states of Punjab and Jammu and Kashmir) were generally becoming exacerbated and a time when Mrs. Gandhi had returned to power following the failure of the coalition Janata party (1977–79). A Ramjanmabhoomi Action Committee was formed in October of 1984, and a "*tala kholo*" ("Open the lock!") campaign was begun. The campaign also included a "chariot journey" (a *rath yātra*), a religious procession to call attention to the Ramjanmabhoomi issue.[201] The campaign was aborted, however, because of the political confusion over the assassination of Mrs. Gandhi on 31 October 1984. The campaign was resumed a year later (October 1985) with the additional demand that the Babri Masjid (the mosque) be torn down and a temple to Lord Rāma be constructed on the site. Moreover, the resumed campaign was now also sponsored by the conservative VHP (the Vishva Hindu Parishad or "World Council of Hindus") together with the tacit support of the conservative Hindu RSS (the Rashtriya Swayamsevak Sangh or the "National Assembly of Volunteers") and the newly reorganized conservative Hindu political party, the BJP or Bharatiya Janata Party.[202] The Babri Masjid-Ramjanmabhoomi controversy, in other words, was rapidly becoming a major political issue and a symbolic rallying point for conservative Hindu and Neo-Hindu sentiment fed up with the supposed appeasement and favoritism continually being shown to minorities such as Sikhs and Muslims.

There was considerable support even within the Congress (I) government of Rajiv Gandhi for the Ramjanmabhoomi cause, and in January of 1986 an application was filed by a lawyer in Faizabad (near Ayodhya) to remove the restrictions on the *pūjā*, or, in other words, open the locks on the mosque. No action was taken at the local level, but the matter was appealed to the district level.[203] The district judge of Faizabad, K. M. Pandey, after briefly inquiring into the law and order situation at the mosque and being assured by the district magistrate and the superintendent of police that there would be no violence, then commented:

> It is clear that it is not necessary to keep the locks at the gates for the purpose of maintaining law and order or the safety of the idols. This appears to be an unnecessary irritant to the applicant and other members of the community. . . .
>
> After having heard the parties it is clear that the members of the other community, namely the Muslims, are not going to be affected by any stretch of imagination if the locks of the gates are opened and the idols inside the premises are allowed to be seen and worshipped by the pilgrims and devotees. It is undisputed that the premises are presently in the court's possession and that for the last 35 years Hindus have had an unrestricted right to worship as a result of the court's orders of 1950 and 1951. If the Hindus are offering prayers and worshipping the idols, though in a restricted way, for the last 35 years, then the heavens are not going to fall if the locks of the gates are removed. The District Magistrate has stated before me today that the members of the Muslim community are not allowed to offer prayer at the disputed site. They are not allowed to go there.[204]

Thus, on 1 February 1986 the order was given to unlock the gates. K. M. Pandey was correct. The heavens did not fall when the locks were removed, but, alas, a process was set in motion that led finally some six years later to the walls of the mosque falling, that is to say, to the destruction of the mosque by a frenzied crowd of conservative Hindus on 6 December 1992.

In the interim between February 1986 and December 1992, the political situation grew increasingly tense, and the Babri Masjid–Ramjanmabhoomi controversy came to dominate almost every aspect of public life. Muslims reacted to the 1986 order by forming the Babri Masjid Action Committee (the BMAC) together with other spin-off (as well as rival) groups in order to stop the Hindu onslaught on the Babri Masjid. Civil suits of various kinds were filed. Muslims were especially alarmed because the court's ruling in 1986 came almost directly on the heels of the Supreme Court's ruling in the Shah Bano Begum case of 1985. The Muslim Women (Protection of Rights on Divorce) Bill of 1986 had allayed their fears to some extent, but there was a growing disquiet over the actions of the Neo-Hindu state, and even more than that, over the increasingly powerful and vocal conservative Hindu sentiment. Conservative Hindus for their part kept up the pressure for a new temple to Rāma at the site of the Babri Masjid. The VHP sponsored an additional campaign to collect bricks from all over Hindu India in order to construct the proposed Rāma temple. Supposedly some 200,000 villages sent bricks, and the foundation stone for the proposed temple to Rāma was laid on 9 November 1989.

In December of 1989 the new coalition (National Front) government of V. P. Singh came into power, a minority government supported by the Communist parties on the left, and the increasingly powerful BJP (Bharatiya Janata Party) on the right. In that election the BJP, which had previously had only a handful of seats, now had a remarkable 86 seats and had become a major support for the V. P. Singh government. The reason for the BJP's growing popularity was clearly its vigorous support for the Ramjanmabhoomi cause. In October of 1990 yet another "chariot journey" (*rath yātra*) was announced, this one to begin at the sacred site of Somnāth in Gujarat (a site reclaimed by Hindus shortly after partition with the strategic support of deputy prime minister Vallabhbhai Patel) and to proceed through the state of Bihar and, finally, to Uttar Pradesh and the Babri Masjid-Ramjanmabhoomi site at Ayodhya. Moreover, this new "chariot journey" was to be led by the president of the Bharatiya Janata Party, the powerful Lal Krishnan Advani, a Hindu from Sindh in what is now Pakistan who had to flee from his homeland at the time of partition and who has been heavily influenced by the conservative Neo-Hindu ideology of the RSS.

The National Front government of V. P. Singh, even though one of its essential supports was the BJP, warned Advani that the "chariot journey" would not be allowed to proceed to Ayodhya because of the serious threat to law and order. Advani and the BJP proceeded anyway, and on 23 October 1990 Advani was arrested and taken to jail. The BJP, of course, immediately removed its support from the V. P. Singh government, and the no confidence vote was held in parliament on 7 November 1990 with V. P. Singh losing the vote 356 to 151.[205] V. P. Singh officially resigned on 8 November 1990, a victim not only of his well-intentioned efforts to implement the Mandal Commission recommendations (as discussed earlier) but also of his efforts to stop Advani's "chariot journey" to Ayodhya.

As already mentioned, the short-lived Chandra Shekhar government was only a brief interim between the National Front government of V. P. Singh and the current Congress (I) government of P. V. Narasimha Rao. Chandra Shekhar was successful in getting the various protagonists in the Babri Masjid–Ramjanmabhoomi controversy to negotiate with one another on a continuing basis, and so likewise was P. V. Narasimha Rao successful initially in fostering discussion and debate about the issue. Everyone appeared more or less to agree that the ultimate resolution of the Babri Masjid-Ramjanmabhoomi controversy should be left to the courts to decide. The land, after all, was "*nazul*" land (land owned by the state), and surely some compromise could be worked out whereby the site could be maintained as some sort of national monument in honor of both Hindu and Muslim traditions. The BJP, however, was continuing to gain political momentum over the whole issue. In the elections of June 1991 (following Rajiv Gandhi's assassination on 21 May 1991), for example, the BJP's representation at the Centre jumped from 86 to 117 and its share of the popular vote nearly doubled from 11 percent to 20 percent.[206] Moreover, BJP governments were in power in the key states of Uttar Pradesh, Rajasthan, Himachal Pradesh and Madhya Pradesh. The BJP continued to hammer away at what it called the "pseudo-secularism" of the Congress (I), a "pseudo-secularism," according to the BJP, that is little more than a cynical coddling and appeasement of minorities (especially Muslims and Sikhs) for the sake of maintaining political power. Swapan Dasgupta, writing in 1991, has expressed the matter as follows:

> [T]he BJP and its allies are now in a position to make an effective bid for power at the centre.
>
> What, in the past 16 months has contributed to this marked shift? The role of Mr. Advani's *rath yatra*, particularly in the aftermath of the Mandal commission controversy, is undoubtedly an important factor. By undertaking a highly symbolic campaign at a moment of great social tension, the BJP leader created an unprecedented Hindu consolidation, the like of which has not been witnessed since the struggle for independence. The tremors of the *rath yatra* and the subsequent *kar seva* ["active service" in helping to build the temple] in Ayodhyā are still being felt in the country. . . .
>
> Mr. Advani has enabled Hindus to assert proudly that they, as a community, have a decisive stake in the governance of India. The BJP leader has, in a sense, made Hindu nationalism "respectable."
>
> Not that such a radical and unexpected assertion has been without its share of spirited opposition. From the articulate, westernised intelligentsia who have correctly diagnosed this saffron resurgence as a fundamental challenge to its cultural hegemonism, to the centre-left political parties who apprehend their vote banks being turned upside down, the Advani challenge has been subjected to ridicule and abuse. Ironically, these have

> proved woefully counterproductive and the appeal of Hindu nationalism has grown in direct proportion to the amount of secularist vitriol. A political phenomenon that was, at best, marginal a decade ago, has today turned into a serious offensive for political power.[207]

Perhaps little more need be said by way of describing the final outcome of the Babri Masjid-Ramjanmabhoomi controversy than the following story from the *New York Times* news service published on Monday, 7 December 1992.

> Ayodhya, India—A screaming mob of thousands of Hindu militants stormed a 16th-century mosque here Sunday [6 December 1992] and demolished it with hammers and their bare hands in less than six hours, triggering bloody Hindu-Muslim clashes across India. . . .
>
> The attack came after Hindu revivalist leaders from political and religious groups called for Hindus from around India to come to Ayodhya, in Uttar Pradesh State in northeastern India, to begin construction of a temple to the Hindu god Ram, also called Rāma, and to destroy the Mosque of Babar. . . .
>
> Prime Minister P. V. Narasimha Rao addressed the nation Sunday night, speaking, he said, "under the grave threat that has been posed to the institutions, principles and ideals on which the constitutional structure of our republic has been built."
>
> The destruction of the mosque, Rao said, "is a matter of great shame and concern for all Indians."
>
> "This is a betrayal of the nation and a confrontation with all that is sacred to all Indians as the legacy which we have inherited as a part of our national ethos," he said.[208]

Hundreds died in the resulting riots all over India, especially in Bombay. As might be expected, Muslim communities suffered the most in the resulting carnage. The prime minister, P. V. Narasimha Rao, was enraged at the BJP, the VHP, the RSS and other conservative Hindu groups together with the various BJP state governments, the leaders of all of which groups had promised the prime minister that the gathering of "volunteers" in Ayodhya on 6 December would be a peaceful rally. Followers of the BJP and other thoughtful observers as well pointed out that the prime minister and the Congress (I) government must also share some responsibility for the final tragedy. There was a clear pattern of needless delay and drift in the government's reaction reaching back at least to 1986 and, arguably, back to 1951.

The resulting violence and perceived betrayal led Narasimha Rao to ban the activities of the BJP, the VHP and the RSS, but since that time the ban has been lifted for the BJP and the RSS. Also, the prime minister dismissed the four BJP state governments (in Uttar Pradesh, Madhya Pradesh, Himachal Pradesh and Rajasthan) and imposed President's rule. New elections in the four states and the Delhi area were finally held in November of 1993. Interestingly, the BJP was able to win only in Rajasthan and the Delhi area, suggesting that people are no longer buying the single-issue Rāma platform of the BJP. Also, it should be noted that the Supreme Court in a ruling on 11 March 1994 upheld the prime minister's decision to dismiss the four BJP state governments in December 1992 on the grounds that the BJP governments at the time of the crisis had acted in a non-secular manner, that is, they had failed to maintain a separation between religion and the state. Up to the present time no final decision has been taken by the government as to when or where a new mosque or a new temple is to be built in the vicinity of Ayodhya. The agony over Ayodhya has not yet been resolved.

As in the other crises already discussed, many of the same common features show up here again: (*a*) a variety of distinct religious "players" (Neo-Hindu conservatives in their quest for a new "rule of Rāma" or *Rāma-rājya*, Rāma *bhakta*-s and Rāma ascetics, Indo-Islamic traditions reaching back to the Mughal period, the Neo-Hindu "secular" or "pseudo-secular" state, Neo-Muslim activists, and so on.), (*b*) a crisis largely growing out of unresolved problems stemming from partition, (*c*) a pattern of long-standing and apparently cynical delay that exacerbates the crisis, (*d*) massive violence and rioting requiring extensive intervention by police, paramilitary and military forces, and (*e*) a residual alienation, hatred, fear and resentment that continues down to the present with very little communication among or between the various participating groups.

What is most interesting about the crisis in Ayodhya, however, is not so much the tension between Hindus and Muslims, important as that is, but rather the tension that shows itself between the various Neo-Hindu forces, and especially the tension between so-called "secular" India and so-called "communal" India. Here perhaps more than anywhere else in our analysis it is important to understand India's hybrid discourse of modernity and what this discourse means for the future of India as a civilisation-state. When the BJP, VHP and RSS look at the Congress (I) and its allies and perceive a cynical, manipulative "pseudo-secularism" operating, and when the Congress (I) and other "modern" political forces look at the BJP, VHP and RSS and perceive a "fundamentalist," obscurantist "communalism" operating, both are noticing important features in the other but both are also seriously distorting a number of other features that also appear to be operating in contemporary Indian social reality.

One way of putting the matter is simply to point out that the two sides, so apparently different, and so given to name-calling ("fundamentalist," "pseudo-secularist," "obscurantist," "manipulative," and so forth) are really remarkably alike in many respects. First, both are very much products of the Indo-Anglian period. The Gandhian-Nehruvian "secular" Neo-Hindu orientation emerged from the older liberal democratic tradition of the Indian National Congress together with such synthesizing and moderate Neo-Hindu religious traditions as the Brahmo Samaj, the Ramakrishna Mission, and so forth. The BJP conservative Neo-Hindu orientation also emerged from the older liberal democratic tradition of the Indian National Congress but together with more strident and aggressive Neo-Hindu traditions such as the Arya Samaj, Savarkar's "Hindutva," the Hindu Mahasabha, and so forth. Both, in other words, are fully modern religious orientations with authentic credentials deeply rooted in the nation's freedom struggle.

Second, both are also examples of what we have called Neo-Hindu "reformist and nationalist" movements in contrast to Neo-Hindu "revisionist and internationalist" movements. Both, in other words, are religious orientations that have been deeply implicated in what we have called the religionization of the political and the politicization of the religious, in contrast to Neo-Hindu traditions such as the Satya Sai Baba movement and others which are explicitly a-political.

Third, both are representative of reformist but nevertheless "high" or "forward caste" orientations. Sometimes in the media the BJP and its allies are referred to in jest as the party of the B-and-B's, namely, the party of Brahmins and Banias, but it should not be overlooked that the Gandhian-Nehruvian "secular" Neo-Hindu orientation was and is also very much a B-and-B operation (with Nehru the quintessential Brahmin and Gandhi the hyperactive Bania). Until recently the Neo-Hindu "secular" Congress has occupied the "commanding heights" of the modern caste structure—see above, for example, the earlier quotation from Khushwant Singh about the proportions of Brahmins in the Neo-Hindu "secular" state—in alliance with the Scheduled Castes, the Scheduled Tribes and strategic minorities (mainly Muslim and Christian groups). The BJP Neo-Hindu conservative orientation is likewise appealing to the highest ruling elites but also to the forward castes just below the highest levels, that is, lower government officials, middle management types, business entrepreneurs, wide segments of the urban middle class, and so forth, together with the higher levels among what the Rudolphs have called "bullock capitalists" or the more successful among the Other Backward Classes.

Fourth, both are in favor of a strong Centre, a market economy which is nevertheless oriented to import substitution and controlled from the "commanding heights," and a willingness to use police, paramilitary and military force to retain power at the Centre both internally (for domestic purposes) as well as externally (for foreign policy purposes). Both also favor policies of non-alignment. Both, in other words, represent rather authoritarian visions of the Neo-Hindu civilisation-state.

Finally, both wish to commandeer the term "secular" for themselves but refuse to allow the term to be used by the other. Thus, the BJP and its allies refer to the Neo-Hindu "secular" state as nothing more than "pseudo-secularism," a cynical and manipulative ideological facade designed to attract low caste and minority votes. The proponents of the Neo-Hindu "secular" orientation return the favor by denouncing the BJP's claim to want a truly "secular" state (in terms of a uniform civil code, the elimination of Article 370 regarding Kashmir, and so forth) as obscurantist "Hindutva" and "communalism."

Earlier along in this chapter I introduced the notion of "civil religion" and suggested that just as there is an "American civil religion," so too it may be helpful to think of a comparable "Indic civil religion." The Gandhian Neo-Hindu vision and its demythologized Nehruvian variant (in terms of "socialism," "secularism," "non-alignment," and so forth) represents a kind of Indic civil religion that has been operative in India since the time of Partition in very much the same way as an American civil religion has been operating in the United States since independence. Robert Wuthnow in his recent book, *The Restructuring of American Religion*, has noticed a marked change in the American civil religion in more recent years, however, having to do with changing values between liberals and conservatives in the United States. The American civil religion, in other words, is being very much contested. Says Wuthnow,

> American civil religion is, nevertheless, deeply divided. Like the religion found more generally in the nation's churches, it does not speak with a single voice, uniting the majority of Americans around common ideals. It has instead become a confusion of tongues speaking from different traditions and offering different visions of what America can and should be. Religious conserva-

> tives and liberals offer competing versions of American civil religion that seem to have very little of substance in common.[209]

It is helpful, I think, to consider the situation in contemporary India along the same lines. One might well say that the Indic civil religion, that is to say, the Gandhian-Nehruvian Neo-Hindu "secular" consensus is now being seriously challenged and contested by the more conservative Neo-Hindu vision of the BJP. There is also, as we have seen, yet a third contender in the struggle over the Indic civil religion, and that is V. P. Singh's more radical program of social transformation and reconstruction beyond the high caste orientations of the Congress (I) and the BJP. There is, in other words, a "confusion of tongues speaking from different traditions and offering different visions" of what India "can and should be." The struggle overall is deeply political and deeply religious, and the final outcome is far from settled.

6

Conclusion: The End as the Beginning

The inner conflict of the coming years will be soul-searing, the sense of frustration and uncertainty acute, but it is at least possible that the combination of spiritual distress, intellectual travail and external influences may produce in course of time a new civilization altogether, related to both Hinduism and the West but different from either. If Hinduism cannot hope to be the heir of all the ages, she may in the course of time become the Mother of the heir.

—Percival Spear, *India, Pakistan, and the West*

Two Closing Tasks

Two tasks remain in concluding our discussion, first, a summary overview of some of the key notions that have emerged in our efforts to understand India's hybrid discourse of modernity, and, second, a few brief suggestions about some possible new beginnings or directions that might be explored in the future. The fulfillment of both tasks must perforce be brief, the former because these notions have been discussed at some length already and need only be highlighted in this concluding summary, the latter because the search for new beginnings is a search best left to the people of India rather than to the musings of this or that scholarly interloper no matter how well-intentioned.

CONCLUDING SUMMARY

By way of providing a brief summary of India's hybrid discourse of modernity, perhaps the best way to proceed is simply to highlight and provide a brief overview of the six basic terms or conceptualizations that have emerged as having unique meaning and importance in our overall analysis and discussion: (1) "religion," (2) "religionization," (3) "Neo-Hindu," (4) "secular" or "secular state," (5) "communityship" and "communalism," and (6) "citizenship."

"Religion"

In the course of our discussion and analysis it became apparent early along that to speak about "religion" in India in terms of the so-called "world religions" is to say not much of anything at all theoretically or analytically. The so-called "world religions" (abstractions such as "Hinduism," "Buddhism," and so forth) are little more than conventional names or simple artifacts of categorization for administrative or journalistic convenience. Regarding "Hinduism," for example, the Rudolphs are surely correct when they observe,

> The obvious candidate for national confessional politics is the "Hindu majority." But this majority, 83 percent according to the 1981 census, is an artifact of categorization. The Hinduism of the "Hindu majority" encompasses a diversity of gods, texts and social practice and a variety of ontologies and epistemologies. Without an organized church, it is innocent of orthodoxy, heterodoxy and heresy.[1]

Or, as Robert Frykenberg has put it, the theoretically vacuous expression, "Hinduism," has led us into "trackless deserts of nonsense."[2] Possibly an argument can be mounted that such conventional names or artifacts of categorization have been used as ways of justifying political power. Kenneth W. Jones, for example, has argued along these lines with respect to the decennial census in India.

> The concept of religion as a community grew from the introduction of a decennial census in 1871. The census defined religious communities, counted them, and examined their characteristics as social and economic units. The granting of separate electorates linked religion, the census reports, political power, and political patronage.[3]

In any case, to speak about "religion" in terms of the "world religions" is to make little progress in understanding the religious dynamics operating in the South Asian environment. Instead (and see above in chapter 4), we have attempted to formulate a much more specific notion of "religion" in terms of the relations between enculturation, socialization and individuation. Moreover, we have devised a typology for identifying "religions" which has allowed us to break free of the "world religions" categories as well as to specify to some degree both diachronic and synchronic features in our formulation of a theoretical notion of "religion." This has enabled us to notice a great variety of "religions" in the South Asian environment (and elsewhere as well), but more than that, it has enabled us to use the term "religion" in a basic anthropological sense that goes far beyond its unreflective use in the discourse of the so-called "world religions."

"Religion," we have argued, is a fundamental anthropological notion on analogy with "culture," "language," and "society." To the extent that our formulation of the notion of "religion" is a cogent one, it means that whereas one might well choose no longer to be a "participant" in one of the "world religions," one does not have an option *not* to be religious, any more than a normal human being does not have an option *not* to have a culture, or a language or a kinship identity. This does not mean that one must be necessarily sympathetic to any traditional worldview or to any particular traditional religious form. Nor does it mean that one must have some sort of "theology" in any traditional sense or an elaborate traditional belief-system of any kind. One might well be hostile or sympathetic, skeptical or pious, critical or accepting, traditional or innovative, and so forth, regarding any or all religious formulations. "Religion," rather, has to do with the development of comprehensive interpretive frameworks regarding the meaning and significance of human existence-as-such within the contexts of enculturation, socialization and individuation, and from such a theoretical perspective even the so-called "non-believer," "non-practitioner," agnostic, or totally indifferent person all have a "religious" dimension that can be identified and analyzed, and more than that, needs to be identified and analyzed if one is to understand any normal person's self-understanding.

In formulating this broader, non-substantive and anthropological notion of "religion," the theoretical work of Thomas Luckmann was an important clue, but a more important basis for our formulation emerged out of the complex spirituality of the South Asian environment itself (and see chapters 2 and 3 for a full discussion), an environment that demanded a conceptualization regarding "religion" that transcended the substantive (and thus historically derived) theoretical categories of European history of religions and Western social science. India has been instructive in exhibiting forms of religion in which determinate cognitive formulation regarding ultimate truth is neither essential nor possible, in which simply "birth and minimal cognitive participation" is sufficient for belonging, and in which the institutional framework need be no larger than the teacher-student (*guru-śiṣya*) relationship.

"Religionization"

Just as the South Asian data required a broader, non-substantive and anthropological notion of "religion," so, too, the South Asian material required a more expansive notion of religious change than the usual Western model of "secularization" provided. To a large extent the notion of "secularization" is historically derived from unreflective "world religions" discourse, and specifically, the unreflective Western "world religions" discourse of Judaism, Christianity and Islam. As modern nation-states and institutions became detached progressively from the older religious traditions, they became "disenchanted" in the Weberian sense, worldly or increasingly "secular." If, however, the notion of "religion" or the "religious dimension" is not necessarily tied to one of the traditional "world religions," then to say that a nation-state or an institution has undergone "secularization" is to say something only about the nation-state's or the institution's treatment of its older pre-modern traditional religious forms, but it is to say almost nothing about possible new religious meanings growing out of the secularization process.

To be sure, there have been classic studies of the rise of Protestantism in terms of "secularization" and there has been work in recent years regarding the emergence of the so-called "new religions" out of secular environments. Much of this discourse, however, is still largely within the "world religions" idiom and heavily dependent on modern Christian (largely Protestant) theoretical notions. T. N. Madan has nicely characterized this discourse as follows:

> Scholars from Max Weber and Ernst Troeltsch to Peter Berger and Louis Dumont have in their different ways pointed to the essential linkages among Protestantism, individualism, and secularization. . . .
>
> This is not the occasion to go into details of the well-grounded idea that secularization is a gift of Christianity to mankind, but it

> is important . . . to note that the privatization of religion, through the assumption by the individual of the responsibility for his or her own salvation without the intervention of the Church, is very much a late Christian idea.[4]

It has only been recently realized, largely as a result of the tremendous explosion of new spiritualities and new religious forms throughout the world in the latter part of the twentieth century, that secularization is itself only a part, and possibly only a relatively minor part, of a larger process that is more adequately called something like "religionization," that is to say, the manner in which "religion" and the "religious dimension" develops and changes over time. There was a tendency earlier to think that secularization and privatization were somehow universal processes that perforce had to occur as nations and peoples entered modernity, just as it was thought that certain Western economic theories and processes were universal and inevitable. Now it has become increasingly clear that these so-called universal processes are historically derived and neither inevitable nor predictable, and that there may be all sorts of models of "religionization" beyond the Western (mainly Protestant) "secularization" model. Most important, of course, has been the growing realization that the "secularization" model itself can be very much a "religious" model in the sense that it often becomes a comprehensive interpretive framework regarding the meaning and significance of human existence-as-such or, in other words, "secularism" as a total way of life, and that it warrants, therefore, no privileged status over and above other religious models. Again, if one detaches the notion of "religion" from the unreflective discourse of the so-called "world religions," then it is hardly surprising that "secularization" can and often does have important "religious" significance, and must take its place as only one among a plurality of models within the larger context of a theory of "religionization" (and see chapter 4 for a full discussion). As Peter Berger has commented: "The secular community would have to abandon its counterpluralistic tendencies and agree to allow all communities of meaning . . . to create their own institutions without interference from an ideologically monopolistic state. . . ."[5] Moreover, Berger continues: "the secular community would *ipso facto* come to understand itself as a denomination within a pluralistic society instead of some sort of state Shinto to which all citizens, including children, owe allegiance."[6]

Here again, the situation in India is instructive. The great religious movements in the nineteenth and twentieth centuries in India, including the Brahmo Samaj, the Arya Samaj, the Ramakrishna Mission, the RSS, the Gandhian-Nehruvian nationalist movement, the Sikh movement, the Kashmiri Muslim movement are all on one level clear examples of "secularization" and "reform" vis-à-vis the older religious and political traditions with which they had been allied. What is more interesting to trace, however, is what they represent as examples of "religionization," as new "comprehensive interpretive frameworks regarding the meaning and significance of human existence-as-such." What we have also found interesting to trace (in chapter 5 primarily), of course, is the manner in which the Neo-Hindu "secular state" is itself likewise an instance of "religionization."

"Neo-Hindu"

Early along we made reference to S. C. Dube's comment: "Hinduism, such as it is, is a loosely structured federation of faiths rather than a faith. . . . Birth and minimal cognitive participation are enough to identify one as belonging to the Hindu faith."[7] In chapters 2 and 3 we traced many of the various religious traditions that make up this Hindu "federation," and we noticed in particular a set of religious traditions that were developing in the nineteenth and twentieth centuries that appeared to represent a clear break with the older traditions and that we identified as "Neo-Hindu." Just as the the terms "Hinduism" or "Hindu" refer to a plural set or "federation," so, too, the term "Neo-Hindu" refers to a specific set of religious traditions. We were able to identify two subdivisions of the basic set, namely, what we referred to as "Neo-Hindu reformist and nationalist movements" and "Neo-Hindu revisionist and internationalist movements." The former were characterized by such features as developing a self-conscious national awareness, the reform of outdated religious practices, the rejection or radical reform of the caste system, a commitment to the emancipation of women, the improvement of social conditions for the poor, the economic progress of the entire nation, and the use of modern techniques of communication. The latter were characterized by such features as devotion to a deified *guru* or teacher, total obedience to the *guru*, the practice of one or another kind of disciplined meditation (*yoga*), the claim that all religions are valid, the claim that ethnic identity has no bearing on practice so long as one is properly initiated, a de-emphasis on social work and political activity, and the use of modern means of communication. We noticed, furthermore, that at least two of the Neo-Hindu groups, that is, the Ramakrishna Mission and the Aurobindo movement can be classified to some extent in each subdivision and represent, as it were, "swing" groups among the Neo-Hindu religions. We also noticed a great range of political views among the Neo-Hindu religious traditions, ranging from the conservative Hindu Mahasabha and the Arya Samaj on one end of the political spectrum to the socialist, "secular" Neo-Hindu orientation of the Gandhian-Nehruvian nationalist movement, on the other end, and even beyond the conventional political spectrum, the non-political or apolitical posture of such Neo-Hindu groups as the Satya Sai Baba or Siddha Yoga movements. In spite of these many differences, however, these traditions all exhibit certain fundamental characteristics that justify the designation "Neo-Hindu": (1) the use of the medium of English in much of their communication, (2) a preference for modern methods of education in contrast to traditional methods, (3) the rejection of the ritual-based hierarchies of the traditional caste system, (4) the self-confident assertion of the value and global importance of certain fundamental Indic notions, such as a broadly pluralistic notion of *dharma*, the practice of meditation (*yoga*) or self-discipline of one kind or another, the need for an exemplary leader or spiritual guide, and so forth, and (5) the utilization of modern means of communication, including newspapers, pamphlets, tracts, film and public broadcasting of all varieties. They all represent modern examples of what I am calling "religionization," that is, the process by means of which new comprehensive interpretive frameworks are generated vis-à-vis the relations between enculturation, socialization and individuation in a given social reality. They are all, of course, examples of "secularization" in terms of older, traditional Hindu notions and practices, but they are truly intellectually interesting as fascinating and innovative examples of "religionization." They have become, in other words, an important and new set of religions that have given shape to contemporary Indian religious self-understanding, and the understanding of these religions qua religions is fundamental for understanding the modern civilisation-state of India.[8]

"Secular" and "Secular State"

Is modern India a "secular state"? Yes, of course, it is a "secular state" in very much the same way as modern India is 83 percent Hindu. That is, to call modern India a "secular state" is not to go far enough in analyzing the nature of the modern Indian civilisation-state. It is to do little more than acquiesce in the public rhetoric of the government. Put somewhat differently, India is, indeed, a "secular state," but it is also much more than that, or perhaps better, the expression "secular state" has a dense and specific meaning, a kind of "overplus" of significance, in the South Asian hybrid discourse of modernity. The "secular state" is the Gandhian-Nehruvian Neo-Hindu civilisation-state that combines in a fascinating, albeit bewildering, manner the Neo-Hindu universalism of the Gandhian nationalist ideology together with its demythologized Nehruvian variant in terms of "socialism," "secularism," control of the "commanding heights," a strong Centre and "nonalignment," along with the liberal democratic traditions of the Indian National Congress, the reformist impulses of such Neo-Hindu religious movements as the Brahmo Samaj, the Arya Samaj, the Ramakrishna Mission and even to some degree the Hindu Mahasabha, and all of this with a quasi-Protestant veneer of individualism and the privatization of religious belief. In terms of India's multi-layered cultural heritage, it is an interesting combination of the Indo-Anglian together with the Indic and the Indo-Brāhmaṇical, and it is very much the conventional mind-set of India's high-caste ruling elite. To use Percival Spear's idiom, it is a breathtaking exercise in the "solution of synthesis." It is also useful to see the Neo-Hindu "secular state," we have argued, as a Gandhian-Nehruvian Indic civil religion that exists alongside the many other religious traditions in modern India, a civil religion mainly of the high caste, English-educated and English-speaking elite in government, the modern, industrialized economy, the professions, communications and the academy. As one Indian commentator put it in the title of an article, it is "Hindu Chauvinism with a Liberal Mask."[9] The BJP, as we have seen, calls the Neo-Hindu "secular state" "pseudo-secularist." V. P. Singh calls it simply the "upper-caste Hindu raj." The Sikhs and the Kashmiri Muslims see it as a repressive, totalitarian Neo-Hindu presence that cynically pursues its aims through arrogant and manipulative negotiations and the barrel of a gun. All of this and more is entailed when the terms "secular" and "secular state" are intoned in India's hybrid discourse of modernity.

"Community-ship" and "Communalism"

As has been mentioned in passing at a number of points in our discussion, the Anthropological Survey of India has identified some 4,599 distinct communities in India, some 325 languages and dialects, and as many as 12 distinct language families. Clearly India's communities within communities within communities represent fundamental and major features of South Asian social reality, not only in terms of the traditional or pre-modern caste system with its religio-hierarchical ranking based on ritual purity but also in terms of the fundamental structure of modern, "secular" India with its Scheduled Castes, Scheduled Tribes, Other Backward Classes, caste associations, sectarian movements, extended families with carefully arranged marriages, and any number of other minority communities based on language, religion or regional culture. The notion of community is so central in understanding what India has been and continues to be that we have coined the notion of "community-ship," to parallel the notion of "citizen-ship," as one way of capturing this dimension of India's hybrid discourse of modernity. Moreover, it is no exaggeration to assert that in modern India the claims of "community-ship" are at least as strong, and in many contexts much stronger, than the claims of "citizen-ship."

If "community-ship" and the responsibilities of "community-ship" are descriptive notions of a positive kind meant to highlight an essential dimension of modern Indian social reality and of modern India's commitment to the well-being of all of its communities, then "communalism" as the selfish and separatist efforts of a particular religious group to act in ways contrary to the larger community or the nation, can be said to be the negation or tragic distortion of "community-ship." Just as the notion of slavery or human bondage contrasts with the notion of the free "citizen" on a personal level, so "communalism" contrasts with "community-ship" on a social level. The responsibilities of "community-ship" are fundamental and basic to the long-term survival of the civilisation-state of India because of its complex and multiform network of communities, and "communalism" is an ever-present threat to that survival.

The notion of "communalism" in India prior to partition, as we noticed earlier, was the antithesis of the notion of "nationalism," and the event of partition became the primary symbol of "communalism" in modern India's hybrid discourse of modernity after independence.[10] Since partition, however, the term "nationalism" has largely been replaced by "secular" and "secularism," and, thus, there has tended to develop in public discourse since independence a clear antithesis between "secularism" and "communalism." This leads to the unfortunate result that any person or community or religion that challenges or calls into question the "secular state" all too quickly becomes tagged with the label "communal" or "communalist," or the closely related label "caste-ist" or "caste-ism." To challenge the Neo-Hindu "secular state" is all too often to be characterized as being anti-national, to be a pawn of "outside forces," to be a threat to the integrity of the nation, and, finally, in extreme cases, to be a threat to the very survival of the nation. In other words, it quickly becomes the worst kind of name-calling, which, ironically enough, is finally a strategy whose motivation is itself a kind of communalism, namely, the communalism of the ruling elite. The Neo-Hindu "secular state," especially since the time of Mrs.

Gandhi, has routinely used this sort of name-calling against the Sikhs in the Punjab, the Kashmiri Muslims in Jammu and Kashmir, the Muslims involved in the Babri Masjid controversy in Ayodhya, and, of course, most recently against the BJP, the RSS and the VHP.

To be sure, it may well be the case that the BJP, the RSS and the VHP have "communalist" elements within them (just as the Neo-Hindu "secular state" has its own "communalist" elements) and that the BJP, RSS and VHP overall are overly defensive about their strident Neo-Hindu identity. It is hardly fair or accurate, however, to describe the BJP and its program as "communalist" in the sense of a narrow pro-Hindu orientation that would exclude all others and destroy the integrity of the nation. A more accurate portrayal is that the Neo-Hindu BJP is simply the more conservative vein within the Neo-Hindu tradition. If the Neo-Hindu "secular state" can be characterized as "Hindu Chauvinism with a Liberal Mask," as mentioned above, then it is legitimate to characterize the Neo-Hindu BJP as "Hindu Chauvinism with a Conservative Mask." It is fully Indo-Anglian and reformist and has authentic nationalist credentials of a conservative kind (through the Hindu Mahasabha, the Savarkar "*Hindutva*" tradition, the Arya Samaj, and so forth). In terms of India's multi-layered cultural heritage, if the Neo-Hindu "secular state," as indicated just above, is an interesting combination of the Indo-Anglian, the Indic and the Indo-Brāhmaṇical, then one would have to say that the Neo-Hindu BJP is an even more interesting combination of the Indo-Anglian, the Indic and, more than a little ironically, the Indo-Islamic. Rāma *bhakti*, *Rāma-rājya* and the exuberant devotionalism so typical of the Neo-Hindu adherents of the BJP, the RSS and the VHP are all very much a product of the Indo-Islamic period in which older Hindu traditions were interacting with Islamic Sufi traditions, the emerging *sant* traditions, and the great regional *bhakti* traditions (and see chapter 3). Indeed, to go one step further, it is possible to detect in the Neo-Hindu BJP and its programs a political style and strident rhetoric not unlike a variety of Islamic protest movements in South Asia and the Middle East. The RSS and the VHP, for example, are not unlike the Muslim Brotherhood or radical groups of Mujahadin of one kind or another throughout the Muslim world. Moreover, one has a sense that if the people of India elect a BJP government at the Centre, it could well be the case that the Neo-Hindu civilisation-state will begin to look more like a Neo-Hindu version of the Islamic Republic of Pakistan or the Islamic Republic of Iran (and see the typology of "Nation-State" religions in chapter 4 above). Whether these quasi-Islamic features within the Neo-Hindu BJP are simply the odd ironies of history or some sort of Freudian "return of the repressed" need not detain us. What has been important is the attempt to clarify how "community-ship" and "communalism" operate in modern India's hybrid discourse of modernity.

"Citizenship"

Given the fact that only a small portion of the population of modern India is within the modern, industrialized sector of the economy and state, and given the fact of the overwhelming presence of discrete communities on all sides together with traditions of personal law that operate within many of the communities, it is not difficult to conclude that India's commitment to equal citizenship and equality before the law is difficult to maintain and ends up all too often as little more than rhetoric and lip-service. As Dipesh Chakrabarty has put it: "the 'codes' of politics in the subaltern domain derive from power-relationships and ideological formations that pre-date colonialism and the importation of the idea of 'citizenship'. . . . For the greater part of our daily experience, class relations express themselves in that other language of politics, which is the politics of a nation without 'citizens.'"[11] The revival of *satī* (widow immolation on the funeral pyre of the husband), wife-burning over dowry disputes, arranged marriages, caste obligations, traditions of personal law and a host of other "community-ship" and "communalist" issues, are all symptomatic of "the politics of a nation without citizens."[12] The inequities in India as outlined and described in the Report of the Backward Classes Commission (the Mandal Report) together with the remarkable statistic that "backward classes" (including Scheduled Tribes and Scheduled Castes) may represent as much as 75 percent of the total population suggest that the modern notion of the individual "citizen" has not progressed very far since independence. That India has made almost no progress in developing a uniform civil code and that it continues routinely to extend the system of "reservations" even though such reservations were to cease ten years after independence are further evidence of "the politics of a nation without 'citizens.'" Even more disturbing are conditions in states such as Punjab and Jammu and Kashmir where human rights are routinely violated and there is very nearly a total police state.

Regarding all of these matters, neither the "liberal" Neo-Hindu "secular state" nor the "conservative" Neo-Hindu BJP orientation appear to offer much of an alternative. Both are in favor of a strong Centre, the use of police and paramilitary forces to sustain that Centre, and a willingness to sacrifice individual rights with alacrity for the sake of law and order. To its credit the conservative Neo-Hindu BJP does favor the development of a uniform civil code, which can be interpreted to mean its serious commitment to individual rights, although its support of a uniform civil code is more than a little motivated by its hostility towards what it considers the pampering of minorities in terms of personal law and other special privileges.

The only other voice currently to be heard in favor of a renewed commitment to equal citizenship and equality before the law together with remedial measures to redress the inequities of Indian society is that of V. P. Singh and his Janata Dal party. He was and is vigorously supportive of the recommendations of the Mandal Report regarding increased reservations for the Other Backward Classes, although it is obviously debatable whether further efforts towards reservations will enhance individual rights and modern notions of citizenship. Many have argued that the system of reservations simply perpetuates "casteism" and "communalism," since it operates on the basis of group-identity which is the antithesis of the notion of the individual "citizen." The counterargument, of course, is that of Rajni Kothari, quoted earlier: "Those in India who complain of 'casteism' in politics are really looking for a sort of politics which has no basis in society." Kothari's comment in this context is profoundly important. In India's hybrid discourse of modernity it is essential to understand that the notion of "citizenship" is inextricably allied with the notion of "community-ship." The two play off one another continuously. In the early years after independence it can be argued plausibly that the two were kept in a reasonable balance. In more recent years, however, again dating primarily from the time of Mrs. Gandhi, the balance has shifted decisively in the direction of "community-ship" and away from "citizenship."

The Search for a New Beginning

T. N. Madan in an interesting article entitled "Secularim in its Place" has commented as follows:

> Now, I submit that in the prevailing circumstances secularism in South Asia as a generally held credo of life is impossible, as a basis for state action impracticable, and as a blueprint for the foreseeable future impotent. . . . Secularism is the dream of a minority which wants to shape the majority in its own image, which wants to impose its will upon history but lacks the power to do so under a democratically organized polity. . . . From the point of view of the majority, "secularism" is a vacuous word, a phantom concept, for such people do not know whether it is desirable to privatize

> religion, and if it is, how this may be done, unless they be Protestant Christians but not if they are Buddhists, Hindus, Muslims or Sikhs.[13]

Ashis Nandy has expressed a similar skepticism about secularism: "To build a more tolerant society we shall have to defy the imperialism of categories of our times which allows the concept of secularism . . . to hegemonize the idea of tolerance, so that any one who is not secular becomes definitionally intolerant."[14]

T. N. Madan and Ashis Nandy are but two of a number of voices that have been raised in recent years about the long-term value and significance of holding fast to the hybrid discourse of the "secular state" in India. Its inadequacies from a religious point of view are becoming increasingly clear. Again, T. N. Madan puts the matter well.

> While society seethes with . . . a vibrant religiosity, the feeble character of the Indian policy of state secularism is exposed. At best, Indian secularism has been an inadequately defined "attitude" . . . of "goodwill towards all religions," *sarvadharma sadbhāva*; in a narrower formulation it has been a negative or defensive policy of religious neutrality (*dharma nirapekshitā*) on the part of the state. In either formulation, Indian secularism achieves the opposite of its stated intentions; it trivializes religious difference as well as the notion of the unity of religions.[15]

The "goodwill towards all religions" mind-set is the pre-partition Gandhian universalist attitude, and the "religious neutrality" mind-set is the Nehruvian demythologized post-partition variant. Both are more than a little influenced by Western and largely "secularized" Protestant notions of individualism and the privatization of religious belief. Both are religious formulations that function on the level of ideas and ideals and impinge hardly at all on the larger social reality. One is entitled to believe whatever one wishes so long as it makes no difference on the level of social reality. One thereby gains a tolerant pluralism on the level of thought but at the price of detaching religious interpretations from social behavior. As J. Duncan M. Derrett has wryly commented: "The unattractive compromise became a fact, and no amount of religion enables an individual to contravene his country's laws, whatever they are. This naturally comforts those who do not think too deeply. . . . Could it be said that this is what has happened and is about to happen in India?"[16]

It would be a mistake, however, to trace the Gandhian-Nehruvian religious formulation of the "secular state" solely to the Western and largely Protestant notions of secularization, individualism and the privatization of religious belief, although it certainly is the case that these Protestant notions appear to be dominant in modern Indian discourse. There is also a deep resonance for such a religious formulation within the Old Indic traditions themselves, that is, the Indo-Brāhmaṇical, the Indo-Śramaṇical and the Indic. There is almost a kind of Weberian elective affinity between some traditions of cognitive pluralism and tolerance, on the one hand, and modern notions of the "secular state," on the other, whether in India or elsewhere. It is, therefore, no accident that, *mutatis mutandis*, an American civil religion could look very much like an Indic civil religion and appear within the same subsection of a typology of religions (and see chapter 4).

In any case, while such a "secular" religious formulation may have worked reasonably well in modern contexts in which alternative religious formulations or religions generally are not salient features of social life, as, for example, in areas in which religionization has occurred along the lines of a Protestant "secularization" model like the United States or Western Europe, it would appear to be the case that such a "secular" religious formulation has been a failure in the modern South Asian environment where religionization has unfolded in dramatically different ways as, for example, among Sikh communities in the Punjab, Neo-Muslim groups in Jammu and Kashmir, sectarian movements of one kind or another in various parts of India, and all sorts of other unusual manifestations of religion in contemporary India. The "secular state" appears to have had only two strategies by way of dealing with the varieties of religionization occuring in modern India, either something along the lines of the comment that "one must give the minorities what they want," or something along the lines of anti-national, communal, name-calling together with the repressive use of police and paramilitary forces. In other words, the "secular" religious formulation appears to have no way of mediating between the various manifestations of religionization. It appears to have only the either-or options of total capitulation or violent repression. Says T. N. Madan: "Though forty years have passed and the Midnight's Children are at the threshold of middle life, tempers continue to rage, and occasionally (perhaps too frequently) blood even flows in some places, as a result of the mutual hostility between the followers of different religions."[17]

T. N. Madan concludes his interesting essay, "Secularism in its Place," with the following comment:

> I must conclude; but I really have no conclusions to offer, no solutions to suggest. Let me hasten to say, however, that I am not advocating the establishment of a Hindu state in India—not at all. It simply will not work.[18]

Likewise the present writer has no definitive or quick solutions by way of finding a new direction for the future. Moreover, as mentioned at the outset of this concluding chapter, the pursuit of a new beginning is best left for the people of India to decide. There would appear to be certain new developments, however, or perhaps better, exploratory possibilities emerging at the present time in modern India's hybrid discourse of modernity, and I would like briefly to mention some of these. One might think of them simply as possible agenda items for an on-going cultural debate that will be unfolding in the years ahead as the people of India fashion their destiny, an on-going debate not unlike the one that has always been unfolding through the centuries.

The Possibility of Developing a "Multi-Religious State"

There could be merit in exploring the possibility of a middle ground between the extremes of a Neo-Hindu "secular state," on the one hand, and a supposed "Hindu" state, on the other. The one extreme (the Neo-Hindu secular state) eliminates the possibility of discourse about religion in matters of public policy and education, thereby totally detaching the claims of religion from matters of public policy and state functioning. The other extreme (a supposed "Hindu" state) subordinates the possibility of discourse about religion in matters of public policy and education to the discourse of one contrived interpretation among the Hindu federation of faiths, thereby also detaching the claims of religion from matters of public policy and state functioning with the exception, of course, of the contrived single interpretation. Both extremes are in an important sense anti-pluralist and, finally, anti-nationalist, anti-pluralist in the sense that only one option is truly recognized in each extreme, namely, the secular option in the Neo-Hindu secular state and the purported "Hindu" in the Hindu state, and anti-nationalist in the sense that both extremes repress (in the political sense as well as the Freudian sense) crucial components in the identity of the civilisation-state of India.

As a third option which mediates the extremes, consideration might be given to the possibility of developing the Republic of India as a "multi-religious state." No one religious tradition would be favored or established, but all would be recognized (including secularist and agnostic traditions) and "enfranchised," as it were, in matters of public policy, especially in the areas of research, education and communication. Just as there is an All India Institute of Medical Sciences or an Indian Council for Philosophical Research, so there could be an All India Institute for Research in Religion or an Indian Council for Research in Religion. Membership in such an institute or council would be determined by the participating religious groups that take part, in consultation, of course, with appropriate government officials. Whether there would be a Department of Religious Affairs or simply an Institute or Council for coordinating research, education and communication regarding issues related to religion would have to be determined as planning develops. Funding for such an institute or council would likewise be determined and provided by the groups taking part. Instead of pretending that religion should have no place in public policy and public life, efforts could be directed to determine its reasonable and appropriate place. Some minimal Centre funding would probably be required for setting up an appropriate mechanism for trying to fashion a multi-religious state, but such minimal funding would not violate Article 27 of the Constitution, inasmuch as Article 27 only prohibits the use of tax monies "for the promotion or maintenance of any particular religion or religious denomination." Tax money presumably could be used to foster research, education and communication with respect to issues of religion in general in a "multi-religious state." Article 28(1), however, which prohibits religious instruction "in any educational institution wholly maintained out of state funds," would have to be modified. A broad program of education in the history of religions or religious studies would be an important component in the education curriculum on all levels in a "multi-religious state."

Obviously the setting up of a "multi-religious state" would be a difficult and complex undertaking, fraught with problems and dangers. There would have to be safeguards in place to protect the equal status of all participating religious groups together with clearly established guidelines of civility between the various religious groups. Safeguards would also have to be in place to protect the religious groups from being coopted or coerced by the authority of the state. Criteria for the maintenance of free expression as well as free exercise in research, education, communication and overall practice would have to be assured. There is, of course, no model to follow in this regard. India would be undertaking a remarkable experiment in interreligious "community-ship," but it is probably fair to say that no state is better equipped in terms of long and enduring experience with cultural pluralism and toleration than is the civilisation-state of India to undertake such a task.

It should be noted, finally, that developing a "multi-religious state" is not at all a new idea in modern India. At the time of independence, as D. E. Smith has pointed out, C. Rajagopalachari proposed something very much along these lines.

> And if India's government is to be an institution integrated with her people's lives, if it is to be a true democracy and not a superimposed western institution staged in Indian dress, religion must have an important and recognized place in it, with impartiality and equal reverence for all the creeds and denominations prevailing in India. This alone would be historically consistent with the peaceful revolution brought about by our Nation's Father [Gandhi].[19]

Perhaps this old idea from the time of independence, dismissed at the time as being naive and unworkable, should be given a renewed hearing as India approaches the half century mark of her independence. It would allow a clear public space for religion, and it would enable the civlisation-state of India to draw freely from its rich, pluralistic heritage. Presumably it was something along these lines that Percival Spear had in mind when he commented, as quoted in the epigraph to the present chapter: "If Hinduism cannot hope to be the heir of all the ages, she may in the course of time become the Mother of the heir."[20]

The Possibility of "Decentering the Centre" and Descending from the "Commanding Heights"

This possibility requires little comment since it is already being seriously debated and to some extent implemented at the present time in India. Especially since the election of P. V. Narasimha Rao, there has been a determined effort in the direction of "liberalization" in terms of government rules and regulations, outside investment, and the involvement of India in the global economy. As many voices in India are suggesting, this needs to be coupled also with greater decentralization between the states and the Centre. There may have been considerable merit in the early decades after independence with the policies of import substitution, government control of the "commanding heights," and strong control from the Centre for the sake of rapid industrialization and the establishment of a modern polity as quickly as possible. Given the current situation in the states of Punjab and

Jammu and Kashmir, however, together with the unrest in the Northeast and elsewhere in India, the strong Centre is rapidly becoming perceived as a repressive and violent Centre. The careful constitutional balance between states and Centre has shifted considerably in recent years in the direction of excessive centralization, partly because of centrifugal—often referred to by Indian commentators as "fissiparous"—forces such as the separatist movements in Punjab, Jammu and Kashmir and elsewhere, but also partly because of a deliberate policy by Mrs. Gandhi of what the Rudolphs have called "deinstitutionalization," that is, transforming established bureaucratic institutional functioning into relations of personal power and personal loyalty between the Centre and the states.[21] In any case, whatever the reasons, it is probably important, as many thoughtful commentators in India are currently suggesting, for India to move away from excessive centrism and to permit as much local political autonomy as possible in the years just ahead.

The Possibility of Some Sort of South Asian "Confederation"

Here again is an old idea that may be ripe for reconsideration in the current climate in South Asia. In December of 1985 India for the first time joined with six other South Asian regional powers (Bangladesh, Bhutan, the Maldives, Nepal, Pakistan and Sri Lanka) to form the South Asian Association for Regional Cooperation (SAARC), a body designed to provide a forum for the discussion of conflicts, area development and general cooperation in the South Asian region.[22] SAARC's accomplishments thus far have been only modest, but it does represent for the first time since partition an attempt to provide an institutional structure for overcoming some of the hostility and lack of communication between the various regional powers in South Asia. As was mentioned earlier in chapter 4, Sheikh Abdullah, the "Lion of Kashmir," often toyed with the idea of an institutional "confederation" between India, Pakistan and Jammu and Kashmir, and one wonders if some sort of revised notion of "confederation" could provide a way out of the impasse that currently exists between India, Pakistan and Jammu and Kashmir as well as the state of Punjab. "Confederation" need not mean total independence. It could mean developing the notion of a "state within a state" with respect to Punjab and Jammu and Kashmir in India and the Tamil-majority area in Sri Lanka. It could also become a basis for developing a greater coalescence of interests between India, Pakistan, Bangladesh and Sri Lanka within the context of an upgraded SAARC. In any case, it appears to be inevitable that a plebiscite will have to be held in Jammu and Kashmir, either under international auspices or possibly under a simpler bilateral agreement between India and Pakistan or under the auspices of SAARC, just as it is inevitable that local elections will eventually have to take place in the state of Punjab involving all of the Sikh communities, and it is probably the better part of wisdom, as many Indian commentators have recognized, for India to work with the process of accommodation through some sort of "confederation" than to attempt to hold off the inevitable with massive military repression.

The Possibility of a Uniform Civil Code

We have already discussed at some length the need for a uniform civil code in order to enhance the notions of citizenship and equality before the law in India. There is widespread support in India for this, not only among Neo-Hindu groups such as the BJP but also in Muslim communities in various parts of India. One way to proceed would be to form an All India Commission for a Uniform Civil Code made up of representatives from the legal community as well as all religious communities that function with any kind of "personal law" (mainly Hindu, Muslim, Parsi and Christian groups) and to charge such a commission to present a draft uniform civil code for all citizens within the territory of India within a period of five years. Efforts could be pursued not only to hold hearings all around India but to consult widely with Muslim communities outside of India, including the Islamic Republic of Pakistan, Bangladesh, Indonesia, and so forth. The time has surely come, as most thoughtful observers in India are fully aware, for Article 44 of the Directive Principles of State Policy to be transferred to the section of Fundamental Rights.

The Possibility of Revisioning "Community-ship" away from a Reservations Policy Based on Group Identity

This last agenda item is particularly difficult, since it is not clear how India can or should maintain its joint commitments to what we have called "community-ship" and citizenship. More than most other nation-states, the civilisation-state of India has had a remarkable and enviable track record in seriously trying to address problems of "community-ship." The legacy of the caste system and colonialism together with the modern rebirth of the caste system in the form of the politics of caste associations has necessitated a self-conscious policy of compensatory discrimination in India, largely for Scheduled Castes and Scheduled Tribes at the Centre but also for Other Backward Classes as well on the level of policy in many states. There is some evidence that the policy of reservations has over the past forty years of independence made a positive difference in the lives of many untouchables and tribals. At the time of independence, for example, the percent of persons from Scheduled Castes and Tribes in government jobs was negligible whereas in recent years the percent has reached a significant 9 percent.[23] This is an important achievement, but as we noted earlier, the policy of reservations for Scheduled Castes and Scheduled Tribes was supposed to cease after ten years of independence, that is, in 1960. Because caste and group interests have become entrenched, the date for ending reservations has been routinely extended at the end of each subsequent decade for yet another decade (in 1960, 1970, 1980 and most recently in 1990).

As we have discussed earlier, there is now the additional recommendation of the Mandal Commission that reservations be expanded to cover Other Backward Classes up to a total of 49.5 percent of the total population (including Scheduled Castes and Scheduled Tribes). In other words, instead of cutting back on reservations, the Mandal Commission recommends that reservations be greatly increased in numbers, and we have already discussed how V. P. Singh and P. V. Narasimha Rao have attempted to implement these recommendations. Noble as these commitments to compensatory discrimination are with respect to balancing the social inequities in Indian life, the words of D. E. Smith, written some thirty years ago, are still very much to the point.

> There is a profound contradiction between the objective of a casteless society and the method of elevating the backward on a caste basis. . . .
>
> India has taken a gigantic administrative shortcut. By identifying certain castes as underprivileged, the state has reduced its problem to the relatively simple one of verifying a given applicant's membership in one of these castes. This procedure is not followed by any modern state, even where a high correlation exists between economic need and membership in certain religious or ethnic groups. . . .
>
> Equality before the law and equal protection of the laws can only mean that the state deals with the individual as a citizen and not as a member of a group. . . . India's administrative shortcut is proving a very costly one, for the price being paid is the perpetuation of caste and the general weakening of the foundations of the secular state.[24]

While we have commented favorably about Rajni Kothari's point that "those in India who complain of 'casteism' in politics are looking for a sort of politics which has no basis in society," it is much worth debating whether caste-oriented reservations will ever really accomplish the overcoming of social, educational and economic backwardness. Perhaps the framers of India's Constitution were right, namely, that the policy of reservation should have ceased in 1960.

This need not at all mean that India's commitment to compensatory discrimination should be scrapped. It means only that the policy of reservations by caste or backward class should cease. It would still be possible to take into account the social, and hence caste, identity of all individuals in developing programs in education, social welfare, and regional development. Scholarships, special training programs, grants-in-aid and a host of other "affirmative action" avenues would still be open for further exploration and implementation. Whether such measures instead of a policy of reservations will be any more successful, only time can determine. In any case, there is no more challenging and fascinating debate to take place in the years to come than that between India's joint commitment to both "community-ship" and citizenship.

"Abide with Me . . ." ". . . Mother Great and Free"

This book opened with reference to the ceremony "Beating the Retreat" and to the use in the ceremony of the music of the old Christian hymn "Abide with Me." Through these chapters we have moved from the great abiding truths—"Abide with me"—of Indic civilization as embodied in its dense and complex cultural layers (the Indus Valley, the Indo-Brāhmaṇical, the Indo-Śramaṇical, the Indic, the Indo-Islamic and the Indo-Anglian) to the current period of the onset of evening—"fast falls the eventide"—when distinctions have become somewhat blurred, when shadows have lengthened and distorted what had been so clear, when ropes have become increasingly mistaken for snakes, and when illusory dreams of ignorance have become the only respite from the fearful night of alienation. Indeed, "the darkness deepens," as the old hymn continues. But then the hymn takes a turn back to the beginning— "Lord with me abide"—and gives expression to that which abides and will continue to abide even when all else has disappeared.

> When other helpers fail, and comforts flee;
> Help of the helpless, O abide with me.

The Old Indic inflection of the "Lord" here, of course, diverges a good deal from the steadfast father God of the New Indic stiff-collared, nineteenth-century Anglican cleric and his older Islamic colleague, the Muslim mullah. That which abides in the Old Indic sensibilities is, rather, closer to the notion of a loving and powerful mother.

> Mother, I bow to thee!
> Rich with thy hurrying streams,
> Bright with thy orchard gleams,
> Cool with thy winds of delight,
> Dark fields waving, Mother of might,
> Mother free.
> . . .
> With many strengths who are mighty and stored,
> To thee I call, Mother and Lord!
> Thou who savest, arise and save!
> . . .
> Every image made divine
> In our temples is but thine.
> Thou art Durga, Lady and Queen,
> With her hands that strike and her swords of sheen,
> Thou art Lakshmi lotus-throned,
> And the Muse a hundred-toned.
> Pure and perfect without peer,
> Mother, lend thine ear.
> . . .
> Mother sweet, I bow to thee
> Mother great and free![25]

Nehru in the Epilogue to *The Discovery of India* also gives eloquent expression to that which abides in India, and it seems fitting to close this book with a portion of that expression.

> The discovery of India—what have I discovered? It was presumptuous of me to imagine that I could unveil her and find out what she is today and what she was in the long past. . . .
>
> India is a geographical and economic entity, a cultural unity amidst diversity, a bundle of contradictions held together by strong but invisible threads. . . .
>
> She is a myth and an idea, a dream and a vision, and yet very real and present and pervasive. There are terrifying glimpses of dark corridors which seem to lead back to primeval night, but

also there is the fullness and warmth of the day about her. Shameful and repellent she is occasionally, perverse and obstinate, sometimes even a little hysteric, this lady with a past. But she is very lovable and none of her children can forget her wherever they go or whatever strange fate befalls them. For she is part of them in her greatness as well as her failings, and they are mirrored in those deep eyes of hers that have seen so much of life's passion and joy and folly and looked down into wisdom's well. Each one of them is drawn to her, though perhaps each has a different reason for that attraction or can point to no reason at all, and each sees some different aspect of her many-sided personality. From age to age she has produced great men and women, carrying on the old tradition and yet ever adapting it to changing times. . . .[26]

Notes

Chapter 1. Introduction: Beating The Retreat

1. The hymn, known as "Eventide," was composed by William H. Monk (1823–89) and with lyrics by the Rev. Henry Francis Lyte (1793–1847). Lyte wrote the lyrics for the hymn in 1847; Monk's tune was composed in 1861. The hymn was one of Gandhi's favorites.

It should be noted that in the ceremony "Beating the Retreat," only the title of the hymn is printed in the official program. The words of the first verse of the hymn are not printed. I would like to thank Leroy S. Rouner for permitting me to use this anecdote about "Beating the Retreat" which I first used in an essay published in a collectionof essays edited by him. See Leroy S. Rouner, ed. *Celebrating Peace* (Notre Dame, Indiana: Univ. of Notre Dame Press, 1990).

2. Alfred North Whitehead, *Process and Reality* (New York: Macmillan 1929; reprint by Harper and Row, 1957), p. 318.

3. *Ibid.*, p. 513.

4. K. M. Panikkar, *The State and the Citizen* (Bombay: Asia Publishing House, 1956), p. 28.

5. Quoted in Ainslie Embree, *Imagining India* (Delhi: Oxford University Press, 1989; edited by M. Juergensmeyer), p. 10.

6. *Ibid.*, pp. 10-11.

7. G. W. F. Hegel, *The Philosophy of History*, trans. J. Sibree (New York: Dover Publications, 1956), pp. 160-6l.

8. *Ibid.*, p. 513.

9. *Ibid.*

10. W.H. Morris-Jones, "India's Political Idioms," quoted in Thomas R. Metcalf, ed., *Modern India: An Interpretive Anthology* (London: Collier Macmillan, 1971), pp. 273–74 and 277).

11. Amulya Ratna Nanda, ed., *Census of India* 199l, Paper-l, Provisional Population Totals (Delhi: Government of India, Samrat Press, 199l), p. 19 and *passim*.

12. Joseph W. Elder, "Society," in Marshall M. Bouton, ed., *India Briefing, 1987* (Delhi: Oxford University Press, 1987), pp. 109–ll0.

13. Francis Robinson, ed., *The Cambridge Encyclopedia of India, Pakistan, Bangladesh, Sri Lanka, Nepal, Bhutan and the Maldives* (Cambridge: Cambridge University Press, 1989), p. 63. It should be noted that these figures are only rough estimates and are already somewhat dated. Also, whenever possible in each instance the figure represents only people from India. In other words, the figures do not include Pakistan, Bangladesh, and so forth. Finally, it should be noted that there are numerous other places around the world with Asian Indian populations of less than 100,000.

14. Lloyd I. and Susanne H. Rudolph, *In Pursuit of Lakshmi* (Chicago: University of Chicago Press, 1987), p. 9. Many of these figures may undergo considerable alteration as a result of the 1991 census which is currently being analyzed and the results of which will be published serially over the next several years.

15. *Census of India* 1991, p. 55.

16. Robin Wright, "Poverty's Shadow Haunting New Democracies," *Los Angeles Times*, 25 Februrary 1992, p. H4.

17. B.P. Mandal, *Report of the Backward Classes Commission*, first part, volumes I and II (Delhi: Government of India, 1980), p. 50. The issues of caste and community will be discussed at length in the sequel (see chapters 3 and 5). Suffice it to say at this point that these percentages are somewhat controversial with respect to the "OBCs" (Other Backward Classes). The Mandal Commission Report estimates OBCs at a full 50% of the population. The Rudolphs (*In Pursuit of Lakshmi*, p. 54) argue for a much smaller percentage of 25% for OBCs, suggesting that the OBCs represent the "status aspect" of the economic category of "bullock capitalists," that is to say, self-employed, yeoman-like "middle peasants" who own a pair of bullocks and a small plot of land. According to the Rudophs, these "middle peasants" have benefitted greatly from the "green

revolution" in India and since the 1970s have been becoming a "hegemonic agrarian class," making up some 34% of all agricultural households and controlling over 50% of the land. Caste groups among the OBCs that have become prominent include Yadavas, Kurmis, Koeris, Vokkaligas, and others.

18. The Constitution of India (as on the lst April 1986), (Delhi: Government of India, 1986), p. xviii.

19. The Constitution, p. 194 (Eighth Schedule).

20. *The Indian Voice*, I, no. 33 (January 3, 1992): 15.

21. *Ibid.*

22. Rudolph and Rudolph, *In Pursuit of Lakshmi*, p. 397.

23. *Ibid.*, p. 22.

24. *Ibid.*, pp. 49–50.

25. Achin Vanaik, *The Painful Transition: Bourgeois Democracy in India* (London: Verso, 1990), p. 284.

26. Rudolph and Rudolph, *In Pursuit of Lakshmi*, p. 50.

27. *Ibid.*, pp. 52–53.

28. *Ibid.*, p. 54.

29. *Ibid.*

30. *Ibid.*, pp. 22–23.

31. *Ibid.*, p. 25.

32. *Ibid.*

33. *Ibid.*, p. 2.

34. *Ibid.*, p. 5l.

35. *Ibid.*, pp. 58–59.

36. *Ibid.*, p. 54. Regarding the percentage of those who make up the "Other Backward Classes," see above, note 16.

37. E. Wayne Nafziger, *The Economics of Developing Countries* (Englewood Cliffs, N.J.: Prentice Hall, 1990), p. 69.

38. Dipesh Chakrabarty, "Invitation to a Dialogue," in Ranajit Guha, ed., *Subaltern Studies IV: Writings on South Asian History and Society* (Delhi: Oxford University Press, 1985), p. 374.

39. Immanuel Wallerstein, *The Politics of the World-Economy: The States, the Movements and the Civilizations* (Cambridge: Cambridge University Press, 1987), pp. 126–27.

40. *Census of India* 1981, Series-1, Paper 3, "Household Population by Religion and Head of Household," (Delhi: Government of India, 1984), *passim.*

41. *Census of India* 1991, p. 1. It should be stressed that these figures are only rough estimates. There have been some claims that Muslims are deliberately undercounted and that their total may be considerably more than the census indicates. The same may well be true for the "Hindu" classification. I have made allowances for such discrepancies by citing figures between 82% and 83% for Hindus and 11.5% and 12% for Muslims. As overall rough estimates, however, the figures are reasonable enough.

42. The Rudolphs argue for precisely such a refiguring, namely, 62% "Hindu" and 38% "non-Hindu," *In Pursuit of Lakshmi*, p. 37.

43. Agehananda Bharati refers to a "cautious estimate" of "one million" monastics in India. K. Klostermaier, surveying both Indian and western sources, estimates 8-15 "professional religious" or monastics. See Agehananda Bharati, *Hindu Views and Ways and the Hindu-Muslim Interface* (New Delhi: Munshiram Manoharlal, 1981), p. 53; and Klaus K. Klostermaier, *A Survey of Hinduism* (New York: State University of New York Press, 1989), p. 329.

44. Bharati, *Hindu Views and Ways*, pp. 9ff., 11ff., 48ff., 51ff., and *passim.*

45. Figures are available for Assam only from the 1971 census. All other figures are from the census of 1981.

46. Myron Weiner, "India's Minorities: Who Are They? What Do They Want?" in J.R. Roach, ed., *India 2000: The Next Fifteen Years* (Riverdale, Maryland: The Riverdale Co., 1986), pp. 100–134.

47. David B. Barrett, *World Christian Encyclopedia* (Oxford: Oxford University Press, 1982), pp. 373–375. See also the articles "India, Christianity in," "Malabar Christians," "North India, Church of," and "South India, Church of," in F.L. Cross and E.A. Livingstone, eds., *The Oxford Dictionary of the Christian Church* (London: Oxford University Press, 1974; second edition), pp. 698–99, 860–861, 981, and 1293-94.

48. Barrett, *World Christian Encyclopedia*, p. 374.

49. W.H. McLeod, *The Sikhs: History, Religion and Society* (New York: Columbia University Press, 1989), p. 45.

50. Bharati, *Hindu Views and Ways*, p. 81.

51. The two best treatments of the background to Operation Blue Star are Rajiv A. Kapur, *Sikh Separatism: The Politics of Faith* (London: Allen and Unwin, 1986), especially p. 226ff.; and Mark Tully and Satish Jacob, *Amritsar: Mrs. Gandhi's Last Battle* (London: Jonathan Cape, 1985), *passim.*

52. K. Sandhu and R. Vinayak, "Punjab: Area of Darkness," *India Today*, 15 July 1992, pp. 22–27.

53. Stephen Hay, ed., *Sources of Indian Tradition*, volume 2 (New York: Columbia University Press, 1988; second edition), pp. 324–32 and pp. 339–48. See especially Ambedkar's speech entitled "Why Accept Buddhism?," translated by Eleanor Zelliot and Rekha Damle, pp. 347–48.

54. *Ibid.*, p. 339.

55. Barrett, *World Christian Encyclopedia*, p. 373.

56. For a brief but useful account of the Sino-Indian problem and the issue of Tibet during the Nehru era, see Stanley Wolpert, *A New History of India* (New York: Oxford University Press, 1989), pp. 351–70.

57. A solid summary treatment of Jain traditions is Padmanabh S. Jaini, *The Jaina Path of Purification* (Berkeley: University of California Press, 1979). For a general discussion of the early foundations of the tradition, see pp. 1–41. For a useful survey of Jain institutions in the regional history of the subcontinent, see pp. 274–315. An excellent recent collection of essays on Jainism is Michael Carrithers and Caroline Humphrey, eds., *The Assembly of Listeners: Jains in Society* (Cambridge: Cambridge University Press, 1991), *passim*.

58. *Ibid.*, p. 33 and 33n.

59. *Ibid.*, pp. 4–6.

60. Michael Carrithers, "Jainism," in F. Robinson, ed., *The Cambridge Encyclopedia of India, Pakistan, Bangladesh, Sri Lanka, Nepal, Bhutan, and the Maldives* (Cambridge: Cambridge University Press, 1989), pp. 331–32.

61. Jaini, *The Jaina Path of Purification*, pp. 274–315.

62. John Hinnells, "Judaism" and "Zoroastrianism," in F. Robinson, *Cambridge Encyclopedia of India*, pp. 360–62.

63. *Ibid.*

64. *Ibid.*

65. R. E. Frykenberg, "The Emergence of Modern 'Hinduism' as a Concept and as an Institution: A Reappraisal with Special Reference to South India," in G. D. Sontheimer and H. Kulke, eds., *Hinduism Reconsidered* (Delhi: Manohar, 1991), p. 32.

66. Peter Hardy, "Islam and Muslims in South Asia," in R. Israeli, ed., *The Crescent in the East*: Islam in Asia Major (London: Humanities Press, 1982), pp. 39–40.

67. Wilfred C. Smith, *The Meaning and End of Religion* (New York: Harper and Row, 1972; reprrint of the original 1962 edition), pp. 51–118.

68. Frits Staal, "The Himalayas and the Fall of Religion," in D. E. Klimburg-Salter, ed., *The Silk Route and the Diamond Path* (Los Angeles: University of

California Press, 1982), pp. 38–51; and Frits Staal, *Rules Without Meaning* (New York: Peter Lang, 1989; Toronto Studies in Religion, volume 4), 387ff.

69. Ernest Gellner, *Nations and Nationalism* (Oxford: Basil Blackwell, 1983), p. 4.

70. *Ibid.*, p. 5.

71. *Ibid.*, p. 7.

72. Benedict Anderson, *Imagined Communities: Reflections on the Origin and Spread of Nationalism* (London: Verso, 1983), pp. 14–16.

73. Anthony Giddens, *The Nation-State and Violence* (Berkeley: University of California Press, 1987), p. 121.

74. *Ibid.*, pp. 79–80.

75. *Ibid.*

76. *Ibid.* pp. 4–5.

77. *Ibid.*, pp. 267–76.

78. *Ibid.*, p. 267.

79. *Ibid.*, p. 269.

80. *Ibid.*, p. 274.

81. Ravinder Kumar, "India: A 'Nation-State' or a 'Civilisation-State'?," *Occasional Papers on Perspectives in Indian Development*, Centre for Contemporary Studies, Nehru Memorial Museum and Library, Number VIII (Delhi: Teen Murti House, May 1989), p. 41.

82. *Ibid.*, p. 6.

83. *Ibid.*, p. 42.

84. Rudolph and Rudolph, *In Pursuit of Lakshmi*, pp. 63–64 and 66.

85. Percival Spear, *India, Pakistan and the West* (London: Oxford University Press; third edition), p. 38.

86. For a good summary statement of "modernization" theory, see Robert Wuthnow, "Understanding Religion and Politics," *Daedalus*, 120, no. 3 (Summer 1991): 2–5. For a good treatment of "secularization," see Peter Berger, *The Sacred Canopy* (New York: Doubleday Anchor Books, 1969), pp. 105–71.

87. Edward Said, *Orientalism* (New York: Vintage Books, 1978), p. 86.

88. Ronald Inden, *Imagining India* (Oxford: Basil Blackwell, 1990), p. 37.

89. For recent discussions of Orientalism that are somewhat more analytical than either Said or Inden, see Carol A. Breckenridge and Peter van der

Veer, eds., *Orientalism and the Postcolonial Predicament* (Philadelphia: University of Pennsylvania Press, 1993), especially part I, pp. 23–185.

90. For Wallerstein's original formulation, see Immanuel Wallerstein, *The Modern World-System: Capitalist Agriculture and the Origins of the European World-Economy in the Sixteenth Century* (New York: Academic Press, 1974). For a more recent treatment, see Immanuel Wallerstein, *The Politics of the World-Economy: The States, the Movements and the Civilizations* (Cambridge: Cambridge University Press, 1984), see especially pp. 27–145.

91. For a recent treatment of world-system theorizing in India, see Sugata Bose, ed., *South Asia and World Capitalism* (Delhi: Oxford University Press, 1990), passim.

92. Ranajit Guha, ed., *Subaltern Studies I-VI: Writings on South Asian History and Society* (Delhi: Oxford University Press, 1982–85)

93. *Ibid.*, vol. IV, 330ff.

94. *Ibid.*, vol. IV, 229ff.; vol. II, 116ff., and vol. IV, 101ff.

95. *Ibid.*, vol. IV, p. 373.

96. *Ibid.*, p. 374.

97. *Ibid.*, p. 375.

98. A stimulating example of subaltern therorizing is Partha Chatterjee, *Nationalist Thought and the Colonial World: A Derivative Discourse* (Minneapolis: University of Minnesota Press, 1993; first published by United Nations University, 1986). A methodological problem in the book, however, is the old problem of the self-referential paradox. Chatterjee challenges the "fundamentals of Western bourgeois thought" but does so through the very structures of "the rational tones of Western scholarship." His attack on Western thought is finally also an attack on his own analysis! This is not unlike Derrida's attack on the so-called Western logocentric paradigm. At every step of its analysis it is dependent upon the very paradigm it is attacking, as Derrida, of course, recognizes. It is incorrigibly Western and Hegelian. Finally, such analyses lead into a cul-de-sac intellectually. One would hope that subaltern theorizing will finally be able to escape the Western paradigm *tout ensemble* and give us some genuinely creative and new critical reflection. Possibly the resources for a genuinely new critical reflection might be available within traditions of traditional Indian philosophizing.

99. I am borrowing the term "religionization" from an essay by Roland Robertson, "Church-State Relations and the World System," in T. Robbins and R. Robertson, eds., *Church-State Relations: Tensions and Transitions* (New Brunswick: Transaction Books, 1987), pp. 39–51 and especially pp. 46–47. Robertson, however, uses the term quite differently from the manner in which I use the term later (chapter 4). Robertson uses the term "religionization" to play

off its opposite, namely, the "politicization of religion." One then has the interesting dichotomy of the "politicization of religion" over against the "religionization of the political" or the "religionization of the state." My use of the term "religionization" is much broader than that and relates to the general task of developing a theory of religion.

100. Inden, *Imagining India*, pp. 1–48.

Chapter 2. Discontinuity as Continuity (i): Old Indic Formations

1. The best account of the role of Lord Cornwallis (1738–1805) in the American War of Independence is the first volume of the two-volume biography of Cornwallis by Franklin and Mary Wickwire, *Cornwallis and the War of Independence* (London: Faber and Faber, 1971), and see especially chapter 16 (entitled "The World Turned Upside Down"), pp. 354–88, for a detailed account of the siege and surrender at Yorktown. For the subsequent career of Cornwallis, see Franklin and Mary Wickwire, *Cornwallis: The Imperial Years* (Chapel Hill: University of North Carolina Press, 1980), *passim*. For a detailed treatment of Cornwallis's time in Bengal, see A. Aspinall, *Cornwallis in Bengal* (Manchester: University of Manchester, 1931), especially the overall assessment, pp. 163–76. See also W. S. Seton-Karr, *Rulers of India: The Marquess Cornwallis and the Consolidation of British Rule* (Oxford: Clarendon Press, 1898), especially the overall assessment, pp. 178–97. For the relation between Charles Cornwallis and other figures of the time such as Charles Grant, John Shore, and others, see Ainslie T. Embree, *Charles Grant and British Rule in India* (New York: Columbia University Press, 1962), pp. 95–120 and 136–40. For good bibliographical surveys of the extensive literature on Cornwallis, see F. and M. Wickwire, *Cornwallis and the War of Independence*, pp. 463–68, and *Cornwallis: The Imperial Years*, pp. 307–19. The single best printed source for the original papers of Charles Cornwallis continues to be Charles Ross, ed., *Correspondence of Charles, First Marquis Cornwallis*, 3 vols. (London: John Murray, 1859).

2. F. and M. Wickwire, *Cornwallis and the War of Independence*, pp. 2–3.

3. *Ibid.*, p. 3. The text of the tune, "The World Turned Upside Down," can be traced to an issue in 1767 of the London publication, *Gentleman's Magazine*. The author of the text is unknown. It carries the subtitle, "The Old Woman Taught Wisdom," and the first verse goes as follows: "Goody Bull and her daughter together fell out.

> Both squabbled and wrangled and made a great rout!
> But the cause of the quarrel remains to be told,
> Then lend both your ears and a tale I'll unfold,
> Derry down, down, hey, derry down,
> Then lend both your ears and a tale I'll unfold.

The music for the text is the popular English tune, "Down Derry Down."In five additional verses the story of a great conflict between mother and daughter is described, a conflict which is finally mediated by a "Farmer Pitt." The tune can be interpreted as describing the war between Britain (the mother, Goody Bull) and her colonies in North America (the disobedient daughter). "Farmer Pitt" is supposedly none other than the great William Pitt, the powerful advocate in Britain for the American cause. For the text of the entire song together with the music, see Lee Vinson, ed., *The Early American Songbook* (Englewood Cliffs, N.J.: Prentice-Hall, 1974), pp. 58–60. The Wickwires in *Cornwallis and the War of Independence,* pp. 391–92, comment as follows about the tradition that this song was played at the surrender at Yorktown:

> The incident was recorded by Count Matheiu Dumas, *Memoirs of His Own Time,* 2 vols. (Philadelphia, 1839). . . . Modern scholars who have studied the Yorktown campaign in great detail question that the British ever played "The World Turned Upside Down." So many bands—French, British, German and American—were at Yorktown that one would be surprised if the tune, a very popular one, were not played sometime during the surrender ceremony. There is no reason to suppose British musicians did not play it, and, in any event, it was particularly appropriate. . . . On that warm October day the world did turn upside down. The British knew it, and their musicians may well have expressed it. . . . Events may not have gone precisely as Dumas described them, but most eyewitnesses agreed on the general outlines of the ceremony, and it was sufficiently close to Dumas' picture to warrant our using his version.

4. F. and M. Wickwire, *Cornwallis: The Imperial Years,* p. 24.

5. Many of the innovations and reforms brought about by Cornwallis would undergo considerable change by the middle of the nineteenth century, especially after the North Indian rebellion in 1857–58 when the East India Company was phased out in favor of direct British imperial rule, but it is fair enough to say that the basic foundations of the British Raj in India were first put in place by the bureaucratic and legal reforms of Cornwallis between 1786 and 1793.

6. Seton-Karr, *Rulers of India,* pp. 99–100.

7. Aspinall, *Cornwallis in Bengal,* p. 168.

8. Cornwallis's wife, Jemima, had died already in 1779 while he was on leave from the American War of Independence. He had, in fact, determined not to return to the American War after 1778, but the grief over the death of his wife impelled him to want to get out of England, thus paving the way for his return to America and his humiliation at Yorktown. He and Jemima had two children, a son, Charles, and a daughter, Mary. Cornwallis also had two younger brothers and two sisters, all of whom were his responsibility since he was the eldest

sibling at the time of his father's death in 1762 (when Cornwallis himself was only 24 and only recently returned from the Seven Years War). He arranged for one of his younger brothers to pursue a career in the Church of England. Eventually that brother became the Bishop of Lichfield and Coventry. He arranged a military career for his other younger brother, and that brother eventually rose to the rank of admiral. He arranged for the marriage of the older of his two sisters, but that sister died while giving birth to her first child. His other, younger sister married a relatively poor man against the wishes of the family and proved to be a financial burden on Cornwallis throughout his life. For a good discussion of the life of the family, see F. and M. Wickwire, *Cornwallis and the War of Independence*, pp. 30–46.

9. F. and M. Wickwire, *Cornwallis: The Imperial Years*, pp. 261–67.

10. Seton-Karr, *Rulers of India*, pp. 193 and 197.

11. Fernand Braudel, *The Mediterranean and the Mediterranean World in the Age of Philip II*, trans., S. Reynolds (New York: Basic, 1972); Michel Foucault, *The Archaeology of Knowledge*, trans., A. M. Sheridan (New York: Harper and Row, 1972); and Bridget and Raymond Allchin, *The Rise of Civilization in India and Pakistan* (Cambridge: Cambridge University Press, 1982).

12. B. and R. Allchin, *The Rise of Civilization*, p. 13.

13. W. Norman Brown, "The Content of Cultural Continuity in India," *Journal of Asian Studies*, 20 (August 1961): 433–34; also reprinted in T. R. Metcalf, ed., *Modern India*: An Interpretive Anthology (London: Macmillan, 1971), p. 20.

14. *The Indian Voice*, 1, no. 33 (3 January 1992): 15.

15. This is a fairly standard periodization, although my naming of the various layers is somewhat new. In particular, the expression "Indo-Anglian" deserves some comment. It is an expression used in discussions of contemporary Indian literature in the medium of English. That is, instead of such older expressions as "Anglo-Indian" or "Indo-British" literature, there is a growing preference for "Indo-Anglian" literature, that is, Indian literature written in India but in the medium of English.

Generally speaking, there has been too much emphasis, in my judgment, on "Hindu," "Vedic," "Sanskritic" and "Brahmanical" components in treatments of the history of the subcontinent and not nearly enough emphasis on Buddhist, Jain, Bhakti, Tantric, Islamic and Christian components. This is basically the result of the history of western scholarship on South Asia, with the various groups of Orientalists (namely, Islamicists, Indologists and Buddhologists) compartmentalized over against historians of religions, missiologists and theologians, and with all of these various groups more or less out of touch with one another or suspicious of one another. Hence, discourses about matters South Asian have been very much a Tower of Babel with ample blame to be distributed on all sides. In naming the various layers or levels of South Asian civilization, therefore, I have tried to develop a terminology that is somewhat more balanced. My basic category is "Indic," which is meant to include both Sanskritic and Middle Indic (Buddhist, Jain, and so forth) traditions. So-called "classical Hindu" and "Purāṇic" traditions, beginning about the time of the Gupta dynasty, are, thus, combined with Mahāyāna Buddhist, Jain, Tantric and other traditions into what I am calling simply "Indic (Hindu-Buddhist-Jain)." Similarly, rather than buy into some sort of "two-nation" hypothesis or some variant thereof, I have characterized the coming of Islam as simply the "Indo-Islamic" period and include therein almost all regional traditions of so-called "Hindu Bhakti." Similarly, rather than refer to a "modern period" or a period of "Westernization" or "modernization," I much prefer the expression "Indo-Anglian." If Pakistan were in the purview of the present book, I would be inclined to include an additional "layer" to be identified as something like "Indo-Islamic-Anglian."

Regarding the issue of periodization, my treatment resembles (at least in terms of chronology) the scheme set forth by R. C. Majumdar, "Evolution of Religio-Philosophic Culture in India," in H. Bhattacharya, ed., *The Cultural Heritage of India*, vol. 4 (Calcutta: The Ramakrishna Mission Institute of Culture, 1956), pp. 31–62. It is also in keeping with Ainslie T. Embree, ed., *Sources of Indian Tradition* (New York: Columbia University Press, 1988; revised edition), vol. 1, pp. xxvii–xxxii, and Volume II, pp. xxv-xxvii (the latter volume edited by Stephen Hay). It likewise conforms for the most part with the chronology of M. Winternitz, *A History of Indian Literature*, vol. 3, trans. S. Jha (Delhi: Motilal Banarsidass, 1963 and 1967), pp. 455–731.

I have also kept one eye on the history of Indian philosophy in my chronology, and my periodization is roughly in keeping with what I take to be the best periodizations currently available in the secondary literature, namely, those of Erich Frauwallner and Richard Robinson. The former, Frauwallner, sees three basic phases in the development of Indian philosophy (a *first phase* from the time of the Veda through the development of the classical systems and concluding at the end of the first millenium C.E.., that is, from 1500 B.C.E. up through 1000 C.E.; a *second phase* from the middle of the first millenium C.E. up through the present in traditional contexts, including the great Vaiṣṇava and Śaiva theologies, that is, 500 C.E. up through the present; and, finally, a *third phase*, from the nineteenth century to the present, a "new" Indian philosophy under European influence. See Erich Frauwallner, *Geschichte der indischen Philosophie*, Band I (Salzburg: Otto Muller, 1953), pp. 11–29. The other periodization, that of Richard Robinson, is a good deal more sophisticated. He identifies four overall phases: an *Archaic Period* (with three subphases of "Early," 900–500 B.C.E.., late Ṛg Veda to Buddha, "Middle," 500–200 B.C.E., Buddha to Early Gītā, and "Late," 200 B.C.E.–200 C.E., Gītā to Nāgārjuna); a *Classical Period* (again with three subphases of "Early," 200–400 C.E., Nāgārjuna to Dignāga, "Middle," 400–800, Dignāga to Śankara, and "Late," 800–1300, Śankara to Madhva); a *Medieval Period* (1300–1800); and a *Modern Period* (1800–present). See Richard Robinson, "Classical Indian Philosophy, Parts I and II," in Joseph W. Elder, ed., *Chapters in Indian Civilization*, volume 1—Classical and Medieval India (Dubuque, Iowa: Kendall Hunt Publishing, 1970), p. 146.

16. This is largely the historical method outlined by Jean-Paul Sartre in his *Critique de la raison dialectique*, and called simply *"la méthode progressive-regressive"* (the "progressive-regressive method"), as set forth in a prolegomenon to that work entitled *"Questions de méthode."* See Jean-Paul Sartre, *Critique de la raison dialectique, précédé de Questions de méthode*, tome 1 (Paris: Gallimard, 1985 edition of the original 1960 publication), pp. 72-173. An English translation is available: Jean-Paul Sartre, *Search for a Method*, trans. Hazel E. Barnes (New York: Random House, 1968), pp. 85–166. *Mutatis mutandis*, it would be fair to say that my own historical method in the present book is very much in keeping with this basic orientation.

17. B. and R. Allchin, *The Rise of Civilization*, pp. 347–49.

18. *Ibid.*, pp. 347 and 97.

19. A. L. Basham, *The Wonder That Was India* (New York: Grove Press, 1959), pp. 10–14; and S. Wolpert, *A New History of India* (New York: Oxford University Press, 1989; 3rd ed.), pp. 4–5.

20. B. and R. Allchin, *The Rise of Civilization*, p. 97.

21. *Ibid.*

22. *Ibid.*, p. 99.

23. The name "Indus," it should perhaps be noted, is the origin of the word "Hindu." The original Indian name of the river is Sindhu. The ancient Iranians had difficulty in pronouncing an initial "S" and changed it to "H-indu." The Greeks referred to the river as the "Indos," and the later Arabs referred to it as "al-Hind." Eventually the name came to be applied to the people of the entire subcontinent, namely, the "Hindi," the "Hindus" and the "Indians." In ancient times Indians themselves referred to their country as Bhārata-varṣa (the "the Land of the Sons of Bharata," a legendary ruler), Jambudvīpa (the "continent of Jambu" or of the rose-apple tree), Āryāvartta (the "abode of the noble or excellent ones") and Brahmāvartta (the "abode of the brahmanical people").

24. Basham, *The Wonder That Was India*, pp. 14–28. The best recent discussion of the Indus Valley civilization is to be found in B. and R. Allchin, *The Rise of Civilization*, pp. 166–225.

25. Basham, *The Wonder That Was India*, pp. 28–31, and B. and R. Allchin, *The Rise of Civlization*, pp. 298–308.

26. Wendy D. O'Flaherty, trans., *The Rig Veda:* An Anthology (New York: Penguin Books, 1981), p. 31.

27. *Ibid.*, pp. 25–26.

28. By far the best overall treatment of the rise of speculative thinking in this period are still the definitive essays of Franklin Edgerton entitled, "The Origins of Hindu Speculations" and "The Upaniṣads, and the Fundamental Doctrines of Later Hindu Thought," in his "Interpretation of the Bhagavad Gita" in *The Bhagavad Gita*, trans. and interpreted by Franklin Edgerton (New York: Harper and Row, 1964; reprint of the 1944 Harvard Oriental Series edition), pp. 111-131.

29. It should be stressed that I am not claiming that either Advaita Vedānta or Sāṃkhya as full-blown philosophical systems are present in Upaniṣadic speculations. I am only suggesting that the seeds or incipient trends that will later become Advaita Vedānta and Sāṃkhya are to be found in the Upaniṣads, and thus essential to mention at this place in the historical narrative. The textual base for the Advaita Vedānta "seeds" may be found in Taittirīya, Aitareya, Bṛhadāraṇyaka and Chāndogya Upaniṣad-s. Sāṃkhya "seeds" may be found in Chāndogya, Kaṭha and Śvetāśvatara Upaniṣad-s. For a discussion of relevant historical issues, see Gerald J. Larson, *Classical Sāṃkhya: An Interpretation of its History and Meaning* (Delhi: Motilal Banarsidass, 1979; 2nd rev. ed.), pp. 75–153.

30. Ravinder Kumar, "India: A 'Nation-State' or a 'Civilisation-State'?," p. 14.

31. *Ibid.*, pp. 14–15.

32. Padmanabh S. Jaini, "Śramaṇas: Their Conflict with Brāhmaṇical Society," in Joseph W. Elder, ed., *Chapters in Indian Civilization*, volume 1, pp. 41–81.

33. *Ibid.*, p. 42.

34. The interesting historical question of the precise relation between the Indo-Brāhmaṇical and Indo-Śramaṇical in terms of origins is beyond the scope of the present essay. For useful recent discussions of these issues, see Patrick Olivelle, trans., *Sāṃnyāsa Upaniṣads* (New York: Oxford University Press, 1992), pp. 11–112; and Johannes Bronkhorst, *The Two Traditions of Meditation in Ancient India* (Stuttgart: Franz Steiner Verlag, 1986). Bronkhorst (currently professor in the Oriental Language and Civilization Section of the University of Lausanne, Switzerland) has completed a sequel to the previously mentioned work, entitled *The Two Sources of Indian Asceticism* (Bern: Peter Lang, Inc., 1993), p. 113.

35. Embree, *Sources of Indian Tradition*, volume I, p. 58; and Jaini, *The Jaina Path of Purification*, pp. 47–77.

36. As mentioned earlier in chapter 1, the best current treatment of the Jain tradition overall is Padmanabh S. Jaini, *The Jaina Path of Purication*, especially pp. 274–315.

37. This is basically the content of the so-called first "sermon" or "discourse" of Gautama. It is entitled, "The Discourse Setting into Motion the Wheel of the Law" (*dhammacakkappavatana-sutta* in Pāli) and is found in the Pāli Canon, Sāṃyutta-nikāya, section V (Mahāvagga), subsection 56, discourse 16. It is anthologized in Embree, *Sources of Indian Tradition*, vol. 1, pp. 100–101.

38. Edward Conze, *Buddhist Thought in India* (London: Allen and Unwin, 1962), pp. 92–106.

39. Jaini, "Śramaṇas," pp. 63–81. The best overall treatment of early Buddhist thought and meditational practice is still Edward Conze, *Buddhist Thought in India.* For exhaustive treatments of the history of Buddhist traditions in India, see E. Lamotte, *History of Indian Buddhism*, trans. S. Webb-Boin (Louvain: Peeters Press, 1988); Hajime Nakamura, *Indian Buddhism* (Delhi: Motilal Banarsidass, 1987); and A. K. Warder, *Indian Buddhism* (Delhi: Motilal Banarsidass, 1970).

40. Edward Conze, *A Short History of Buddhism* (Bombay: Chetana, Ltd., 1960), pp. ix–xii and 1–83.

41. Quoted in Ainslie Embree, ed., *Sources of Indian Tradition*, vol. 1, p. 131.

42. Ronald Inden, *Imagining India* (Oxford: Basil Blackwell, 1990), p. 229ff.

43. Louis Dumont, *Homo Hierarchicus* (Chicago: University of Chicago Press, 1980), p. 301. See also the excellent discussion of Stanley Tambiah, *World Conqueror and World Renouncer: A Study of Buddhism and Polity in Thailand Against a Historical Background* (Cambridge: Cambridge University Press, 1976) for a full treatment of early and later Buddhist views.

44. R. C. Majumdar, "Evolution of Religio-Philosophic Culture in India," pp. 37–46.

45. *Ibid.* Also, see the dated but still useful discussion of the rise of devotional cults in India in R. G. Bhandarkar, *Vaiṣṇavism, Śaivism and Minor Religious Systems* (Varanasi: Indological Book House, 1965; reprint of 1913 edition), pp. 1–13 and 102–128.

46. See above, note 24 of the present chapter.

47. Ravinder Kumar, "India: A 'Nation-State' or a 'Civilisation-State'?," p. 6.

48. For a solid discussion of the significance of Kauṭilya's *Arthaśāstra* within the overall context of the development of the notion of the state in ancient India, see Romila Thapar, *From Lineage to State: Social Formations in the Mid-First Millenium B.C. in the Ganga Valley* (Bombay: Oxford University Press, 1984), especially pp. 70–154.

49. A.L. Basham, *The Wonder That Was India*, p. 57. Regarding the use of the terms "feudalism" and "quasi-feudalism," Basham comments:

> Authorities differ on the definition of a feudal system. Some would confine the term to the complex structure of contractual relations covering the whole of society from king to villein, which prevailed in medieval Europe. Others use the term so loosely that they apply it to any system where political power is chiefly in the hands of those who own land. Most British historians would prefer the narrower definition, according to which ancient India never had a true feudal system. Something very like European feudalism did evolve among the Rājputs after the Muslim invasions. . . . Ancient India had, however, a system of overlordship, which was quasi-feudal, though never as fully developed as in Europe, and resting on a different basis. (*Ibid.*, pp. 93–94.)

50. Ronald Inden, *Imagining India*, pp. 162–270.

51. The approximate dates refer to periods in which these regional polities were prominent. They are derived from Basham, *The Wonder That Was India*, pp. xvii–xviii. For brief but useful thumbnail sketches of historical developments among these regional polities, see Basham, *The Wonder That Was India*, pp. 57–78, and Wolpert, *A New History of India*, pp. 70–103. For a more detailed treatment, see R. C. Majumdar, H. C. Raychaudhuri, and K. Datta, *An Advanced History of India* (New York: St. Martin's Press, 1967), pp. 107–264.

52. Basham, *The Wonder That Was India*, p. 77.

53. Romila Thapar, *A History of India* (London: Penguin, 1966), pp. 227–37.

54. *Ibid.*

55. The expression "Slave" dynasty is a misnomer. Many non-Muslim soldiers became "slaves" as a result of Muslim conquests. After converting to Islam, however, they frequently became major figures at court and on occasion even became Sultans as in the case of Qutb ud-Din Aibak. In fact, however, Aibak had already been manumitted from slave-status by Muhammand of Ghur; so, too, Iltutmish and Balban, the other "slave" sultans. See Majumdar, Raychaudhuri and Datta, *An Advanced History of India*, p. 271n.

56. *Ibid.*, p. 74.

57. S. C. Dube and V. N. Basilov, eds., *Secularization in Multi-Religious Societies* (New Delhi: Concept Publishing Co., 1983), p. 1.

58. There are various listings of the ten *avatāra*-s of Viṣṇu, the most well-known of which includes the following: Matsya (fish), Kūrma (tortoise), Varāha (boar), Narasiṃha (man-lion), Vāmana (dwarf), Paraśurāma ("Rāma with an axe" who destroys evil warriors), Rāma, Kṛṣṇa, Buddha and Kalkin (a future

"incarnation" yet to come). Regarding the history of the tradition and the various lists of *avatāra*-s, see P. V. Kane, *History of Dharmaśāstra*, Vol II, Part II, pp. 717 ff.

59. *Ibid.*, pp. 716–17.

60. For an interesting comparison between *devapūjā* in Hindu contexts and Jain contexts, see Jaini, *The Jaina Path of Purification*, pp. 293–98.

61. Romila Thapar, *A History of India*, vol. 1 (London: Penguin Books, 1966), pp. 179–93.

62. Embree, *Sources of Indian Tradition*, vol. 1, pp. 344–78.

63. Thapar, *A History of India*, p. 188.

64. For a discussion of the composition and historical importance of the text, see Gerald J. Larson, "The Bhagavad Gītā as Cross-Cultural Process: Toward an Analysis of the Social Locations of a Religious Text," *Journal of the American Academy of Religion* (December 1975): 651–69.

65. For the definitive and exhaustive discussion of all aspects of *dharma*, see, of course, P. V. Kane, *History of Dharmaśāstra*, 5 vols. (Poona: Bhandarkar Oriental Research Institute, 1930–1962; Government Oriental Series, Class B, No. 6). See also Gerald J. Larson, "The *Trimūrti* of *Dharma* in Indian Thought: Paradox or Contradiction," *Philosophy East and West* 22, no. 2 (April 1972): 145–53.

66. For a good recent discussion, see Patrick Olivelle, *Sāṃnyūsa Upaniṣads*, pp. 19–112.

67. The literature on "caste" is vast and has generated much controversy up to the present time. For a balanced perspective regarding the various issues, the following should be consulted: (*a*) P. V. Kane, *History of Dharmaśāstra*, vol. 2, pp. 19–179 and vol. 5, pp. 1632–43; (*b*) J. F. Hutton, *Caste in India* (Oxford: Oxford University Press, 196l; 3rd ed.); (*c*) Louis Dumont, *Homo Hierarchicus*, trans., M. Sainsbury, L. Dumont and B. Gulati (Chicago: University of Chicago Press, 1980); (*d*) McKim Marriott and Ronald B. Inden, "Caste Systems," *Encyclopaedia Britannica*, Macropaedia 3:982–91 (Chicago: Bentons, 1974; 15th ed.); and (*e*) McKim Marriott, "Constructing an Indian Ethnosociology," in McKim Marriott, ed., *India through Hindu Categories* (New Delhi: Sage Publications, 1990; *Contributions to Indian Sociology*, Occasional Studies, no. 5).

68. For a stimulating recent discussion of scholarly distortions about the caste system and an important corrective treatment of the subject, see Ronald Inden, *Imagining India*, especially pp. 49–84. Regarding issues of caste mobility, see the classic discussion of the matter in M. N. Srinivas, *Social Change in Modern India* (Berkeley: University of California Press, 1966), pp. 1–45; and more recently, M. N. Srinivas, *The Cohesive Role of Sanskritization and Other Essays* (Delhi: Oxford University Press, 1989), especially pp. 1–72.

69. Useful discussions of these matters may be found in Romila Thapar, *From Lineage to State*, and see especially p. 138ff. for her account of the relevant *Matsya-purāṇa* passages. Also, see Inden, *Imagining India*, pp. 162–212. Useful excerpts from Kauṭilya's *Arthaśāstra* and related texts may be found in Embree, *Sources of Indian Tradition*, vol. 1, pp. 237–53.

70. Dumont, *Homo Hierarchicus*, pp. 287–313.

71. Inden, *Imagining India*, pp. 162–212.

72. For a good discussion of this issue, see Karl H. Potter, *Indian Metaphysics and Epistemology: The Tradition of Nyāya-Vaiśeṣika up to Gaṇgeśa* (Princeton: Princeton University Press, 1977), pp. 23–37.

73. Useful brief discussions of the history of Indian philosophy in this Indic period are (*a*) Richard Robinson, "Classical Indian Philosophy, Parts I–IV," pp. 127–227; (*b*) Karl H. Potter, *Presuppositions of India's Philosophies* (Englewood Cliffs, N.J.: Prentice-Hall, 1963); (*c*) C. Sharma, *Indian Philosophy: A Critical Survey* (New York: Barnes and Noble, 1962), pp. 36–277; (*d*) M. Hiriyanna, *The Essentials of Indian Philosophy* (London: George Allen and Unwin, 1973), p. 84ff.; and (*e*) S. Chatterjee and D. Datta, *An Introduction to Indian Philosophy* (Calcutta: University of Calcutta, 1968), pp. 25–52 and 71–420. A detailed treatment of the history and literature of Indian philosophy is, of course, S. N. Dasgupta, *A History of Indian Philosophy*, 5 vols. (Cambridge: Cambridge University Press, 1922–1955). For an exhaustive bibliography on Indian philosophy, see Karl H. Potter, ed., *The Encyclopedia of Indian Philosophies: Bibliography*, vol. 1 (Princeton: Princeton University Press, 1983; revised edition).

74. Jaini, *The Jaina Path of Purification*, pp. 81–82.

75. The best one-volume treatment of Buddhist thought in India during our period is still Edward Conze, *Buddhist Thought in India*, pp. 119–269.

76. Gerald James Larson, "An Old Problem Revisited: The Relation between Sāṃkhya, Yoga and Buddhism," in *Studien zur Indologie und Iranistik* 15 (1989): 129–46.

77. P. V. Kane, *History of Dharmaśāstra*, vol. 2. pp. 906–16, 917–29, and 930–75.

78. *Ibid.*, pp. 938–39. See also Patrick Olivelle, *Sāṃnyāsa Upaniṣads*, pp. 19–112.

79. P. V. Kane, *History of Dharmaśātra*, vol. 2, p. 948ff.

80. The Kumbha Melā, which means something like "pot-festival" in Hindi, is an auspicious astrological time for sacred bathing in the rivers near the cities of Allahabad, Hardwar, Ujjain and Nasik. The use of the term "pot" (*kumbha*) has various explanations, ranging from "pot" being the sign of Aquarius all the way to the old Hindu myth of the "pot" which contained the nectar of immortality and was fought over by the gods and demons at the time

of the churning of the ocean of milk. Every three years the festival moves from city to city and, thus, it occurs at Allahabad, the most auspicious place, every twelfth year. Hundreds and thousands of monks, mendicants and *sādhu*-s gather for these festivals, and the festivals become an occasion for the various monastic orders to meet with one another, resolve various conflicts, and generally maintain a loose or relaxed sort of on-going communication.

Chapter 3: Discontinuity as Continuity (ii): New Indic Formations

1. Inden, *Imagining India*, p. 228ff.

2. For here and following, see Wolpert, *A New History of India*, pp. 104–86. For more detailed treatments, see Romila Thapar, *A History of India*, volume 1, pp. 266–336, and Percival Spear, *A History of India*, vol. 2 (London: Penguin, 1965), pp. 15–80. For exhaustive treatments, see R. C. Majumdar, ed., *The Delhi Sultanate*, vol. 4, and the *The Mughul Empire*, vol. 7 of the massive series, The History and Culture of the Indian People (Bombay: Bharatiya Vidya Bhavan, 1984).

3. Ira M. Lapidus, *A History of Islamic Societies* (Cambridge: Cambridge University Press, 1988), p. 120.

4. Perhaps the best, brief overview of the faith of Islam continues to be Wilfred C. Smith, *Islam in Modern History* (New York: The New American Library, 1957), pp. 17–47.

5. Lapidus, *A History of Islamic Societies*, p. 41.

6. Wolpert, *A New History of India*, p. 107.

7. For the best current treatment of the history of Islam in one volume with excellent sections on the spread and development of Islam in India, see Ira M. Lapidus, *A History of Islamic Societies*, pp. 3–136, 437–66, and 718–48.

8. Lapidus, *A History of Islamic Societies*, pp. 441–42.

9. *Ibid.*, p. 454.

10. Wolpert, *A New History of India*, pp. 129–30.

11. Lapidus, *A History of Islamic Societies*, p. 452.

12. Embree, *Sources of Indian Tradition*, vol. 1, p. 388.

13. From the time of Sultan Muhammad of Ghur up through the Mughal period, Persian became the official court language. It was preferred to Arabic by the various Turko-Afghan Muslims and Central Asian Muslims, partly because Persian was viewed as a more cosmopolitan medium and partly (perhaps mainly) because it was easier to learn than Arabic. For a brief, excellent

discussion of cultural developments in the Mughal period, see Majumdar et al., *An Advanced History of India*, pp. 559–94.

14. Embree, *Sources of Indian Tradition*, vol. 1, pp. 475–83.

15. Romila Thapar, *A History of India*, pp. 300–301.

16. R. D. Minor, "Cow, Symbolism and Veneration," in *The Abingdon Dictionary of Living Religions*, ed., K. Crim (Nashville: Abingdon, 1981), p. 198.

17. David N. Lorenzen, "Warrior Ascetics in Indian History," *Journal of the American Oriental Society* 98, no. 1 (January-March 1978): 61–75.

18. A useful survey is still G. W. Briggs, *Gorakhnāth and the Kānphaṭa Yogīs* (Delhi: Motilal Banarsidass, 1973; reprint of the original 1938 edition). For a more recent discussion, see Charlotte Vaudeville, trans., *Kabīr*, vol. 1 (Oxford: Clarendon Press, 1974), pp. 81–119.

19. *Ibid.*, pp. 85–89; also for the Hindu and Buddhist backgrounds, see David N. Lorenzen, *The Kāpālikas and Kālāmukhas: Two Lost Śaivite Sects* (Berkeley: University of California Press, 1972), and Benoytosh Bhattacharyya, *An Introduction to Buddhist Esoterism* (Delhi: Motilal Banarsidass, 1980; reprint of 1931 edition).

20. For here and following, see Hans Bakker, *Ayodhyā*, part I, chapters 7–8 (Groningen: Egbert Forsten, 1986), pp. 119–153; R. G. Bhandarkar, *Vaiṣṇavism, Śaivism and Minor Religious System*; Embree, *Sources of Indian Tradition*, vol. 1, chapter 12 ("The Songs of Medieval Hindu Devotion"), pp. 342–78; J. N. Farquhar, *An Outline of the Religious Literature of India* (Delhi: Motilal Banarsidass, 1967; reprint of 1920 Oxford University Press edition); J. N. Farquhar, *Modern Religious Movements in India* (Delhi: Munshiram Manoharlal, 1967; reprint of the 1914 Oxford edition); Ann Feldhaus, trans., *The Deeds of God in Ṛddhipur* (New York: Oxford University Press, 1984); J. S. Hawley and M. Juergensmeyer, trans., *Songs of the Saints of India* (New York: Oxford University Press, 1988); David N. Lorenzen, *Kabir Legends* (Albany: State University of New York Press, 1991); Philip Lutgendorf, *The Life of a Text:* Performing the *Rāmcaritmānas* of Tulsidas (Berkeley: University of California Press, 1991); Susmita Pande, *The Medieval Bhakti Movement* (Meerut: Kusumanjali Prakashan, 1989); Peter van der Veer, *Gods on Earth* (Delhi: Oxford University Press, 1989), pp. 85–114; and, Charlotte Vaudeville, trans., *Kabir*, vol. 1, pp. 81–119.

21. Vaudeville, *Kabir*, pp. 110–17.

22. McLeod, *The Sikhs*, pp. 16–31.

23. Hawley and Juergensmeyer, *Songs of the Saints of India*, pp. 3–7.

24. R.D. Ranade, *Mysticism in India: The Poet-Saints of Maharashtra* (Albany: State University of New York Press, 1983; reprint of the 1933 edition); and see also Anne Feldhaus, trans., *The Deeds of God in Ṛddhipur*, especially pp. 3–36.

25. For the best recent treatment of Tulsīdās's *Rāmcaritmānas*, see Lutgendorf, especially pp. 1–52.

26. Embree, *Sources of Indian Tradition*, vol. 1, pp. 381–82.

27. Thapar, *A History of India*, vol. 1, p. 319.

28. Embree, *Sources of Indian Tradition*, vol. 1, p. 409.

29. Eric Stokes, *The English Utilitarians and India* (Oxford: Clarendon Press, 1959), pp. 27–3l.

30. Percival Spear, *India, Pakistan and the West*, p. 187.

31. *Ibid.*, pp. 177–91.

32. Wolpert, *A New History of India*, p. 180ff.; Spear, *A History of India*, vol. 2, pp. 61–115.

33. Ravinder Kumar, "India: A 'Nation-State' or 'Civilisation-State'?," pp. 17–18.

34. David Kopf, *British Orientalism and the Bengal Renaissance* (Berkeley: University of California Press, 1969), especially pp. 13–64.

35. Gerald James Larson, "Modernization and Religious Legitimation in India, 1835–1885," in B. L. Smith, ed., *Religion and the Legitimation of Power in South Asia* (Leiden: E. J. Brill, 1978), pp. 28–41.

36. For the best current discussions of modern Islamic movements in South Asia, see Kenneth W. Jones, *Socio-Religious Reform Movements in British India*, The New Cambridge History of India, III-l (Cambridge: Cambridge University Press, 1989); and Fazlur Rahman, "Islam," in *The Cambridge Encyclopedia of India, Pakistan, Bangladesh and Sri Lanka*, pp. 352–55. Also, see the following (in alphabetical order) for useful discussions: Mumtaz Ahmad, "Islamic Fundamentalism in South Asia: The Jamaat-i-Islami and the Tablighi Jamaat of South Asia," in M.E. Marty and R.S. Appleby, eds., *Fundamentalisms Observed* (Chicago: University of Chicago Press, 199l), pp. 457–530; J. N. Farquhar, *Modern Religious Movements in India*, p. 91ff.; Ira M. Lapidus, *A History of Islamic Societies*, pp. 718–48; Bruce B. Lawrence, *Defenders of God* (New York: Harper and Row, 1989), pp. 227–45; Barbara D. Metcalf, ed., *Moral Conduct and Authority* (Berkeley: University of California Press, 1984); Annemarie Schimmel, *Islam in the Indian Subcontinent* (Leiden: E.J. Brill, 1980); W. C. Smith, *Islam in Modern India* (New York: Mentor Books, New American Library, 1957); and Syed Shahabuddin and T. P. Wright, "India: Muslim Minority Politics and Society," in John L. Esposito, ed., *Islam in Asia* (New York: Oxford University Press, 1987), pp. 152–76.

37. Fazlur Rahman, "Islam," p. 353.

38. *Ibid.*, and Kenneth W. Jones, *Socio-Religious Reform Movements in British India*, p. 57ff.

39. Rahman, "Islam," pp. 353–54; and Jones, *Socio-Religious Reform Movements in British India*, pp. 63–70.

40. It is Fazlur Rahman who uses the term "protestant" to describe the Deoband tradition, "Islam," p. 353. The expressions "Anglo-Islamic" and "Neo-Muslim" are my own. The expression "Neo-Hindu" has been widely used to refer to nineteenth century reform movements by Paul Hacker, Agehananda Bharati, *et al.* For my own use of the expression "Neo-Hindu," see the discussion in the next section and in the concluding chapter.

41. Useful detailed discussions of each of these "revivalist" movements may be found in Fazlur Rahman, "Islam," and Kenneth W. Jones, *Socio-Religious Reform Movements in British India*. Sometimes these "revivalist" movements are called "fundamentalist," but, in my view, that is a serious misnomer. The term "fundamentalism" deserves to be left in its appropriate American Protestant milieu. It is confusing to apply it outside of its proper context.

42. Older but still useful discussions of new religious movements in India up through the early twentieth century are J. N. Farquhar, *Modern Religious Movements in India*, pp. 29–353 and H. Bhattacharya, ed., *The Cultural Heritage of India*, volume 4, The Religions (Calcutta: The Ramakrishna Mission Institute of Culture, 1937), pp. 613–728. The more recent bibliography, of course, is vast, but some of the more important and readable treatments include the following: Kenneth W. Jones, *Socio-Religious reform Movements in British India*, pp. 15–183 and 184–209; A. Bharati, "Religious Revival in Modern India," in *The Cambridge Encyclopedia of India, Pakistan, Bangladesh and Sri Lanka*, pp. 345–50; A. Bharati, *Hindu Views and Ways and the Hindu-Muslim Interface*, pp. 1–22 and 41–96; P. H. Ashby, "Hinduism," and M. Juergensmeyer, "Hinduism in America," both in *The Abingdon Dictionary of Living Religions*, ed. K. Crim (Nashville: Abingdon Press, 1981), pp. 315–18 and 318–21 respectively; Daniel Gold, *The Lord as Guru* (New York: Oxford University Press, 1987), pp. 55–115 and 201–13; Daniel Gold, "Organized Hinduisms: From Vedic Truth to Hindu Nation," in *Fundamentalisms Observed*, pp. 531–93; Peter van der Veer, *Gods on Earth* (Delhi: Oxford University Press, 1988), pp. 1–43, 66–182, and 268–74; T.N. Madan, "Religion in India," *Daedalus*, 118, no. 4 (Fall 1984): 115–46; Lawrence A. Babb, "The Puzzle of Religious Modernity," in J. Roach, ed., *India 2000* (Riverdale, Maryland: The Riverdale Co., 1986), pp. 55–79; and the various essays in G. D. Sontheimer and H. Kulke, eds., *Hinduism Reconsidered* (Delhi: Manohar, 1991).

43. Here again, of course, the bibliographical literature is vast. For the general historical background regarding the rise of the Neo-Hindu reform movements, especially in Bengal, see David Kopf, *British Orientalism and the Bengal Renaissance* (Berkeley: University of California Press, 1969). For useful and readable overviews of the period as a whole, see Wolpert, *A New History of India*, pp. 201–370 and Percival Spear, *India, Pakistan and the West*, pp. 175–242. For a more detailed treatment of the history of the modern period, see Majum-

dar, Raychaudhuri and Datta, *An Advanced History of India*, pp. 765–1001. See also the excellent bibliographies in all of these works. Finally, for a most useful compilation of primary documents relating to the modern period, see Stephen Hay, ed., *Sources of Indian Tradition*, vol. 2, especially chapters 1–4 and 7, pp. 1–172, 275–333, and the bibliography, pp. 413–18.

44. Hay, *Sources of Indian Tradition*, vol. 2, pp. 15–35.

45. *Ibid.*, pp. 44–52.

46. *Ibid.*, pp. 52–62.

47. *Ibid.*, pp. 62–83.

48. *Ibid.*, p. 152.

49. *Ibid.*, pp. 148–59.

50. *Ibid.*, pp. 102–20 and 140–48.

51. The best treatment of the RSS, its history and ideology, is W. K. Andersen and S. D. Damle, *The Brotherhood in Saffron* (New Delhi: Vistaar Publications, 1987). For the writings of Savarkar, see Hay, *Sources of Indian Tradition*, vol. 2, pp. 289–95.

52. Hay, *Sources*, pp. 243–74, and, of course, M. K. Gandhi, *Gandhi: An Autobiography*, trans. Mahadev Desai (Boston: Beacon Press, 1957).

53. Hay, *Sources*, pp. 296–324.

54. J. N. Farquhar, *Modern Religious Movements in India*, p. 443.

55. *Ibid.*, p. 444.

56. Kenneth W. Jones, *Socio-Religious Reform Movements in British India*, pp. 213–14.

57. For purposes of quick reference, see A. Bharati, "Religious Revival in Modern Times, Hinduism," pp. 345–50, and various entries in the *Abingdon Dictionary of Living Religions*, cited earlier. For a useful collection of essays about the future of new religions, see D. G. Bromley and P. E. Hammond, eds., *The Future of New Religious Movements* (Macon, Georgia: Mercer University Press, 1987).

58. For useful discussions, see Rohit Barot, "Caste and Sect in the Swaminarayana Movement," in Richard Burghart, ed., *Hinduism in Great Britain* (London: Tavistock Publications, 1987), pp. 67–80; H. T. Dave, *Life and Philosophy of Shree Swaminarayan, 1781–1830* (London: Allen and Unwin, 1974); and R. B. Williams, *A New Face of Hinduism: The Swaminarayan Religion* (Cambridge: Cambridge University Press, 1984).

59. See L. A. Babb, *Redemptive Encounters: Three Modern Styles in the Hindu Tradition* (Berkeley: University of California Press, 1986), pp. 15–89;

Mark Juergensmeyer, *Radhasoami Reality: The Logic of a Modern Faith* (Princeton: Princeton University Press, 1991); and A. P. Mathur, *Radhasoami Faith: A Historical Study* (Delhi: Vikas, 1974).

60. R. S. Ellwood, Jr., *Religious and Spiritual Groups in Modern America* (Englewood Cliffs, N.J.: Prentice-Hall, 1973); and Paramahamsa Yogananda, *Autobiography of a Yogi* (Los Angeles: Self-Realization Fellowship, 1973).

61. M. Craske, *The Dance of Love: My Life with Meher Baba* (North Myrtle Beach: Sheriar Press, 1980); and C. B. Purdom, *The God-Man* (London: Allen and Unwin, 1964).

62. D. G. Bromley and L. D. Shinn, eds., *Krishna Consciousness in the West* (Lewisburg: Bucknell University Press, 1989); Charles R. Brook, *The Hare Krishnas in India* (Princeton: Princeton University Press, 1989); D. Haberman, *Acting as a Way of Salvation* (New York: Oxford University Press, 1987); E. B. Rochford, *Hare Krishna in America* (New Brunswick, NJ: Rutgers University Press, 1985); and L. D. Shinn, *The Dark Lord: Cult Images and the Hare Krishnas in America* (Philadelphia: The Westminster Press, 1987).

63. Gene R. Thursby, "Siddha Yoga: Swami Muktananda and the Seat of Power," in T. Miller, ed., *When Prophets Die: The Postcharismatic Fate of New Religions* (Albany: State University of New York Press, 1991); and Catherine Wessinger, "Woman Guru, Woman Roshi: The Legitimation of Female Religious Leadership in Hindu and Buddhist Groups in America," in C. Wessinger, ed., *Women's Leadership in Marginal Religions: Explorations Outside the Mainstream* (Urbana and Chicago: University of Illinois Press, 1993).

64. W. S. Bainbridge and D. H. Jackson, "The Rise and Decline of Transcendental Meditation," in B. Wilson, ed., *The Social Impact of New Religious Movements* (New York: The Rose of Sharon Press, 1981); and A. Campbell, *The Mechanics of Enlightenment: An Examination of the Teaching of Maharishi Mahesh Yogi* (London: Gollancz, 1977).

65. L. A. Babb, "Satya Sai Baba's Magic," *Anthropological Quarterly* 56 (1983): 116–24; L. A. Babb, *Redemptive Encounters: Three Modern Styles in the Hindu Tradition* (Berkeley: University of California Press, 1986), pp. 159–201; and Charles S. J. White, "The Sai Baba Movement: Approaches to the Study of Indian Saints," *Journal of Asian Studies* 31 (1972): 863–78. See also Antonio Rigopoulos, *The Life and Teachings of Sai Baba of Shirdi* (Albany: State University of New York Press, 1993).

66. Percival Spear, *India, Pakistan and the West*, p. 38.

Chapter 4. The Minority as Majority

1. Ludwig Wittgenstein, *The Blue and the Brown Books* (New York: Harper and Row, 1958), see especially pp. 132–35.

2. For useful discussions of "absences" in classical Indian philosophy, see S. Chatterjee, *The Nyāya Theory of Knowledge* (Calcutta: University of Calcutta Press, 1965), pp. 175–82; and B. K. Matilal, *The Navya-Nyāya Doctrine of Negation* (Cambridge, Mass.: Harvard University Press, 1968; Harvard Oriental Series, vol. 46), pp. 108 and 148ff.

3. Chatterjee, *The Nyāya Theory of Knowledge*, pp. 177–78, and Matilal, *The Navya-Nyāya Doctrine of Negation*, p. 108.

4. Chatterjee, *The Nyāya Theory of Knowledge*, pp. 176–77, and Matilal, *The Navya-Nyāya Doctrine of Negation*, p. 108.

5. See the discussions of the Indo-Islamic and Indo-Anglian periods in chapter 3 for a fuller treatment.

6. One further technical or logical comment. I shall be referring in what follows to the "absence of a separation" between various concepts and things. This amounts, of course, to a double negation, since "the absence of a separation" is another way of saying "the absence of an absence of identity." I proceed in this way in order to highlight the distinctive features of the Old Indic formations.

7. S. Schayer, "Das mahāyānistische Absolutum nach der Lehre der Mādhyamikas," in *Orientalistische Literatur-Zeitung* 38 (1935): 405, and cited in Richard Robinson, "The Classical Indian Axiomatic," in *Philosophy East and West* 17 (1967): 145.

8. E. H. Johnston, *Early Sāṃkhya* (London: Royal Asiatic Society, 1937), p. 38.

9. For further discussion of the Sāṃkhya view, see Gerald J. Larson, *Classical Sāṃkhya*, (Delhi: Motilal Banarcidass, 1979, second edition), pp. 154–235.

10. I have treated these issues at some length in Gerald James Larson, "An Eccentric Ghost in the Machine," *Philosophy East and West* 33, no. 3, (July 1983): 219–33; see also Gerald James Larson and Ram Shankar Bhattacharya, eds., *Sāṃkhya: A Dualist Tradition in Indian Philosophy* (Princeton: Princeton University Press, 1987), p. 73ff.

11. J. N. Mohanty, "A Fragment of the Indian Philosophical Tradition—Theory of Pramāṇa," in *Philosophy East and West* 38, (July 1988): 252–53.

12. *Ibid.*

13. Karl H. Potter, *Presuppositions of India's Philosophies* (Englewood Cliffs, N.J.: Prenctice-Hall, 1963), p. 66.

14. Chatterjee, *The Nyāya Theory of Knowledge*, p. 265.

15. See the first verse as found in Larson, *Classical Sāṃkhya*, p. 255.

16. The now classic discussion of the "individual" in Western thought and in South Asian traditions is to be found in Louis Dumont, *Homo Hierarchicus*, trans., M. Sainsbury, L. Dumont and B. Gulati (Chicago: University of Chicago Press, 1980). See also Louis Dumont, *From Mandeville to Marx* (Chicago: University of Chicago Press, 1977), and Louis Dumont, "A Modified View of Our Origins: The Christian Beginnings of Modern Individualism," *Religion* 12 (1982): 1–27. For interesting discussions of Dumont's work, see T. N. Madan, ed., *Way of Life: King, Householder, Renouncer—Essays in Honour of Louis Dumont* (Delhi: Motilal Banarsidass, 1982), and J. F. Richards and Ralph W. Nicholas, eds., "Symposium: The Contributions of Louis Dumont," *The Journal of Asian Studies* 35, no. 4 (August 1976): 579–650 (including essays by P. Kolenda, J. D. M. Derrett, J. M. Mdasson, S. Barnett, L. Fruzzetti, A. Ostor and M. Francillon).

17. Geddes MacGregor, "Reincarnation," *Dictionary of Religion and Philosophy* (New York: Paragon House, 1991), pp. 531–32.

18. For a full discussion of the Sāṃkhya view, see Larson, *Classical Sāṃkhya*, pp. 189ff., and Larson and Bhattacharya, *Sāṃkhya*, pp. 53ff.

19. The classic discussion of the problem in early Buddhist literature is to be found in the *Milindupanha*, conveniently anthologized as "Rebirth is Not Transmigration," in Henry Clarke Warren, ed. and trans., *Buddhism in Translations* (New York: Atheneum, 1973), pp. 234–41.

20. I have already referred to the now classic treatment of this family resemblance, at least in terms of the Judeo-Christian tradition, in the work of Louis Dumont. See above, note 16 for appropriate bibliographical references.

21. Again, see note 16 for appropriate references to the work of Louis Dumont.

22. *Ibid*.

23. *Ibid*.

24. The best current statement of Marriott's work may be found in McKim Marriott, "Constructing an Indian Ethnosociology," McKim Marriott, ed., *India through Hindu Categories*, in Contributions to Indian Sociology, Occasional Studies 5 (New Delhi: Sage Publications, 1990), pp. 1–39. For a more general treatment of his views regarding the caste system, see McKim Marriott and Ronald B. Inden, "Caste Systems," *Encyclopaedia Britannica* (1974), Macropaedia 3: 982–91. See also an interesting discussion of Marriott's work (by T. N. Madan, R. S. Khare, L. A. Babb, M. Moffat, G. J. Larson, K. N. Sharma and S. Derne) in *Contributions to Indian Sociology* 24, no. 2 (July-December 1990): 175–263.

25. Madhav Deshpande, "History, Change and Permanence: A Classical Indian Perspective," in Gopal Krishna, ed., *Contributions to South Asian Studies I* (Delhi: Oxford University Press, 1979), p. 9, 18–19, and 21.

26. Mohanty, "A Fragment of the Indian Philosophical Tradition," p. 258. See also Richard Robinson,

27. Larson and Bhattacharya, *Sāṃkhya*, pp. 65-83.

28. *Ibid.*

29. Matilal, *The Navya-Nyāya Doctrine of Negation*, p. 52.

30. Frykenberg, "The Emergence of Modern Hinduism," p. 32, and Hardy, "Islam and Muslims in South Asia," pp. 39–40.

31. W. C. Smith, *The Meaning and End of Religion*, pp. 51–118.

32. Frits Staal, *Rules without Meaning*, p. 387ff.

33. Regarding the matter of definition, I have been influenced by D. E. Smith's useful attempt to define the complex notion of the "secular state" by way of identifying certain key relations that come into play. In a similar way, I think that it is helpful to think about the complex notion of "religion" in terms of certain key relations. See D. E. Smith, *India as a Secular State* (Princeton: Princeton University Press, 1963), p. 4. Regarding the matter of constructing a typology, I have been influenced by Ernest Gellner's attempt to identify certain key types of nation-states in terms of three basic variables. In a similar way, I have attempted to construct a typology of religions in terms of certain basic variables. See Ernest Gellner, *Nations and Nationalism* (Oxford: Basil Blackwell, 1983), pp. 88–109.

34. By "normal" or "acculturated" I mean any human organism that has undergone normal human development whether that be in an archaic or ancient tribal context or in a contemporary, "modern" context. I would agree with the following observation by Jean-Paul Sartre in his *Critique of Dialectical Reason*, tome 1, trans. Alan Sheridan-Smith (London: New Left Books, 1976), pp. 677–78: "the free praxis of the isolated individual loses its suspicious appearance as a Robinsonade; *there is no such thing* as an isolated individual (unless isolation is treated as a special structure of sociality). . . . [T]he community *is no less abstract* than the isolated individual: there are revolutionary pastorals on the group which are the exact counterpart of Robinsonades."

35. For a stimulating discussion of the notion of "worldview" and its relation to the notions of "religion" and "ideology," see Ninian Smart, *Beyond Ideology*: Religion and the Future of Western Civilization (London: Collins, 1981).

36. Ludwig Feuerbach, *The Essence of Christianity*, trans. George Eliot (New York: Prometheus Books, 1989; first published 1841), p. 12ff. For a useful secondary account of the "species-notion" or *Gattungs-begriff* in Feuerbach, see M. W. Wartofsky, *Feuerbach* (Cambridge: Cambridge University Press, 1982), p. 162ff. I owe the expression "the meaning of human existence-as-such" not simply to Feuerbach's *Gattungs-begriff* but to Schubert Ogden's comparable phrase

"existence as such," as found in Schubert Ogden, "Theology and Religious Studies: Their Difference and the Difference It Makes," *Journal of the American Academy of Religion* 46, no. 1 (1978): 3–17.

37. Melford E. Spiro, "Some Reflections on Cultural Determinism and Relativism with Special Reference to Emotion and Reason," in R. A. Shweder and R. A. Le Vine, eds. *Culture Theory: Essays on Mind, Self and Emotion* (Cambridge: Cambridge University Press, 1984), p. 323.

38. *Ibid.*

39. *Ibid.*, p. 324.

40. *Ibid.*, p. 329.

41. Luckmann, *The Invisible Religion*, p. 45.

42. *Ibid.*, p. 49.

43. *Ibid.*, p. 69.

44. *Ibid.*, p. 51.

45. This is not at all to suggest that the "cognitive indeterminacy" end of the continuum is in any sense non-cognitive. In other words, the expression "cognitive indeterminacy" does not imply irrationality. It means, rather, the highly cognitive claim that ultimate truth transcends what can be determinately said. The great minds of India such as Śaṅkara, Nāgārjuna, Vasubandhu, and others, have arrived at positions of "cognitive indeterminacy" on the basis of rigorous cognitive and critical intellectual analysis. See the first section of the present chapter ("The Problem of Coherence in Indian History and Civilization") for a full discussion of these matters.

46. Let me repeat that the expression "cognitive indeterminacy" does not mean non-cognitive or irrational. It refers, rather, to the highly cognitive claim that ultimate truth goes beyond or transcends determinate formulation. To use the formulation developed by the Buddhist philosopher Nāgārjuna, it can be said that ultimate truth is neither cognitive, nor non-cognitive, nor both cognitive and non-cognitive, nor neither cognitive nor non-cognitive. Ultimate truth, in other words, cannot be formulated in terms of assertions or propositions and a two-valued logic.

47. See Chapter 1 and the subsection entitled "The Terms 'State,' 'Nation-State,' and 'Civilization' for a discussion of Giddens's views.

48. It may seem somewhat surprising that such religious traditions as the Islamic Republic of Iran and the American civil religion should appear in the same subtype or subset, but the clearcut macro-communal and highly political orientation within the nation-state framework together with essentially modern notions of individuality and citizenship place such traditions in clear affinity with one another. Here, it seems to me, is a good example of how jour-

nalistic references to Islamic "fundamentalism" with respect to the Islamic Republic of Iran have completely missed the point of what is really happening in modern Iran. It is hardly a "fundamentalist" movement in any meaningful sense. It is, rather, a future-oriented, revolutionary recasting of Shi'ite Islam in a modern institutional setting.

49. With the dichotomy 'shamanic-ecstatic' and 'ascetic-enstatic' I have in mind to some extent what might be called, to use a Jungian idiom, "extravertive" as contrasted with "introvertive" religious experience. Shamanism is a spirituality that focusses on losing one's ordinary identity and going "outside" (hence, *ek-stasis*, "to stand out," "to displace") in order to be given a new birth and a new identity. See Eliade's discussion of the "ecstatic" spirituality of Shamanism in Mircea Eliade, *Shamanism: Archaic Techniques of Ecstasy*, trans. W. R. Trask (New York: Pantheon Books, 1964; Bollingen Series 76). With the expression 'ascetic-enstatic' I have in mind Nietzsche's well-known use of the expression, "ascetic-priest," and also Richard Rorty's use of the same expression in his treatment of Heidegger and other thinkers in the Western tradition who are always looking to ground subjectivity. Nietzsche and Rorty, of course, use the expression pejoratively. I wish to use the expression descriptively in contrast to 'shamanic-ecstatic' and so I have changed the expression to 'ascetic-enstatic.' The term "enstasis" (en-stasis, "to stand in," "to go in") is coined by Eliade to refer to a spirituality that focuses on introspection and inner meditation, as, for example, in South Asian Yoga, in contrast to the "going out" or loss of identity characteristic of shamanic, ecstatic spirituality. See Eliade, *Shamanism*, p. 417. For an engaging, although thoroughly tendentious, discussion of the notion of the "ascetic-priest," see Richard Rorty, "Heidegger, Kundera and Dickens," in Richard Rorty, *Essays on Heidegger and Others*, Philosophical Papers, vol. 2 (Cambridge: Cambridge University Press, 1991), pp. 66–82.

50. See above, notes 47 and 48 as well as the discussion of coherence in the first part of the chapter for explanations on how the expressions "cognitive indeterminacy" and "without determinate qualities" (*nirguṇa*) are being used.

51. Rajni Kothari, *Politics and the People: In Search of a Humane India*, vol. 2 (Delhi: Ajanta Publications, 1990; second edition), p. 485.

Chapter 5. The Secular as Religion and the Community as Citizen

1. D. E. Smith, *India as a Secular State*, p. 4.

2. *Ibid.*

3. *Ibid.*, pp. 499–500.

4. W. H. Morris-Jones, "India's Political Idioms," pp. 273–74 and 277.

5. Franklin Edgerton, *Buddhist Hybrid Sanskrit Grammar and Dictionary*, vols. I and II (Delhi: Motilal Banarsidass, 1970; reprint of Yale University Press edition, William Dwight Whitney Linguistic Series).

6. See section of chapter 3, entitled "The Indo-Anglian (c. 1757–present)."

7. For a detailed discussion of the period, see Gerald James Larson, "Modernization and Religious Legitimation in India: 1835–1885," pp. 30–39. See also the discussion, supra, chapter 3, under "The Indo-Anglian (c. 1757–present)."

8. Syed Ahmed Khan, *Writings and Speeches*, quoted in S. Hay, *Sources of Indian Tradition*, vol. 2, p. 192.

9. *Ibid.*, p. 195.

10. D. E. Smith, *India as a Secular State*, pp. 88–89.

11. *Ibid.*, p. 86.

12. For an engaging, albeit ideological and tendentious, presentation of the view of communalism as a product of the modern imperialist system, see Bipan Chandra, *Communalism in Modern India* (Delhi: Vani Educational Books, 1984).

13. For a good discussion of the issue, see Wolpert, *A New History of India*, pp. 319–20.

14. Quoted in ibid., pp. 316–17.

15. *Ibid.*

16. Quoted in D. E. Smith, *India as a Secular State*, p. 459.

17. *Ibid.*, pp. 459–60.

18. Jinnah, *Recent Speeches and Writings*, cited in Hay, *Sources of Indian Tradition*, vol. 2, pp. 229–30.

19. Quoted in D. E. Smith, *India as a Secular State*, pp. 148–49.

20. Quoted in Wolpert, *A New History of India*, p. 331.

21. *Ibid.*

22. *Ibid.*, p. 348.

23. *Ibid.*

24. D. E. Smith, *India as a Secular State*, p. 140.

25. W. Norman Brown, *The United States, India and Pakistan* (Cambridge, Mass.: Harvard University Press, 1963), p. 104, and quoted in M. D. Lewis, ed., *Gandhi: Maker of Modern India?* (Boston: D. C. Heath and Co., 1965), p. 102.

26. M. K. Gandhi, *An Autobiography: The Story of My Experiments with Truth,* trans., Mahadev Desai (Boston: Beacon Press, 1957), pp. xii–xiv. A useful collection of Gandhi's writings culled from the more than ninety volumes of the collected works is Raghavan Iyer, ed., *The Essential Writings of Mahatma Gandhi* (Delhi: Oxford University Press, 1990).

27. *Ibid.*, pp. 503–4.

28. Jawaharlal Nehru, *The Discovery of India*, ed., Robert I. Crane (New York: Doubleday Anchor Books, 1960), p. 274.

29. *Ibid.*, p. 281.

30. *Ibid.*, p. 279.

31. *Ibid.*

32. *Ibid.*, pp. 280–81.

33. *Harijan*, 23 March 1948, quoted in D. E. Smith, *India as a Secular State,* p. 149.

34. *Ibid.*, p. 10.

35. *Ibid.*, pp. 40–41.

36. Nehru, *Toward Freedom*, p. 71, quoted in D. E. Smith, ed., *Religion and Political Modernization* (New Haven: Yale University Press, 1974), p. 145.

37. *Ibid.*

38. S. Radhakrishnan, "Foreword," in S. Abid Hussain, *The National Culture of India* (Bombay: Jaico Publishing House, 1956), pp. vii–viii, and quoted in D. E. Smith, *India as a Secular State*, p. 147.

39. J. Nehru, *Independence and After* (New York: John Day Company, 1950), p. 122, cited in D. E. Smith, *India as a Secular State*, p. 155.

40. D. E. Smith, *India as a Secular State*, p. 149.

41. See our discussion of a typology of religions in chapter 4.

42. S. C. Dube and V. N. Basilov, eds., *Secularization in Multi-Religious Societies*, p. 1.

43. The term "demythologization" derives from a tradition of biblical interpretation inaugurated by the New Testament scholar and theologian, Rudolf Bultmann (1884–1976). According to Bultmann, much of the narrative in the New Testament presupposes a mythological worldview, including a three-storied universe (heaven, earth and hell), spirits and demons, and so forth. It is possible, however, to separate the mythological components from the essential faith (what Bultmann called the "kerygma" or the basic proclamation of faith), or, in other words, to "demythologize" the biblical text. More-

over, instead of using the old mythological language of the Bible, it is possible to "demythologize" and to recast the message of the New Testament into modern, Heideggerian existentialist language, thereby making the biblical proclamation much more attractive and appealing to modern, critical people. It strikes me that this is a useful way of thinking about the manner in which Nehru appropriated and recast the Gandhian religious vision. Clearly Nehru accepted the core of the Gandhian proclamation or what he called the "spiritualization of politics." At the same time Nehru wanted to translate or recast the Gandhian religious idiom into a more modern discourse, and just as Bultmann used Heideggerian existentialist language to translate the New Testament "kerygma" or proclamation, so Nehru used the language of democratic socialist ideology (of a largely Fabian variety) for recasting the Gandhian message. For a good statement of Bultmann's own position, see Rudolf Bultmann, *Jesus Christ and Mythology* (London: SCM Press, 1960). For an excellent critical discussion of the process of "demythologization," see John Macquarrie, *The Scope of Demythologizing*: Bultmann and His Critics (New York: Harper and Brothers, 1960). For an excellent discussion of how Nehru was able to combine Gandhian notions, socialist ideology and his own sense of what is essential for modern India, see Robert D. Baird, "Religion and the Legitimation of Nehru's Concept of the Secular State," in B. L. Smith, ed., *Religion and the Legitimation of Power in South Asia* (Leiden: E. J. Brill, 1978), pp. 73–86.

44. Robert N. Bellah, "Civil Religion in America," *Daedalus* 96 (1967): 1–21.

45. *Ibid.*, p. 1.

46. *Ibid.* Cf. Sidney E. Mead, *The Nation with the Soul of a Church* (New York: Harper and Row, 1975) for the development of the notion of the "religion of the Republic," and cf. Will Herberg, *Protestant, Catholic, Jew* (New York: Doubleday, Anchor Books, 1973) for a discussion of the "American way of life" as a form of idolatry. For the best general discussion of the American civil religion, see Catherine L. Albanese, *America: Religions and Religion*, chapter 11 "Civil Religion: Millenial Politics and History" (Belmont, Cal.: Wadsworth Publishing Co., 1981), pp. 283–309.

47. M. N. Roy, *India's Message (Fragments of a Prisoner's Diary)*, quoted in S. Hay, *Sources of Indian Tradition*, vol. 2, pp. 300–301.

48. B. R. Ambedkar, *What Congress and Gandhi Have Done to the Untouchables*, 2nd edition (Bombay, 1946), quoted in M. D. Lewis, ed., *Gandhi: Maker of Modern India?*, pp. 51–52.

49. *Ibid.*, p. 54.

50. *Ibid.*

51. Ambedkar's Neo-Buddhist movement has already been described briefly above in chapter 1 in the section entitled "Religions" and under the sub-

section entitled "Buddhists." For a good recent assessment of Ambedkar and the progress of untouchables generally, see Eleanor Zelliot, "Dalit: New Perspectives on India's Untouchables," in P. Oldenburg, ed., *India Briefing, 1991* (Boulder: Westview Press in cooperation with the Asia Society, 1991), pp. 97–121.

52. Subhas Chandra Bose, *The Indian Quarterly Register* (1928), quoted in S. Hay, *Sources of Indian Tradition*, vol. 2, pp. 306–7.

53. V. D. Savarkar, *Hindu Rashtra Darshan* (Bombay, 1949), quoted in M. D. Lewis, *Gandhi: Maker of Modern India?*, p. 45.

54. *Ibid.*, pp. 46–47.

55. Rudolph and Rudolph, *In Pursuit of Lakshmi*, p. 39.

56. *The Indian Voice* vol. 1, no. 33 (3 January 1992): 15.

57. George Johnson, "The Princes and the Raj," in F. Robinson, ed., *The Cambridge Encyclopedia of India Pakistan, Bangladesh, Sri Lanka, Nepal, Bhutan and the Maldives* (Cambridge: Cambridge University Press, 1989), pp. 139–42.

58. Eleanor Zelliot, "Dalit: New Perspectives on India's Untouchables," pp. 97–121.

59. The 25% figure is cited by Rudolph and Rudolph, *In Pursuit of Lakshmi*, p. 52. The 52% figure is cited by the Mandal Commission Report, p. 56.

60. Khushwant Singh, "Brahmin Power," in *Sunday*, 23–29 December 1990, p. 19. Khushwant Singh comments further: "My statistics come from a pen friend, Brother Stanny, of St. Anne's Church of the Dhule in Maharashtra. He has compiled figures of different castes in government employment during British rule in 1935 and as they were 35 years after Independence in 1982."

61. Barbara Crossette, *India Facing the Twenty-First Century* (Bloomington: Indiana University Press, 1993), pp. 36–37.

62. Dipesh Chakrabarty, "Invitation to a Dialogue," pp. 373–74, and see chapter 1, note 38.

63. *Ibid.*, p. 376.

64. For an excellent treatment of Patel's life and work, see the recent Rajmohan Gandhi, *Patel: A Life* (Ahmedabad: Navajivan Publishing House, 1990). For a good discussion of Patel's role in bringing about the accession of Hyderabad, Junagadh and Kashmir, see p. 433ff.

65. Paul R. Brass, *Language, Religion and Politics in North India* (Cambridge: Cambridge University Press, 1974), pp. 17–20.

66. The Constitution of India, Diglot Edition (Hindi and English), p. 5.

67. For an excellent discussion of the use of the word "only" with extensive documentation from relevant court cases, see Ved Prakash Luthera, *The Concept of the Secular State and India* (Calcutta: Oxford University Press, 1964), pp. 64–81.

68. *Ibid.*, p. 70. The citation is from *Anjali* v. *The State of West Bengal*, AIR (1951) Cal. 822 at 829.

69. The Constitution of India, p. 6.

70. *Ibid.*

71. C. H. Alexandrowicz, "The Secular State in India and in the United States," *Journal of the Indian Law Institute* 2 (1960): 273–96; D. E. Smith, *India as a Secular State*, especially pp. 163–332; and Ved Prakash Luthera, *The Concept of the Secular State and India*, pp. 21–23 and 150–55.

72. The Constitution of India, pp. 9–10.

73. *Ibid.*, p. 14.

74. *Ibid.*

75. *Ibid.*, p. 15.

76. D. E. Smith, *India as a Secular State*, p. 276 and see also the overall discussion on law, pp. 265–91.

77. Quoted in J. D. M. Derrett, *Religion, Law and the State in India* (New York: The Free Press, 1968), p. 39.

78. *Ibid.*

79. For the detailed and definitive treatment of traditional Hindu and Muslim law and its relation to modern law in India, see J. Duncan M. Derrett, *Religion, Law and the State in India*, especially pp. 35–55, 321–51, 437–81, and 513–54. For a good discussion of the Sanskrit sources for civil and religious law, see A. B. Keith, *A History of Sanskrit Literature* (London: Oxford University Press, 1920), chapter XXII, "Civil and Religious Law," pp. 437–49. For the most recent and best book on classical Indian law in a Western language, see Robert Lingat, *The Classical Law of India*, trans., J. Duncan M. Derrett (Berkeley: University of California Press, 1973). Finally, Ludo Rocher has written extensively on matters of Indian law in numerous articles and reviews over the years. Two articles in particular are worth noting, first, Ludo Rocher, "'Lawyers' in Classical Hindu Law," *Law and Society Review* 3 (1969): 383–402; and second, Ludo Rocher, "Hindu Conceptions of Law," *The Hastings Law Journal* 29 (1978): 1284–1305.

80. J. Duncan M. Derrett, *Religion, Law and the State in India*, p. 517.

81. D. E. Smith, *India as a Secular State*, p. 271.

82. Cited in *ibid.*, p. 273.

83. *Ibid.*, pp. 281-291.

84. The Constitution of India, p. 15. .

85. *Ibid.*, pp. 111–12.

86. *Ibid.*, p. 113.

87. *Ibid.*, p. 114.

88. *Ibid.*, p. 115.

89. *Ibid.*, p. 116.

90. Some of the more important works of Marc Galanter are the following: "The Religious Aspects of Caste: A Legal View," in D. E. Smith, ed., *South Asian Politics and Religion* (Princeton: Princeton University Press, 1966), pp. 277–310; "Hinduism, Secularism and the Indian Judiciary," in *Philosophy East and West* 21, no. 4 (October 1971): 467–87; "Who Are the Other Backward Classes?," in *Economic and Political Weekly*, 28 October 1978, pp. 1812–28; *Competing Equalities* (Berkeley: University of California Press, 1984); and most recently, *Law and Society in Modern India* (New York: Oxford University Press, 1990). In addition to Galanter, there is, of course, a vast bibliography concerning the caste system and its modern variants. We have already referred to the work of Srnivas, Dumont and McKim Marriott in earlier chapters. Mention should perhaps also be made to the important work of the social anthropologist, André Béteille. Three titles are especially informative in terms of changing patterns in social stratification in India, two of which are based on fieldwork and the third on comparative theoretical analysis. They are as follows: André Béteille, *Caste, Class and Power: Changing Patterns of Stratification in a Tanjore Village* (Berkeley and Los Angeles: University of California Press, 1965); André Beteillé, *Studies in Agrarian Social Structure* (Delhi: Oxford University Press, 1973); and André Béteille, *Essays in Comparative Sociology* (Delhi: Oxford University Press, 1987).

91. Marc Galanter, "The Religious Aspects of Caste: A Legal View," pp. 277–79.

92. *Ibid.*, p. 289.

93. *Ibid.*, p. 309.

94. Marc Galanter, *Competing Equalities*, p. 561.

95. *Ibid.*, p. 567.

96. Cited in ibid., *Competing Equalities*, p. 561.

97. Rajni Kothari, *Caste in Indian Politics*, quoted in *Report of the Backward Classes Commission* (Mandal Report), 1980, pp. 18 and 62.

98. Especially useful for the current scene are the series of books produced by the Asia Society and Westview Press entitled, *India Briefing*. Seven volumes have been published thus far, one each for the years 1987 through 1993. The 1994 volume is due later in the present year. The series was edited in the first two volumes by M. M. Bouton. The volumes for 1989 and 1990 were edited by M. M. Bouton and Philip Oldenburg. The volume for 1991 was edited by Philip Oldenburg, and the volume for 1992 was edited by Leonard A. Gordon and Philip Oldenburg. See *India Briefing*, 1987, 1988, 1989, 1990, 1991, 1992 and 1993 (Boulder, Colorado: Westview Press, 1987-1993). Also, Stanley Wolpert's *A New History of India*, fourth edition, 1992, is useful for an impressionistic overview of events through 1991. See Stanley Wolpert, *A New History of India* (New York: Oxford University Press, 1992; 4th ed.), and especially pp. 434–46. The best journalistic source for reliable, continuing reporting is, of course, the news magazine, *India Today*. Also, *India Abroad*, out of New York, and *L.A. India*, out of Los Angeles, provide useful summaries and some helpful analysis of current events. Unfortunately, American newspapers, even *The New York Times* and *The Los Angeles Times*, are for the most part rather thin in their coverage of South Asia.

99. For the facts in the following quick survey, I have relied for the most part on the series of books mentioned just above, namely, *India Briefing*, from 1987 through 1993.

100. Rudolph and Rudolph, *In Pursuit of Lakshmi*, p. 69ff.

101. Paul Brass, "Political Parties and Electoral Politics," in M. M. Bouton and P. Oldenburg, eds., *India Briefing, 1989*, pp. 64–65.

102. Rudolph and Rudolph, *In Pursuit of Lakshmi*, p. 79ff.

103. Paul Brass, "Political Parties and Electoral Politics," pp. 64–65.

104. For an interesting account of the Congress (I) involvement with Bhindranwale, see Mark Tully and Satish Jacob, *Amritsar: Mrs. Gandhi's Last Battle* (London: Jonathan Cape, 1985), pp. 52–62.

105. Paul Brass, "Political Parties and Electoral Politics," pp. 64–65.

106. Wolpert, *A New History of India*, pp. 216 and 238.

107. For a thoughtful and careful overview of the Sikh traditions, see W. H. McLeod, *The Sikhs: History, Religion and Society* (New York: Columbia University Press, 1989). For a fuller treatment, exhaustive up through the period of the early 1960s, see Khushwant Singh, *A History of the Sikhs*, 2 vols. (Princeton: Princeton University Press, 1963–66).

108. By far the best book on the emergence of the Sikh community is that of Rajiv A. Kapur, *Sikh Separatism: The Politics of Faith*, especially chapters 4–6, pp. 105–9, for a detailed treatment of the period up to 1925, and pp. 194–250 for a useful sketch of developments from partition to Operation Blue Star. A second valuable account is that of M. J. Akbar, *India: The Siege Within* (Harmondsworth: Penguin Books, 1985), pp. 103–209. An engaging and somewhat more popular account of the history of the Sikh crisis is to be found in Mark Tully, *Amritsar: Mrs. Gandhi's Last Battle*, especially pp. 52–72 for the background regarding the rise of Bhindranwale, and pp. 155–73 for details regarding Operation Blue Star. For a useful collection of articles, editorials and essays regarding the Sikh crisis, Operation Blue Star, the assassination of Mrs. Gandhi and the continuing problems in the Punjab, see Patwant Singh and Harji Malik, eds., *Punjab: The Fatal Miscalculation* (Delhi: Crescent Printing Works, 1985).

109. Kapur, *Sikh Separatism*, pp. 96–97.

110. *Ibid.*, pp. xiv–xv.

111. *Ibid.*, pp. 92–93.

112. McLeod, *The Sikhs*, p. 67ff.

113. Kapur, *Sikh Separatism*, pp. 185–91.

114. *Ibid.*

115. *Ibid.*

116. *Ibid.*, pp. 190–91.

117. *Ibid.*, pp. 20–22.

118. *Ibid.*, pp. 205–6.

119. *Ibid.*, p. 206.

120. Quoted in Kapur, *Sikh Separatism*, p. 207.

121. McLeod, *The Sikhs*, p. 102.

122. Kapur, *Sikh Separatism*, pp. 211–16.

123. *Ibid.*, p. 217.

124. Mark Tully, *Amritsar*, pp. 45–48; McLeod, *The Sikhs*, pp. 114–15; and Kapur, *Sikh Separatism*, pp. 218–20.

125. McLeod, *The Sikhs*, p. 114.

126. Mark Tully, *Amritsar*, p. 52ff.

127. Kapur, *Sikh Separatism*, p. 218ff.

128. *Ibid.*, p. 226ff.

129. *Ibid.*, p. 223ff.

130. *Ibid.*, p. 242.

131. *Ibid.*, p. 243; and Wolpert, *A New History of India*, p. 423.

132. L. I. Rudolph, "The Faltering Novitiate: Rajiv at Home and Abroad in 1988," in *India Briefing, 1989*, pp. 5–9; and P. Oldenburg, "Politics: How Threatening a Crisis?," in *India Briefing, 1991*, pp. 21–23; and Walter Andersen, "Lowering the Level of Tension," in *India Briefing, 1992*, pp. 31–33.

133. See, for example, the article by K. Sandhu and R. Vinayak, "Punjab: Area of Darkness," *India Today*, 15 July 1992, pp. 22–27, which gives little hope for the long-term survival of the Beant Singh government.

134. I have found the following two recent treatments of Kashmir especially helpful: M. J. Akbar, *India: The Siege Within*, pp. 213–314; and Phillips Talbot, "Kashmir's Agony," in P. Oldenburg, ed., *India Briefing, 1991*, pp. 123–42.

135. Talbot, "Kashmir's Agony," pp. 125–126.

136. *Ibid.*, pp. 127–28.

137. *Ibid.*

138. *Ibid.*

139. Akbar, *India: The Siege Within*, pp. 223–35.

140. *Ibid.*

141. Talbot, "Kashmir's Agony,"pp. 130–31.

142. Akbar, *India: The Siege Within*, pp. 237–38.

143. Cited in *ibid*.

144. *Ibid.*

145. *Ibid.*, p. 241ff.

146. Talbot, "Kashmir's Agony," pp. 133–34.

147. *Ibid.*, pp. 126–27.

148. *Ibid.*, p. 131.

149. *Ibid.*, p. 133.

150. Akbar, *India: The Siege Within*, p. 243ff.

151. *Ibid.*

152. Talbot, "Kashmir's Agony," p. 133, and Akbar, *India: The Siege Within*, p. 249.

153. Cited in Talbot, "Kashmir's Agony," p. 134.

154. *Ibid.*, p. 135.

155. Akbar, *India: The Siege Within*, pp. 261–62.

156. *Ibid.*, p. 271.

157. *Ibid.*, p. 284–86.

158. *Ibid.*, p. 287–90.

159. Talbot, "Kashmir's Agony," pp. 138–41.

160. *Ibid.*, p. 139.

161. *Ibid.*

162. For a good account of Jagmohan's actions against Farooq Abdullah in 1984, see Akbar, *India: The Siege Within*, pp. 285–87.

163. Bob Drogin, "Trapped in a Vale of Tears," *Los Angeles Times*, 29 August 1992, p. A1 and A11.

164. *Ibid.*

165. For a useful background summary of the Hazratbal Mosque crisis, see Harinder Baweja, "Hazratbal Siege: Operation Blunder," *India Today*, 15 November 1993, pp. 18–29.

166. *Mohd. Ahmed Khan* vs. *Shah Bano Begum and Others*, A.I.R. (All India Reporter) 1985 Supreme Court Cases, pp. 556–74.

167. The *mahr* or "dowry" is an agreed upon amount paid by a bridegroom to support his wife in preparation for and during marriage and which remains her property. It can be paid in full at the time of marriage or a portion can be set aside to be paid later or at the time of the dissolution of a marriage. In the event of divorce, the wife retains the entire dowry. In the case of an unconsummated marriage, the wife retains only half. The *'iddah* or "period of waiting" is a period of three months or three menstrual cycles in the case of divorce or four months and ten days after the death of a husband before a woman may be remarried. In the case of divorce, a husband is expected to pay support during this period. The reason for the waiting period in the case of divorce is twofold: first, it provides an interval for normal menstrual functioning so that issues of paternity are not ambiguous in any subsequent marriage; second, it provides an interval during which a possible reconciliation might take place. See Cyril Glasse, ed., *The Concise Encyclopedia of Islam* (San Francisco: Harper Collins, 1989), p. 248 and 179.

168. *Mohd. Ahmed Khan* vs. *Shah Bano Begum*, p. 574.

169. *Ibid.*, pp. 572–73.

170. For readable and brief account of the whole episode, see Ainslie T. Embree, "Religion and Politics," in M. M. Bouton, ed., *India Briefing, 1987*, pp. 58–60.

171. *Ibid.*, p. 60.

172. *Ibid.*

173. *Ibid.*, p. 65.

174. *Ibid.*, p. 66.

175. Rudolph and Rudolph, *In Pursuit of Lakshmi*, p. 45.

176. *Ibid.*, pp. 38–39.

177. For an interesting discussion of the manner in which the Bill violates the Constitution, see Lucy Carroll, "The Muslim Women (Protection of Rights on Divorce) Bill 1986: A Retrogressive Precedent of Dubious Constitutionality," *Journal of the Indian Law Institute* 28 (1986): 364–76.

178. P. Koteswar Rao, "Shah Bano's Case and Uniform Civil Code—A Survey of Public Opinion among the Muslim Community at Tirupati," *Journal of the Indian Law Institute* 27 (1985): 572–77.

179. F. Ahmed, R. Menon and J. M. Ansari, "Young Muslims: Forging a New Identity," *India Today*, 31 October 1992, pp. 22–31.

180. The Constitution, p. 116.

181. Government of India, *Report of the Backward Classes Commission*, first part (volumes I and II), 1980, submitted by B. P. Mandal, Chairman of the Commission, to President Neelam Sanjiva Reddy on 31 December 1980, 130 pp. Hereafter, the Mandal Report.

182. See pp. 28–29 of the Mandal Report for an excellent summary of Supreme Court cases regarding reservation and compensatory discrimination.

183. The Mandal Report, p. 14.

184. *Ibid.*, p. 30.

185. *Ibid.*, p. 18.

186. *Ibid.*, pp. 18–19.

187. *Ibid.*, p. 19.

188. *Ibid.*

189. *Ibid.*, p. 52.

190. For the most balanced, fair and thoughtful assessment of the complex historical evidence regarding the disputed site, see Sushil Srivastava, *The Disputed Mosque: A Historical Inquiry* (New Delhi: Vistaar Publications, 1991),

especially pp. 125–31 for his summary conclusions. For a good treatment of the conservative Neo-Hindu interpretation of the evidence, see Koenraad Elst, *Ram Janmabhoomi vs. Babri Masjid: A Case Study in Hindu-Muslim Conflict* (New Delhi: Voice of India, 1990), and more recently, Koenraad Elst, *Ayodhya and After: Issues Before Hindu Society* (New Delhi: Voice of India, 1991). For a useful collection of essays, documents and court judgments together with a thoughtful presentation of the Muslim interpretation of the controversy, see Asghar Ali Engineer, ed., *Babri-Masjid Ramjanambhoomi Controversy* (Delhi: Ajanta Publications, 1990).

191. Pratapaditya Pal, "Whose Shrine Is It?," *The Saturday Statesman*, Calcutta, 13 April 1991, p. 2.

192. For the definitive treatment of the history of the city of Ayodhya, see the masterful work by Hans Bakker, *Ayodhyā* (Gronigen: Egbert Forsten, 1986; Gronigen Oriental Studies, volume I).

193. *Ibid.*, pp. 9–10.

194. For an excellent recent discussion of the significance of "Sita's kitchen," see Ramachandra Gandhi, *Sita's Kitchen* (Albany: State University of New York Press, 1993).

195. *Ibid.*, p. 61.

196. *Ibid.*, p. 148.

197. Srivastava, *The Disputed Mosque*, p. 127.

198. *Ibid.*, pp. 14–16.

199. *Ibid.*

200. *Ibid.*, p. 17.

201. *Ibid.*, p. 12.

202. *Ibid.*

203. *Ibid.*

204. *Ibid.*, pp. 12–13.

205. Wolpert, *A New History of India*, p. 439.

206. Walter Andersen, "Lowering the Level of Tension," *India Briefing, 1992*, p. 16.

207. Swapan Dasgupta, "Battle for Ram," *The Times of India*, Monday, 15 April 1991, p. 6.

208. New York Times News Service Story, *Santa Barbara News Press*, Monday, 7 December 1992, p. A3.

209. Robert Wuthnow, *The Restructuring of American Religion* (Princeton: Princeton University Press, 1988), p. 244.

CHAPTER 6: CONCLUSION: THE END AS THE BEGINNING

1. Rudolph and Rudolph, *In Pursuit of Lakshmi*, p. 37.

2. Frykenberg, "The Emergence of Modern 'Hinduism,' " p. 32.

3. Kenneth W. Jones, *Socio-Religious Reform Movements in British India*, p. 184.

4. T. N. Madan, "Secularism in its Place," *The Journal of Asian Studies* 46, no. 4 (November 1987): 753.

5. Peter L. Berger, "From the Crisis of Religions to the Crisis of Secularity," in M. Douglas and S. M. Tipton, eds., *Religion and America* (Boston: Beacon Press, 1982), p. 22.

6. *Ibid.*

7. S. C. Dube and V. N. Basilov, eds., *Secularization in Multi-Religious Societies*, p. 1. For the expression "Neo-Hindu," see note 40, Chapter 3.

8. Much the same can be said about various "Neo-Muslim" groups that have formed through the nineteenth and twentieth centuries. These also deserve serious study as examples of "religionization" and are undoubtedly fundamental for understanding the emergence of the Islamic Republic of Pakistan and the Islamic Republic of Bangladesh as well as a number of other religio-political movements in the Middle East and South and Southeast Asia.

9. Cited in A. T. Embree, "Religion and Politics," in *India Briefing*, 1987, p. 74, and referring to Vir Sanghvi, "Hindu Chauvinism with a Liberal Mask," *Sunday Mail*, 6 April 1986.

10. See the section in chapter 5 entitled "The Community as Citizen" for a full discussion. For the antithesis "nationalism"–"communalism" before partition becoming the antithesis "secularism"–"communalism" after partition, see D. E. Smith, *India as a Secular State*, p. 140.

11. Dipesh Chakrabarty, "Invitation to a Dialogue," p. 375–76.

12. For a good discussion of a variety of contemporary social issues, see Barbara Crossette, *India Facing the Twenty-first Century*. Regarding the issue of *satī* in particular, see S. Narasimhan, *Sati: Widow Burning in India* (New York: Doubleday Anchor, 1990). See also an unpublished paper by Professor John S. Hawley (Barnard College, Columbia Univerisity, New York City) entitled "*Satī* as a Focus for Hindu Revivalism."

13. T. N. Madan, "Secularism in its Place," pp. 748–49.

14. Ashis Nandy, "An Anti-Secularist Manifesto," *Seminar* 314 (October 1985): 24.

15. T. N. Madan, "Secularism in its Place," p. 750.

16. J. Duncan M. Derrett, *Religion, Law and the State in India*, pp. 556–57.

17. T. N. Madan, "Secularism in its Place," p. 750.

18. *Ibid.*, p. 758.

19. C. Rajagopalachari, "The Place of Religion in Future India," *Message of India*, 1959, volume I, p. 83, and quoted in D. E. Smith, *India as a Secular State*, p. 151.

20. Percival Spear, *India, Pakistan and the West*, p. 242.

21. Rudolph and Rudolph, *In Pursuit of Lakshmi*, p. 79.

22. Wolpert, *A New History of India*, p. 430.

23. Khushwant Singh, "Brahmin Power," p. 19. See also the article by Eleanor Zelliot, "Dalit: New Perspectives on India's Untouchables," pp. 97–121.

24. D. E. Smith, *India as a Secular State*, pp. 320–2l.

25. *Bande Mātaram*, "Hail to the Mother," the famous poem of Bankim Chandra Chatterjee, quoted in S. Hay, ed., *Sources of Indian Tradition*, volume 2, pp. 134–35.

26. Nehru, *The Discovery of India*, pp. 412–13.

Select Bibliography

Abu-Lughod, Janet L. *Before European Hegemony: The World System A.D. 1250–1350*. New York: Oxford University Press, 1989.

Ahmad, Imtiaz. "Religion in Politics." *Economic and Political Weekly*. 8 January 1972: 81–86.

Ahmad, Mumtaz. "Islamic Fundamentalism in South Asia: The Jamaat-i-Islami and the Tablighi Jamaat." *Fundamentalisms Observed*. Volume I. Eds. Martin E. Marty and R. Scott Applesby. Chicago: University of Chicago Press, 1991: 457–530.

Ahmed, Farzan, *et al*. "Young Muslims: Forging a New Identity." *India Today*. 3l October 1992: 22–29.

Aiyar, Shahnaz A. "The VHP: Flexing its Muscles." *India Today*. 30 April 1991: 32–34.

Akbar, M. J. *India: The Siege Within*. Harmondsworth: Penguin, 1985.

Albanese, Catherine L. *America: Religions and Religion*. Belmont, Cal.: Wadsworth Publishing Co., 1981.

Alexandrowicz, C. H. "The Secular State in India and in the United States." *Journal of the Indian Law Institute.* Vol. 2 (1960): 273–96.

Allchin, Bridget and Raymond. *The Rise of Civilization in India and Pakistan.* Cambridge: Cambridge University Press, 1982.

Andersen, Walter K. and Shridhar D. Damle. *The Brotherhood in Saffron: The Rashtriya Swayamsevak Sangh and Hindu Revivalism.* New Delhi: Vistaar Publications, 1987.

Anderson, Benedict. *Imagined Communities: Reflections on the Origin and Spread of Nationalism.* London: Verso, 1983.

Arberry, A. J., ed. *Religion in the Middle East: Three Religions in Concord and Conflict.* Volume 2: Islam. Cambridge: Cambridge University Press, 1969.

Aspinall, A. *Cornwallis in Bengal.* Publications of the University of Manchester Historical Series No. LX. Manchester: Manchester University Press, 1931.

Awasthi, Dilip and S. A. Aiyar. "RSS-BJP-VHP: Hindu Divided Family." *India Today.* 30 November 1991: 14–21.

Awasthi, Dilip and Yubaraj Ghimire. "Politics of Opportunism." *India Today.* 15 August 1992: 14–21.

Babb, Lawrence A. "The Puzzle of Religious Modernity." *India 2000: The Next Fifteen Years.* Ed. James R. Roach. Riverdale, Maryland: The Riverdale Co, 1986.

———. *Redemptive Encounters: Three Modern Styles in the Hindu Tradition.* Berkeley: University of California Press, 1986.

———. "Satya Sai Baba's Magic." *Anthropological Quarterly.* Volume 56 (1983): 116–24.

Badhwar, Inderjit. "Hindus: Militant Revivalism." *India Today.* 31 May 1986: 30–39.

Badhwar, Inderjit and Prabhu Chawla. "Politics of Nihilism." *India Today.* 15 October 1990: 12–23.

Baig, M. R. A. *The Muslim Dilemma in India.* Delhi: Vikas Publishing, 1974.

Bainbridge, W. S. and D. H. Jackson. "The Rise and Decline of Transcendental Meditation." *The Social Impact of New Religious Move-*

ments. Ed. Brian Wilson. New York: The Rose of Sharon Press, 1981.

Baird, Robert D. "Human Rights Priorities and Indian Religious Thought." *A Journal of Church and State*. Vol. XI. No. 2 (Spring 1969): 221–38.

———, ed. *Religion and Law in Independent India*. Delhi: Manohar, 1994.

———. "Religion and the Legitimation of Nehru's Concept of the Secular State." *Religion and the Legitimation of Power in South Asia*. Ed. Bardwell L. Smith. Leiden: E. J. Brill, 1978: 73–86.

———. "Religion and the Secular: Categories for Religious Conflict and Religious Change in India." *Journal of Asian and African Studies*. Vol. XI. Nos. 1–2 (1979): 47–63.

———, ed. *Religion in Modern India*. Delhi: Manohar, 1981.

Bakker, Hans. *Ayodhyā*. Groningen Oriental Studies I. Groningen: Egbert Forsten, 1986.

———. "Ayodhyā: A Hindu Jerusalem." *Numen*. Vol. XXXVIII. Fasc. 1 (June 1991): 80–109.

Bakshi, P. M. "Reservations for Backward Classes: Some Reflections." *Journal of the Indian Law Institute*. Vol. 27 (1985): 318–35.

Balakrishnan, S. "Ayodhya: The Communal Tinderbox." *The Illustrated Weekly of India*. 5 November 1989: 30–33.

Barot, Rohit. "Caste and Sect in the Swaminarayana Movement." *Hinduism in Great Britain*. Ed. Richard Burghart. London: Tavistock Publications, 1987.

Barrett, David B. *World Christian Encyclopedia*. Oxford: Oxford University Press, 1982.

Basham, A. L. *The Origins and Development of Classical Hinduism*. Ed. Kenneth Zysk. Boston: Beacon Press, 1989.

———. *The Wonder That Was India*. New York: Grove Press, 1954.

Basu, Kajal, ed. "Reservations: Caste vs. Class." *India Today*. 31 May 1991: 33–41.

Baweja, Harinder. "Hazratbal Siege: Operation Blunder." *India Today*. 15 November 1993: 18–24.

———. "Kashmir: Severe Setback." *India Today*. 15 January 1993: 80–82.

———. "Kashmiri Pandits: Living on the Edge." *India Today*. 15 July 1992: 48–49.

Baxi, Upendra. "The Struggle for the Redefinition of Secularism in India: Some Preliminary Reflections." Unpublished essay, 1991.

Bedi, Rajesh and Ramesh. Sadhus: *The Holy Men of India*. New Delhi: Brijbasi Printers, 1991.

Bellah, Robert N. "Civil Religion in America." *Daedalus*. Vol. XCVI (1967): 1–21.

Berger, Peter L. "From the Crisis of Religion to the Crisis of Secularity." *Religion and America*. Eds. Mary Douglas and Steven M. Tipton. Boston: Beacon Press, 1982.

———. *The Sacred Canopy*. New York: Doubleday Anchor, 1969.

Bergesen, Albert, ed. *Crises in the World-System*. Political Economy of the World-System Annals, Vol. 6. Beverly Hills: Sage Publications, 1983.

Béteille, André. *Caste, Class, and Power: Changing Patterns of Stratification in a Tanjore Village*. Berkeley: University of California Press, 1965.

———. *Essays in Comparative Sociology*. Delhi: Oxford University Press, 1987.

———. "Individualism and Equality." *Current Anthropology*. Vol. 27. No. 2 (1986): 121–34.

———. "Religion as a Subject for Sociology." *Economic and Political Weekly*. 29 August 1992: 1865–70.

———. "Secularism and the Intellectuals." *Economic and Political Weekly*. Forthcoming 1994.

———. *Studies in Agrarian Social Structure*. Delhi: Oxford University Press, 1973.

Bhalla, G. S., et al., eds. *India, Nation-State and Communalism*. New Delhi: Patriot Publishers, 1989.

Bhandarkar, R. G. *Vaiṣṇavism, Śaivism and Minor Religious Systems*. 1913. Repr. Varanasi: Indological Book House, 1965.

Bharati, Agehananda. *Hindu Views and Ways and the Hindu-Muslim Interface*. New Delhi: Munshiram Manoharlal, 1981.

Bhattacharya, Benoytosh. *An Introduction to Buddhist Esoterism.* Delhi: Motilal Banarsidass, 1980.

Bhattacharya, H., ed. *The Cultural Heritage of India. The Religions.* Vol. 4. Calcutta: The Ramakrishna Mission Institute of Culture, 1937.

Biardeau, Madeleine. *Hinduism: The Anthropology of a Civilization.* Trans. Richard Nice. French Studies in South Asian Culture and Society III. Delhi: Oxford University Press, 1989.

Bonner, Arthur. *Averting the Apocalypse: Social Movements in India Today.* Durham: Duke University Press, 1990.

Bose, Arun. *India's Social Crisis: An Essay on Capitalism, Socialism, Individualism, and Indian Civilization.* Delhi: Oxford University Press, 1989.

Bose, Ashish, comp. *Demographic Diversity of India: 1991 Census State and District Level Data: A Reference Book.* Delhi: B. R. Publishing Corp., 1991.

———. *Population of India: 1991 Census Results and Methodology.* Delhi: B. R. Publishing Corp., 1991.

Bose, Sugata, ed. *South Asia and World Capitalism.* Delhi: Oxford University Press, 1990.

Bouton, Marshall M., ed. *India Briefing, 1987.* Delhi: Oxford University Press, 1987.

———, ed. *India Briefing, 1988.* Boulder: Westview Press, 1988.

Bouton, Marshall M. and Philip Oldenburg, eds. *India Briefing, 1989.* Boulder: Westview Press, 1989.

———, eds. *India Briefing, 1990.* Boulder: Westview Press, 1990.

Brass, Paul R. *Language, Religion and Politics in North India.* Cambridge:University Press, 1974.

Braudel, Fernand. *The Mediterranean and the Mediterranean World in the Age of Philip II.* Trans. S. Reynolds. New York: Basic Books, 1972.

Breckenridge, Carol A. and Peter van der Veer, eds. *Orientalism and the Postcolonial Predicament.* Philadelphia: University of Pennsylvania Press, 1993.

Briggs, G. W. *Gorakhnāth and the Kānphaṭa Yogis.* 1938. Repr Delhi: Motilal Banarsidass, 1973.

Bromley, David G. and Larry D. Shinn, eds. *Krishna Consciousness in the West*. Lewisburg: Bucknell University Press, 1989.

Bromley, David G. and Phillip E. Hammond, eds. *The Future of New Religious Movements*. Macon, Georgia: Mercer University Press, 1987.

Bronkhorst, Johannes. *The Two Sources of Indian Asceticism*. Bern: Peter Lang, 1993.

———. *The Two Traditions of Meditation in Ancient India*. Stuttgart: Franz Steiner, 1986.

Brook, Charles R. *The Hare Krishnas in India*. Princeton: Princeton University Press, 1989.

Brown, W. Norman. "The Content of Cultural Continuity in India." *Journal of Asian Studies*. Vol. XX (August 1961): 427–34.

———. *Man in the Universe: Some Cultural Continuities in India*. Berkeley: University of California Press, 1970.

Burghart, Richard and Audrey Cantlie, eds. *Indian Religion*. Collected Papers on South Asia No. 7. London: Curzon Press, 1985.

Buhler, G., trans. *The Laws of Manu*. Sacred Books of the East. Vol. 25. 1886. Repr. Delhi: Motilal Banarsidass, 1988.

Bultmann, Rudolf. *Jesus Christ and Mythology*. London: SCM Press, 1960.

Campbell, A. *The Mechanics of Enlightenment: An Examination of the Teaching of Maharishi Mahesh Yogi*. London: Gollancz, 1977.

Carman, John Braisted. *The Theology of Rāmānuja: An Essay in Interreligious Understanding*. New Haven: Yale University Press, 1974.

Carrithers, Michael and Caroline Humphreys, eds. *The Assembly of Listeners: Jains in Society*. Cambridge: Cambridge University Press, 1991.

Carroll, Lucy. "The Muslim Women (Protection of Rights on Divorce) Act 1986: A Retrogressive Precedent of Dubious Constitutionality." *Journal of the Indian Law Institute*. Vol. 28 (1986): 364–76.

Chacko, Arun. "The Muslims: Settling for Secularism." *India Today*. 30 April 1991: 36–38.

Chandra, Bipan. *Communalism in Modern India*. Delhi: Vani Educational Books, 1984.

Chandra, Sudhir. "Secular Potential of Early Indian Nationalism." *Economic and Political Weekly*. 26 April 1980: 773–75.

Chatterjee, Margaret. *Gandhi's Religious Thought*. Notre Dame: Notre Dame University Press, 1983.

Chatterjee, Partha. *Nationalist Thought and the Colonial World*. Minneapolis: University of Minnesota Press, 1986.

Chatterjee, S. and D. Datta. *An Introduction to Indian Philosophy*. Calcutta: University of Calcutta, 1968.

Chatterjee, Satischandra. *The Nyāya Theory of Knowledge*. Calcutta: University of Calcutta, 1965.

Chatterji, P. C. *Secular Values for Secular India*. New Delhi: Lola Chatterji, 1984.

Chaudhuri, K. N. *Asia Before Europe: Economy and Civilisation of the Indian Ocean from the Rise of Islam to 1750*. Cambridge: Cambridge University Press, 1990.

Chopra, P. N., ed. *Religions and Communities of India*. New Delhi: Vision Books, 1982.

Coburn, Thomas B. "Where Was God Born? The Myth-History Controversy in Contemporary North India." Unpublished essay, October 1991.

Cohn, Werner. "Is Religion Universal? Problems of Definition." *Journal for the Scientific Study of Religion*. Vol. II. No. 1 (Fall 1962): 25–35.

Conze, Edward. *Buddhist Thought in India*. London: Allen and Unwin, 1962.

Copeland, E. Luther. "Neo-Hinduism and Secularism." *A Journal of Church and State*. Vol. IX (1967): 200–210.

Coward, Harold G. and K. Kunjunni Raja, eds. *The Philosophy of the Grammarians. Encyclopedia of Indian Philosophies*. Volume V. Princeton: Princeton University Press, 1990.

Cragg, Kenneth. *The House of Islam*. Belmont, Cal.: Dickenson Publishing, 1969.

Craske, M. *The Dance of Love: My Life with Meher Baba*. North Myrtle Beach: Sheriar Press, 1980.

Crim, Keith, ed. *Abingdon Dictionary of Living Religions*. Nashville: Abingdon Press, 1981.

Cross, F. L. and E. A. Livingstone, eds. *The Oxford Dictionary of the Christian Church*. Second Edition. London: Oxford University Press, 1974.

Crossette, Barbara. *India: Facing the Twenty-First Century*. Bloomington: Indiana University Press, 1993.

Damen, Frans L. *Crisis and Religious Renewal in the Brahmo Samaj (1860–64)*. Orientalia Lovaniensia Analecta Volume 9. Leuven: Department Orientalistiek, Katholieke Universitat Leuven, 1981.

Das, Veena. *Structure and Cognition: Aspects of Hindu Caste and Ritual*. Delhi: Oxford University Press, 1977.

Dasgupta, Shashibhusan. *Obscure Religious Cults*. 2nd Edition. Calcutta: K. L. Mukhopadhyay, 1962.

Dasgupta, Surendranath. *Hindu Mysticism*. New York: Frederick UngarPublishing, 1927.

———. *History of Indian Philosophy*. 5 Volumes. Cambridge: Cambridge University Press, 1922–55.

Dasgupta, Swapan. "Battle for Ram: Issue is the Denial of the Temple." *The Times of India*. 15 April 1991: 5.

Dave, H. T. *Life and Philosophy of Shree Swaminarayan 1781–1830*. London:Allen and Unwin, 1974.

Derrett, J. Duncan M. *History of Indian Law (Dharmaśāstra)*. Leiden: E. J. Brill 1973.

———. *Religion, Law and the State in India*. New York: The Free Press, 1968.

Deshpande, G. P. "The Plural Tradition." Symposium: The Hindus and Their Isms. *Seminar*. 313 (1985): 23–25.

Deshpande, Madhav. "History, Change and Permanence: A Classical Indian Perspective." *Contributions to South Asian Studies I*. Ed. Gopal Krishna. Delhi: Oxford University Press, 1979: 1–28.

Deutsch, Eliot. *Advaita Vedanta: A Philosophical Reconstruction*. Honolulu: University of Hawaii Press, 1969.

Dhami, M. S. "Punjab and Communalism." *Seminar*. 314 (1985): 25–38.

Doniger, Wendy and Brian K. Smith, trans. *The Laws of Manu*. London: Penguin, 1991.

Doniger (O'Flaherty), Wendy. *Asceticism and Eroticism in the Mythology of Śiva*. London: Oxford University Press, 1973.

———, trans. *The Rig Veda: An Anthology*. Harmondsworth: Penguin, 198l.

Drekmeier, Charles. *Kingship and Community in Early India*. Stanford: Stanford University Press, 1962.

Drogin, Bob. "Trapped in a Vale of Tears." *Los Angeles Times*. 29 August 1993: A1 and A11.

Dube, S. C. "Harmonizing Dimension in Hindu Civilizational Processes." *Secularization in Multi-Religious Societies*. Eds. S. C. Dube and V. N. Basilov. New Delhi: Concept Publishing Co., 1983: 1–20.

———. *Indian Village*. New York: Harper Colophon Books, 1967.

Dumont, Louis. *Homo Hierarchicus: The Caste System and Its Implications*.Revised English Edition. Trans. Mark Sainsbury, Louis Dumont and Basia Gulati. Chicago: University of Chicago Press, 1980.

———. *From Mandeville to Marx: The Genesis and Triumph of Economic Ideology*. Chicago: University of Chicago Press, 1977.

———. "A Modified View of Our Origins: The Christian Beginnings of Modern Individualism." *Religion*. Vol. 12 (1982): 1–27.

Dushkin, Lelah. "Backward Class Benefits and Social Class in India, 1920–1970." *Economic and Political Weekly*. 7 April 1979: 661–67.

Dyczkowski, Mark S. G. *The Doctrine of Vibration*. Albany: SUNY Press, 1987.

Eck, Diana L. *Banaras: City of Light*. Princeton: Princeton University Press, 1982.

Edgerton, Franklin, trans. *The Beginnings of Indian Philosophy*. Cambridge: Harvard University Press, 1965.

———, trans. *The Bhagavad Gītā*. 2 volumes. Harvard Oriental Series Vols. 38–39. Cambridge, Mass.: Harvard University Press, 1944.

Eisenstadt, S. N. and S. Rokkan, eds. *Building States and Nations*. 2 Volumes. Beverly Hills: Sage Publications, 1973.

Eliade, Mircea. *Yoga: Immortality and Freedom*. Trans. Willard R. Trask. Second Edition. Bollingen Series LVI. Princeton: Princeton University Press, 1969.

———. *Shamanism: Archaic Techniques of Ecstasy*. Trans. Willard R. Trask. New York: Pantheon Books, 1964.

Ellwood, Robert S. *Religious and Spiritual Groups in Modern America*. Englewood Cliffs, N.J.: Prentice-Hall, 1973.

Elst, Koenrad. *Ayodhya and After*. New Delhi: Voice of India, 1991.

———. *Ram Janmabhoomi vs. Babri Masjid: A Case-Study in Hindu-Muslim Conflict*. New Delhi: Voice of India, 1990.

Embree, Ainslie T. *Charles Grant and British Rule in India*. New York: Columbia University Press, 1962.

———. *Imagining India: Essays on Indian History*. Ed. Mark Juergensmeyer. Delhi: Oxford University Press, 1989.

———. "Religion and Politics." *India Briefing, 1987*. Ed. Marshall M. Bouton. Delhi: Oxford University Press, 1987.

———, ed. *Sources of Indian Tradition*. Volume One. Second Edition. New York: Columbia University Press, 1988.

———. *Utopias in Conflict*. Berkeley: University of California Press, 1990.

Engineer, Asghar Ali, ed. *Babri-Masjid Ramjanmabhoomi Controversy*. Delhi: Ajanta Publications, 1990.

———. "Understanding Communalism." *Economic and Political Weekly*. Vol. XIX. No. 18 (May 1984): 752–56.

Esposito, John L., ed. *Islam in Asia: Religion, Politics and Society*. New York: Oxford University Press, 1987.

———, ed. *Voices of Resurgent Islam*. New York: Oxford University Press, 1983.

Farquhar, J. N. *Modern Religious Movements in India*. 1914. Repr. Delhi: Munshiram Manoharlal, 1967.

———. *An Outline of the Religious Literature of India*. 1919. Repr. Delhi: Motilal Banarsidass, 1967.

Faruqi, Ziya-ul-Hasan. *The Deoband School and the Demand for Pakistan*. London: Asia Publishing House, 1963.

Fay, Peter Ward. *The Forgotten Army: India's Armed Struggle for Independence 1942–1945*. Ann Arbor: University of Michigan Press, 1993.

Feldhaus, Ann, trans. *The Deeds of God in Ṛddhipur*. New York: Oxford University Press, 1984.

Feuerbach, Ludwig. *The Essence of Christianity*. Trans. George Eliot. New York: Prometheus Books, 1989.

Foucault, Michel. *The Archaeology of Knowledge*. Trans. A. M. Sheridan. New York: Harper and Row, 1972.

Frauwallner, Erich. *Geschichte der indischen Philosophie*. 2 volumes. Salzburg: Otto Muller, 1953, 1956.

Freitag, Sandria B. *Collective Action and Community: Public Arenas and the Emergence of Communalism in North India*. Berkeley: University of California Press, 1989.

———, ed. *Culture and Power in Banaras: Community, Performance and Environment, 1800–1980*. Berkeley: University of California Press, 1989.

Frykenberg, Robert Eric. "The Emergence of Modern 'Hinduism' as a Concept and as an Institution: A Reappraisal with special Reference to South India." *Hinduism Reconsidered*. Eds. G. D. Sonthheimer and H. Kulke. Delhi: Manohar, 1989: 29–49.

———. "Hindu Fundamentalism and the Structural Stability of India." *Fundamentalisms and the State: Remaking Polities, Economies and Militance*. Volume 3. Eds. Martin E. Marty and F. Scott Applesby. Chicago: University of Chicago Press, 1993: 233–55.

Galanter, Marc. *Law and Society in Modern India*. Ed. Rajeev Dhavan. Delhi: Oxford University Press, 1989.

———. *Competing Equalities*. Berkeley: University of California Press, 1984.

———. "Hinduism, Secularism and the Indian Judiciary." *Philosophy East and West*. Vol. 21. No. 4 (October 1971): 467–87.

———. "The Religious Aspects of Caste: A Legal View." *South Asian Politics and Religion*. Ed. D. E. Smith. Princeton: Princeton University Press, 1966: 277–310.

———. "Secularism, East and West." Review of D. E. Smith's India as a Secular State. *Comparative Studies in Society and History*. Vol. VII. No. 2 (January 1965): 133–59.

———. "Who Are the Backward Classes?" *Economic and Political Weekly*. 28 October 1978: 1812–28.

Gandhi, Mohandas K. *An Autobiography: The Story of My Experiments with Truth*. Trans. Mahadev Desai. Boston: Beacon Press, 1957.

Gandhi, Rajmohan. *Patel: A Life*. Ahmedabad: Navajivan Publishing House, 1990.

Gandhi, Ramachandra. *Sita's Kitchen*. Albany: SUNY Press, 1993.

Geertz, Clifford. *The Interpretation of Cultures*. New York: Basic Books, 1973.

Gellner, Ernest. *Nations and Nationalism*. Oxford: Basil Blackwell Ltd., 1983.

Ghimire, Yubaraj. "Ram Is Still Best." *India Today*. 3l December 1993: 22–24.

Giddens, Anthony. *A Contemporary Critique of Historical Materialism: Power Property and the State*. Vol. l. Berkeley: University of California Press, 198l.

———. *The Nation-State and Violence. A Contemporary Critique of Historical Materialism*. Vol. 2. Berkeley: University of California Press, 1987.

———. *Profiles and Critiques in Social Theory*. Berkeley: University of California Press, 1982.

Glasse, Cyril, ed. *The Concise Encyclopedia of Islam*. San Francisco: Harper- Collins, 1989.

Gold, Daniel. *The Lord as Guru: Hindi Sants in the Northern Indian Tradition*. New York: Oxford University Press, 1987.

———. "Organized Hinduisms: From Vedic Truth to Hindu Nation." *Fundamentalisms Observed*. Vol. I. Eds. Martin E. Marty and R. Scott Applesby. Chicago: University of Chicago Press, 199l: 53l–93.

Gopal, Sarvapalli, Romila Thapar, Bipan Chandra, et al. "The Political Abuse of History: Babri-Masjid-Rama Janmabhumi Dispute." *South Asia Bulletin*. Vol. 9. No. 2 (1989): 65–67.

Gordon, Leonard A. and Philip Oldenburg, eds. *India Briefing, 1992*. Boulder: Westview Press, 1992.

Gould, Harold A. *The Hindu Caste System. The Sacralization of a Social Order*. Vol. I. *Caste Adaptation in Modernizing Indian Society*. Vol. II. Delhi: Chanakya Publications, 1988.

Government of India. *The Constitution of India*. Diglot Edition of 1986. Delhi: Prakashan Niyantrak, Bharat Sarkar, 1986.

Government of India. *Report of the Backward Classes Commission. First Part. Vols. I and II. 1980*. Comp. B. P. Mandal. Shimla: Manager Government of India Press, 1984.

Graubard, Stephen R., ed. "Another India." *Daedalus*. Vol. 118. No. 4 (Fall 1989).

Gross, Robert Lewis. *The Sadhus of India*. Jaipur: Rawat Publications, 1992.

Guha, Ranajit, ed. *Subaltern Studies: Writings on South Asian History and Society*. Six Volumes. Delhi: Oxford University Press, 1982– .

Guha Ranajit and Gayatri Chakravorty Spivak, eds. *Selected Subaltern Studies*. New York: Oxford University Press, 1988.

Gupta, Shekhar, ed. "What Is Secularism?" *India Today*. 15 May 1991: 61–73.

Gupte, Pranay. *Mother India: A Political Biography of Indira Gandhi*. New York: Charles Scribner's Sons, 1992.

Haberman, David L. *Acting as a Way of Salvation: A Study in Rāgānugā-Bhakti Sādhana*. New York: Oxford University Press, 1988.

———. *Journey Through the Twelve Forests: An Encounter with Krishna*. New York: Oxford University Press, 1994.

Habermas, Jürgen. *The Theory of Communicative Action. Reason and the Rationalization of Society*. Vol. One. *Lifeworld and System: A Critique of Functionalist Reason*. Vol. Two. Trans. Thomas McCarthy. Boston: Beacon Press, 1984 and 1987.

Hadar, Leon T. "What Green Peril?" *Foreign Affairs*. Vol. 72. No. 2 (Spring 1993): 27–42.

Halbfass, Wilhelm. *On Being and What There Is: Classical Vaiśeṣika and the History of Indian Ontology*. Albany: SUNY Press, 1992.

———. *Tradition and Reflection: Explorations in Indian Thought*. Albany: SUNY Press, 1991.

Hardy, Peter. "Islam and Muslims in South Asia." *The Crescent in the East*. Ed. R. Israeli. London: Humanities Press, 1982: 39–40.

Harman, S. *Plight of Muslims in India*. London: D. L. Publications, 1977.

Hartsuiker, Dolf. *Sadhus: India's Mystic Holy Men*. Rochester, Vermont:Inner Traditions International, 1993.

Hawley, John Stratton. "Sati as a Focus for Hindu Revivalism." Unpublished essay, 1992.

Hawley, John Stratton and Mark Juergensmeyer, ed. and trans. *Songs of the Saints of India*. New York: Oxford University Press, 1988.

Hay, Stephen, ed. *Sources of Indian Tradition*. Volume Two. Second Edition. New York: Columbia University Press, 1988.

Heesterman, J. C. *The Inner Conflict of Tradition: Essays in Indian Ritual, Kingship and Society*. Delhi: Oxford University Press, 1985.

Hegel, G. W. F. *The Philosophy of History*. Trans. J. Sibree. New York: Dover Publications, 1956.

Herberg, Will. *Protestant, Catholic, Jew*. New York: Doubleday Anchor Books, 1973.

Hess, Linda and Shukdev Singh, trans. *The Bījak of Kabir*. San Francisco: North Point Press, 1983.

Hiriyanna, M. *The Essentials of Indian Philosophy*. London: Allen and Unwin, 1973.

Hudson, Winthrop S. *Religion in America*. Third Edition. New York: Charles Scribner's Sons, 1981.

Hutton, J. F. *Caste in India*. Third Edition. London: Oxford University Press, 1961.

Inden, Ronald. *Imagining India*. Oxford: Basil Blackwell Ltd., 1990.

———. "Orientalist Constructions of India." *Modern Asian Studies*. Vol. 20. No. 3 (1986): 401–46.

Irschick, Eugene F. *Dialogue and History: Constructing South India, 1795–1895*. Berkeley: University of California Press, 1994.

Iyer, Raghavan, ed. *The Essential Writings of Mahatma Gandhi*. Delhi: Oxford University Press, 1990.

Jaini, Padmanabh S. *The Jaina Path of Purification*. Berkeley: University of California Press, 1979.

———. "Śramaṇas: Their Conflict with Brāhmaṇical Society." *Chapters in Indian Civlization*. Volume I. Ed. Joseph W. Elder. Dubuque, Iowa: Kendall-Hunt, 1970.

Johnston, E. H. *Early Sāṃkhya*. London: Royal Asiatic Society, 1937.

Jones, Kenneth W. *Socio-Religious Reform Movements in British India*. *The New Cambridge History of India, III.1*. Cambridge: Cambridge University Press, 1989.

Jordens, J. T. F. *Dayānanda Sarasvatī: His Life and Ideas*. Delhi: Oxford University Press, 1978.

Juergensmeyer, Mark. *Radhasaomi Reality: The Logic of a Modern Faith*. Princeton: Princeton University Press, 1991.

Kakar, Sudhir, ed. *Identity and Adulthood*. Delhi: Oxford University Press, 1979.

———. *The Inner World: A Psychoanalytic Study of Childhood and Society in India*. Second Edition. Delhi: Oxford Univeristy Press, 1981.

Kane, P. V. *History of Dharmaśāstra*. 5 Volumes. Second Edition. Poona:Bhandarkar Oriental Research Institute, 1968–74.

Kapoor, Satish C . "Contemporary Relevance." Symposium: The Hindus and Their Isms. *Seminar*. 313 (1985): 30–37.

Kapur, Rajiv A. *Sikh Separatism:* The Politics of Faith. London: Allen and Unwin, 1986.

Keith, A. B. *A History of Sanskrit Literature*. London: Oxford University Press, 1920.

Kennedy, Paul. *The Rise and Fall of the Great Powers: Economic Change and Military Conflict from 1500–2000*. New York: Random House, 1987.

Khare, R. S. *The Untouchable as Himself*. Cambridge: Cambridge University Press, 1984.

Klostermaier, Klaus K. *A Survey of Hinduism.* Albany: SUNY Press, 1989.

Kohli, Atul. *Democracy and Discontent: India's Growing Crisis of Governability.* Cambridge: Cambridge University Press, 1990.

Kopf, David. *The Brahmo Samāj and the Shaping of the Modern Indian Mind.* Princeton: Princeton University Press, 1979.

———. *British Orientalism and the Bengal Renaissance: The Dynamics of Indian Modernization 1773–1835.* Berkeley: University of California Press, 1969.

Kothari, Rajni. "The Confrontation of Theories with National Realities: Reports of an International Conference." *Building States and Nations.* Eds. S. N. Eisenstadt and S. Rokkan. Beverly Hills: Sage Publications, 1973: 99–115.

———. *Politics and the People: In Search of a Humane India.* 2 volumes. Delhi: Ajanta Publications, 1990.

Kothari, Rajni and Rushikesh Maru. "Caste and Secularism in India: Case-Study of a Caste Federation." *Journal of Asian Studies.* Vol. 25 (November-August 1965–66): 33–50.

Kumar, Krishna. "Hindu Revivalism and Education in North-Central India." *Fundamentalisms and Society: Reclaiming the Sciences, the Family and Education.* Volume 2. Eds. Martin E. Marty and F. Scott Applesby. Chicago: University of Chicago Press, 1993: 536–57.

Kumar, Ravinder. "India: A 'Nation-State' or a 'Civilisation-State'?" Occasional Papers on Perspectives in Indian Development No. VIII. Center for Contemporary Studies. Nehru Memorial Museum and Library. New Delhi: Teen Murti House, 1989.

———. "India's Political Identity." *The Times of India.* 26 August 1991: 6.

———. "The Secular Culture of India." Occasional Papers on History and Society No. XVIII. Nehru Memorial Museum and Library. New Delhi: Teen Murti House, 1984.

———. "Secularism in a Multi-Religious Society: The Indian Context." *Secularization in Multi-Religious Societies.* Eds. S. C. Dube and V. N. Basilov. New Delhi: Concept Publishing Co., 1983: 21–36.

Lakshman, Nikhil. "The RSS: The New Untouchables." *The Illustrated Weekly of India.* 14 August 1988: 8–17.

Lamotte, Etienne. *History of Indian Buddhism*. Trans. S. Webb-Boin. Louvain: Peeters Press, 1988.

Lapidus, Ira M. *A History of Islamic Societies*. Cambridge: Cambridge University Press, 1988.

Larson, Gerald James. "The Bhagavad Gītā as Cross-Cultural Process: Toward an Analysis of the Social Locations of a Religious Text." *Journal of the American Academy of Religion*. Vol. XLIII. No. 4 (1975): 651–69.

———. *Classical Sāṃkhya: An Interpretation of its History and Meaning*. Second Revised Edition. Delhi: Motilal Banarsidass, 1979.

———. "Discourse about 'Religion' in Colonial and Postcolonial India." *Ethical and Political Dilemmas of Modern India*. Eds. Ninian Smart and Shivesh Thakur. New York: St. Martin's Press, 1993.

———. "An Eccentric Ghost in the Machine." *Philosophy East and West*. Vol. 33. No. 3 (July 1983): 219–33.

———. "India through Hindu Categories: A Sāṃkhya Response." *Contributions to Indian Sociology*. Vol. 24. No. 2 (July-December 1990): 303-26.

———. "Mandal, Mandir, Masjid: The Citizen as Endangered Species in Independent India." *Religion and Law in Independent India*. Ed. Robert D. Baird. Delhi: Manohar, 1994.

———. "Modernization and Religious Legitimation in India: 1835–1885." *Religion and the Legitimation of Power in South Asia*. Ed. Bardwell L. Smith. Leiden: E. J. Brill, 1978.

———. "An Old Problem Revisited: The Relation between Sāṃkhya, Yoga and Buddhism." *Studien zur Indologie und Iranistik*. Heft 15 (1989): 129–46.

———. "The Rope of Violence and the Snake of Peace: Conflict and Harmony in Classical India." *Celebrating Peace*. Ed. Leroy S. Rouner. Notre Dame, Indiana: University of Notre Dame Press, 1990.

———. "Some Notes on Religion and Politics in Contemporary India." *Vidyajyoti Journal of Theological Reflection*. Vol. 53. No. 2 (February 1989): 79–87.

———. "The *Trimūrti of Dharma* in Indian Thought: Paradox or Contradiction." *Philosophy East and West*. Vol. XXII. No. 2 (1972): 145–53.

Larson, Gerald James and Ram Shankar Bhattacharya, eds. *Sāṃkhya: A Dualist Tradition in Indian Philosophy. Encyclopedia of Indian Philosophies.* Volume IV. Princeton: Princeton University Press, 1987.

Lawrence, Bruce B. *Defenders of God: The Fundamentalist Revolt against the Modern Age.* New York: Harper and Row, 1989.

Lewis, Bernard. "Islam and Liberal Democracy." *The Atlantic Monthly.* February 1993: 89–98.

Lewis, Martin Deming, ed. *The British in India: Imperialism or Trusteeship.* Lexington: D. C. Heath and Co., 1962.

———, ed. *Gandhi: Maker of Modern India.* Lexington: D. C. Heath and Co., 1965.

Lingat, Robert. *Classical Law of India.* Trans. J. Duncan M. Derrett. Berkeley: University of California Press, 1973.

Lorenzen, David N. *Kabir Legends and Ananta Das's Kabir Parachai.* Albany: SUNY Press, 1991.

———. *The Kāpālikas and Kālāmukhas: Two Lost Śaivite Sects.* Berkeley: University of California Press, 1972.

———. "Warrior Ascetics in Indian History." *Journal of the American Oriental Society.* Vol. 98. No. 1 (January–March 1978): 61–75.

Luckmann, Thomas. *The Invisible Religion: The Problem of Religion in Modern Society.* New York: The Macmillan Co., 1967.

Lutgendorf, Philip. "The King, The Baby, and the Bathwater." Panel: Myth on Earth: Late Twentieth-Century Passions over the Birthplace of Rāma. American Academy of Religion. Unpublished essay, 1992.

———. *The Life of a Text: Performing the Rāmacaritmānas of Tulsidas.* Berkeley: University of California Press, 1991.

Luthera, Ved Prakash. *The Concept of the Secular State and India.* Calcutta: Oxford University Press, 1964.

McLeod, W. H. *The Sikhs: History, Religion and Society.* New York: Columbia University Press, 1989.

McMahon, Robert J. *The Cold War on the Periphery: The United States, India and Pakistan.* New York: Columbia University Press, 1994.

MacGregor, Geddes, comp. *Dictionary of Religion and Philosophy*. New York: Paragon House, 1991.

Macquarrie, John. *The Scope of Demythologizing*. New York: Harper and Row, 1960.

Madan, T. N. "The Double-edged Sword: Fundamentalism and the Sikh Religious Tradition." *Fundamentalisms Observed*. Volume 1. Eds. Martin E. Marty and F. Scott Applesby. Chicago: University of Chicago Press, 1991: 594–627.

———. *Non-Renunciation: Themes and Interpretations of Hindu Culture*. Delhi: Oxford University Press, 1987.

———. "Secularism in Its Place." *The Journal of Asian Studies*. Vol. 46. No. 4 (November 1987): 747–59.

———, ed. *Way of Life: King, Householder, Renouncer. Essays in Honour of Louis Dumont*. Delhi: Motilal Banarsidass, 1982.

Mahmood, Tahir. *Muslim Personal Law: Role of the State in the Subcontinent*. New Delhi: Vikas Publishing, 1977.

Majumdar, R. C. "Evolution of Religio-Philosophic Culture in India." *The Cultural Heritage of India. The Religions*. Volume 4. Ed. H. Bhattacharya. Calcutta: The Ramakrishna Mission Institute of Culture, 1956.

———, ed. *The History and Culture of the Indian People*. 2 Volumes. Bombay: Bharatiya Vidya Bhava, 1984.

Majumdar, R. C., H. C. Raychaudhuri and Kalikinkar Datta. *An Advanced History of India*. New York: St. Martin's Press, 1967.

Mandal Commission Report. See Government of India. *Report of the Backward Classes Commission*.

Mandal, D. *Ayodhya: Archaeology after Demolition: A Critique of the 'New' and 'Fresh' Discoveries*. Tracts for the Times-5. Hyderabad: Orient Longman, 1993.

Mandelbaum, David G. *Society in India*. Volume 1: *Continuity and Change*. Volume 2: *Change and Continuity*. Berkeley: University of California Press, 1970.

Marriott, McKim, ed. *India through Hindu Categories*. Contributions to Indian Sociology. Occasional Studies 5. New Delhi: Sage Publications, 1990.

Marriott, McKim and Ronald Inden. "Caste Systems." *Encyclopedia Britannica*. Macropaedia 3. Chicago: Bentons, 1974: 982–91.

Marshall, P. J., ed., *The British Discovery of Hinduism in the Eighteenth Century*. Cambridge: Cambridge University Press, 1970.

Marty, Martin E. and R. Scott Applesby, eds. Volume 1: *Fundamentalisms Observed*. Volume 2: *Fundamentalisms and Society: Reclaiming the Sciences, the Family and Education*. Volume 3: *Fundamentalisms and the State: Remaking Polities, Economies and Militance*. Chicago: University of Chicago Press, 1991, 1993.

Masani, Zareer. *Indian Tales of the Raj*. Berkeley: Univeristy of California Press, 1987.

Mathur, A. P. *Radhasoami Faith: A Historical Study*. Delhi: Vikas Publishing, 1974.

Matilal, Bimal Krishna. *Logic, Language and Reality: An Introduction to Indian Philosophical Studies*. Delhi: Motilal Banarsidass, 1985.

———. *The Navya-Nyāya Doctrine of Negation: The Semantics and Ontology of Negative Statements in Navya-Nyāya Philosophy*. Harvard Oriental Series Vol. 46. Harvard: Harvard University Press, 1968.

———. *Perception: An Essay on Classical Indian Theories of Knowledge*. Oxford: Clarendon Press, 1986.

Mayer, Peter B. "Tombs and Dark Houses: Ideology, Intellectuals, and Proletarians in the Study of Contemporary Indian Islam." *The Journal of Asian Studies*. Vol. XL. No. 3 (May 1981): 481–502.

Mead, Sidney E. *The Nation with the Soul of a Church*. New York: Harper and Row, 1975.

Mehta, Ved. "The Mosque and the Temple." *Foreign Affairs*. Vol. 72. No. 2 (Spring 1993): 16–21.

Metcalf, Barbara Daly, ed. *Moral Conduct and Authority: The Place of Adab in South Asian Islam*. Berkeley: University of California Press, 1984.

Metcalf, Thomas R., ed. *Modern India: An Interpretive Anthology*. London: The Macmillan Co., 1971.

Miller, Judith. "The Challenge of Radical Islam." *Foreign Affairs*. Vol. 72. No. 2 (Spring 1993): 43–56.

Mishra, Kamalakar. *Kashmir Śaivism: The Central Philosophy of Tantrism.* Cambridge, Mass.: Rudra Press, 1993.

Mishra, Vinay Chandra and Parmanand Singh, eds. *Ram Janmabhoomi Babri Masjid: Historical Documents, Legal Opinions and Judgements.* New Delhi: Bar Council of India Trust, n.d.

Mitter, Sarah S. *Dharma's Daughters: Contemporary Indian Women and Hindu Culture.* New Brunswick: Rutgers University Press, 1991.

Mohanty, J. N. "Consciousness and Knowledge in Indian Philosophy." *Philosophy East and West.* Vol. 29. No. 1 (January 1979): 3–10.

———. "A Fragment of the Indian Philosophical Tradition—Theory of Pramāṇa." *Philosophy East and West.* Vol. 38. No. 3 (July 1988): 251–60.

———. "Indian Theories of Truth: Thoughts on Their Common Framework." *Philosophy East and West.* Vol. 30. No. 4 (October 1980): 439–51.

Mohd. Ahmed Khan vs. *Shah Bano Begum and Others,* A.I.R (All India Reports). Supreme Court Cases 1985: 556–74.

Morris-Jones, W. H. *The Government and Politics of India.* Bombay: B. I. Publications, 1964.

Mukarji, Nirmal and Ashis Banerjee. "Neo-Nationalism." Symposium: The Hindus and Their Isms. *Seminar.* 313 (1985): 26–29.

Muller-Ortega, Paul Edwardo. *The Triadic Heart of Śiva: Kaula Tantricism of Abhinavagupta in the Non-Dual Shaivism of Kashmir.* Albany: SUNY Press, 1989.

Muthama, C. R. "The National Ethos." Symposium: The Hindus and Their Isms. *Seminar.* 313 (1985): 38–40.

Nafziger, E. Wayne. *The Economics of Developing Countries.* Second Edition. Englewood Cliffs, N.J.: Prentice-Hall, 1990.

Naipaul, V. S. *India: A Million Mutinies Now.* New York: Viking, 1990.

Nakamura, Hajime. *Indian Buddhism.* Delhi: Motilal Banarsidass, 1987.

Nanda, Amulya Ratna, comp. *Census of India 1991: Provisional Population Totals.* Paper-1. New Delhi: Samrat Press, 1991.

———. *Census of India 1991: Provisional Population Totals: Rural-Urban Distribution.* Paper-2. New Delhi: Akashdeep Printers, 1991.

———. *Census of India 1991: Provisional Population Totals: Workers and Their Distribution*. Paper-3. New Delhi: Akashdeep, 1991.

Nandy, Ashis. "An Anti-Secularist Manifesto." *Seminar*. 314 (October 1985): 14–24.

Narasimhan, Sakuntala. *Sati: Widow Burning in India*. New York: Doubleday Anchor, 1992.

Nehru, Jawaharlal. *The Discovery of India*. Ed. Robert I. Crane. New York: Doubleday Anchor, 1960.

Oberoi, Harjot. "Sikh Fundamentalism: Translating History into Theory." *Fundamentalisms and the State: Remaking Polities, Economies and Militance*. Volume 3. Eds. Martin E. Marty and F. Scott Applesby. Chicago: University of Chicago Press, 1993: 256–85.

O'Flaherty. See under Doniger, Wendy.

Ogden, Schubert. "Theology and Religious Studies: Their Differences and the Difference It Makes." Journal of the American Academy of Religion. Vol. XLVI. No. 1 (1978): 3–17.

Oldenburg, Philip, ed. *India Briefing, 1991*. Boulder: Westview Press, 1991.

———, ed. *India Briefing, 1993*. Boulder: Westview Press, 1992.

Olivelle, Patrick. *The Āśrama System: The History and Hermeneutics of a Religious Tradition*. New York: Oxford University Press, 1993.

———. *Renunciation in Hinduism: A Medieval Debate*. 2 volumes. Vienna: De Nobili Research Library, 1986-87.

———, trans. *Saṃnyāsa Upaniṣads*. New York: Oxford University Press, 1992.

Oommen, T. K. *State and Society in India: Studies in Nation-Building*. New Delhi: Sage Publications, 1990.

Padoux, André. *Vāc: The Concept of the Word in Selected Hindu Tantras*. Trans. Jacques Gontier. Albany: SUNY Press, 1990.

Pal, Pratapaditya. "Whose Shrine Is It?" *The Saturday Statesman*. 13 April 1991: 2–3.

Pande, Susmita. *Medieval Bhakti Movement*. Meerut: Kusumañjali Prakashan, 1989.

Pandey, Gyanendra. *The Construction of Communalism in Colonial North India*. Delhi: Oxford University Press, 1990.

Panikkar, K. M. *The State and the Citizen*. Bombay: Asia Publishing House, 1956.

Panikkar, Raimundo, trans. *The Vedic Experience: Mantramañjarī*. Berkeley: University of California Press, 1977.

Philips, C. H., ed. *Historians of India, Pakistan and Ceylon*. London: Oxford University Press, 1961.

Pintchman, Tracy. *The Rise of the Goddess in the Hindu Tradition*. Albany: State University of New York Press, 1994.

Potter, Karl H., ed. *Advaita Vedānta up to Sāṃkara and His Pupils. Encyclopedia of Indian Philosophies*. Volume III. Princeton: Princeton University Press, 1982.

———, ed. *Bibliography. Encyclopedia of Indian Philosophies*. Volume I. Revised Edition. Princeton: Princeton University Press, 1983.

———, ed., *Indian Metaphysics and Epistemology: The Tradition of Nyāya-Vaiśeṣika up to Gaṇgeśa. Encyclopedia of Indian Philosophies*. Volume II. Princeton: Princeton University Press, 1978.

———. *Presuppositions of India's Philosophies*. Englewood Cliffs, N.J.. Prentice- Hall, 1963.

Purdom, C. D. *The God-Man*. London: Allen and Unwin, 1964.

Puri, Balraj. *Kashmir: Towards Insurgency*. Tracts for the Times-4. Hyderabad: Orient Longman, 1993.

Pye, Lucian W. *Asian Power and Politics*. Cambridge, Mass.: Belknap Press of Harvard University Press, 1985.

Raghavan, T. C. A. "Origins and Development of Hindu Mahasabha Ideology." *Economic and Political Weekly*. 9 April 1983: 595–600.

Rahman, Fazlur. "Islam." *The Cambridge Encyclopedia of India, Pakistan, Bangladesh, Sri Lanka Nepal, Bhutan and the Maldives*. Ed. Francis Robinson. Cambridge: Cambridge University Press, 1989.

Rajgopal, P. R. *Communal Violence in India*. New Delhi: Uppal Publishing, 1987.

Rajshekar, V. T. "Anti-human." Symposium: The Hindus and Their Isms. *Seminar*. 313 (1985): 41–51.

Ranade, R. D. *Mysticism in India: The Poet-Saints of Maharashtra*. 1933. Repr. Albany: SUNY Press, 1983.

Rao, P. Koteswar. "Shah Bano's Case and Uniform Civil Code—A Survey of Public Opinion among the Muslim Community at Tirupati." *Journal of the Indian Law Institute*. Vol. 27 (1985): 572–77.

Richards, J. F. and Ralph Nicholas, eds. "Symposium: The Contributions of Louis Dumont." *The Journal of Asian Studies*. Vol. XXXV. No. 4 (August 1976): 579–650.

Rigopoulos, Antonio. *The Life and Teachings of Sai Baba of Shirdi*. Albany: SUNY Press, 1993.

Roach, James R., ed. *India 2000: The Next Fifteen Years*. Riverdale, Maryland: The Riverdale Co., 1986.

Robbins, Thomas, Dick Anthony and James Richardson. "Theory and Research on Today's 'New Religions'." *Sociological Analysis*. Vol. 39. No. 2 (1978): 95–122.

Robbins, Thomas and Roland Robertson, eds. *Church-State Relations: Tensions and Transitions*. New Brunswick: Transaction Books, 1987.

Robertson, Roland and William R. Garrett, eds. *Religion and Global Order: Religion and the Political Order*. Volume IV. New York: Paragon House, 1991.

Robinson, Francis, ed. *The Cambridge Encyclopedia of India, Pakistan, Bangladesh, Sri Lanka, Nepal, Bhutan and the Maldives*. Cambridge: Cambridge University Press, 1989.

Robinson, Richard. "Classical Indian Philosophy." *Chapters in Indian Civilization*. Volume 1. Ed. Joseph W. Elder. Dubuque, Iowa: Kendall-Hunt, 1970: 127–227.

Rocher, Ludo. "Can a Murderer Inherit His Victim's Estate? British Responses to Troublesome Questions in Hindu Law." *Journal of the American Oriental Society*. Vol. 107. No. 1 (January–March 1987): 1–10.

———. "Hindu Conceptions of Law." *The Hastings Law Journal*. Vol. 29 (1978): 1284–1305.

———. "Indian Reactions to Anglo-Hindu Law." *Journal of the American Oriental Society*. Vol. 92. No. 3 (July–September 1972): 419–24.

———. "'Lawyers' in Classical Hindu Law." *Law and Society Review*. Vol. 3 (1969): 383–402.

Rochford, E. B. *Hare Krishna in America*. New Brunswick: Rutgers University Press, 1985.

Roof, Wade Clark, ed. *World Order and Religion*. Albany: SUNY Press, 1991.

Rorty, Richard. *Essays on Heidegger and Others*. Philosophical Papers. Volume 2. Cambridge: Cambridge University Press, 1991.

Ross, Charles, ed. *Correspondence of Charles, First Marquis Cornwallis*. 3 volumes. London: John Murray, 1859.

Rouner, Leroy S., ed. *Celebrating Peace*. Notre Dame, Indiana: University of Notre Dame Press, 1990.

Rubinson, Richard, ed. *Dynamics of World Development*. Beverly Hills: Sage Publications, 1981.

Rudolph, Lloyd I. and Susanne H. *In Pursuit of Lakshmi*. Chicago: University of Chicago Press, 1987.

———. *The Modernity of Tradition*. Chicago: University of Chicago Press, 1967.

Said, Edward W. *Orientalism*. New York: Vintage Books, 1979.

Sandhu, Kanwar and Ramesh Vinayak. "Punjab: Area of Darkness." *India Today*. 15 July 1992: 22–27.

Saraswati, Swami Dayananda. *Autobiography*. Ed. K. C. Yadav. Delhi: Manohar, 1976.

Sartre, Jean-Paul. *Critique de la raison dialectique, précédé de Questions de méthode*. Tome I. Paris: Gallimard, 1960.

Schayer, S. "Das mahāyānistische Absolutum nach der Lehre der Mādhyamikas." *Orientalistische Literatur-Zeitung*. Vol. 38 (1935): 405ff.

Schimmel, Annemarie. *Islam in the Indian Subcontinent*. Leiden: E. J. Brill, 1980.

Schomer, Karine and W. H. McLeod, eds. *The Sants: Studies in a Devotional Tradition of India*. Berkeley Religious Studies. Delhi: Motilal Banarsidass, 1987.

Segal, Ronald. *The Crisis of India*. Bombay: Jaico Publishing, 1965.

Sen, Amartya. "The Threats to Secular India." *New York Review of Books*. Vol. XL. No. 7 (8 April 1993): 26–32.

Seshadri, H. V., ed. *R.S.S.: A Vision in Action*. Bangalore: Jagarana Prakashana, 1988.

Seton-Karr, W. S. *The Marquess Cornwallis and the Consolidation of BritishRule*. Rulers of India Series. Oxford: Clarendon Press, 1898.

Shahabuddin, Syed and Theodore P. Wright, Jr. "India: Muslim Minority, Politics and Society." *Islam in Asia*. Ed. John L. Esposito. New York: Oxford University Press, 1987.

Shakir, Moin, ed. *Religion, State and Politics in India*. Delhi: Ajanta Publications, 1989.

———. *Secularization of Muslim Behavior*. Calcutta: The Minerva Associates, 1973.

———. *State and Politics in Contemporary India*. Delhi: Ajanta Publications, 1956.

Sharma, Arvind. "Hinduism and Politics in India." *Movements and Issues in World Religions*. Eds. Charles Gerhard, et al. New York: Greenwood Press, 1987.

———. "The Indo-Pakistani Conflict." *Movements and Issues in World Religions*. Eds. Charles Gerhard, et al. New York: Greenwood Press, 1987.

Sharma, Chandradhar. *Indian Philosophy: A Critical Survey*. New York: Barnes and Noble, 1962.

Shepard, William. "'Fundamentalism' Christian and Islamic." *Religion*. Vol. 17 (1987): 355–78.

Shils, Edward. *The Intellectual between Tradtion and Modernity: The Indian Situation*. The Hague: Mouton and Co., 1961.

Shinn, Larry D. *The Dark Lord: Cult Images and the Hare Krishnas in America*. Philadelphia: Westminster Press, 1987.

Shourie, Arun. *Religion in Politics*. New Delhi: Roli Books International, 1987.

Shweder, R. A. and R. A. Le Vine, eds. *Culture Theory: Essays on Mind, Self and Emotion*. Cambridge: Cambridge University Press, 1984.

Silburn, Lilian. *Kuṇḍalinī: The Energy of the Depths*. Trans. Jacques Gontier. Albany: SUNY Press, 1988.

Singh, Khushwant. "Brahmin Power." *Sunday*. 23–29 December 1990: 19.

———. *A History of the Sikhs*. 2 volumes. Princeton: Princeton University Press, 1963–66.

———. *Need for a New Religion in India and Other Essays*. Ed. Rohini Singh. New Delhi: UBS Publishers, 1991.

Singh, Onkar and Vinod Behl. "The Trishul Cult Again." *The Illustrated Weekly of India*. 7 December 1986: 26–29.

Singh, Patwant and Harji Malik, eds. *Punjab: The Fatal Miscalculation*. New Delhi: Patwant Singh, 1985.

Smart, Ninian. *Beyond Ideology: Religion and the Future of Western Civilization*. London: Collins, 1981.

———. *Doctrine and Argument in Indian Philosophy*. London: Allen and Unwin, 1964.

Smart, Ninian and Shivesh Thakur, eds. *Ethical and Political Dilemmas of Modern India*. New York: St. Martin's Press, 1993.

Smith, Bardwell L., ed. *Religion and the Legitimation of Power in South Asia*. Leiden: E. J. Brill, 1978.

Smith, Brian K. *Classifying the Universe: The Ancient Indian Varṇa System and the Origins of Caste*. New York: Oxford University Press, 1994.

———. *Reflections on Resemblance, Ritual and Religion*. New York: Oxford University Press, 1989.

Smith, Donald Eugene. *India as a Secular State*. Princeton: Princeton University Press, 1963.

———. *Religion and Political Development*. Boston: Little, Brown and Co., 1970.

———, ed. *Religion and Political Modernization*. New Haven: Yale University Press, 1974.

———, ed. *South Asian Politics and Religion*. Princeton: Princeton University Press, 1966.

Smith, Wilfred Cantwell. *Islam in Modern History*. Princeton: Princeton University Press, 1957.

———. *The Meaning and End of Religion*. New York: Harper and Row, 1978.

———. *Modern Islam in India*. Lahore: Sh. Muhammad Ashraf, 1946.

———. *Modernisation of a Traditional Society*. London: Asia Publishing House, 1965.

Sontheimer, Günther D. and Hermann Kulke, eds. *Hinduism Reconsidered*. Delhi: Manohar, 1989.

Spear, Percival. *A History of India: From the Sixteenth Century to the Twentieth Century*. Volume Two. London: Penguin, 1965.

———. *India: A Modern History*. Ann Arbor: University of Michigan Press, 1961.

———. *India, Pakistan and the West*. London: Oxford University Press, 1958.

———. *The Nabobs: A Study of the Social Life of the English in Eighteenth-Century India*. London: Oxford University Press, 1963.

———. *The Oxford History of India: 1740–1975*. Second Edition. Delhi: Oxford University Press, 1978.

Spiro, Melford E. "Some Reflections on Cultural Determinism and Relativism with Special Reference to Emotion and Reason. *Culture Theory: Essays on Mind, Self and Emotion*. Eds. R. A. Shweder and R. A. Le Vine. Cambridge: Cambridge University Press, 1984.

Srinivas, M. N. *The Cohesive Role of Sanskritization and Other Essays*. Delhi: Oxford University Press, 1989.

———. *Social Change in Modern India*. Berkeley: University of California Press, 1969.

Srivastava, Sushil. *The Disputed Mosque: A Historical Inquiry*. New Delhi: Vistaar Publications, 1991.

Staal, Frits. "The Himalayas the Fall of Religion." *The Silk Route and the Diamond Path*. Ed. D. E. Klimburg-Salter. Berkeley: University of California Press, 1982: 38–5l.

———. *Rules without Meaning*. Toronto Studies in Religion, volume 4. New York: Peter Lang, 1989.

Stern, Robert W. *Changing India: Bourgeois Revolution on the Subcontinent*. Cambridge: Cambridge University Press, 1993.

Stokes, Eric. *The English Utilitarians and India*. Oxford: Clarendon Press, 1959.

Swarup, Devendra, ed. *Politics of Conversion*. Delhi: Deendayal Research Institute, 1986.

Tambiah, Stanley J. "The Sources of Charismatic Leadership: Max Weber Revisited." *Comparative Social Dynamics*. Ed. E. Cohen, et al. Boulder: Westview Press, 1985.

———. *World Conqueror and World Renouncer: A Study of Buddhism and Polity in Thailand against a Historical Background*. Cambridge: Cambridge University Press, 1976.

Thapar, Romesh. "The Hindus: A Call to Arms." *The Illustrated Weekly of India*. 7 December 1986: 8–17.

Thapar, Romila. *From Lineage to State: Social Formations in the Mid-First-Millenium B.C. in the Ganga Valley*. Bombay: Oxford University Press, 1984.

———. *A History of India: From the Discovery of India to 1526*. Volume One. London: Penguin, 1966.

———. "Syndicated Moksha?" Symposium: The Hindus and Their Isms. *Seminar*. 313 (1985): 15–25.

Thursby, Gene. "Siddha Yoga: Swami Muktananda and the Seat of Power." *When Prophets Die*. Ed. T. Miller. Albany: SUNY Press, 1991.

Tripathi, B. D. *Sadhus of India: The Sociological View*. Bombay: Popular Prakashan, 1978.

Tully, Mark and Satish Jacob. *Amritsar: Mrs. Gandhi's Last Battle*. London: Jonathan Cape, 1985.

Tully, Mark. *The Defeat of a Congressman and Other Parables of Modern India*. New York: Alfred A. Knopf, 1992.

Vanaik, Achin. *The Painful Transition: Bourgeois Democracy in India*. London: Verso, 1990.

van Aalst, Frank D. "The Secular State, Secularization and Secularism." *Quest*. Vol. 62 (July-September 1969): 24–35.

van Buitenen, J. A. B. "Vedic and Upaniṣadic Bases of Indian Civilization." *Chapters in Indian Civilization*. Volume 1. Ed. Joseph W. Elder. Dubuque, Iowa: Kendall-Hunt, 1970.

van der Veer, Peter. *Gods on Earth: The Management of Religious Experience and Identity in a North Indian Pilgrimage Centre*. Delhi: Oxford University Press, 1989.

———. *Religious Nationalism: Hindus and Muslims in India*. Berkeley: University of California Press, 1994.

Vaudeville, Charlotte, trans. *Kabir*. Volume I. Oxford: Oxford University Press, 1974.

Vinson, Lee, comp. *The Early American Songbook*. Englewood Cliffs, N.J.: Prentice-Hall, 1974.

von Grünebaum, G. E., ed. *Unity and Variety in Muslim Civilization*. Chicago: University of Chicago Press, 1955.

Wallerstein, Immanuel. *The Modern World-System: Capitalist Agriculture and the Origins of the European World-Economy in the Sixteenth Century*. New York: Academic Press, 1974.

———. *The Politics of the World Economy: The States, the Movements and the Civilizations*. Cambridge: Cambridge University Press, 1984.

Warder, A. K. *Indian Buddhism*. Delhi: Motilal Banarsidass, 1970.

Warren, Henry Clarke, ed. and trans. *Buddhism in Translations*. New York: Atheneum, 1973.

Wartofsky, M. W. *Feuerbach*. Cambridge: Cambridge University Press, 1982.

Wayman, Alex. *The Buddhist Tantras: Light on Indo-Tibetan Esotericism*. New York: Samuel Weiser, 1973.

Weber, Max. *The Religion of India: The Sociology of Hinduism and Buddhism*. Trans. Hans H. Gerth and Don Martindale. New York: The Free Press, 1958.

Webster, John C. B. *The Nirankari Sikhs*. Batala: The Christian Institute of Sikh Studies, 1979.

Weiner, Myron. "India's Minorities: Who Are They? What Do They Want?" *India 2000: The Next Fifteen Years*. Ed. James R. Roach. Riverdale, Maryland: The Riverdale Co., 1986: 100–34.

Wessinger, Catherine. "Woman Guru, Woman Roshi: The Legitimation of Female Religious Leadership in Hindu and Buddhist Groups in America." *Women's Leadership in Marginal Religions*. Ed. C. Wessinger. Urbana: University of Illinois, 1993.

Whaling, Frank. *The Rise of the Religious Significance of Rama*. Delhi: Motilal Banarsidass, 1980.

White, Charles S. J. "The Sai Baba Movement: Approaches to the Study of Indian Saints." *Journal of Asian Studies*. Vol. 31 (1972): 863–78.

Whitehead, Alfred North. *Process and Reality*. New York: The Macmillan Co., 1929.

Wickwire, Franklin and Mary. *Cornwallis and the War of Independence*. London: Faber and Faber, 1971.

———. *Cornwallis: The Imperial Years*. Chapel Hill: The University of North Carolina Press, 1980.

Wilkinson, T. S. and M. M. Thomas, eds. *Ambedkar and the Neo-Buddhist-Movement*. Madras: The Christian Literature Society, 1972.

Williams, J. Paul. "The Nature of Religion." *Journal for the Scientific Study of Religion*. Vol. II. No. 1 (Fall 1962): 3–14.

Williams, Raymond B. *A New Face of Hinduism: The Swaminarayan Religion*. Cambridge: Cambridge University Press, 1984.

Winternitz, Maurice. *A History of Indian Literature*. 3 volumes. Trans. S. Jha. Delhi: Motilal Banarsidass, 1963 and 1967.

Wittgenstein, Ludwig. *The Blue and the Brown Books*. New York: Harperand Row, 1958.

Wolpert, Stanley. *India*. Berkeley: University of California Press, 1991.

———. *Jinnah of Pakistan*. New York: Oxford University Press, 1984.

———. *A New History of India*. 4th Edition. New York: Oxford University Press, 1993.

The World Bank. *World Development Report 1993: Investing in Health*. New York: Oxford University Press, 1993.

———. *World Development Report 1991: The Challenge of Development*.New York: Oxford University Press, 1991.

———. *World Development Report 1990: Poverty*. New York: Oxford University Press, 1990.

Wright, Robin. "Islam, Democracy and the West." *Foreign Affairs*. Vol. 71. No. 3 (Summer 1992): 131–45.

———. "Poverty's Shadow Haunting New Democracies." *Los Angeles Times*. 25 February 1992: H4.

Wuthnow, Robert. *The Restructuring of American Religion: Society and Faith since World War II.* Princeton: Princeton University Press, 1988.

———. "Understanding Religion and Politics." *Daedalus*. Vol. 120. No. 3 (Summer 1991): 1–20.

Yocum, Glenn E. "The Goddess and the Guru: Two Models of Universal Order in Tamil India." *Religion and Global Order: Religion and the Political Order.* Volume IV. Ed. Roland Robertson and William R. Garrett. New York: Paragon House, 1991: 87–117.

Yogananda, Paramahamsa. *Autobiography of a Yogi.* Los Angeles: Self-Realization Fellowship, 1973.

Zelliot, Eleanor. "Dalit: New Perspectives on India's Untouchables." *India Briefing, 1991.* Ed. Philip Oldenburg. Boulder: Westview Press, 1991.

Index